ACCOUNTING FOR HUNGER

The challenge of global hunger is now high on the agenda of governments and international policy-makers. This new work contributes to addressing that challenge, by looking at the obstacles which stand in the way of implementing a right to food in the era of globalisation. The book has several functions: to describe the current situation of global hunger, to consider how it relates both to the development of food systems and to the merger of the food and energy markets, and to explain how the right to food contributes to identifying solutions at the domestic and international levels. The right to food, it argues, can only be realised if governance improves at the domestic level, and if the international environment enables governments to adopt appropriate policies, for which they require a certain policy space. The essays in this book demonstrate how improved accountability at the national level and reform of the international economic environment in the areas of trade, food aid and investment go hand in hand in the move towards full realisation of the right to food, while reforms at the domestic level are key to effectively tackling hunger (including reforms that improve accountability of government officials). The current regimes of trade, investment and food aid, as well as the development of biofuels production—all of which contribute to define the international context in which states implement such reforms—should be reshaped if these national efforts are to be successful. The title—*Accounting for Hunger*—emphasises the point that accountability at both the domestic and international levels must be improved if sustainable progress is to be achieved in combating global hunger. The implication is that the extraterritorial human rights obligations of states (their obligations to respect the right to food beyond their national territories, for instance in their food aid, investment or trade policies) and the strengthening of global governance of food security (as is currently being attempted with the reform of the Committee on World Food Security in Rome) have a key role to fulfil: domestic reforms will not achieve sustainable results unless the international environment is more enabling of the efforts of governments acting individually.

Volume 36 in the series Studies in International Law

Studies in International Law
Recent titles in this series

The International Court of Justice and Self-Defence in International Law
James A Green

State Liability in Investment Treaty Arbitration: Global Constitutional and Administrative Law in the BIT Generation
Santiago Montt

Reappraising the Resort to Force: International Law, Jus ad Bellum and the War on Terror
Lindsay Moir

International Law and Dispute Settlement: New Problems and Techniques
Edited by Duncan French, Matthew Saul and Nigel White

The Democratic Legitimacy of International Law
Steven Wheatley

Reflections on the UN Declaration on the Rights of Indigenous Peoples
Edited by Stephen Allen and Alexandra Xanthaki

Contracting with Sovereignty: State Contracts and International Arbitration
Ivar Alvik

Multi-Sourced Equivalent Norms in International Law
Edited by Yuval Shany and Tomer Broude

The Distinction and Relationship between *Jus ad Bellum* and *Jus in Bello*
Keiichiro Okimoto

International Humanitarian Law and Terrorism
Andrea Bianchi and Yasmin Naqvi

Promises of States under International Law
Christian Eckart

The Militarisation of Peacekeeping in the Twenty-First Century
James Sloan

Accounting for Hunger: The Right to Food in the Era of Globalisation
Edited by Olivier De Schutter and Kaitlin Y Cordes

For the complete list of titles in this series, see the 'Studies in International Law' link at www.hartpub.co.uk/books/series.asp

Accounting for Hunger

The Right to Food in the Era of Globalisation

Edited by

Olivier De Schutter
and
Kaitlin Y Cordes

·HART·
PUBLISHING

OXFORD AND PORTLAND, OREGON
2011

Published in the United Kingdom by Hart Publishing Ltd
16C Worcester Place, Oxford, OX1 2JW
Telephone: +44 (0)1865 517530
Fax: +44 (0)1865 510710
E-mail: mail@hartpub.co.uk
Website: http://www.hartpub.co.uk

Published in North America (US and Canada) by
Hart Publishing
c/o International Specialized Book Services
920 NE 58th Avenue, Suite 300
Portland, OR 97213-3786
USA
Tel: +1 503 287 3093 or toll-free: (1) 800 944 6190
Fax: +1 503 280 8832
E-mail: orders@isbs.com
Website: http://www.isbs.com

© The editors and contributors severally, 2011

The editors and contributors have asserted their right under the Copyright, Designs and Patents Act 1988, to be identified as the authors of this work.

All rights reserved. No part of this publication may be reproduced, stored in a retrieval system, or transmitted, in any form or by any means, without the prior permission of Hart Publishing, or as expressly permitted by law or under the terms agreed with the appropriate reprographic rights organisation. Enquiries concerning reproduction which may not be covered by the above should be addressed to Hart Publishing Ltd at the address above.

British Library Cataloguing in Publication Data
Data Available

ISBN: 978-1-84946-226-6

Typeset by Forewords Ltd, Oxford
Printed and bound in Great Britain by
TJ International Ltd, Padstow, Cornwall

Acknowledgements

The editors would like to thank Okeoma Moronu and Julia Szybala for their assistance in editing footnotes.

Kaitlin Cordes would like to thank Andrew Idrizovic for his constant help and support.

Contents

Acknowledgements   v
Author Biographies   ix

1. Accounting for Hunger: An Introduction to the Issues   1
Olivier De Schutter and Kaitlin Cordes

Part I: Addressing Power Imbalances in the Food Systems

2. The Impact of Agribusiness Transnational Corporations on the Right to Food   27
Kaitlin Y Cordes

3. The Transformation of Food Retail and Marginalisation of Smallholder Farmers   65
Margaret Cowan Schmidt

4. Biofuels and the Right to Food: An uneasy partnership   95
Ann Sofie Cloots

Part II: Trade and Aid: An Enabling International Environment   135

5. International Trade in Agriculture and the Right to Food   137
Olivier De Schutter

6. How to Phase Out Rich Country Agricultural Subsidies Without Increasing Hunger in the Developing World   193
Jennifer Mersing

7. Invoking the Right to Food in the WTO Dispute Settlement Process: The Relevance of the Right to Food to the Law of the WTO   211
Boyan Konstantinov

8. Food Aid: How It Should Be Done   239
Loreto Ferrer Moreu

Index   265

Author Biographies

Olivier DE SCHUTTER is the UN Special Rapporteur on the right to food since 2008. A professor at the Catholic University of Louvain and at the College of Europe, he is a regular Visiting Professor at Columbia University. In 2004–8, he was General Secretary of the International Federation for Human Rights (FIDH). His publications are in the areas of economic and social rights, economic globalisation, and fundamental rights in the EU.

Kaitlin Y CORDES holds a juris doctor from Columbia University School of Law, where she was a James Kent Scholar, a Harlan Fiske Stone Scholar, and a Managing Editor of *A Jailhouse Lawyer's Manual*. She earned a bachelors of art in political science and international studies from Northwestern University. A human rights advocate, she has worked with a number of social justice and human rights organisations, most recently with Human Rights Watch. In 2009–2010, she served as an adviser to the UN Special Rapporteur on the right to food, Olivier De Schutter. After law school, she clerked for Justice Virginia A. Long of the Supreme Court of New Jersey.

Ann Sofie CLOOTS has a Candidate in Law and a Master in Law from Katholieke University Leuven (KUL), as well as an LLM from Columbia University School of Law, where she was a Harlan Fisk Stone Scholar, an honorary Fulbright fellow, and a BAEF fellow. She has interned at the Permanent Representation of Belgium with the United Nations in Geneva (Human Rights Council). Since January 2009, she has worked as an associate at Cleary Gottlieb Steen & Hamilton LLP, Brussels in its corporate and competition practice. She is a member of the Brussels Bar.

Margaret COWAN SCHMIDT earned a bachelor's degree from the University of Michigan and a juris doctor from Columbia University School of Law. While in law school, Ms Cowan Schmidt studied at the European University Institute in Florence and was a case law editor for the Columbia Journal of European Law. Ms Cowan Schmidt is currently an associate in the Washington, D.C. office of an international law firm, where her practice ranges from regulatory matters to litigation. Ms Cowan Schmidt has also been an active participant in her firm's pro bono practice, where she has represented asylum applicants, worked on an amicus brief to be submitted to an international human rights tribunal, and provided legal research and analysis to several other human rights and development organisations.

Boyan KONSTANTINOV graduated from Sofia University in Bulgaria (LL.B. 2001) and Columbia University School of Law (LL.M. 2008), where he was a Fulbright Scholar and Columbia Human Rights Fellow. He has several years of experience in the NGO sector, working in capacity development in Central and Eastern Europe and the former Soviet Union. Boyan is currently consulting for UNDP's Bureau for Development Policy, working on international trade, intellectual property rights, and access to essential medicines.

Jennifer L MERSING graduated from the College of William & Mary with a B.A. in International Relations and from Columbia University School of Law with a J.D. She is currently an associate in the Energy, Infrastructure, and Project Finance Practice Area at a large law firm. Prior to law school, she worked as a Junior Research Fellow in the Trade, Equity and Development Project at the Carnegie Endowment for International Peace.

Loreto Ferrer MOREU earned a degree in law and a degree in economics from Carlos III University (Madrid), a Master in Development and International Aid from Universidad Complutense (Madrid), and a Master of Arts in Human Rights from Columbia University (New York). She has served as a technical advisor to the Spanish Agency for International Development Cooperation (AECID), and worked as a Political Affairs Officer with the United Nations Department of Political Affairs, Americas Division. She currently works as a project manager at ALMACIGA, an NGO based in Madrid, working on issues related to the human rights of indigenous peoples in Latin America. Since 2006, she has also worked as an independent consultant on issues related to the human rights of indigenous peoples.

1

Accounting for Hunger: An Introduction to the Issues

OLIVIER DE SCHUTTER AND KAITLIN Y CORDES

APPROXIMATELY ONE BILLION people will be hungry in 2011, up from 923 million at the beginning of 2008, 854 million in 2005 and 820 million in 1996.[1] Almost all of these people whose calorie intake is too low to meet their basic physiological needs are located in developing countries—about 98%, according to the UN Food and Agriculture Organization (FAO). In these countries, at least 2.5 billion individuals today lack the essential micronutrients that are needed to lead a healthy and active life.[2] Deficiencies of vitamin A and zinc still rank among the leading causes of death through disease in developing countries, where, together, these deficiencies in newborn children and infants account for 9% of under-five deaths.[3] Between one-fifth and one-quarter of child deaths can be attributed to low birthweight and childhood underweight.[4]

---

[1] See Food & Agriculture Organization of the UN (FAO), 'The State of Food Insecurity in the World: Economic Crises—Impacts and Lessons Learned' (2009) 11 (estimating number of hungry people at 1.02 billion). In 2010, the figure was considered to be slightly lower, thanks to the recovery of the global economy after the financial and economic crisis of 2008 and 2009 (see (FAO), 'The State of Food Insecurity in the World: Economic Crises—Addressing Food Insecurity in Protracted Crises' (2010) 9). However, at the end of 2010, the figure is probably above the mark of one billion because of the impacts of the food price spikes of all staple foods except rice.

[2] One-third of the 8.8 million child deaths worldwide is attributable to malnutrition. RE Black, LH Allen, ZA Bhutta, LE Caulfield, M de Onis, M Ezzati, C Mathers and J Rivera, 'Maternal and Child Undernutrition: Global and Regional Exposures and Health Consequences' (2008) 371 *Lancet* 243.

[3] Ibid, 253.

[4] It was estimated in 2004 that 35% of child deaths could be attributed to childhood underweight and maternal low body-mass index leading to intrauterine growth restriction and low birthweight. See SM Fishman, LE Caulfield, M de Onis, et al, 'Childhood and Maternal Underweight' in M Ezzati et al (eds), *Comparative Quantification of Health Risks: Global and Regional Burden of Disease Attributable to Selected Major Risk Factors* (Geneva, World Health Organization, 2004) 39–161. The figure would now be around 22%, as the prevalence of stunting has declined in most regions. See Black, above n 2, 254.

But hunger is not a natural disaster. It is a legacy of choices made in the past. It stems from a series of decisions that, in retrospect, appear short-sighted, and were based on a wrong diagnosis of the causes of hunger, leading to incorrect prescriptions to remedy it. The single most important proximate cause of structural hunger today is that developing countries have either not invested sufficiently in agriculture or have invested in the wrong kind of agriculture, with little impact on the reduction in rural poverty. In fact, for almost 30 years, starting in the early 1980s, neither the private sector nor governments were interested in investing in agriculture. Under the structural adjustment policies that were launched at the time, the public sector in developing countries was drastically downsized: extension services were dismantled, public research in agriculture limited, and support to farmers in developing countries significantly reduced.[5] As an indicator of this lack of investment, public spending in 14 agriculture-based countries, including 12 countries of sub-Saharan Africa, decreased on average from 6.9% of gross domestic product (GDP) in 1980 to 4% in 2004, although the share of agriculture in those countries' GDP remained roughly constant during those years and although 70–80% of the population of those countries depend on the agricultural sector.[6] Official development assistance (ODA) also moved away from agriculture, which was not seen as offering a strong potential for development. In 2008, for example, the World Bank reported that the share of agriculture in ODA declined from 18% in 1979 to 3.5% in 2004, and that it declined in absolute terms from 8 billion USD (in 2004 dollars) in 1984 to 3.4 billion in 2004.[7]

As the state and donors retreated from agriculture, it was hoped that private investors would enter the sector, filling in the financing gaps. But they did not. Rather, as a result of both the huge subsidies provided by the governments of Organisation for Economic Co-operation and Development (OECD) countries to their producers and the growth of highly competitive types of agriculture in certain developing countries, overproduction of basic food commodities was massive, creating a structural decline in the prices of raw agricultural commodities on the international markets. In addition, despite the entry into force in 1995 of the Agreement on Agriculture as part of the agreements establishing the World Trade Organization (WTO), producers in many developing countries continued to face acute barriers in their access to the high-value markets of OECD countries, including the tariffs imposed by those countries as well

---

[5] For an assessment of the impact of structural adjustment policies on agriculture, see S Commander (ed), *Structural Adjustment and Agriculture: Theory & Practice in Africa & Latin America* (London, Overseas Development Institute, 1989).

[6] World Bank, 'World Development Report 2008: Agriculture for Development' (2007), table 1.3, 41 (WDR 2008). The share of agriculture in total GDP remained stable throughout the period, at an average of 28.9% for the 14 countries concerned.

[7] Ibid, 41.

as non-tariff barriers such as public and private standards. With the exception of certain tropical commodities, the private sector therefore had limited interest in investing in agriculture in developing countries, where it would confront highly unequal competition from producers located elsewhere. The result was that many low-income countries, particularly in sub-Saharan Africa, increasingly specialised in the production of a narrow range of raw agricultural commodities, rendering them highly vulnerable to price changes on the international markets both as regards their export revenues and as regards their food security at home. The situation was exacerbated by a lack of diversification of the economies of the least-developed countries (LDCs). For those countries, the poorest in the developing world, the pattern according to which the international division of labour was organised during the colonial era—with the colonies supplying the centre with raw materials and buying processed foods and manufactured goods produced by the colonial power—was not questioned: instead, it was further reinforced by the push towards export-led agriculture.[8]

In one respect at least, this is now changing. Within the past few years, agri-food companies have begun to view an increase in direct investment in agriculture as a means to lower their costs and ensure the long-term viability of their supplies. As commodity buyers grow larger and more concentrated, they seek to respond to the requirements of their food industry clients through increased vertical coordination, tightening their control over suppliers. Foreign direct investment in agriculture has begun to increase as a result: according to the UN Conference on Trade and Development, it went from an average of 600 million USD annually in the 1990s to an average of 3 billion in 2005–07.[9] More recently, the global food price crisis of 2007–08 led both governments and private investors to realise that the era of low and decreasing prices for agricultural commodities may be coming to an end; that suitable farmland and freshwater might in the future become scarce commodities; and that, as the growth in demand for agricultural commodities is gradually outpacing the ability for the supply side to respond, investing in agriculture might be highly profitable and of strategic importance for the future stability of agricultural supplies.[10]

But simply increasing food production to meet future needs, although

[8] See H-J Chang, *Kicking Away the Ladder: Development Strategy in Historical Perspective* (London, Anthem Press, 2002); H-J Chang, *Bad Samaritan: The Guilty Secrets of Rich Nations & the Threat to Global Prosperity* (London, Random House, 2007); ES Reinert, *How Rich Countries Got Rich and Why Poor Countries Stay Poor* (London, Constable, 2007).
[9] UN Conference on Trade and Development, 'World Investment Report 2009: Transnational Corporations, Agricultural Production and Development' (2009).
[10] On the impacts of the global food price crisis of 2007–08 on policymakers and the private sector, see J Clapp and MJ Cohen (eds), *The Global Food Crisis. Governance Challenges and Opportunities* (Waterloo, ON, Wilfrid Laurier University Press, 2009).

necessary, is not sufficient. It will not enable significant progress in combating hunger and malnutrition unless doing so is combined with higher incomes for the poorest—particularly small-scale farmers and agricultural workers in developing countries. As a result of the past history that was briefly sketched above, many poor countries have been caught in a vicious cycle, in which poverty in the rural areas accelerates rural flight, leading to the expansion of the number of people living in sub-standard conditions at the outskirts of the large cities. More than one in six people—43% of the population in developing countries—already live in slums; by 2030, while the global population will have increased from the current 6.9 billion to an estimated 8.3 billion,[11] it is estimated that the number of people living in slums will have grown to one in three individuals.[12] Accordingly, governments and other actors have sought to increase food production to ensure the provision of low-priced food that is affordable to the urban poor. This solution, however, not only pitted the interests of farmers and agricultural workers against those of the urban populations in low-income countries. It also made importing subsidised foods dumped on the international markets look like a desirable option for many governments, despite the heightened vulnerability this creates due to increasingly volatile prices and the impacts on local food producers. And the narrow focus on increasing food supplies encouraged the development of modes of production that perhaps fit the requirements of the dominant low-cost food economy, but which result in considerable social and environmental externalities that are not accounted for in the price of food. This is the impasse that we now face.

In the remainder of this introductory chapter, we describe the conviction that has animated us in preparing this collection of essays. We then review the contents of the book, providing context and perspective for each chapter. In order to do so, we briefly recall the main changes that the global food systems have experienced in recent years, and the dilemmas that they now confront as they are being reshaped.

---

[11] During the twentieth century, world population increased from 1.65 billion to 6 billion, and experienced the highest rate of population growth (averaging 2.04% per year) during the late 1960s. The largest annual increase in world population (86 million) took place in the late 1980s. The rate of population growth is currently around 1.2% per year, and the annual increase is now approximately 75 million. Over the next generation, the fastest increases in population will take place in Africa: the population of the continent, now at one billion, increases by about 24 million people each year, and it will have doubled by 2050. See UN Population Division, 'The World at Six Billion', UN document ESA/P/WP.154 (12 October 1999).

[12] See UN Habitat, 'The Challenge of Slums: Global Report on Human Settlements 2003' (2003).

SUPPORTING THE ABILITY OF DEVELOPING COUNTRIES TO FEED THEMSELVES

We are convinced that moving from a vicious to a virtuous cycle is possible. We can significantly improve agricultural productivity where it has been stagnant, and thus raise production where it needs most to be raised—in poor, food-deficit countries—while at the same time increasing the incomes of small farmers and preserving ecosystems. This would slow down the trend towards urbanisation in those countries, which places on the public services of those countries a stress with which they are often unable to cope. It would contribute to rural development, with important multiplier effects on the other sectors of local economies if the benefits are spread across a large number of rural poor rather than concentrated in the hands of a few large landowners.[13] And it would preserve the ability of the generation following ours to meet its own needs. To achieve this, however, pouring money into agriculture will not be sufficient: what matters most will be to create the conditions that will allow small-scale farmers to be rewarded for their work. Improving the viability of small-scale farming should go hand in hand with improving the protection of the rights of agricultural wage workers, including their right to a living wage. There are 450 million of these workers—often former peasants who became landless or quasi-landless—globally, and a significant number of them receive wages too low to feed themselves adequately; this is one reason why large plantations have been able

---

[13] The question of linkages between agriculture and the other sectors of the economy has been a classic theme of economic literature since the early 1960s. See, eg BF Johnston and JW Mellor, 'The Role of Agriculture in Economic Development' (1961) 4 *The American Economic Review* 566. The argument that growth in agriculture can benefit other sectors is sometimes based on the view that it will increase demand for inputs and lead to growth in agro-processing activities, respectively upstream and downstream of the production process on the farm. However, since most agricultural inputs and machinery are imported, and since crops can be sold abroad as raw commodities, whether such a 'production' linkage will occur depends on the organisation of the commodity chain in the country concerned. A far more significant linkage results from the fact that increased incomes in rural areas will raise demand for locally traded goods or services: recent research estimates this 'consumption' linkage to be typically four to five times more important than the 'production' linkage. L Christiaensen, L Demery and J Kuhl, 'The (Evolving) Role of Agriculture in Poverty Reduction—an Empirical Perspective' [2011] *Journal of Development Economics* forthcoming; originally published as World Bank Policy Research Working Paper No 4013 (2006). This linkage—in fact a Keynesian argument—is particularly likely where agricultural growth is widely spread across large segments of a very poor population. It presupposes, of course, that the rural population will buy locally produced goods and locally provided services, and that supply can meet this increase in demand. See C Delgado, J Hopkins and VA Kelly, 'Agricultural Growth Linkages in Sub-Saharan Africa', International Food Policy Research Institute Research Report 107 (Washington, DC, 1998). The important implication is that the diversification of the economy—the strengthening of the industry and the services sectors—must precede the growth of a market for manufactured products and services by the increase of incomes in rural areas: you do not accelerate a process that has not been launched.

to achieve a level of competitiveness that allowed them to capture an increasingly share of markets, as well as the land and water on which farming depends, in many regions relegating smaller farmers to the more hilly and arid soils.

How can this be done? The reason why increasing the overall levels of production will not suffice to combat global hunger is because hunger is the result of poverty and not of inadequate aggregate volumes of food production. The lessons drawn from the path-breaking study by Amartya Sen on twentieth-century famines can be extended, in this regard, to more structural types of hunger.[14] Indeed, the number of the hungry has risen at the same time that the levels of cereals production are breaking record after record on a worldwide basis. For instance, in 2009, the figures of global hunger hovered around all-time high levels, yet cereals harvests that year only modestly fell short of the record high levels of 2008, when 2287 million tons were produced.[15] The number of hungry people has thus continued to increase despite the fact that, on average, increases in annual grain production have consistently exceeded demographic growth.[16]

To successfully combat hunger, therefore, we must not focus only on improving supply. Instead, we must take as our departure point an identification of the obstacles faced by those who are victims of hunger. And we must recognise this basic fact: the majority of the hungry live in rural areas and either depend on small-scale farming for their subsistence or are employed in sub-standard conditions on large plantations. In total, at least 1.5 billion individuals depend on small-scale farming for their livelihoods. They live mostly from subsistence agriculture on less than two hectares of land.[17] Among them, a significant proportion, most of who are net buyers of food, are hungry. The unfair competition between these independent farmers and larger production units results in an underclass of waged agricultural workers being exploited and more farmers being driven off their land.[18] It is by supporting these victims of hunger that we can hope to achieve durable victories against hunger.

---

[14] See AK Sen, *Poverty and Famines. An Essay on Entitlement and Deprivation* (Oxford, Oxford University Press, 1981).

[15] O De Schutter, UN Special Rapporteur on the Right to Food, 'Seed Policies and the Right to Food: Enhancing Agrobiodiversity, Encouraging Innovation', 2, delivered to the General Assembly, UN document A/64/170 (2009).

[16] See Annie Shattuck and Eric Holt-Giménez, 'Moving from Food Crisis to Food Sovereignty' (2010) 13 *Yale Human Rights & Development Law Journal* 421, 422: 'Over the last twenty years, food production has risen steadily at over 2% a year. Meanwhile, over the same period, population growth has slowed to 1.09% per year, with an average growth rate of 1.2%' (internal citations omitted).

[17] WDR 2008, above n 6, at 3.

[18] It is estimated that smallholders represent approximately half of the one billion hungry people in the world, and that waged agricultural workers represent one fifth of victims of hunger. See UN Millennium Project, 'Halving Hunger: It Can be Done, Summary Version of the Report of the Task Force on Hunger' (2005) 6.

This book is guided by a sense of urgency. It is time now to descend from the lofty heights of the commodity prices on the international markets to the situation of those who work in the fields or survive from petty trade on the outskirts of cities. Poor farmers do not sell on the Chicago Board of Trade; poor consumers buy their bag of rice from the local market, not from the commodities exchanges; and the wages of agricultural workers does not rise with commodity prices. By ignoring that perspective on hunger, we fail to see the political economy problems that arise in the food production and distribution chains. We see hunger as a problem of supply and demand, when it is primarily a problem of a lack of access to productive resources such as land and water, of unscrupulous employers and traders, of an increasingly concentrated input providers sector or of insufficient safety nets to support the poor. Too much attention has been paid in the past to addressing the mismatch between supply and demand on the international markets—as if global hunger were the result of physical scarcity at the aggregate level—while too little attention has been paid both to the imbalances of power in the food systems and to the failure of the international economic environment to support efforts aimed at improving the ability of small-scale farmers in developing countries to feed themselves, their families and their communities. These are the core intuitions at the basis of the two parts of the book.

PART I: ADDRESSING POWER IMBALANCES IN THE FOOD SYSTEMS

The Changing Nature of Food Supply Chains

In part I of the book, it is this shift of perspective that we seek to achieve. We note, first, that the recent increase in direct investment in agriculture, referred to above, is part of a larger transformation of the global supply chains in the agrifood sector.[19] Commodity buyers today are larger and more concentrated than previously: for example, according to some estimates, the five largest traders in grains (Cargill, Bunge, Archer Daniels Midland (ADM), Glencore and Dreyfus) control 75% of international trade in grains. These actors seek to respond to the requirements of their food industry clients by increasing vertical coordination and

---

[19] See in particular T Reardon and JA Berdegué, 'The Rapid Rise of Supermarkets in Latin America: Challenges and Opportunities for Development'(2002) 20(4) *Development Policy Review* 317; T Reardon et al, 'Supermarkets and Horticultural Development in Mexico: Synthesis of Findings and Recommendations to USADI and GOM', Report submitted by MSU to USAID/Mexico and USDA/Washington (August 2007); T Reardon et al, 'Agrifood Industry Transformation and Small Farmers in Developing Countries' (2009) 37 *World Development* 1717.

tightening their control over suppliers, while wholesalers and retailers seek to secure stability of supply either by the acquisition of production units or, more often, by the use of explicit contracts (long-term arrangements with producers) or techniques such as preferred supplier lists. The processing industry is also rapidly consolidating, after an initial period during the 1980s and early 1990s during which parastatal large-scale processors were dismantled. This sector is increasingly globalised and dominated by large transnational corporations; even at the domestic level, it was common for private monopolies to replace public monopolies during the privatisations of the 1980s and 1990s in the import–export sector.[20] The retail sector has also witnessed increased multi-nationalisation. Global retailers and fast food chains are now expanding to reach China, India, Russia, Vietnam and, increasingly, Southern and Eastern Africa, and retailers are diversifying from processed foods to semi-processed foods and, increasingly, fresh produce, replacing the more traditional food markets.

In this process of expansion and consolidation, the procurement system too has been modernised. In addition to public standards, private standards imposed by retailers have gained increased importance: these private standards now include not only requirements related to food safety, but also social and environmental requirements included in codes of conduct.[21] Procurement is also increasingly centralised, as the procurement shed (the area from which companies source) expands from national to regional and global networks.

The result is that concentration in the food production and distribution chains has been significantly increasing.[22] The resulting market structure gives buyers considerable bargaining strength over their suppliers, with potentially severe implications for the welfare both of producers and consumers. The intergovernmental initiatives that currently exist

---

[20] J Ziegler, C Golay, C Mahon and SA Way, *The Fight for the Right to Food: Lessons Learned* (Basingstoke: Palgrave Macmillan, 2011) 71.

[21] On compliance with social and environmental standards as a condition of access to global markets, see in particular S Ponte, *Standards, Trade and Equity: Lessons from the Speciality Coffee Industry* (Copenhagen, Centre for Development Research, 2002).

[22] For example, in the Brazilian soybean market, there are roughly 200,000 farmers attempting to sell to five main commodity traders. Three large transnational commodity buyers (ADM, Cargill and Barry Callebaut) dominate the Ivorian cocoa industry. Food processors sometimes also achieve the same degree of concentration: in 1996, two transnational food and beverage companies, Nestlé and Parmalat, shared 53% of the Brazilian dairy processing market, driving off a large number of cooperatives that were led to sell their facilities to those companies. For these and other examples, see P Gibbon, 'The Commodity Question: New Thinking on Old Problems, Human Development Report Office', Occasional Paper 2005/13; B Vorley, 'Food Inc: Corporate Concentration From Farm to Consumer' (UK Food Group, 2003); M Anderson, 'A Question of Governance: To Protect Agribusiness Profits or the Right to Food?' (Agribusiness Action Initiatives, 2009); A Sheldon and R Sterling, 'Estimating the Extent of Imperfect Competition in the Food Industry: What Have We Learned?' (2003) 54(1) *Journal of Agricultural Economics* 89.

to encourage companies to act responsibly are unable to tackle this structural dimension.[23] Concentration in buying markets is particularly worrying, even more so than concentration in selling markets, because dominance in buying markets can be achieved with a relatively smaller market share: for instance, the UK Groceries Market Investigation concluded in 2000 that retail grocers with as little as 8% of the total retail market have substantial buyer power over sellers.

The bargaining power of buyers and retailers is strengthened by a number of factors.[24] In respect of food processors and commodity purchasers, buyer power increases if the geographic selling market is very narrow and if the options for the producer are limited as a result. This may occur if the transport infrastructure is weak or if the agricultural product concerned is extremely perishable. For example, a poultry farmer cannot sell to any processing plants outside a particular radius of his farm, because live poultry may not be viably transported over large distances. This strengthens the bargaining position of poultry processing plants in the area over their suppliers, especially if, as is usually the case, there are a number of poultry farmers in the area. In addition, this gives such processing plants an incentive to engage in tacit collusion to locate their plants at suitable distances from each other, in order to wield greater power over poultry farmers.[25]

Similarly, buyer power may be further strengthened if farmers may not turn their resources to the production of other agricultural goods, or exit the market, except at very great expense. Coffee is a prime example of such low production substitutability: the land on which coffee is cultivated is generally very hilly and located at high altitudes, making it difficult for farmers to grow anything else. Thus, when the price of coffee falls below a profitable level, farmers often do not have the option to cultivate other crops. Instead, they produce even more coffee in an attempt to bring in income in the short-term, thereby depressing coffee prices even further.[26] Entering this 'productivity trap' is not irrational: coffee farmers have to pay for their basic necessities, and they therefore cannot afford to exit the market even temporarily.

As for retailers, buyer power arises from the fact that suppliers need large networks of outlets in order to take advantage of economies of

---

[23] For example, in their current version as last revised in 2000, the OECD Guidelines for Multinational Enterprises have no provision on fair prices to be paid to producers, or on a living wage for workers. Therefore, quite apart from the uneven performance of the mechanisms established to monitor compliance with these guidelines, they are clearly insufficient to ensure that the outcomes of relationships in the food chain will be more equitable.

[24] We gratefully acknowledge the assistance of Aravind Ganesh in the preparation of the following paragraphs.

[25] P Carstensen, 'Buyer Power, Competition Policy and Antitrust: the competitive effects of discrimination among suppliers' (2008) 53 *Antitrust Bulletin* 271, 306.

[26] See R Patel, *Stuffed and Starved* (London, Portobello, 2007) 8–11.

scale, meaning that retailers controlling large swathes of outlets generally obtain very strong bargaining positions. This bargaining strength is enhanced if the market concerned does not possess a strong wholesale sector that could counterbalance retailer power. The pressure that retailers place on wholesalers and food manufacturers ultimately bears upon farmers: food processors and wholesalers who find their profit margins squeezed by the demands of retailers will resort to demanding increasingly lower prices of the farmers from whom they purchase their inputs.

Due to the deeply unequal bargaining positions of food producers and consumers on the one hand, and buyers and retailers on the other hand, the latter can continue to pay relatively low prices for crops even when the prices increase on regional or international markets, and they can continue to charge high prices to consumers even if prices fall on those markets. This explains the fact that, despite the burst of the commodities market bubble in July 2008, which led to lower prices until the new price spike of the fourth quarter of 2010, food prices have consistently remained high on the local markets in many developing countries. Indeed, in a number of these countries, prices were higher in July 2009 than they were a year earlier,[27] and they have continued to remain at high levels.[28] Because certain traders occupy dominant positions in these countries and because competition regimes are non-existent or ineffective, those traders often feel no pressure to allow consumers to benefit from the falling prices on international markets.

In OECD countries, although the revenues of farmers can increase as prices on regional or international markets rise, the revenues of food processors and retailers generally increase in even larger proportions. For example, while in the 1950s farmers in the United States received 40–50% of the food dollar, today they receive around 20%.[29] The situation of smallholders in developing countries is more fragile still. Often, in the absence of proper storage facilities, they have no choice but to sell their crops during the harvest period, when the prices are lowest, even if they then have to buy food, later in the year, at much higher prices.[30] To the

---

[27] See O De Schutter, 'Crisis into Opportunity: Reinforcing Multilateralism', UN document A/HRC/12/31 (September 2009) ¶ 5; FEWSNET (Famine Early Warning Network), 'Price Watch: Urban Food Markets' (USAID, October 2009).

[28] See I Ortiz, J Chai and M Cummins, 'Return of the Food Crisis: The Threat to Poor Households and Policies to Safeguard a Recovery for All', UNICEF Social and Economic Policy Working Paper (January 2011).

[29] University of Georgia College of Agriculture and Environmental Sciences, 'Changes in US Agriculture from the 1950s to the 1990s' (2008).

[30] On the importance of the price variations across seasons for the livelihoods of the poor in developing countries, see in particular R Chambers, R Longhurst and A Pacey, *Seasonal Dimensions to Rural Poverty* (London, Pinter/Totowa, NJ, Allanheld Osmun, 1981); A Ferro-Luzzi and F Branca, 'Nutritional Seasonality: the Dimensions of the Problem' in S Ulijaszek and S Strickland (eds), *Seasonality and Human Ecology* (Cambridge, Cambridge

extent that they do not market their produce themselves, they also often face a very limited number of buyers who can store the food, process it and sell it to the end consumer. The first obstacle can be overcome by the expansion of storage facilities in rural areas, at the local level, or by mechanisms such as warrantage, through which a farmer can place crops in a warehouse at harvest time, using it as a collateral to obtain a loan, which is redeemed during the lean season, at which time the farmer can sell the crops at higher prices. The second obstacle has to do with excessive concentration at certain segments of the food chain, which constitutes an important market failure in the food system.

The vast majority of smallholders produce crops for local consumption. Here, the main answer is to improve information about prices, allowing producers to improve their bargaining position vis-à-vis buyers; to improve infrastructure, in order to allow them to transport more easily their crops to markets, where they can obtain better prices from other buyers; and to encourage the formation of strong cooperatives, both in order to allow farmers to achieve economies of scale in the storage, transportation, processing and marketing of food, and in order to strengthen their bargaining position.

Smallholders wishing to have access to the high-value markets of industrialised countries face distinct problems. In many cases, they have been left out from the potential benefits of the development of global supply chains. While these supply chains have developed at a rapid pace, linking an increasing number of food producers to the international markets, the development of local, national and regional food systems has lagged behind in most poor countries. In poor countries, these markets have not commanded quite the same degree of attention from governments. Because producers exporting their crops were a source of revenue for the state—both in export duties and in foreign currency— they have benefited from some levels of public support, whereas food producers supplying the local markets have been almost entirely neglected until recently. As a result of this imbalance, farmers often must choose between serving the low-value local markets, without appropriate support from the state, or linking to the high-value export markets, in which they face both powerful competitors from other countries and large agribusiness companies whose bargaining power is far more significant than their own. The position of small-scale farmers in linking to export markets is particularly weak since commodity buyers generally prefer sourcing from large producers, both because of the lower transaction costs involved and because larger producers have easier access to capital and thus to non-land farm assets such as storage, greenhouses and

University Press, 1993); and S Devereux, B Vaitla and S Hauenstein Swan, *Seasons of Hunger: Fighting cycles of quiet starvation among the world's rural poor* (Action Against Hunger/Pluto Press, London, 2008).

irrigation systems. Small farmers can only compensate for this disadvantage by their lower labour costs (provided there is some substitutability between capital and labour, which depends on the crops concerned) or if buyers view them as a less risky sourcing option, given that larger farmers have more market options and thus can be less reliable.[31] Small-scale farmers therefore pay a high entry fee into global supply chains: due to the structural obstacles they face, they can only compete by paying low wages to those working on the farm, who are often family members. In addition, entering into such agreements often locks them into a situation of high dependency towards the buyer, especially when they commit to sell exclusively to one buyer. The resulting lack of real choice or alternatives for farmers in developing countries—particularly the smaller farmers—significantly weakens their position as sellers of crops.

The consolidation of the agrifood industry has also led to a number of practices that may be particularly detrimental to producers. For instance, a dominant buyer may demand from sellers a discount from the market price that reflects the savings made by the seller due to increased production. Such a 'discount' may be an explicit reduction in price, or it may come in the form of passing on to the seller certain costs associated with functions normally carried out by the buyer, such as the grading of livestock or stocking of shelves. This effectively means that the dominant buyer alone captures the savings or an inequitably large proportion thereof, which cannot then be passed on to other buyers. This puts non-dominant buyers at a competitive disadvantage in the downstream market, leading to the dominant buyers also becoming dominant on the selling markets.[32] This can also lead to increased concentration on the producer side, as smallholders are pushed out of the market because only large suppliers enjoying economies of scale are able either to afford such volume discounts or to resist dominant buyer demands for them. Another practice that can harm producers is to adjust the terms of supply. Of the 52 practices investigated by the UK Competition Commission in the Groceries Market Investigation, 26 were concerned with 'practices that have the potential to create uncertainty for suppliers regarding their revenues or costs as a result of the transfer of excessive risks or unexpected costs to suppliers'.[33] For

---

[31] See, eg JM Codron et al, 'Supermarkets in Low-Income Mediterranean Countries: Impacts on Horticulture Systems' (2004) 22 *Development Policy Review* 587.
[32] See PW Dobson and R Inderst, 'Differential Buyer Power and the Waterbed Effect: Do Strong Buyers Benefit or Harm Consumers?' (2007) 28 *European Competition Law Review* 393.
[33] UK Competition Commission, Groceries Market Investigation, ¶9.52, 166–67.

example, flexibility and 'just in time' supply is increasingly required.[34] Other similar practices have also been documented.[35]

Reforming the Food Supply Chains

These are some of the issues addressed by the contributions collected in part I of the book. Chapter 2, written by Kaitlin Cordes, examines the ways in which agribusiness transnational corporations (TNCs) can affect the right to food through the various relations they entertain with the other actors in the food chain. Agribusiness TNCs have exceptional power within the global food system, as subsectors have become progressively more concentrated, thus enabling agribusiness TNCs to affect nearly every aspect of the global food system. Agribusiness TNCs influence decisions over which food is grown in various locations, how land is used, which seeds are used and whether they can be saved, how water is allocated and what research is undertaken. They also directly and indirectly employ a significant amount of the global population and, given their market power, influence the prices paid to farmers and farmworkers at the lowest end of the agribusiness chain. Cordes examines the impact of two different sectors of the food industry on the right to food: the food processing sector, which trades in commodities and also processes and manufactures the food that much of the world eats, and the biotechnology sector, which produces the seeds, agrochemicals and other inputs that are used in most global agriculture production. She first addresses the influence of the food processing industry on the right to food. In particular, she looks at the market power of commodity traders, which enables them to influence the prices paid to producers around the world. She also looks at the influence of food and beverage companies, using the examples of the beverage industry's impact on the right to water and the influence of food companies over prices and conditions in the cocoa industry. The chapter then discusses the impact of biotechnology companies, examining the influence of those companies on access to resources and the right to food, especially through intellectual property rights regimes. Cordes concludes with recommendations for agribusiness TNCs, governments, and policymakers focused on improving the impact of agribusiness TNCs on the right to food.

In chapter 3, Margaret Cowan expands our understanding of the influence of private actors within the global food system by focusing

---

[34] T Lang, 'Food Industrialisation and Food Power: Implications for Food Governance' (2003) 21 *Development Policy Review* 555.

[35] ActionAid, 'Who Pays?'. See also Collateral Damage (Banana Link, 2006) (describing how price pressures from UK retailers have forced banana producers to cut wages, replace permanent labourers with temporary contract workers and suppress trade union rights).

on the role of global retailers in the food distribution system and their impact on smallholder farmers. The transformation of food retail and rapid supermarket consolidation have had dramatic impacts on access to food. Although the buying practices of powerful retailers have increased their capacity to deliver affordable, high-quality food to consumers, the same practices have also reinforced low wages and payments to those who produce our food. Cowan first documents the rise of supermarkets in industrialised and developing countries. She then examines the modernisation of procurement systems, including flexible production and 'just in time' delivery, the creation of private standards, and the rise of 'preferred supplier' relationships, and addresses the impact of such systems on consumers. Currently, food retailers often enjoy retailer buyer power, which allows them to purchase from suppliers at more favourable terms than would be expected under competitive conditions. This, in turn, means that food retailers often pay lower prices and pass risks to vulnerable smallholder farmers. US and EU antitrust and competition laws have been inadequately tailored to the realities of modern food retailer practices and their anticompetitive effects. Given this environment, it is important to improve smallholder access to global supply chains in a way that increases smallholder security. This will require coordinated efforts of public and private bodies, including providing smallholders with access to resources, improving domestic infrastructure, and coordinating agricultural policies and marketing initiatives at the regional level. Cowan concludes her contribution by exploring government policies that can increase smallholder security and examining the role that private sector and non-governmental organisations can play to support smallholders.

Imbalances in power pose real problems in the current development of food chains, and governments should prioritise remedying those imbalances, for instance by better use of competition regimes and by supporting farmers' organisations where they are weak. Similar imbalances also exist as a result of the increased competition for natural resources, particularly farmland and water. Since 2009–10, the issue of large-scale acquisitions or leases of farmland in developing countries— what non-governmental organisations refer to as 'land-grabbing'—has attracted an enormous amount of attention, commensurate with the scope of the phenomenon: based on press reports, the World Bank notes, for instance, that 'investors expressed interest in 56 million ha of land globally in less than a year [between 1 October 2008 and 31 August 2009]', which represents double the size of France's farmland and two-fifths of all farmland in the EU.[36] Although this race towards farmland can be

---

[36] World Bank, 'Rising Global Interest in Farmland: Can It Yield Sustainable and Equitable Benefits?' (September 2010) xxxii. It is important to note that this figure refers to the projects reported, though the actual implementation lags behind quite significantly.

explained by a number of drivers,[37] it can be described generally as an attempt by both public investors (directly or through sovereign wealth funds or publicly owned companies) and private investors to secure access to land, in order to meet the food and energy needs of cash-rich but resource-poor countries.[38] As noted by Mann and Smaller, this results in 'shifting land and water uses from local farming to essentially long-distance farming to meet home state food and energy needs',[39] thus allowing investors to circumvent the international markets and creating

> a new dynamic of global importance. It is no longer just the crops that are commodities: rather it is the land and water for agriculture themselves that are increasingly becoming commodified, with a global market in land and water rights being created.[40]

The choice of major advanced economies to favour the switch to biofuels in transport through blending mandates and subsidies has been a significant factor behind this global rush towards farmland.[41] Many observers note that these policies have significantly increased the risk that poor farmers will be evicted from their land.[42] Indeed, an inventory presented

---

According to the Bank, almost 30% are still in an exploratory stage (that is, they have not obtained government approval); 18% have been approved but have not started yet; more than 30% are at initial development stages; and only 21% have initiated actual farming, often on a scale much smaller than intended. Ibid, 36.

[37] On these various drivers, see, eg listed in chronological order of publication, International Fund for Agricultural Development (IFAD), 'The Growing Demand for Land: Risks and Opportunities for Smallholder Farmers', a discussion paper prepared for the Roundtable organised during the thirty-second session of IFAD's Governing Council (18 February 2009); L Cotula, S Vermeulen, R Leonard and J Keeley, *Land Grab or Development Opportunity?* (London/Rome, IIED, FAO and IFAD, 2009) 62 (based on detailed examination of land deals in Sudan, Ethiopia, Madagascar, Mozambique and Tanzania); Deutsche Gesellschaft für Technische Zusammenarbeit (GTZ), 'Foreign Direct Investment (FDI) in Land in Developing Countries', German Federal Ministry for Economic Cooperation and Development, Eschborn, December 2009; M Kugelman and SL Levenstein (eds), *Land Grab? The Race for the World's Farmland* (Washington, DC, Woodrow Wilson International Center for Scholars, 2009); A-C Gerlach and P Liu, 'Resource-Seeking Foreign Direct Investment in African Agriculture: A Review of Country Case Studies', FAO Commodity and Trade Policy Research Working Paper No 31 (September 2010); World Bank, ibid.

[38] For a discussion of the impacts on the rights of land users, see O De Schutter, 'The Green Rush: The Race Towards Farmland and the Rights of Land Users' (2011) 52(2) *Harvard International Law Journal* (forthcoming).

[39] H Mann and C Smaller, 'Foreign Land Purchases for Agriculture: What Impact on Sustainable Development?', Sustainable Development Innovation Briefs, United Nations Department of Economics Social Affairs, no 8 (New York, January 2010) 1–2.

[40] Ibid. See also Gerlach and Liu, above n 37, 5: '[T]his new trend differs from more traditional forms of international investment in the agro-food sector which were mainly targeting markets. Through the new investment forms, investors seek to gain access to natural resources, in particular land and water'.

[41] It should be noted, however, that energy from biomass can serve a number of uses, of which transport is only a minor part. See FAO, 'The State of Food and Agriculture 2008. Biofuels: Prospects, Risks and Opportunities' (Rome, 2008) 11.

[42] See UN Energy, 'Sustainable Bioenergy: A Framework for Decision Makers' (New York, 2007) 24; FAO, ibid, 83: 'Expansion of biofuel production will, in many cases, lead

16 *Olivier De Schutter and Kaitlin Y Cordes*

by the World Bank in April 2010, which listed 389 large-scale acquisitions or long-term leases of land in 80 countries, noted that while 37% of the so-called investment projects are meant to produce food (crops and livestock), agrofuels account for 35% of such projects.[43] More recently, in what remains the largest survey conducted to date on large-scale investments in land, the World Bank reviewed 405 projects with commodity data. The review showed that 37% of these projects focus on food crops, 21% on industrial or cash crops and 21% on biofuels, with the remainder distributed among conservation and game reserves, livestock and plantation forestry in order, inter alia, to capture carbon credits.[44] Energy crops thus represent a significant driver in this overall trend towards large-scale acquisitions or leases of farmland.

In chapter 4, Ann Sofie Cloots examines the impacts on the right to food of this competition between food and fuel for arable lands. This chapter explains the reasons behind the biofuels boom, the subsequent debate over their value and impact, and their place in the international trade regime. Cloots notes that, although many people have pointed to biofuels as an important solution to address climate change, the environmental gains of switching to such fuels are mixed. She then addresses the multiple potential impacts of expanded production of crops for fuel from the perspective of the right to food, the most obvious of which is the potential for rising food prices due to competition over arable land. In addition, increased biofuels production could lead to deforestation and negative effects on biodiversity, the concentration of economic power through intellectual property rights, water pollution, and an increased use of fertilisers and pesticides to grow crops for biofuels. On the other hand, the increased use of biofuels has the potential to create more employment opportunities at many stages along the supply chain. Biofuels could also contribute to improving local energy supplies and could drive development in rural areas that traditionally lack affordable energy options. After discussing these potential impacts, Cloots evaluates biofuels from the perspective of the right to food. In doing so, she examines states' obligations to respect, protect and fulfil the right to food, as well as the responsibilities of companies regarding the right to food. She concludes that, although domestic policies are important, the

---

to greater competition for land. For smallholder farmers, women farmers and/or pastoralists, who may have weak land-tenure rights, this could lead to displacement'. L Cotula, N Dyer and S Vermeulen, *Fuelling Exclusion? The Biofuel Boom and Poor People's Access to Land* (London, International Institute for Environment and Development (IIED) and the FAO, 2009); R Smolker et al, 'The Real Cost of Agrofuels: Impacts on Food, Forests, Peoples and the Climate' (Global Forest Coalition and Global Justice Ecology Project, 2008).

[43] The figures are from presentations made by the World Bank, most recently at its annual conference held in Washington, DC on 24–25 April 2010. See 'The World Bank in the Hot Seat' [May 2010] *GRAIN*.

[44] See World Bank, above n 36, 51.

problems raised by biofuels cannot be resolved by countries in isolation. She thus argues for the creation of a transnational framework to address the impacts of biofuels production.

PART II: TRADE AND AID: AN ENABLING INTERNATIONAL ENVIRONMENT

The Dependency of Poor Developing Countries on the International Markets

Part II of the book addresses what might be called the addiction of poor developing countries to cheap food dumped on international markets. It examines how this addiction has been encouraged by a perverse system of international trade and the misguided use of food aid. And it explores potential solutions to overcome the burden of this dependency. Since the 1980s, the 49 least-developed countries have shifted from being net food exporters to being net food importers, and their food bills have significantly increased as a result. The FAO estimates that their food bills have risen from 45 to 70% of those countries' total merchandise exports, placing them in a particularly vulnerable situation as the international markets become less reliable and as prices of food commodities will be subjected to more frequent spikes than in the past, particularly as a result of weather-related events linked to climate change.[45] While part of this shift can be explained by the persistent strong demographic growth in these countries, the major factor leading to this situation was the lowering of import tariffs during the 1980s as part of the structural adjustment imposed on these countries as a condition for being able to continue to borrow on international markets. At the time, the poor countries were encouraged to specialise into a limited range of tropical commodities, and to increase their dependence on international markets to feed their populations. Food on international markets would remain cheap and abundant, they were led to believe, as it was heavily subsidised by OECD countries' governments, and it thus made more sense to purchase food under such conditions than to produce it themselves. The result was that the fast-growing urban populations in least-developed countries increasingly consumed imported (often processed) foods, instead of buying locally produced (and fresher) foods. Instead of links being strengthened between the countryside and the cities, these worlds grew apart from each other. This created more rural poverty, and more inequality in the rural areas: deprived of access to markets, local farmers produced no

---

[45] Statement by the FAO at the WTO Ministerial Conference, fifth session, Cancún, Mexico, 10–14 September 2003, WTO document WT/MIN(03)/ST/61.

more than they could consume themselves or sell locally, except for the few larger producers who entered the global commodity chains.

The resulting shortfalls in production in poor countries, which rendered them vulnerable to price shocks on international markets and to regular balance-of-payments problems, can hardly be said to be compensated by the delivery of food aid. There are important distinctions to be made, of course, between the three distinct modalities under which food aid is provided. It is now well acknowledged that the shipment of donor-country-sourced commodities (ie food transfers) is only justified in the relatively exceptional case where there is a lack of food availability in the region concerned, and that cash-based food aid, allowing food transfers paid for by donor funding in so-called 'triangular' purchases, are otherwise a highly preferable option. Moreover, where the local producers can meet local demand and where the need for food aid stems from an insufficient purchasing power for the poorest segment of the population, aid should take the form of vouchers or cash transfers, enabling recipients to obtain food from the local market.[46] However, questions still regularly surface about how to combine emergency responses—which have gained significantly in importance over the past 20 years as a proportion of the total food aid provided—with the need to promote local food markets and food security in food-aid-recipient countries. And, although there is a growing consensus on the desirability of providing greater flexibility, including through the use of locally and regionally procured food transfers and cash or voucher transfers, and on the importance of food aid being provided with a clear exit strategy in order to avoid dependency, these commitments remain unfulfilled in practice.

Emergency measures in any case are not a substitute for more structural measures to secure longer-term food supply, particularly through support for agriculture in developing countries. Yet, in the choice of such measures, conflicts may emerge between short-term and long-term considerations. Developing countries have been critical of the distortions resulting from the agricultural subsidies benefiting producers from developed countries, particularly in the EU, the US and Japan. In a much-publicised report presented in 2005, the UN Development Programme (UNDP) noted: 'When it comes to world agricultural trade, market success is determined not by comparative advantage, but by comparative access to subsidies—an area in which producers in poor

---

[46] See O De Schutter, 'The Role of Development Cooperation and Food Aid in Realizing the Right to Adequate Food: Moving from Charity to Obligation', UN document A/HRC/10/005 (March 2009). The report includes a number of recommendations concerning the reform of the Food Aid Convention, which is still under discussion at the time of writing. See also, in particular, CB Barrett and DG Maxwell, *Food Aid after Fifty Years: Recasting its Role* (London and New York, Routledge, 2005); FAO, 'The State of Food and Agriculture 2006. Food Aid for Food Security?' (Rome, 2006.)

countries are unable to compete'.[47] Developed countries' subsidies to their agricultural producers were estimated at the time to amount to 350 billion USD per year. This, in turn, the UNDP noted in the same report, represents a loss of 34 billion USD per year for developing countries, whose producers are confronted with the dumping of heavily subsidised agricultural products on the world markets; this sum did not even include the dynamic and spillover effects on communities that depend on the agricultural sector for investment and employment. Many therefore see the recent increase in the prices of food commodities as an opportunity to finally end this massive distortion of trade, by making it easier for developed states to justify lowering the level of support to their farmers.

Things are not so simple, however. There exist significant differences between different groups of developing countries on this issue. The Cairns Group (Argentina, Brazil, Chile, Colombia, Costa Rica, Indonesia, Malaysia, the Philippines, South Africa, Thailand and Uruguay) have a strong comparative advantage in agriculture and would clearly benefit from the removal, or at least the lowering, of the trade-distorting subsidies of developed countries. In contrast, other developing countries are net food-importing countries, and their populations would, in general and in the short term, be hurt by the inflationary impact of the removal of subsidies, aggravating the negative impact on food security of the current peak in food prices.[48] In addition, due to the lack of investment in agriculture for many years, many farmers from this second group of countries might not be able to benefit from the removal of trade-distorting agricultural subsidies, or from the resulting increase in prices on the international markets. What is needed, therefore, is to plan a transition. We need to move from a situation in which the poorest developing countries depend on the availability of cheap food on the international markets to feed themselves—on average, the LDCs import 20% of the food that they consume—to a situation in which the local food systems are strengthened, and links between local food producers and urban consumers are rebuilt.

---

[47] UNDP, 'Human Development Report 2005: International Cooperation at a Crossroads: Aid, Trade and Security in an Unequal World', 130.
[48] See A Panagariya, 'Agricultural Liberalisation and the Least Developed Countries: Six Fallacies' [2005] *World Economy: Global Trade Policy* 1277. See also J Stiglitz and A Charlton, *Fair Trade for All: How Trade Can Promote Development* (Oxford, Oxford University Press, 2005) 233. See chapter 5 for more on this.

Limiting the Dependency

These are the issues discussed by the chapters collected in part II of this volume. In chapter 5, Olivier De Schutter examines whether trade liberalisation in agricultural commodities can provide a solution to the problem of global hunger. The Preamble of the Marrakech Agreement establishing the WTO recognises that, far from being an end in itself, the encouragement of trade by the establishment of a rules-based system of international trade and by the gradual lowering of barriers to trade should serve the ends of human development. De Schutter argues that, if this objective is to be fulfilled, and if trade is to contribute to the realisation of the right to adequate food, the regime of international trade needs to recognise the specificity of agricultural products, rather than to treat them as any other commodities. It should also allow more flexibility to developing countries, particularly in order to shield their agricultural producers from the competition from industrialised countries' farmers.

For countries that have a competitive agricultural sector, the expansion of international trade in agricultural commodities can have a growth-enhancing effect and improve their trade balance. However, this chapter notes that these benefits should be balanced against other potential impacts on the right to food, and it documents three such potential impacts. First, the development of global supply chains results in an increased dependency on international trade, for both net food-exporting countries and for net food-importing countries. This may lead to a loss of export revenues for agricultural exporters when the prices of export commodities go down, as well as to threats to local producers when low-priced imports arrive on the domestic markets, against which these producers may be unable to compete. Conversely, when prices rise, the dependency of low-income net food-importing countries on food imports can lead to balance-of-payments problems against which the mechanisms currently established within the WTO have failed to protect them. Secondly, the expansion of global supply chains increases the role of large transnational corporations in the agrifood sector, vis-à-vis both producers and consumers. As already noted above, this creates a potential for abuses of market power in increasingly concentrated global food supply chains and may increase the divide of domestic farming sectors between subsistence farming on the one hand and export agriculture in cash crops on the other. Thirdly, the expansion of trade in agricultural commodities has potential impacts on the environment and on human health and nutrition, impacts that usually receive little attention in international trade discussions, despite their close relationship to the right to adequate food. Trade liberalisation in agricultural commodities is thus far from constituting an unmitigated good, particularly for the LDCs whose agricultural sectors have been severely hurt by dumping practices in the past, and which should prioritise regaining their ability to feed themselves—in other words, managing a transition towards less trade rather than more trade.

Chapter 6, by Jennifer Mersing, considers the key question highlighted above: how to phase out rich country agricultural subsidies without increasing hunger in the developing world? Rich country agricultural subsidies, including export subsidies and domestic support schemes, can dramatically affect agricultural producers in developing countries. Mersing describes this impact in the context of the 2007–08 food price crisis and increased hunger in developing countries; she contends that the underlying factors for that crisis remain and will contribute to increased food prices again in the near future. Although the current multilateral framework for international trade has led to some changes in the composition of rich countries' subsidies, they continue to have a distorting affect on the global agricultural market. They can also undercut producers in developing countries. Indeed, many developing countries have been pushing for a reduction in agricultural subsidies in rich countries. For developing countries that have a comparative advantage in the production of agricultural products, reducing those distorting subsidies, combined with strengthening their own agricultural sectors, could lead to numerous positive outcomes. However, as noted above, phasing out such subsidies will not benefit everyone in all developing countries. In countries that are net food importers, doing so may lead to increased food costs for consumers. Thus, while reducing or removing agricultural subsidies in rich countries is important for many developing countries, efforts must be undertaken simultaneously to protect vulnerable populations in developing countries from a potential increased risk of hunger. Mersing provides recommendations for actions that governments in both developed and developing countries could take to phase out distorting agricultural subsidies without increasing global hunger.

In chapter 7, Boyan Konstantinov explores the potential for invoking the right to food in the WTO dispute settlement process. The author begins the discussion by tracing the development of the contemporary definition of the right to food, the history of trade liberalisation and negotiations within the WTO related to agriculture. Although international trade can have a substantial impact on human rights, the WTO is often seen as failing to address human rights issues. This includes a failure to address concerns related to the right to food, despite the impact of developed countries' subsidies and dumping practices. While some scholars contend that the WTO is not authorised to address human rights, others argue that the system should be changed to be more sensitive to human rights issues. Even if the WTO wished to address human rights issues, however, it has limited ability to do so, because its decisions are generally the result of complex multilateral negotiations. Konstantinov highlights several potential opportunities for invoking human rights within the WTO system. One of the best options is to raise human rights concerns in dispute settlement procedures. Those procedures allow adjudicating bodies to make decisions that bind the concerned parties, regardless of whether they consent. To date, there have not been any dispute settlement cases based on human rights considerations. Moreover, it is unclear how WTO adjudicating bodies would address them. Despite this uncertainty, it is possible that human rights or right-to-food considerations could be invoked in the dispute settlement procedures. Konstantinov explores this possibility, and then analyses the advantages and disadvantages attached to invoking the right to food in dispute settlement procedures.

Chapter 8, by Loreto Ferrer Moreu, discusses how food aid should be undertaken to ensure that states fulfil their obligations towards the right to food. Effective food aid requires accountability at both the national and international levels. Ferrer Moreu examines the current international framework of food aid, and identifies three trends in food aid: the consolidation of a human-rights-based approach to food aid, the revitalisation of the obligation to cooperate and the emergence of the concept of food security as it relates to food aid. She emphasises the distinctions to be made between the three traditional categories of food aid: programme food aid, project food aid and emergency food aid. Each type of food aid has different goals, and not all are primarily driven by efforts to feed the hungry. Ferrer Moreu analyses the implementation of food aid programmes, projects and emergency assistance, and highlights problems that arise with each type of food aid. One overarching problem is the lack of political will to implement international agreements effectively. The author argues that food aid is often not an appropriate solution. There are, however, certain circumstances in which food aid is useful. These include short-term humanitarian assistance, the provision of longer-term safety nets for asset protection, and limited, targeted and efficient development interventions for asset building among chronically poor or vulnerable populations. Moreover, if local markets are functioning well, then food aid should not be used; rather, cash transfers or employment creation efforts would be better solutions to address local needs. If local markets are not functioning well, then food for food aid should be purchased in nearby markets—primarily through local purchases or triangular transactions. Ferrer Moreu concludes by providing other suggestions on better ways to approach food aid. She also points to the concept of food sovereignty as a guiding framework that enables states to address the root causes of hunger while fulfilling their obligations regarding the right to food.

Like in part I of the book, the authors in this part have framed their analyses using the human right to adequate food as their departure point. The realisation of the right to adequate food should not only guide the efforts that states make at the domestic level; it should also direct the development of a more equitable multilateral trading system, as well as the reform of food aid. While the right to adequate food is recognised under Article 25 of the Universal Declaration of Human Rights,[49] Article 28 of the Declaration states that 'everyone is entitled to a social and international order in which the rights and freedoms set forth in this Declaration can be fully realized'. This provision is certainly one of the most underestimated clauses of the Declaration. It recognises the co-dependency of national and international measures in the fulfilment of human rights. The right to adequate food can only be fully realised by states within a multilateral trading system that enables them to pursue policies aimed at realising the right to food. Such a system should not only refrain from imposing obligations that directly infringe upon the right to food, but should also ensure that all states have the policy space they require to take measures that contribute to the progressive realisation of the right to food under their jurisdiction, and that they are able to use it. As stated by the Committee on Economic, Social and Cultural Rights, the body of independent experts that monitors compliance with the International Covenant on Economic, Social and Cultural Rights,[50] this instrument requires that they 'move as expeditiously as possible towards that goal' by making 'full use of the maximum available resources'.[51]

The obligation to move towards the realisation of the right to food must be facilitated, not impeded, by the organisation of the multilateral trade regime. Indeed, Article 11(2) of the Covenant itself, which recognises the 'fundamental right of everyone to be free from hunger', also requires states to adopt, 'individually and through international cooperation, the measures, including specific programmes, which are needed, taking into account the problems of both food-importing and food-exporting countries, to ensure an equitable distribution of world food supplies in relation to need'. It thus refers to food imports (and the corresponding exports) as a means to ensure the fundamental right to be free from hunger. The drafters of the Covenant thus seemed to assume that the right to food may require that food will have to travel from

---

[49] GA Res. 217 A (III), UN document A/810 (1948), 71.
[50] Adopted on 16 December 1966, GA Res. 2200(XXII), UN GAOR, 21st session, Supp No 16, US document A/6316 (1966), 993 UNTS 3. The right to adequate food is referred to under Art 11 of the International Covenant on Economic, Social and Cultural Rights. There are also references to the human right to food in Arts 24 and 27 of the Convention on the Rights of the Child, and in the International Convention on the Elimination of All Forms of Discrimination against Women (Art 12(2)).
[51] UN Committee on Economic, Social and Cultural Rights, General Comment No 12 (1999), 'The Right to Adequate Food (Art 11)', UN document E/C.12/1999/5, ¶ 9.

regions that have a surplus to regions that have a deficit in food. Yet, for the reasons already explained above, the relationship between the right to food and trade in agricultural commodities should be examined without presuming that hunger or malnutrition are necessarily the result of a lack of food availability. We therefore need to shift the perspective from aggregate values—from the benefits of trade for the country as a whole—to the impacts of trade on the most vulnerable and food insecure. Just as increases in production in any one country are not sufficient to combat hunger if, in that country, a group of the population lacks the purchasing power to buy the food that is available on the markets,[52] the expansion of volumes of traded goods is not an answer to hunger if it leads, not to poverty reduction and decreasing inequalities, but to the further marginalisation of those who are not benefiting from trade and may instead be made more vulnerable by trade liberalisation.

This volume highlights current problems within the global food system and seeks to explain how reforms at both the domestic level and the international level are crucial in order to address global hunger effectively. Approaches that are based on the right to food and focused on the accountability of domestic and transnational actors, as well as trade and aid regimes overall, are the best way forward for improving individual food security and ensuring that governments meet their obligations to protect, respect and fulfil the right to food. This collection of essays therefore explores the ways in which food is produced and distributed; it examines the trade and aid regimes that shape global food distribution; and it sees accountability as key in order to improve the right to food around the world. The authors are not in agreement on all issues, and specific policy prescriptions made in different chapters may therefore conflict with one another,[53] but they share a common conviction that the current organisation of the food system is unsustainable, and that it is in urgent need of repair. Their effort is a contribution towards that goal.

---

[52] AK Sen, above n 14. See also J Drèze and AK Sen, *Hunger and Public Action* (Oxford, Oxford University Press, 1989).

[53] The authors were all participants in a seminar on 'Globalization and Human Rights' directed by Olivier De Schutter at Columbia University School of Law during the spring of 2008. All the chapters originated from that seminar, except for chapter 5. They were subsequently revised, and updated in 2011.

Part I

Addressing Power Imbalances in the Food Systems

2

The Impact of Agribusiness Transnational Corporations on the Right to Food

KAITLIN Y CORDES

THE RIGHT TO food stands out as one of the most urgent, and compelling, human rights in a world that already produces more than enough food to feed its current population,[1] yet in which a child below 10 'dies from hunger and malnutrition-related diseases'[2] every five seconds. No private actors have as great an impact on the right to food as agribusiness transnational corporations (TNCs). From influencing the scope and quality of the food that the world produces, purchases and consumes, to directly and indirectly employing a significant amount of the world's population, agribusiness shapes both the global food system and access to food. Indeed, agribusiness influences agricultural production in nearly every country in the world; it is the thread that ties together the starving coffee farmer in Uganda,[3] the struggling dairy farmer in Pakistan,[4] the harassed corn farmer in the US[5] and the worried rice farmer in Thailand.[6]

---

[1] J Ziegler, UN Special Rapporteur on the Right to Food, 'Report of the Special Rapporteur on the Right to Food, Delivered to the Human Rights Council', UN document A/HRC/7/ (2008).

[2] Ibid.

[3] S Morris, 'Unfair Trade Winds: What do Ecuadorean Bananas, Ugandan Coffee and English Apples Have in Common? No Power', *The Guardian*, 17 May 2003 (discussing extremely low prices paid to coffee farmers in Uganda).

[4] Since entering Pakistan in 1988, one agribusiness company 'almost has a monopoly of the UHT milk market' and 'has been accused of exploiting Pakistani dairy farmers by buying up their milk for less than it costs to produce and selling it back to local people at inflated prices'. B Vorley, 'Food, Inc: Corporate Concentration from Farm to Consumer (UK Food Group, 2003) 59.

[5] D Barlett and JB Steele, 'Monsanto's Harvest of Fear', *Vanity Fair*, May 2008 (discussing agribusiness company's tactics to intimidate farmers it believes use its genetically modified seeds without its permission, even those who have never bought or planted such seeds).

[6] M Macan-Markar, 'Green Groups Will Take GM Crops Issue to Court', *IPS News*, 9 January 2008 (noting that EU has said it will not import rice from Thailand that has been

Agribusiness TNCs[7] have unprecedented power in the global food system. Nearly every sector of the global food system has become progressively more consolidated in recent decades, as large 'multinational agroenterprises increasingly dominate the agribusiness sector along the value chain'.[8] Less than a dozen corporations control one-third of the global commercial seed market.[9] Four cocoa traders dominate 40% of the global cocoa market.[10] Two companies control 40% of the grain exports from the US.[11] This domination by large agribusiness TNCs affects the global food supply in numerous ways, with many implications for the right to food. It determines what food is grown where, promoting export crop production at the expense of more diversified crop production for domestic consumption.[12] It allows agribusiness TNCs to influence how land is used, which seeds are used and how they are saved, and how water is allocated. It facilitates biotechnology research that focuses more on the needs of large corporations than on those of poor people in developing countries.[13]

Moreover, agribusiness employs, directly and indirectly, an extraordinary number of people. The Food and Agriculture Organization of the UN (FAO) states that 'agribusiness is one of the main generators of employment and income worldwide'.[14] While most agribusiness TNCs are headquartered in western countries,[15] many of the people producing the commodities on which the food industry is based are located in developing countries. Due to their market power, however, agribusiness TNCs greatly influence both the high cost of inputs needed to grow

genetically modified, and discussing concern that allowing GM rice to be produced in Thailand will detrimentally affect poor rice farmers).

[7] Although small and medium enterprises exist in the agribusiness sector, some of which are important domestic players, this chapter focuses solely on transnational corporations, which overwhelmingly control and influence almost all aspects of the agribusiness industry.

[8] World Bank, 'World Development Report 2008: Agriculture for Development', Focus D, 135 (2008).

[9] Ziegler, above n 1, ¶ 42, *citing* Erosion, Technology and Concentration Action Group, 82 Communiqué, Nov/December 2003.

[10] World Bank, above n 8, 136.

[11] Sophia Murphy, *Concentrated Market Power and Agricultural Trade*, EcoFair Trade Dialogue Discussion Papers, 14 (August 2006).

[12] See, eg Charles D Brockett, *The Right to Food and United States Policy in Guatemala*, 6 Hum. Rts. Q., 366 (1984).

[13] World Bank, above n 8, 158.

[14] The Food and Agriculture Organization of the UN [hereinafter FAO], Agribusiness Development, www.fao.org/WAICENT/faoINFO/AGRICULT/ags///subjects/en/agribusiness/index.html.

[15] As of 2008, eight out of the top 10 agricultural companies, ranked by agricultural sales, were American, while the other two were located in New Zealand and Switzerland. See Hoover's Industry Snapshots, 2008: Agriculture (2008). The top 10 food manufacturers, ranked by food sales, were all based in the US or Europe. See Hoover's Industry Snapshots, 2008: Food (2008).

food and the low prices paid for commodities. Agribusiness TNCs thus deeply affect the ability of those at the lowest end of the agribusiness chain—both the farmers who are paid low prices for the commodities they grow and the workers on farms and plantations who receive low wages for their work—to earn sufficient income to afford to purchase 'quantitatively and qualitatively adequate and sufficient food'.[16]

This chapter examines the role of agribusiness TNCs in respect of the right to food. Part I briefly discusses the scope of agribusiness TNCs, the definition of the right to food and the possible ways in which TNCs can have an impact on the right to food. Part II explores the impact of two different sectors of the food industry on the right to food: the food processing sector, which trades in commodities and also processes and manufactures the food that much of the world eats, and the biotechnology sector, which produces the seeds, agrochemicals and other inputs that are used in most global agriculture production. It first examines the impact of food processing companies on the right to food, focusing in particular on the market power of commodity traders and the influence wielded by large food and beverage companies. It then discusses the impact of biotechnology companies on the right to food, examining in particular the influence of those companies on access to resources. Part III discusses recommendations for improving the role of agribusiness TNCs, so that they can have a more positive impact on the right to food.

I. AGRIBUSINESS AND THE RIGHT TO FOOD: HOW DO THEY RELATE?

'Agribusiness' is a term that is widely used, but not always understood. Vilified by many activists, promoted by some aid agencies, dressed up as 'life sciences' by parts of the industry, agribusiness covers a wide array of businesses and activities. The FAO defines agribusiness as 'the collective business activities that are performed from farm to fork. It covers the supply of agricultural inputs, the production and transformation of agricultural products and their distribution to final consumers.'[17] Similarly, the Agribusiness Council, an industry group based in the US, describes agribusiness as 'encompass[ing] all aspects of agricultural production, processing and distribution. This includes food, . . . agricultural chemicals and pharmaceuticals . . .; in short; all of the major elements essential to the establishment and operation of efficient agro-food enterprises.'[18]

Transnational corporations are business enterprises or 'clusters of

---

[16] Ziegler, above n 1, ¶ 16.
[17] FAO, above n 14.
[18] The Agribusiness Council, www.agribusinesscouncil.org.

economic entities' that operate in at least two countries.[19] Agribusiness TNCs are thus transnational corporations that are primarily focused on some aspect of food production, 'from farm to fork'.[20] The term encompasses companies that develop seeds and agrochemicals, trade in commodities, process and manufacture food and beverage products, and retail food.[21] The largest agribusiness TNCs are almost all incorporated in the US or Europe.[22]

The right to food is one of the most basic economic, social and cultural rights imaginable, because it addresses one of the most fundamental needs faced by all humans. It has been described as 'above all, the right to be able to feed oneself in dignity'.[23] The UN Committee on Economic, Social and Cultural Rights states that the right to food 'is realized when every man, woman and child, alone or in community with others, has physical and economic access at all times to adequate food or means for its procurement'.[24] The former UN Special Rapporteur on the right to food, Jean Ziegler, has elaborated on this definition, stating that it is

> the right to have regular, permanent and unrestricted access, either directly or by means of financial purchases, to quantitatively and qualitatively adequate and sufficient food corresponding to the cultural traditions of the people to which the consumer belongs, and which ensures a physical and mental, individual and collective, fulfilling and dignified life free of fear.[25]

This right includes the right to have access to resources and to the means to ensure and produce one's own subsistence, including land, small-scale irrigation, seeds, credit, technology, and local and regional markets, especially in rural areas and for vulnerable and discriminated groups, traditional fishing areas, a sufficient income to enable one to live in dignity, including for rural and industrial workers, and access to social

---

[19] The draft Norms on the Responsibilities of Transnational Corporations and Other Business Enterprises with Regard to Human Rights (hereinafter 'Norms on the Responsibilities of Transnational Corporations') defined a 'transnational corporation' as 'an economic entity operating in more than one country or a cluster of economic entities operating in two or more countries – whatever their legal form, whether in their home country or country of activity, and whether taken individually or collectively'. UN Economic and Social Council (ECOSOC), Sub-Committee on the Promotion and Protection of Human Rights, 'Norms on the Responsibilities of Transnational Corporations and Other Business Enterprises with Regard to Human Rights', ¶ 20, UN document E/CN.4/Sub.2/2003/12/Rev.2 (26 August 2003).

[20] FAO, above n 14.

[21] This chapter covers the most common types of agribusiness TNCs except retailers, which are discussed in chapter 3 of this volume by Margaret Cowan.

[22] See Hoover's Industry Snapshots, 2008: Agriculture, above n 15; see also Hoover's Industry Snapshots, 2008: Food, above n 15.

[23] Ziegler, above n 1, ¶ 16.

[24] ECOSCO Committee on Economic, Social nd Cultural Rights, 'General Comment 12: The Right to Adequate Food', ¶ 6, UN document E/C.12/1999/5 (12 May 1999).

[25] Ziegler, above n 1, ¶ 16.

security and social assistance for the most deprived. The right to food also includes the right to have access to safe drinking water.[26]

Agribusiness TNCs potentially can have an impact on the right to food at nearly every stage of the production chain. First, agribusiness TNCs can affect farmers who are growing crops or raising livestock. Farmers growing crops are often pressured to raise crops for export production, which reduces their own food security, increases land consolidation, and consequently restricts their ability to raise food for themselves and to access land. To grow export crops, farmers often buy seeds produced by large agribusiness biotechnology firms. Those seeds, some of which are genetically modified, are often patented and sold with restrictions on their use, inhibiting farmers' access to seeds. The use of those seeds also often requires expensive agrochemicals, including pesticides and herbicides, which can lead to cycles of debt and reduce the income that farmers can earn. Farmers raising livestock confront similar issues, with agribusiness TNCs influencing their choice of livestock, the feed they use for the livestock and, in some situations, the income that they earn through contract farming arrangements.

Secondly, farmers often sell their products to large commodity traders and processors, or to retailers, as discussed in Margaret Cowan's chapter (chapter 3 below). Those traders and processors have vast market power that allows them to dictate the amount of money that they will pay for products. Farmers therefore are sometimes at risk of receiving very low prices for the crops they produce,[27] which ironically can lead to insufficient income to purchase food for themselves.[28] Those low prices, combined with the high prices of inputs, can lead to cycles of debt for small-scale farmers. This debt can be exacerbated by farmers' insecure land tenure, leading in some cases to farmers losing their ability to earn a livelihood from farming and instead becoming agricultural workers on

---

[26] Ibid, ¶ 17.

[27] For example, when farmers enter into contract farming arrangements to supply products to firms, they generally have an unequal status during negotiations and are in a weak bargaining position. '[T]he concern with unfair conduct by contracting firms is justified by empirical evidence that imbalanced power in contractual relations can lead to noncompetitive behaviour by the dominant party. In the case of contracting agribusiness firms, this can be expressed, inter alia, by the imposition of low prices, by deductions of highly set input costs, by early termination of contracts, by the manipulation of quality attributes or by the design of biased contractual clauses.' CAB da Silva, 'The Growing Role of Contract Farming in Agri-Food Systems Development: Drivers, Theory and Practice' (FAO Agricultural Management, Marketing and Finance Service, 2005) 23.

[28] Low prices paid for products, along with other factors such obstacles to access to land, mean that 'approximately 500 million people depending on small-scale agriculture are hungry'. O De Schutter, UN Special Rapporteur on the Right to Food, 'Report of the Special Rapporteur on the Right to Food, Delivered to the UN General Assembly', UN document A/65/281 (2010).

large-scale plantations, often with sub-standard conditions.[29] Moreover, the low prices that are paid for commodities can also result in even lower wages for workers on plantations that are either owned by or source to large agribusiness TNCs, leading to workers receiving insufficient income to purchase adequate food.

Thirdly, once food commodities have been processed and manufactured into different food products, food and beverage companies market and set the price for food, which subsequently has an impact on consumers and their ability to afford qualitatively and quantitatively adequate food. Pricing is, of course, also greatly influenced by retailers, which is beyond the scope of this chapter. In addition, food and beverage companies can affect the right to food via the marketing and manufacturing of nutritionally poor food. This phenomenon is also not addressed in this chapter.

The next section examines in greater detail some of the ways in which agribusiness TNCs have an impact on the right to food.

II. AGRIBUSINESS AND ITS IMPACT ON THE RIGHT TO FOOD: SECTOR ANALYSIS

A. Food Processors: Buying, Selling and Manufacturing

The food processing industry, which is part of the agribusiness industry, can be further divided into commodity traders and processors, and food and beverage manufacturers. Although there is some overlap between these two groups, which is unsurprising given the amount of integration that exists, many of the largest companies based on 'agricultural sales' are distinct from the largest companies based on 'food sales'.[30] TNCs within those two categories of food processors have varying levels of market power and influence, depending in part on the commodity. While both categories of companies thus have an important role with respect to the right to food, they vary in how and to what extent they do so.

(i) Commodity Buyers and Sellers

Commodities play an extremely important role in the global food system. Certain commodities, including wheat, corn and soy, form the

---

[29] Ibid: 'Whether because small-scale farming has become non-viable or because they have been expelled from the land in the absence of effective security of tenure, many such farmers become agricultural workers on large-scale plantations, where they are often paid lower than subsistence wages and left without social or legal protection'.

[30] For example, in 2007, only Cargill and Smithfield Foods ranked among the top 10 companies in terms of both agricultural sales and food sales. Hoover's Industry Snapshots, above n 15.

basis for most manufactured food products in western countries, and are important staples in many developing countries. In 2007–08, increasing prices for many basic commodities caused food riots around the world.[31] Commodities such as coffee, tea and cocoa are grown by millions of people around the world, and are consumed by millions more. Fluctuations in the commodity prices of those more luxury goods, although not seen very often by western consumers, can be devastating for those who grow them as export crops in developing countries. Some of the most commonly traded agricultural food commodities are corn, oats, rice, soy (traded as soybeans, soybean meal and soybean oil), wheat, cocoa, coffee and sugar.[32] Other important agricultural commodities include palm oil, tea, bananas and meat.[33]

Commodity traders and processors that purchase commodities from farmers wield immense power over the price paid to producers around the world. Tea farmers in India, cocoa farmers in Côte d'Ivoire, soy farmers in Brazil and wheat farmers in the US all share a common dependence on powerful commodity traders.

The sheer influence of commodity buyers and sellers can be attributed to their market power. Market power is defined as 'the ability to affect price, to reduce competition and to set standards for a sector of economic activity'.[34] This can be parsed further into seller power, which is 'the ability to set customer prices above competitive levels', and buyer power, which is 'the ability to set supplier prices below competitive levels'.[35] Market power is usually achieved through the consolidation of businesses through growth and mergers, and their subsequent economic concentration.[36] It is this concentration that enables the consolidated businesses to 'significantly affect prices for goods'[37] and thus hold market power.

Businesses achieve this consolidation through either horizontal consolidation or vertical coordination or integration.[38] Horizontal coordination occurs when two or more businesses, or their assets, merge and combine, when the businesses are 'in the same industry and . . . engaged in the same stage of the production cycle'.[39] Horizontal concentration thus refers to when 'only a few firms dominate a given point in a production

---

[31] See S Erlanger, 'UN Addresses Food Production, Poverty and Rising Prices', *International Herald Tribune*, 16 April 2008.
[32] See World Bank Pink Sheet (April 2008).
[33] Ibid.
[34] Murphy, above n 11, 9.
[35] Ibid.
[36] Democratic Staff of the Sub-Committee on Agriculture, Nutrition, and Forestry, 108th Congress, 'Economic Concentration and Structural Change in the Food and Agriculture Sector: Trends, Consequences and Policy Options' (Comm Print, 2004) 2.
[37] Ibid.
[38] Ibid, 3.
[39] Ibid, 3.

chain'.[40] Most commodity processing markets are horizontally concentrated.[41] Vertical coordination or integration arises when businesses at different stages of the production cycle acquire or coordinate with each other.[42] This leads to vertical concentration, when 'the same firm or few firms dominate more than [one] point on a production chain'.[43] It is possible for a firm to have market power due both to horizontal concentration and to vertical concentration, exerting power throughout the food production chain.[44]

Globalisation is often viewed as a third way of concentrating the food system, apart from horizontal and vertical concentration. Because horizontal and vertical concentration are often measured in the domestic market context, globalisation, contract farming and global commodity chains are considered other avenues for concentrating business and creating market power worldwide. It has thus been argued that 'the food systems of the world are becoming so integrated by the transnational corporations (TNCs) that it often makes little sense to speak of the food system of a single country'.[45] Global commodity chains in agriculture are often buyer-driven, because the 'buyer sources products wherever the price and quality are right and ships them to where there is a market to buy the final good'.[46]

The market power of commodity traders and processors has many implications for the global system and the right to food. First, commodity traders and processors help determine what food is produced where. The commodity market, and commodity traders and processors, in addition to other actors, promote the expansion of export crop production in developing countries. The expansion of export crop production can lead to food insecurity by creating monoculture production and thereby decreasing food sovereignty within countries; it also often leads to the concentration of land. Secondly, the market power of commodity traders and processors often widens the price spread, and enables commodity traders and processors to set very low prices for farmers. The market power of commodity traders and processors can also affect prices for

---

[40] Murphy, above n 11, 14.
[41] Cargill and Archer Daniels Midland Company (ADM) are examples of horizontal concentration in the US grain market: together, they export a large percentage of US grains. Ibid.
[42] 'Economic Concentration and Structural Change in the Food and Agriculture Sector', above n 36, 3.
[43] Murphy, above n 11, 14.
[44] Ibid, 15. Cargill again is an example of a firm that has vertical concentration; this includes owning its own grain elevators throughout the Americas and its own transportations systems. Oligopoly Watch, 'Oligopoly Brief: Cargill' (18 January 2004).
[45] WD Heffernan, 'The Influence of the Big Three—ADM, Cargill and ConAgra', Farmer Cooperatives in the 21st Century, presented at the West Des Moines Marriott, Des Moines, Iowa (9–11 June 1999).
[46] Murphy, above n 11, 16.

retailers and consumers, although the increasing influence and market power of retailers continues to shift the power dynamics. Aside from widening the price spread, it can also lead to deliberate pricing manipulation in some cases. Thirdly, this market power gives commodity traders the ability to influence access to markets and to set standards within a given sector. Finally, the market power of commodity traders enables them to wield strong influence over government policymakers in many countries, which can sometimes lead to enhanced market environments that favour commodity traders at the expense of small farmers.

The immense power of commodity traders and processors varies in its articulations, yet its existence remains constant. To better understand how the market power of commodity traders can affect the right to food, this section examines several commodities to illustrate the influence of traders down the production chain. Specifically, it focuses on the commodities markets in soy, wheat and cocoa, all of which are extremely important commodities in the global food system. Those markets and production chains share important characteristics, yet also illustrate the different ways in which commodity traders can influence the right to food.

(a) Soy

Soy is one of the most important commodities in the world. It is in the majority of processed food products that Westerners consume.[47] The vast majority of soy produced, however, is not 'consumed directly as human food';[48] rather, most of it is processed into oil for the food industry and soy meal pellets for animal feed.[49] It is estimated that up to 80% of soy production is used as livestock feed.[50] The soy market is extremely concentrated.[51] This concentration affects farmers in two ways: 'as primary producers of soybeans and as livestock or dairy producers who depend on soy-based feed'.[52]

Although the US traditionally led the world's soy exports, Brazil and Argentina now produce and export an increasingly large share of the world's soy.[53] Brazil has become the world's largest soy exporter,[54] and

---

[47] R Patel, *Stuffed and Starved: The Hidden Battle for the World Food System* (Brooklyn, NY, Melville House Publishing, 2008) 166.
[48] Vorley, above n 4, 42.
[49] Ibid.
[50] D Howden, 'Eating the Amazon: The Fight to Curb Corporate Destruction, *The Independent*, 17 July 2006.
[51] The main soy traders are Bunge, ADM, Cargill and Louis Dreyfus. Vorley, above n 4, 42.
[52] Ibid.
[53] Ibid.
[54] Howden, above n 50.

the largest soy farm in the world is believed to be located in Brazil.[55] Soy production in Brazil has become a contentious issue, however. Critics allege that soy production there has led to the deforestation of the Amazon,[56] and has subsequently caused the loss of both land and livelihood of the indigenous peoples who live in the forest and depend on the forest for food.[57]

The increased production of soy in Brazil has been directly promoted by soy traders, who have opened a port for soy located three hours away from the national park in which soy farming occurs; soy is shipped directly from that port to Europe.[58] Moreover, soy traders have helped finance this production. Because much of the soy production has been undertaken on illegally deforested land, farmers growing soy without title to land are unable to procure loans from banks. Soy traders, however, have been willing to provide loans to those farmers to enable them to continue production,[59] thus facilitating deforestation and affecting the right to food of those living in the Amazon.

Additionally, allegations have arisen of poor labour conditions on some of the Brazilian soy farms.[60] Those extremely poor labour conditions likely have an impact on the ability of affected workers to earn sufficient income to attain adequate food. Although soy commodity traders do not directly set the prices paid to workers on soy farms, they do set the prices they pay for soy. This influence on producers via the prices they pay likely has a direct impact on the prices that producers can pay workers. Moreover, regardless of the extent to which commodity traders influence the wages and labour conditions on soy farms, their market power in the production chain illustrates the potential they have to help ensure that workers' and farmers' right to food is not violated.

(b) Wheat

Wheat is an extremely important globally traded commodity. Wheat produced for export is primarily produced in developed countries—

---

[55] R Carroll and T Phillips, 'King of Soya: Environmental Vandal or Saviour of the World's Poor?', *The Guardian*, 3 March 2008.

[56] Note that soy production has led to deforestation in two ways. First, soy 'producers buy up land already cleared by cattle ranchers who then acquire cheaper land deeper in the Amazon jungle, replacing virgin forest with vast pastures'. Additionally, 'soy is also directly penetrating the Amazon'. Ibid; see also Howden, above n 50.

[57] Howden, above n 50: '[T]he remote and impoverished communities . . . have found themselves in the way of big agrobusiness. The region is home to 220,000 people from 180 different indigenous groups, many of whom live deep in the forest and are dependent on the rainforest and the river for everything from food and tools to medicines and shelter.'

[58] Ibid.

[59] Ibid.

[60] In 2008, 41 workers were 'extracted' from soy farms from '"slave-like" conditions'. Carroll, above n 55.

the US, Canada and Australia are three of the largest exporters—but it is mostly imported by developing countries.[61] The concentration of commodity traders and their subsequent market power thus have important implications for the right to food in developing countries.

The importance and influence of wheat commodities on the situation of people in wheat-importing countries was highlighted during the global food crisis of 2007–08. The price of wheat rose by 130% between March 2007 and March 2008, leading, along with rising prices of other food commodities, to food riots around the world.[62] From Egypt to Italy, people protested their inability to afford grain products.[63] Those riots arose in the context of a highly concentrated market, with three TNCs controlling most of the global grain market. The question of who profits the most in this highly concentrated market, however, is more nuanced. In the UK, for example, larger retailers have competed to lower bread prices, leading to accusations of 'devaluing the whole sector' and creating an industry in which no company can profit.[64] In Canada, millers and retailers have both been accused of raising prices for consumers while lowering the prices they paid to farmers.[65]

In developing countries, it is unclear if any entity profited from the increased wheat prices. However, given the high concentration of the global grain industry and the continuing struggles of citizens in developing countries to purchase sufficient food, it is arguable that commodity traders might have at least an indirect impact on the right to food, and that they could do more in respect of their impact on the right to food.

(c) Cocoa

Cocoa and chocolate production is a $60 billion global industry.[66] North America and Western Europe consume two-thirds of all cocoa products in the world,[67] while West Africa grows 70% of the global cocoa supply.[68] Cocoa farming is labour intensive, and often occurs on small family farms.[69] There are 4–5 million cocoa farmers worldwide; approximately

---

[61] Vorley, above n 4, 39.
[62] Erlanger, above n 31.
[63] Ibid.
[64] Vorley, above n 4, 40–41.
[65] Vorley, above n 4, 41.
[66] International Institute of Tropical Agriculture, 'Alternatives to Slash-and-Burn' (2006), available at www.asb.cgiar.org/pdfwebdocs/STCP/STCP%20description.pdf.
[67] A Ewing and E Schrage, 'Business and Human Rights in Africa: The Cocoa Industry and Child Labour' (2005) 18 (summer) *The Journal of Corporate Citizenship* 101.
[68] World Cocoa Foundation, 'Cocoa Farming: Fast Facts', available at www.worldcocoafoundation.org/for-the-media/fast-facts.asp.
[69] Ewing, above n 67.

40–50 million people 'depend upon cocoa for their livelihood'.[70] The route from cocoa farms in West Africa to consumers in Western Europe and North America is very indirect; intermediaries include middlemen, local exporters, international traders and major cocoa brands.[71] The international traders and processors are extremely influential, as they are 'fairly concentrated, with four companies . . . controlling around 40% of cocoa grinding'.[72] Indeed, cocoa traders, cocoa grinders and confectionary manufacturers are now all highly concentrated, which has meant that '[d]eveloping countries' claim on value added declined from around 60% in 1970–72 to around 28% in 1998–2000'.[73]

Cocoa farms in Côte d'Ivoire, which alone exports over 40% of the world's cocoa beans,[74] commonly use child labour[75] and some use forced labour.[76] A 2002 survey of Côte d'Ivoire cocoa farms reported that around 625,000 children worked on the farms; although an estimated 96.7% of those children were related to the farmer, nearly 5,000 to 10,000 children were estimated to have been 'trafficked to or within the country to work full- or part time in the cocoa sector'.[77] The US Department of State noted in 2010 that 'children continued to work under hazardous conditions on cocoa farms' in Côte d'Ivoire,[78] while media reports in 2007 and 2008 claimed that some of those children were as young as three or four.[79]

The government of Côte d'Ivoire has attributed the use of forced labour on cocoa farms to the low prices paid by manufacturers,[80] while impoverished farmers in Côte d'Ivoire explain that they use children to work in the fields because they do not get a 'just price'.[81] Moreover, exporters often pass the many levies and export taxes imposed by the Ivorian government on to the farmers, further decreasing the prices

[70] World Cocoa Foundation, above n 68.
[71] Ewing, above n 67.
[72] Vorley, above n 4, 50.
[73] World Bank, above n 8, 136; see also Vorley, above n 4.
[74] Ewing, above n 67, 100; see also Chocolate Manufacturers Association, available at www.chocolateusa.org/Resources/statistical-information.asp.
[75] H Hawksley, 'Child Cocoa Workers Still "Exploited"', BBC News, April 2, 2007, available at www.news.bbc.co.uk/2/hi/africa/6517695.stm.
[76] Vorley, above n 4, 50; see also US Department of State, 'Country Reports on Human Rights Practices 2006: Côte d'Ivoire', released on 6 March 2007, available at www.state.gov/g/drl/rls/hrrpt/2006/78730.htm (citing 2002 International Institute for Tropical Agriculture survey).
[77] US Department of State, 'Country Reports on Human Rights Practices 2009: Côte d'Ivoire', released 11 March 2010, available at www.state.gov/g/drl/rls/hrrpt/2009/af/135949.htm.
[78] Ibid.
[79] Hawksley, above n 74; see also C Parenti, 'Chocolate's Bittersweet Economy: Seven Years after the Industry Agreed to Abolish Child Labor, Little Progress Has Been Made', Fortune, 4 February 2008.
[80] Vorley, above n 4, 50.
[81] Parenti, above n 79.

that those farmers receive.[82] The Ivorian cocoa industry's dependence on child labour or forced labour demonstrates the desperation of cocoa farmers that arises from the low prices that they are paid. This subsequently implicates the right to food: because cocoa farmers in the Côte d'Ivoire receive insufficient income for their cocoa products, they are unable to purchase sufficient food without resorting to illegal labour and human rights abuses.

Cocoa exports from Côte d'Ivoire are dominated by international commodity traders.[83] Those exporters 'do not own plantations and do not directly employ child workers'.[84] Instead, they purchase cocoa beans from middlemen.[85] However, the commodity traders influence and shape the cocoa market in Côte d'Ivoire in several important ways. First, they control cocoa exports from Côte d'Ivoire. Exporters claim that they are 'just an intermediary . . . between the farmers and international markets in London'.[86] Yet they clearly profit from their engagement with cocoa trading. For example, in October 2006, the price of cocoa on the world market was around US$1.52/kg. The official 'farm gate price' paid to cocoa farmers at that time, however, was set at US$0.70/kg, and in reality was only about US$0.35–0.56/kg.[87] The exporters are arguably in a better position than any other actors in the production chain to effect pricing increases and improvements. Secondly, exporters loan money to local farmers' cooperatives.[88] Although loans by commodity traders to farmers are not inherently problematic, farmers have stated that borrowing money from some companies has led to indebtedness, which in turn has led to increased child labour in the cocoa fields.[89] The situation mirrors what is occurring in Brazil, where commodity

---

[82] Global Witness, 'Hot Chocolate: How Cocoa Fuelled the Conflict in Côte d'Ivoire' (June 2007) 19–23.
[83] The determination of which companies dominate cocoa exports from Côte d'Ivoire depends in part on how exports are measured. Ivorian law limits the amount of cocoa that any single exporter can buy during the main harvest, but does not limit the amount that exporters can buy the rest of the year. In 2005–06, the largest exporter of cocoa from the main harvest was thus a Singaporean company, while a Cargill subsidiary was the second largest exporter and ADM was the fourth largest exporter. Ibid, 18. However, some companies have invested in cocoa-processing within Côte d'Ivoire, which allows them to 'bypass tonnage limits applied to unprocessed cocoa bean exports'. There are four TNCs that have done this: ADM, Cargill, CEMOI and Barry Callebaut. Ibid, 17. Others have reported that ADM, Cargill and Callebaut 'dominate the Ivorian market' (Vorley, above n 4, 50), and that Cargill, Archer Daniels Midland, Barry Callebaut and Saf-Cacao are the 'big cocoa exporters' (Parenti, above n 79).
[84] Parenti, above n 79.
[85] Ibid.
[86] Ibid.
[87] Global Witness, above n 82, 18.
[88] Parenti, above n 79.
[89] Ibid.

traders' loans to soy farmers encourage unsustainable soy production for export.[90]

The cocoa industry in Côte d'Ivoire illustrates the impact of concentrated commodity traders on the right to food. In a country that provides 40% of the world's cocoa supply, where exports are effectively dominated by a handful of agribusiness TNCs, where a large percentage of the total population works in the cocoa sector[91] and where most cocoa farmers struggle to make ends meet,[92] it is clear that agribusiness TNCs influence farmers' income and thus have an impact on the farmers' right to food. Indeed, commodity traders and processors in the Ivorian cocoa industry are perhaps in the best position to increase the prices that are paid to farmers, which would have a strong and positive impact on the ability of farmers to access sufficient food without having to rely on child labour or forced labour.

(ii) Food and Beverage Companies

Although food and beverage companies are almost always further removed from farmers than commodity traders, they are extremely influential actors in the global food system. Food and beverage companies choose which food to manufacture, influence tastes around the world, and have an enormous impact on both the prices that consumers pay and those that are paid to farmers. Food and beverage companies are where much of the 'value' is added in the food production chain.

The role of food and beverage companies with respect to the right to food is often less clear cut than that of commodity traders and processors, but is no less important. This section focuses on two different ways in which food and beverage companies have influenced the right to food: producing soft drinks in developing countries and sourcing cocoa from, and thus indirectly shaping production in, developing countries.

(a) The Soft Drinks and Beverage Industry and the Right to Water

The right to food 'includes the right to have access to safe drinking water'.[93] Soft drink and beverage companies have received much criticism for their use of water to produce beverages in developing countries. One example is the criticism that Coca-Cola has received for its production activities in India, where citizens have alleged that a Coca-Cola plant, the Hindustan Coca Cola Beverages Private Ltd, and its

---

[90] Howden, above n 50.
[91] Global Witness, above n 82, 17.
[92] Parenti, above n 79.
[93] Ziegler, above n 1, ¶ 17. Note, however, that the right to food and the right to water are increasingly seen as separate but related rights.

'intensive extraction of groundwater led to a depletion of ground water levels in the area'.[94] Moreover, citizens claim that the groundwater that was left was 'severely contaminated, . . . [which rendered it] unfit for human consumption and irrigation'.[95]

A committee set up by the Indian government found in 2004 that both the Coca-Cola and PepsiCo plants in Kerala were 'responsible for "causing pollution of water, depleting ground water and reducing crop yields"'.[96] That contamination and depletion of groundwater directly affected the surrounding citizens' right to have access to safe drinking water. In addition, the companies indirectly might have had another impact on the citizens' right to food, as the plants' negative effect on water quality and quantity allegedly led to reduced crop yields. Besides inhibiting their ability to produce food, a reduction in crop yields can also affect the ability of farmers to earn sufficient income to purchase food, as well as rendering them incapable of continuing to provide employment for agricultural labourers.[97]

In response to the 'struggle'[98] against the Coca-Cola bottling plant in Kerala, The Coca-Cola Company created an 'integrated water strategy'.[99] The goal of the strategy is to become water neutral by 'return[ing] to communities and to nature an amount of water equivalent to what we use in all of our beverages and their production'.[100] PepsiCo, meanwhile, has undertaken grant-making and partnership 'initiatives . . . targeted to drive sustainable water practices'.[101] Those efforts are important steps to remedying the right-to-food issues that are associated with the beverage industry, although the extent to which they adequately address the impact of the beverage industry on individuals' rights to food and water is not yet clear.

(b) Food and Beverage Companies in the Cocoa Industry

The cocoa industry provides an interesting lens through which to consider the overlapping influences of food and beverage companies and

---

[94] FIAN International, International Fact Finding Mission to India, 'Investigating some Alleged Violations of the Human Right to Water in India: Report of the International Fact Finding Mission to India' (January 2004) 14.
[95] Ibid.
[96] Ibid, 15, citing the JPC Report tabled on 4 February 2004.
[97] Ibid, 15.
[98] Business for Social Responsibility, 'Drinking it In: The Evolution of a Global Water Stewardship Program at The Coca-Cola Company', 2 (March 2008).
[99] Ibid, 4.
[100] 'The Coca-Cola Company, Environment, Water Stewardship—Water Conservation Goal', available at www.thecoca-colacompany.com/citizenship/water_pledge.html.
[101] Press Release, 'PepsiCo Announces Initiatives With the Earth Institute and H2O Africa To Drive Sustainable Water Practices', 22 January 2008, available at www.csrwire.com/News/10775.html.

commodity traders on the right to food. As discussed above, millions of small farmers in developing countries are dependent on cocoa production. Forty per cent of all cocoa is produced in Côte d'Ivoire, where farmers are typically impoverished by the low prices they are paid by middlemen and commodity traders. Commodity traders operating within the producing countries—sometimes through subsidiaries—have been pressured to reconsider their impact on labour conditions and prices.

Food and beverage companies that manufacture chocolate products are generally at least one step further removed than commodity traders and processors from producing countries and their farmers. The largest manufacturers of cocoa products, Mars, Hershey's and Nestlé, all purchase cocoa from commodity traders. Most do not source directly from producing countries,[102] although there are some 'integrated multinational processors and manufacturers' that do have 'significant presence and representation' in certain countries.[103] In the search for accountability over labour conditions and low prices, however, commodity traders have stated that they are merely the middlemen.[104] Thus, consumer pressure, the success of which is often tied to brand targeting, has focused more on the large food and beverage companies for their role in creating the labour conditions—driven in part by the poor prices paid to farmers—in the cocoa industry. Indeed, the voluntary 'Harkin-Engel Protocol', which was entered into by the US chocolate industry in an effort to address child labour in cocoa production, was signed by more chocolate manufacturers than cocoa commodity traders.[105]

Food and beverage companies have already set a precedent for assuming some responsibility over the conditions of cocoa farmers. Cadbury, for example, has created an initiative to assist its cocoa suppliers in Ghana, which 'is aimed at helping farmers increase production and improve the quality of the beans'.[106] Cadbury states that this effort will help the

---

[102] Deborah Orr, 'Slave Chocolate?', Forbes, 24 April 2006.

[103] USAID, 'Indonesia Cocoa Bean Value Chain Case Study', Micro Report #65, 4. Mars, for example, which does not purchase cocoa directly from Côte d'Ivoire, acts as an integrated processor and manufacturer in Indonesia, thereby sustaining some presence in the country. Ibid; see also Orr, above n 102.

[104] Parenti, above n 79.

[105] Chocolate Manufacturers Association, 'Protocol for the Growing and Processing of Cocoa Beans and their Derivative Products in a Manner that Complies with ILO Convention 182 Concerning the Prohibition and Immediate Action for the Elimination of the Worst Forms of Child Labor' (19 September 2001), available at www.cocoaverification.net/Docs/Harkin-Engel%20Protocol.pdf. This is also known as the 'Harkin-Engel Protocol' because of the leading roles that Senator Harkin and Congressman Engel took in its creation. The Protocol was signed by representatives of Guittard; M&M/Mars, Inc; World's Finest Chocolate, Inc; Archer Daniels Midland Company; Nestlé Chocolate & Confections USA; Blommer Chocolate Company; Hershey Food Corporation; and Barry Callebaut AG.

[106] C Eyre, 'Cadbury to Protect Ghanaian Chocolate Production', Foodproductiondaily. com, 28 January 2008.

company protect its supply while also having 'a lasting impact on the lives of cocoa farmers' by, inter alia, increasing income through increased production.[107] Similarly, Nestlé and Mars have committed to a non-government organisation (NGO)-led sustainable cocoa initiative that 'aims to establish a traceability system for all farmers in the Ivory Coast'.[108] To some extent, the manufacturers' acknowledgement of a degree of responsibility supports the arguments by other stakeholders that they should be more accountable for the labour conditions of their suppliers.[109]

The manufacturers' efforts are perhaps more noteworthy for establishing some degree of their responsibility for farmers in producing countries than they are for the potential that those specific initiatives hold. While all of the initiatives could potentially have a positive impact on the livelihood of farmers, it is not clear whether any will improve the situations of farmers and workers. For example, increased cocoa production, which is one of the goals of Cadbury's programme, on its own will not help all cocoa farmers equally; rather, a glut of cocoa on the market could actually lower the prices paid to farmers. It is possible that new 'ethical cocoa supply' initiatives in West African countries could help manufacturers ensure that their suppliers produce crops under acceptable labour conditions that allow them to earn a sufficient income to feed themselves and their families. Some recent efforts have shown promise.[110] On the other hand, however, it is important to remember that those initiatives are occurring in a context where multiple initiatives have already been attempted by cocoa industry stakeholders in efforts to improve conditions in the supply chain without much success.[111]

Although chocolate manufacturers have acknowledged some influence over suppliers in developing countries, and despite the enormous profits that they generate from cocoa sales,[112] they are also sensitive to

---

[107] Ibid.

[108] C Eyre, 'Mars, Nestlé Promise Ethical Cocoa Supply', *Foodproductiondaily.com*, 7 February 2008.

[109] Nestlé has been sued for its complicity in the use of child slavery in Ivorian cocoa fields. See Orr, above n 102. Note also that the Harkin-Engel Protocol arose as a way for the industry to avoid proposed US regulations that would require labelling chocolate products as 'slave-free'.

[110] For example, in December 2010, US Secretary of State Clinton gave Mars the 2010 Award for Corporate Excellence for its efforts to improve the situation of cocoa farmers and workers in Ghana. See 'Mars Awarded for Cocoa Farm Sustainability Work', *Supply-Management.com*, 20 December 2010.

[111] The most marked example of this is the Harkin-Engel Protocol, which the cocoa industry points to when criticised. See Parenti, above n 79. Note also that Mars had already entered into a partnership with a German development agency several years ago to promote profitable and sustainable cocoa production. See Vorley, above n 4, 50.

[112] The worldwide chocolate market is immense, worth about 90 billion Swiss francs. See P Heynike, Head of Chocolate, Biscuits and Confectionery, Nestlé, 'Speech to 141st Annual General Meeting of Nestlé SA' (10 April 2008), available at www.nestle.com/MediaCenter/SpeechesAndStatements/SpeechesAndStatements.htm. Nestlé posted overall profits of over $9.7 billion in 2007. See also 'Nestlé Price Rises Help Drive Up

commodity prices. Rising commodity prices have worried some manufacturers.[113] That sensitivity demonstrates the difficulty of finding the actors within the production chain that are best situated to increase the prices paid to farmers. It also illustrates the inherent problems of expecting public companies to undertake efforts that might affect their bottom line. Despite those problems, however, chocolate manufacturers are clearly positioned to assist cocoa farmers in ways that would have a positive impact on the farmers' right to food.

B. Biotechnology/'Life Sciences'

The biotechnology sector of the agribusiness industry produces the seeds, agrochemicals and other inputs that are central to global agriculture production. The biotechnology sector, which has partially rebranded itself as 'life sciences',[114] has been immensely influential in determining the types of crops grown and the types of livestock raised. It has also set global research and development priorities. In addition, the biotechnology sector has heavily promoted the use of genetically modified seeds throughout the world. Although many tout the potential of biotechnology to improve farmers' livelihoods and address food shortages in some countries, the World Bank has acknowledged that 'the benefits of biotechnology, driven by large, private multinationals interested in commercial agriculture, have yet to be safely harnessed for the needs of the poor'.[115]

The agribusiness TNCs in this sector have 'consolidated horizontally and vertically into a small number of multinational firms'.[116] A diminishing number of TNCs thus control an increasing amount of the agrochemical and seed global markets, as well as hold an increasing percentage of US patents.[117] The concentration and market power of the biotechnology agribusiness TNCs have enabled them to have several substantial impacts on the right to food. First, biotechnology TNCs have used intellectual property rights and other methods to restrict

2007 Profits', *Reuters*, 21 February 2008. In 2007, Forbes ranked Mars the eighth largest private American company, with revenue of $21 billion. See 'America's Largest Private Companies', *Forbes*, 8 November 2007.

[113] Nestlé, for example, managed to increase its revenue in 2007 by passing the higher commodity prices on to consumers. *Reuters*, ibid.
[114] Barlett, above n 5.
[115] World Bank, above n 8, 158.
[116] Ibid, 135.
[117] Ibid, 136. As the former UN Special Rapporteur on the Right to Food, Jean Ziegler, has pointed out, '[j]ust 10 corporations, including Aventis, Monsanto, Pioneer and Syngenta, control one-third of the US$ 23 billion commercial seed market and 80% of the US$ 28 billion global pesticide market'. Ziegler, above n 1, ¶ 43, citing Erosion, Technology and Concentration Action Group, 82 Communiqué, November/December 2003.

access to seeds and technology. Secondly, they have promoted genetically modified seeds, technology and agrochemical inputs to farmers in developing countries that are often ill suited to the farmers' needs, thereby reducing the farmers' ability to produce sufficient food, as well as their ability to earn sufficient income to purchase food. Thirdly, agribusiness TNCs in this sector have begun to undertake the same strategies with respect to livestock, consequently replicating the same problems for farmers as with crop production—lack of access to resources, cycles of debt due to expensive inputs and a subsequent inability to earn sufficient income to purchase food.

(i) The Use and Misuse of Intellectual Property Rights to Restrict Access to Seeds and Technology

Intellectual property rights and the use of them by agribusiness TNCs have important implications for the right to food. In the agribusiness sector, intellectual property rights, 'such as patents or plant breeders' rights',[118] can provide 'incentives . . . to develop seeds that either produce higher yields or have specific characteristics which will improve food security and agro-biodiversity management'.[119] Biotechnology research and development has 'the potential to enhance the competitiveness of market-oriented smallholders and overcome drought and disease in production systems important to the poor'.[120] Strict intellectual property rights touching on agriculture in developing countries, however, also have the potential to restrict farmers' access to resources, especially seeds and technology.[121] That restriction on access to seeds and technology can have a direct impact on farmers' right to food, which includes a right to resources.

The intellectual property rights framework in agriculture is shaped by international treaties and institutions, and implemented through national laws. Although several treaties and institutions guide intellectual property rights in agriculture, the most important are the Agreement on Trade-Related Aspects of Intellectual Property Rights (TRIPS Agreement) and the International Convention for the Protection of New Varieties of Plants (UPOV Convention).

The TRIPS Agreement, which was negotiated in the Uruguay Round of Multilateral Trade Negotiations, is 'the most comprehensive multilateral agreement that sets detailed minimum standards for the protection

---

[118] P Cullet, 'Food Security and Intellectual Property Rights in Developing Countries', IELRC Working Paper (2003), available at www.ielrc.org/content/w0303.pdf.
[119] Ibid.
[120] World Bank, above n 8, 158.
[121] Cullet, above n 118, 4–5.

and enforcement of intellectual property rights'.[122] It is binding on all WTO members, and 'sets the minimum standards—requirements for the grant of rights, the time limitations on protection, permitted exceptions to the use of rights and modes of enforcement—to be implemented by each WTO member'.[123] It requires that 'patents shall be available for any inventions, whether products or processes, in all fields of technology, provided that they are new, involve an inventive step and are capable of industrial application'.[124] Exceptions to this requirement include 'measures to protect public health and nutrition'.[125]

The TRIPS Agreement permits states to 'exclude from patentability ... plants and animals other than micro-organisms'.[126] It requires, however, that members protect plant varieties 'either by patents or by an effective *sui generis* system or by any combination thereof'.[127] Thus, although there is some room for countries to not enact patent laws for plant varieties, it is very narrow. A *sui generis* system would be very similar to patent protection, and would likely be based on the UPOV Convention.[128]

The UPOV Convention, originally adopted in 1961, was designed to provide intellectual property protection to the seed industry without creating patent rights.[129] The 1978 Revision included a '"farmer's privilege" [that allowed] farmers to re-use propagating material from the previous year's harvest and to freely exchange seeds of protected varieties with other farmers'.[130] The 1991 Revision, however, greatly strengthened plant breeders' rights, and the farmer's privilege is now optional.[131]

For the purpose of examining agribusiness TNCs' impact on the right to food, it is useful to look at the impact of the TRIPS Agreement on the right to food. The Office of the UN High Commissioner for Human Rights, in undertaking a human rights analysis of TRIPS, has stated that 'the TRIPS Agreement could affect the enjoyment of several rights—in

---

[122] UN High Commissioner for Human Rights, 'Report of the High Commissioner on the Impact of the Agreement on Trade-Related Aspects of Intellectual Property Rights on Human Rights', delivered to the Committee on Economic, Social and Cultural Rights, UN document E/CN.4/Sub.2/2001/13 (27 June 2001) ¶ 5.
[123] Ibid, ¶ 6.
[124] World Trade Organization (WTO), 'Agreement on Trade Related Aspects of International Property Rights' (hereinafter TRIPS Agreement), Art 27(1).
[125] UN High Commissioner for Human Rights, above n 122, ¶ 6.
[126] TRIPS Agreement, above n 124, 27(3)(b).
[127] Ibid.
[128] See, eg GRAIN, 'The End of Farm-Saved Seed?: Industry's WISH list for the Next Revision of UPOV', *GRAIN Briefing* (February 2007) 2 (discussing the 1991 revision of UPOV, under which plant variety protection is very similar to patents, and which 'is now being rapidly rolled out across developing countries as a result of the WTO TRIPS agreement').
[129] Ibid; see also Cullet, above n 118, 11.
[130] Cullet, above n 118, 11.
[131] Ibid.

particular the right to food, the right to development, the human rights of indigenous peoples'.[132] Since the right to food has been defined to include 'the right to have access to resources and to the means to ensure and produce one's own subsistence, including land, small scale irrigation and seeds, credit, technology and local and regional markets',[133] TRIPS and intellectual property rights are important frameworks that can have an impact on the right to food. The use of those intellectual property rights by agribusiness TNCs thus also has potential implications for the right to food.

The use of intellectual property rights in agriculture introduces several concerns with respect to the right to food. First, it is possible that 'over-patentability' might 'stifle innovation in the private and public sector rather than promote it'.[134] Too many patents could render plant breeders unable to innovate because they are restricted from using materials. Aside from frustrating the efforts of more public-oriented researchers, this could reduce the competitiveness of the market, placing farmers in developing countries at the mercy of large agribusiness TNCs. Secondly, stronger intellectual property rights might focus more research and development on commercially valuable products that are not designed to meet the needs of farmers in developing countries. This scenario is already a problem, and will be addressed in more detail below. Thirdly, intellectual property rights can lead to the displacement of traditional plants and livestock, as varieties protected by patents are heavily promoted. That displacement can create monocultures, which in turn will lead to a loss of biodiversity.[135] More importantly, monoculture production can also reduce farmers' ability to produce food for their own consumption, making them more reliant on markets for their food security.[136] Fourthly, intellectual property rights regimes that promote patented or otherwise protected seeds and then restrict the use of such seeds can have a very direct impact on the right to food. To date, patenting 'specific plant varieties has meant that a few agricultural corporations have virtual monopolies on the genome of important global crops'.[137] Agribusiness TNCs that then seek protection through intellectual property rights in order to restrict farmers' access to seeds, by requiring 'farmers to relinquish the right to save or replant seed from a harvest or to sell or trade that seed to other persons',[138] likewise affect the right to food.

Restricting access to seeds is one of the most problematic ways in

---

[132] UN High Commissioner for Human Rights, above n 122, ¶ 2.
[133] Ziegler, above n 1, ¶ 17.
[134] Cullet, above n 118, 5.
[135] AR Chapman, 'The Human Rights Implications of Intellectual Property Protection' [2002] *Journal of International Economic Law* 872.
[136] See, eg Cullet, above n 118, 6.
[137] Chapman, above n 135.
[138] Ibid.

which agribusiness TNCs using intellectual property regimes have an impact on the right to food. Aside from the fact that access to seeds has been explicitly articulated as one of the aspects of the right to food, restricting access to seeds can also lead to farmers' inability to save seeds and therefore either produce sufficient food or produce sufficient crops to sell in order to purchase food. Indeed, farmers around the world have struggled with restrictions on seed. While restrictions on seed use have led to enormous cycles of debt in the US, restrictions in developing countries have led to cycles of debt that consequently inhibit farmers' ability to earn sufficient income to purchase sufficient food and thus indirectly affect their right to food.

Agribusiness TNCs' use of intellectual property rights to prohibit the saving of seeds in the US illustrates the potential problems that arise with intellectual property rights in agriculture. Farmers historically 'have saved seed from season to season: they planted in the spring, harvested in the fall, then reclaimed and cleaned the seeds over the winter for re-planting the next spring'.[139] And until the 1980s, seeds were not patentable in the US.[140] The determination that biotechnology patents could be granted for seeds, and an increasing consolidation of the seed market, led to a small number of biotechnology TNCs in the US with large market power. That market power, in turn, has greatly influenced the seeds that farmers plant, as well as their subsequent ability to use them.[141]

As stated above, the TRIPS Agreement requires that all countries that are members of the WTO, including developing countries, enact some kind of intellectual property regime that includes either the patentability of plant varieties or the protection of plant varieties through 'an effective *sui generis* system or by any combination thereof'.[142] Developing countries have taken different routes in addressing this obligation. Many developing countries have chosen to adopt a plant varieties protection

---

[139] Barlett, above n 5.
[140] Ibid.
[141] Perhaps the most notable example in the US is the influence of Monsanto, which controls much of the bioengineered and conventional seed market in the country. According to one article, the company requires that all farmers purchasing its patented seeds 'sign an agreement promising not to save the seed produced after each harvest for re-planting, or to sell the seed to other farmers'. Ibid. Farmers using those seeds are thus forced to repurchase seeds every year. That requirement, along with the expensive inputs that accompany the seeds, has led to severe debts for many farmers. The same article alleges that the company has been vigilant in the US in ensuring that the agreements are followed, including using lawsuits to guarantee that farmers do not infringe upon their reuse agreements. The company's enforcement efforts extend not only to those farmers who have knowingly or unknowingly violated the use agreements, but also to farmers who have never even purchased or knowingly used Monsanto's patented seeds. Ibid. Monsanto's response to the allegations in the article is available online at www.democracynow.org/pdf/MonsantoResponse.pdf.
[142] TRIPS Agreement, above n 124, 27(3)(b).

scheme that is modelled after the 1978 UPOV Convention, which 'harmonized conditions and norms for protecting new varieties while giving farmers the right to save and exchange seed'.[143] Some developing countries, however, have chosen to protect plant varieties with patents, while others have 'explicitly recognize[d] framework farmers' rights to save and exchange seed (derived from the 2004 international treaty of the Food and Agriculture Organization of the UN [FAO]) and to share benefits arising from the use of farmers' genetic resources'.[144]

Some developing countries have come under pressure from countries with which they trade to adopt 'TRIPS plus' regimes, under which stronger intellectual property rights are adopted than are required by the TRIPS Agreement.[145] Those include the extension of patent life beyond the TRIPS-imposed minimum, as well as situations 'where countries implement TRIPS-consistent legislation before they are obliged to do so'.[146] Developed countries, through bilateral and regional trade agreements, have 'often put pressure on developing countries to adopt even stronger protection—such as that based on the 1991 Convention of UPOV, which makes selling and exchanging seed of protected varieties illegal'.[147] That pressure is often the result of lobbying by biotechnology firms that develop seeds and related technology.[148]

Restricting the ability of small farmers in developing countries to save, use and sell seeds can have severe and negative impacts on their right to food.[149] Millions of small farmers in developing countries around the world are struggling to make ends meet; requiring them to purchase seeds every year only fuels their cycles of debt. In India, for example, the Plant Variety Protection Act of 2001, which allows farmers to save

---

[143] World Bank, above n 8, 167.
[144] Ibid.
[145] UN High Commissioner for Human Rights, above n 122, ¶ 27: 'The use of trade pressure to impose 'TRIPS plus'-style IP legislation has been noted before CESCR. This could lead member States to implement IP standards that do not take into account the safeguards included under the TRIPS Agreement which could lead to IP systems that are inconsistent with States' responsibilities under human rights law' (footnote omitted)).
[146] Ibid; see also Oxfam, 'Make Trade Fair for the Americas: Agriculture, Investment and Intellectual Property: Three Reasons to Say No to the FTAA', Oxfam Briefing Paper, 28 (discussing use of free trade agreements to push for TRIPS plus legislation).
[147] World Bank, above n 8, 167. Western development agencies, such as USAID, have also been accused of advocating for stronger intellectual property rights in the biotechnology sector. See, eg A Kwa, 'UGANDA: Privatization of Seeds Moving Apace', IPS, 21 February 2008.
[148] Moreover, it has been alleged that at least one biotechnology firm has also lobbied the government of a developing country for a national law with stronger intellectual property rights in agriculture. Kwa, ibid (discussing draft Plant Variety Protection Bill in Uganda and stating that 'seeds companies including the likes of Monsanto have been lobbying the government for such intellectual property protection').
[149] See Oxfam, above n 146, 27: 'The use of patents threatens to restrict the ability of small farmers to conserve, use, and sell seeds, which would seriously impact on their means of survival'.

and sell seeds, has not been fully implemented, and millions of farmers have been persuaded by the extension networks through which agribusiness TNCs operate to use patented seeds.[150] Those seeds, along with the expensive inputs that they require, have pushed many Indian farmers into debt, which is often exacerbated by crop failures and high interest rate loans from moneylenders.[151] It is estimated that 'almost half of India's 100 million farming families are in debt'.[152] The inability to repay crop loans and subsequent desperation of many small farmers in India has led to over 150,000 farmer suicides since 1997.[153]

Farmers in other developing countries have expressed concern that implementing stronger intellectual property regimes, and allowing and promoting the use of patented seeds, will lead to increased debt for small farmers and thus have an impact on their ability to survive. In Uganda, farmers and extension workers acknowledge that some patented seeds enable higher yields. Yet the requirements that farmers repurchase seeds each season can mean that farmers 'who are poor and can't go to the market then cannot eat'.[154] Activists in Indonesia have expressed similar concern over patented seeds, stating that the seeds are not 'suitable' for poor farmers, who cannot afford to repurchase seeds each year.[155]

Agribusiness TNCs defend their use of intellectual property rights to protect patents by pointing to the large amount of money they spend on research and development.[156] Indeed, intellectual property rights in general are designed to create incentives to undertake important research and development efforts.[157] However, it is clear that the use of intellectual property protections by agribusiness TNCs can have a detrimental impact on farmers' right to food, especially in developing countries. Finding a balance between the property rights of agribusiness and the right to food of farmers is thus imperative.

---

[150] K Acharya, 'INDIA: Patented Seeds Edge Out Local Varieties', *Inter Press News Service*, 26 June 2006.
[151] K Mukherjee, 'Farm Bonanza Fails to Save India's Dying Farmers', *Reuters*, 14 March 2008.
[152] Ibid.
[153] Ibid.
[154] Kwa, above n 147.
[155] AP Simamora, 'Gov't Should Rethink the Use of Hybrid Rice', *The Jakarta Post*, 16 October 2007.
[156] For example, Monsanto has defended its aggressive actions to protect the use of its patented seeds by stating that it 'spends more than $2 million a day in research to identify, test, develop and bring to market innovative new seeds and technologies that benefit farmers'. Barlett, above n 5 (quoting Monsanto spokesman Darren Wallis).
[157] UN High Commissioner for Human Rights, above n 122, ¶¶ 10–11.

(ii) Promotion of Seeds and Inputs that are Ill-Suited to Farmers' Needs

Apart from their potentially crippling use of intellectual property rights and patents, agribusiness TNCs also have an impact on the right to food in less direct, but no less detrimental, ways. First, agribusiness TNCs often undertake research and development that ignores the needs of developing countries. Secondly, agribusinesses often promote certain seeds and chemicals in developing countries that are not well suited to the poor farmers to whom they market their products. This is particularly the case with respect to agribusinesses' promotion of genetically modified (GM) seeds in lieu of conventional seeds, which has several implications for the right to food.

Agribusiness TNCs have not focused their research and development efforts on the needs of developing countries. As the former Special Rapporteur on the right to food, Jean Ziegler, has pointed out,

> [n]o serious investments have been made in any of the five most important crops of the poorest countries—sorghum, millet, pigeon pea, chickpea and groundnut. Only 1% of research and development budgets of multinational corporations are spent on crops that might be useful for the developing world in arid regions.[158]

The World Bank attributes the lack of attention to the needs of developing countries to the 'difficulty of appropriating the benefits'.[159] This failure to focus on developing countries' needs is particularly problematic for sub-Saharan Africa, which confronts particular challenges that require increased research and development funding. Those challenges include the difficulties that sub-Saharan African countries encounter in capturing spillover technology, due to the number of 'orphan crops' they cultivate and the region's low 'agroecological distance'.[160] Although the lack of research and development focused on the needs of developing countries is understandable when considering the market incentives involved, it certainly affects the food of people in developing countries. It is particularly problematic from a right-to-food perspective when agribusiness TNCs nevertheless market and promote their seeds in developing countries.

Determining how to promote research and development efforts that are focused on the needs of developing countries is particularly important given the fact that agribusiness TNCs aggressively market their seeds, chemicals and products in developing countries. Those inputs are often ill suited to the needs of the farmers to whom the companies market.

---

[158] Ziegler, above n 1, ¶ 43, citing PL Pingali and G Traxler, 'Changing Focus of Agricultural Research: Will the Poor Benefit from Biotechnology and Privatization Trends?' [2002] *Food Policy* 27.

[159] World Bank, above n 8, 167.

[160] Agroecological distance measures the potential for capturing spillovers. Ibid, 168.

Many commercial seeds require other commercial agrochemicals, such as fertilisers, herbicides and pesticides, to be effective. The high prices of those agrochemicals contribute greatly to farmers' debt around the world. Even when the price of the commodities that farmers grow is high, the high costs of necessary inputs can render farmers unable to earn a sufficient living.[161] Indeed, the high price of required inputs has been one of the explanations given for the farmer suicide phenomenon in India.[162] Thus, even apart from the patent protections and requirements that seeds not be saved, reused, sold or shared, agribusiness TNCs promote inputs that can contribute directly to the debt cycles of poor farmers.

Agribusiness TNCs' promotion of GM seeds provides a particularly interesting illustration of the impact of those companies on the right to food. The commercial seed market, and especially the GM seed market, has become increasingly concentrated. The myriad ways through which biotechnology agribusiness TNCs influence the right to food are all replicated in their promotion of GM seeds, while GM seeds present even more problems for small farmers. Note that not all biotechnologically engineered seeds are genetically modified. First-generation biotechnology is 'fairly cheap and easily applied, . . . [and has] already been adopted in many developing countries'.[163] Second-generation biotechnology uses 'genomics to provide information on genes important for a particular trait'.[164] This has also been used in developing countries, and its use is predicted to increase in the future.[165] Genetic modification of seeds, or transgenic technology, is a process through which 'a gene or set of genes [that] convey specific traits [is transferred] within or across species'.[166]

The debate over whether genetic modification should be used continues to play out on the world stage. Genetic modification is heavily promoted by the handful of biotechnology companies that control the seed market, with companies arguing that GM seeds increase crop yields, reduce pesticide use and provide a clear way to address hunger.[167] Other stakeholders, however, have criticised genetic modification for 'perceived and potential environmental and health risks'.[168] Many crops in the US are already grown with GM seeds, and the US has urged other countries

---

[161] See, eg 'Farmers Fleeing Ancient Centre of Philippine Rice', *Reuters*, 23 April 2008.
[162] B Dogra, 'INDIA: Organic Farming, Answer to Farmers' Suicides?', *Inter Press News Service*, 18 July 2006.
[163] World Bank, above n 8, 162–63.
[164] Ibid, 163.
[165] Ibid.
[166] Ibid.
[167] See Friends of the Earth International, 'Monsanto: Who Benefits from GM Crops?', Executive Summary (January 2006) 7.
[168] World Bank, above n 8, 163.

to accept GM technology.[169] Much of Europe, however, has refused to permit its use.[170]

The promotion and use of genetically modified seeds affect the right to food of small farmers in two ways that are distinct from the use of other patented seeds. First, GM seeds can easily cross-breed with non-GM seeds. Strong intellectual property rights in some countries could lead to determinations that even unintentional cross-breeding renders a cross-bred seed the property of the patent owner.[171] GM seeds thus pose a particular danger to small farmers in developing countries; the use of GM seeds by some farmers could contaminate other farmers' fields, thereby rendering their seeds the property of an agribusiness TNC. Secondly, GM seeds have been promoted as the way to eradicate hunger throughout the world. Whether this is true is highly doubtful, yet the promotion of GM seeds for this goal threatens to skew the perception of GM seeds, as well as divert research and funds in developing countries to less efficient efforts.

That second consequence—confusion over the ability of genetic modification technology to eradicate hunger—is arguably the most important aspect of the debate over GM seeds. The agribusiness industry has argued that GM seeds are the best way to eradicate poverty and hunger, as they increase yields and decrease production costs.[172] The industry also argues that GM seeds allow farmers to use fewer pesticides.[173]

Arguments in favour of GM seeds have been increasingly raised in the context of the 2007–08 food crisis and its lingering effects. Between 2007 and 2008, commodity prices increased exponentially.[174] Although the increased commodity prices did not lead to increased prices for many farmers,[175] they did lead to food riots throughout the world.[176] Some

---

[169] See, eg E Rosenthal, 'Both Sides Cite Science to Address Altered Corn', *New York Times*, 26 December 2007.
[170] See S Dube, 'GM-Free Victory as Trials are Scrapped', *Western Mail*, 6 June 2006; see also Rosenthal, above n 169.
[171] See, eg Dube, ibid: 'Canadian farmer Percy Schmeiser faced a million-dollar patent-infringement lawsuit from Monsanto after his crops became contaminated with its GM rapeseed in 1996. The Supreme Court of Canada ruled that he no longer owned his seeds and crops because they contained the patented GM genes.'
[172] Friends of the Earth International, above n 167.
[173] Ibid.
[174] Erlanger, above n 31.
[175] Note that farmers in the US eagerly anticipated the following growing season, as it was the first time in years in which they had the potential to make good money due to high commodity prices. D Streitfeld, 'A Global Need for Grain that Farm Can't Fill', *New York Times*, 9 March 2008. However, most farmers in developing countries still struggled to make ends meet; the higher price for food commodities failed to trickle down to the price that farmers are paid. See, eg 'Farmers Fleeing Ancient Centre of Philippine Rice', *Reuters*, 23 April 2008.
[176] Erlanger, above n 31.

people used the food crisis to argue that GM seeds should be introduced in more countries and favoured over non-GM seeds.[177]

It is highly doubtful, however, that GM crops are the best way to address the current global food situation. Although GM crops are generally viewed as higher yielding,[178] even their supporters also acknowledge that they might increase yield risk.[179] Moreover, there is no overwhelming evidence that GM crops in the long run are higher yielding, or better suited to the countries in which they are being promoted. Indeed, most GM seeds were not designed to increase yields or decrease production costs. Rather, many were designed for the express purpose of being used with other inputs.[180] As the former Special Rapporteur on the right to food observed,

> The design of genetically modified seeds for example, has largely been about creating vertical integration between seed, pesticides and production to increase corporate profits. The FAO revealed that 85% of all plantings of transgenic crops are soybean, maize and cotton, modified to reduce input and labour costs for large-scale production systems, but not designed 'to feed the world or increase food quality'.[181]

Several studies have concluded that GM technology is not the best way to eradicate poverty or increase yields. Most importantly, a report drafted by the International Assessment of Agricultural Knowledge, Science and Technology for Development, a group convened by the UN and composed of over 400 experts from around the world, determined after a three-year study that GM crops are not the best way to address hunger, and that farmers would be better served by using more traditional farming methods.[182] The report has been accepted by over 60 countries. The US, Australia and Canada have expressed reservations and refused to sign the final agreement, however, while some biotechnology companies walked out of discussions in protest.[183]

In addition, a report released in 2008 concluded that GM crops are actually less productive than conventional crops.[184] The findings, which compared GM soy crops to conventional soy crops, suggest that there

---

[177] A Pollack, 'In Lean Times, Biotech Grains Are Less Taboo', *New York Times*, 21 April 2008.
[178] Ziegler, above n 1, ¶ 43.
[179] World Bank, above n 8.
[180] For example, Monsanto's Roundup-resistant seed, which is one of the most commonly planted GM seeds, was developed to resist Monsanto's Roundup herbicide, so that farmers could reduce the time they spent weeding. See, eg R Weiss, '2 Reports At Odds On Biotech Crops', *Washington Post*, 14 February 2008.
[181] Ziegler, above n 1.
[182] Synthesis Report of the International Assessment of Agricultural Knowledge, Science and Technology for Development, Executive Summary, released April 2008; see also 'GM Debate Overshadows Key UN Agriculture Report', *Farmers Guardian*, 18 April 2008.
[183] *Farmers Guardian*, ibid.
[184] See G Lean, 'Exposed: The Great GM Crops Myth', *The Independent*, 20 April 2008.

are two reasons for the reduced productivity of GM crops. First, while researchers work on genetically modifying crops, conventional crops are also being developed, which can create a 'time lag [that] could lead to a "decrease" in yields'.[185] Secondly, it is possible that the process of modifying crops genetically 'depresses productivity'.[186]

Moreover, most experts acknowledge that hunger is not caused by an insufficient amount of food in the world, but by 'very low incomes and unequal access to land, water, credit and markets'.[187] Even the 2007–08 food crisis was not due to a shortage of food worldwide. Thus, the use of GM crops, even if they could increase yields, might do nothing to alleviate hunger.

The debate over GM crops has several implications with respect to the right to food. Most importantly, the focus on GM crops as an antidote to hunger threatens to divert important resources, energy, and research and development away from efforts that might have a greater impact on food security. Indeed, research on the effectiveness of GM technology in Africa has found that efforts have not been adequately focused on addressing farmers' needs and have diverted important resources towards less important projects.[188]

In addition, the promotion of GM seeds might further the concentration of seed markets around the world. NGOs and others have expressed concerns that this could lead to monopolies in the seed market and increased prices in the future.[189] Moreover, the introduction of GM crop production in developing countries might prevent farmers in those countries from exporting their crops to countries that have strict laws about importing GM crops. That concern has been expressed, for example, by representatives of small farmers in Thailand.[190]

Biotechnology agribusiness TNCs thus play an important role with respect to the right to food. From their use of intellectual property protection to their promotion of inputs that are ill suited to the needs of poor farmers in developing countries, these TNCs can influence the type of food produced, the ability of farmers to earn a sufficient income, and the capacity of countries to maximise the production of appropriate and sufficient food for their citizens.

---

[185] Ibid (stating that even the 'fervently pro-GM US Department of Agriculture' has acknowledged this time lag).
[186] Ibid.
[187] J Ziegler, 'Third Annual Report by the Special Rapporteur on the Right to Food, Delivered to the General Assembly', UN document A/58/330 (28 August 2003) ¶ 29.
[188] A deGrassi, 'Genetically Modified Crops and Sustainable Poverty Alleviation in Sub-Saharan Africa' (Third World Network—Africa, 2003).
[189] Ziegler, above n 187.
[190] M Macan-Markar, 'THAILAND: Green Groups Will Take GM Crops Issue To Court', *IPS News*, 9 January 2008.

(iii) Livestock

The debate over the role of biotechnology TNCs has focused mostly on the commercial seed market, which is highly concentrated throughout the world and very influential over the markets of most important food commodities. Biotechnology firms, however, also are important actors in the livestock industry. Although less globalised than the seed market, the livestock industry is already extremely concentrated in the US and is becoming increasingly globalised in several different ways, all of which also affect the right to food to varying degrees.

First, biotechnology companies patent 'inputs' for livestock, such as feed and hormones. Secondly, breeding companies have aggressively marketed western breeds in developing countries. Thirdly, US livestock breeders and processors, which are already highly concentrated in the US, have begun to expand their operations abroad.

The livestock industry is becoming increasingly concentrated.[191] At the same time, biotechnology companies that dominate the commercial seed market have also worked to develop patented inputs for livestock.[192] Companies have also begun to utilise the same aggressive tactics to promote products that are used in the commercial seed market. For the moment, the development of patented inputs for livestock has little impact on the right to food. However, the aggressive promotion of expensive inputs in the US possibly foreshadows what could happen in developing countries in the future. It is thus conceivable that the use of expensive inputs for livestock could lead to cycles of debt similar to those faced by farmers who use high levels of agrochemicals in crop production.

Not only have companies begun to patent and aggressively market expensive inputs for the livestock industry, but breeding companies (self-described 'livestock genetics' companies) have continued to develop and market hybrid breeding lines. Similar to commercial seeds that cannot regenerate, breeding companies have created hybrid lines with a 'biological lock', which ensures that 'hybrids have to be permanently bred from pure lines'.[193] This allows breeding companies to retain their market power and prevent competition. Moreover, the breeding industry has become increasingly consolidated, as more companies become vertically or horizontally integrated.[194]

Western breeding companies have also begun to aggressively market their breeds in developing countries. This has often occurred with the

---

[191] S Gura, 'Livestock Breeding in the Hands of Corporations', *Seedling*, January 2008.
[192] One example is artificial bovine growth hormone that increases milk production. See, eg Barlett, above n 5.
[193] Gura, above n 191.
[194] Ibid.

help of development and not-for-profit organisations. In some respects, imported breeds hold great potential for small farmers in developing countries. Holstein cattle, for instance, which have been promoted in Uganda by western breeding companies as well as by international charities, generally produce much higher yields of milk than indigenous cattle.[195] Small farmers in Uganda that have been given Holsteins through the Heifer International programme have been able to improve their milk yields, increase their income and purchase more food.[196]

However, the introduction of western breeds also has the potential to negatively affect small farmers, as well as the right to food of citizens in developing countries. At an individual level, small farmers raising imported breeds must contend with different required inputs; Holsteins, for example, require more food and expensive inputs than indigenous cattle in Uganda. Imported Holsteins are also not well adapted to their new climates, and are more susceptible to the diseases that exist in the importing countries.[197] Farmers and governments thus must balance the risks and benefits of imported livestock. With high maintenance, imported livestock can yield more milk and thus improve small farmers' ability to purchase food. On the other hand, there is also a greater risk that the livestock will not survive or will require increasing amounts of inputs, thereby negating any benefits of imported livestock and possibly posing even greater problems. At a national level, imported livestock pose risks to national food sovereignty and security. Importing livestock threatens to render native species extinct, thereby reducing a country's biodiversity while wiping out species that are best adapted to a country. This could potentially create great food insecurity.[198]

Thirdly, US livestock breeders and processors, which are already highly concentrated in the US, have begun to expand their operations abroad, threatening to create greater market concentration worldwide.[199] More significantly for the right to food, however, is the expansion of contract farming for livestock production in developing countries. For example, poultry breeders and processors, which are already very consolidated

---

[195] A Rice, 'A Dying Breed', *New York Times*, 27 January 2008.
[196] Ibid.
[197] Ibid.
[198] For example, since 1994, 13 of the 15 indigenous breeds of pigs in Vietnam have either become extinct or are in danger of becoming extinct because of cross-breeding with imported varieties. In Kenya, Red Maasai sheep were bred almost completely out of existence in a span of 15 years. It was then discovered that the imported sheep were ill suited to Kenya, partly because they did not have the resistance to intestinal parasites that the indigenous breeds have developed. However, '[b]y the time that was discovered, . . . purebred Red Maasai were almost impossible to find'. Ibid.
[199] For example, Smithfield, which is the largest of the four corporations that dominate the US hog market, has extended its operations to Europe. Food & Water Watch, 'The Trouble with Smithfield: A Corporate Profile' (2007). Tyson, the largest poultry breeder and processor in the US, has begun to undertake joint ventures in developing countries. See, eg L Atarah, 'Playing Chicken: Ghana vs the IMF', *CorpWatch*, 14 June 2005.

in the US, have begun to expand their operations to other countries via contract farming. Contract farming allows poultry companies to produce poultry even more cheaply in developing countries for export to the world market.[200] Although contract farming in general has been promoted as a way to increase agricultural investment and support farmers in developing countries, it can sometimes produce cycles of debt in developing countries. This seems particularly true in the livestock industry, as small farmers who enter into contracts with large agribusiness corporations are required to provide expensive inputs.[201] Livestock contract farming often shifts the risk away from international breeders and onto the small farmers.[202] The combination of debt and risk is particularly problematic in a volatile export market, and has definite implications for struggling farmers' right to food.

III. RECOMMENDATIONS AND CONCLUSION

Agribusiness TNCs can have an impact on the right to food in a variety of ways. Given that enough food exists to feed every man, woman and child, yet millions of people die every year because they cannot access sufficient food, it is imperative to consider how to address the factors that affect the realisation of the right to food. Agribusiness TNCs, of course, are not the only actors influencing the right to food: governments, trade rules and other factors play important roles in the allocation of resources within the global food system. Agribusiness, however, is undoubtedly influential with respect to the right to food. Agribusiness TNCs provide food for people throughout the world, yet they also assist in structuring the food system in ways that prevent people from realising their right to food. Considering how agribusiness TNCs could improve their impact on the right to food is thus extremely important.

Whether agribusiness TNCs have a legal obligation in respect of the right to food is a separate issue requiring its own analysis. Some fora have found that transnational corporations do have some legal obligations with respect to certain human rights. This chapter, however, does not seek to argue that agribusiness TNCs do or do not have a legal obligation regarding the right to food; rather, it contends that, given the number of people around the world whose right to food is affected by agribusiness TNCs and given TNCs' ability to address those issues, many reasons exist—including but not limited to those related to business, brand protection and ethics—for agribusiness TNCs to consider improving their impact on the right to food. Moreover, there

---

[200] GRAIN, 'Contract Farming in the World's Poultry Industry', *GRAIN*, January 2008.
[201] Ibid.
[202] Ibid, 16.

are just as many reasons for governments, farmers, consumers and other stakeholders to push for improvements in the conduct and impact of agribusiness TNCs.

Considering the diverse ways in which agribusiness TNCs can have an impact on the right to food, it is impossible to provide a complete list of recommendations for improving agribusiness's role with respect to the right to food. The following suggestions, however, attempt to address some of the important steps that agribusiness TNCs, governments and policymakers can undertake to improve the impact of agribusiness TNCs on the right to food of people throughout the world.

A. Recommendations for Agribusiness TNCs

Agribusiness companies have wide-ranging and distinct sets of partners, suppliers and consumers; each agribusiness TNC therefore has unique and varied impacts on the right to food. Ensuring that every agribusiness TNC does not negatively affect the right to food would thus require that each agribusiness TNC undertake due diligence efforts on all of its operations and the operations of those in its supply chain.[203] Aside from more detailed company-specific assessments, there are several basic steps that each group of agribusiness TNCs could undertake to ensure that they do not negatively affect the right to food of people throughout the world.

(i) Commodity Traders and Processors

Commodity traders and processors occupy a unique position in the global food system. The market power of these TNCs renders them immensely influential and often enables them to set the prices that they pay for commodities. Those prices frequently are very low, affecting the ability of farmers in developing countries to earn a sufficient income and obtain sufficient food. An important first step for commodity traders and

---

[203] The importance of due diligence is highlighted by the former Special Representative of the Secretary-General on the issue of human rights and transnational corporations and other business enterprises ('Special Representative'). The Special Representative has developed a framework for business and human rights issues under which states have a duty to protect human rights, while TNCs have a duty to respect human rights. He argues that the key to respecting human rights is to require TNCs to conduct due diligence on the ways in which their operations, and those of their suppliers, have an impact on human rights. See The Special Representative of the Secretary-General on the issue of human rights and transnational corporations and other business enterprises, 'Promotion and Protection of All Human Rights, Civil, Political, Economic, Social and Cultural Rights, Including the Right to Development: Protect, Respect and Remedy: a Framework for Business and Human Rights', UN document A/HRC/8/5 (advanced edited version), 7 April 2008.

processors therefore would be to ensure transparency in the production chains of commodities in which they trade. Greater transparency of production chains would enable farmers, consumers, suppliers, policymakers and governments to better understand the prices that are paid to actors within the production chain, and would ensure that any efforts to improve wages and prices for farmers and agricultural workers were not diverted to other actors.

Of course, greater transparency alone will not improve the prices that farmers receive for their crops—prices that are increasing crucial, especially for the poorest farmers in developing countries. Commodity traders and processors should ensure that farmers and workers receive prices that allow them to earn enough money to purchase a sufficient amount of food without resorting to the use of illegal labour. Agribusiness TNCs that profit from commodities despite the depressed prices that are paid to farmers often argue that the best way to improve the income of small farmers is to increase their productivity and yields. That solution, however, shifts responsibility away from the TNCs. Moreover, although increased yields are helpful on an individual level, they can lead to decreased commodity prices overall. There is thus no substitute for improving prices that are paid to farmers.

(ii) Food and Beverage Companies

Most food and beverage companies have a different position in the global food system than commodity traders and processors, tending to have more influence over consumers and less direct influence over farmers. That is not universally true, however, and to the extent that food and beverage companies do wield influence over farmers, they should consider undertaking the same steps that are suggested for commodity traders to address their impact on right to food. In the coffee sector, for example, coffee roasters often have greater power than coffee traders; coffee roasters should therefore consider pushing for greater transparency in the production chain and ensuring that higher prices are paid to coffee farmers.

Even in sectors where food and beverage companies do not wield as much power over commodity prices, TNCs should undertake efforts to ensure that their suppliers respect the right to food. Food manufacturers that use soy or cocoa, for example, should only purchase those commodities from commodity traders and processors that can guarantee that farmers are paid an adequate price to enable them to purchase sufficient food.

(iii) Biotechnology Agribusiness TNCs

There are several steps that biotechnology agribusiness TNCs should undertake to ensure that they do not have a negative impact on the right to food. First, biotechnology TNCs should cease directly or indirectly lobbying the governments of developing countries to implement stronger intellectual property regimes. Secondly, they should guarantee that poor farmers in developing countries can save, share and reuse seeds. Although strong intellectual property protections and prohibitions on seed use provide important incentives for research in developed countries, permitting more flexible seed use in developing countries could positively affect farmers' ability to produce or purchase sufficient food. Agribusiness TNCs could thus consider adapting and improving upon the approach of pharmaceutical companies to intellectual property rights in developing countries, where some intellectual property protections have been waived to ensure the fulfilment of the right to health. Of course, pharmaceutical companies have also been strongly criticised for their use of intellectual property rights in developing countries and should not be considered a perfect model. Agribusiness TNCs would therefore have to greatly improve upon the approach taken by pharmaceutical companies in developing countries in order to properly address their impact on the right to food.

Thirdly, agribusiness TNCs should use caution when marketing and promoting their products in developing countries. Such TNCs sometimes aggressively promote their products in developing countries, without considering whether the products are appropriate for the small farmers to whom they market. The restrictions on seed use and related expensive inputs, however, often lead to cycles of debt and desperation for small farmers in developing countries. Agribusiness TNCs must develop a more ethical solution to this dilemma.

Fourthly, agribusiness TNCs should focus more of their research and development on the needs of farmers in developing countries. Agribusiness TNCs currently fail to address those needs sufficiently, although they continue to market their products in developing countries. The minimal research and development that they do allocate to the needs of developing countries is often designed more to promote the TNCs' reputations than to address the actual needs of poor farmers. Agribusiness TNCs should thus commit to focusing a larger percentage of their research and development efforts on developing country needs. At the very least, agribusiness TNCs should not dissemble by claiming to undertake research and development efforts designed to meet the needs of small farmers in developing countries when their efforts fail to do so adequately.

B. Recommendations for Governments and Policy Makers

Just as individual agribusiness TNCs must undertake their own assessments to discover the many ways through which they can improve their impact on the right to food, so must countries determine the best methods through which they can protect the right to food as it relates to agribusiness TNCs operating in their countries. There are several steps that all countries could undertake to ensure that agribusiness TNCs respect the right to food.

First, countries should ensure that their intellectual property regimes balance TNCs' right to intellectual property protection with their citizens' right to food. Countries should refrain from implementing TRIPS plus legislation, and should use intellectual property regimes to proactively protect the rights of their small farmers.

Secondly, countries should be very careful when deciding whether to allow or promote the production of GM crops within their borders. Countries should ensure that those decisions are informed by science, and should carefully weigh whether the use of GM seeds will contribute positively to their food security and food sovereignty. Countries should also guarantee that protections are put in place for small farmers using GM seeds, as well as for farmers whose non-GM seeds might be tainted by GM seeds.

Thirdly, developing countries should seek to create incentives for TNCs to undertake research and development efforts that are focused on the needs of their farmers. Intellectual property regimes should also foster technology transfers between developed and developing countries.[204] Moreover, any government research and development efforts that are undertaken jointly with TNCs should be evaluated on how well the efforts address farmers' needs; countries must be careful that they do not divert scarce resources to ineffective or less important research projects in collaboration with TNCs. Countries should also increase the participation of small farmers in the development of research efforts and agricultural policies.[205]

Fourthly, producing countries must ensure that minimum prices and wages are paid to farmers and agricultural workers. Merely setting minimum prices for commodities fails to ensure that farmers actually receive those prices. Countries should thus create systems that track and enforce payments to small farmers. Governmental labour inspectors should be properly trained and compensated, and must be allowed to inspect farms freely and without prior notice.

Fifthly, countries should monitor the operations of agribusiness TNCs

---

[204] See Cullet, above n 118, 24.
[205] See deGrassi, above n 188, 57; see also World Bank, above n 8, 172.

within their borders to ensure that TNCs do not directly violate the right to food. Violations of the right to food, such as unduly restricting access to water, should be remedied by governments through the judicial system or by mediation between aggrieved parties. Governments should also implement laws that proactively protect their citizens from gross violations of the right to food by agribusiness TNCs.

C. Conclusion

Agribusiness TNCs provide important services within the global food system and generate employment throughout the world. The concentration of agribusiness TNCs and their subsequent market power, however, indicate that agribusiness TNCs have an influential role with respect to the right to food of millions of people throughout the world. Although agribusiness TNCs sometimes facilitate the realisation of the right to food, all too often they instead negatively affect the right to food of small producers, workers and consumers, especially in developing countries. It is therefore very important to think critically about how to harness the power of agribusiness TNCs so that they respect the right to food.

Addressing the problems related to the impact of agribusiness TNCs on the right to food will require many approaches by multiple actors around the world. Agribusiness TNCs, governments, farmers, workers and consumers all have roles to play in improving the food system to ensure that the right to food is respected by agribusiness TNCs. Given the influence of agribusiness TNCs over the food security of people throughout the world, prioritising efforts to improve their impact is critical to reducing hunger and realising the right to food globally.

3

The Transformation of Food Retail and Marginalisation of Smallholder Farmers

MARGARET COWAN SCHMIDT

THE TRANSFORMATION OF food retail has dramatically affected access to food. Rapid supermarket consolidation has concentrated influence over supply chains into the hands of a small number of highly integrated retailers that are, in turn, reliant on industrialised farming and centralised distribution networks. The role of corporate food retailers in realising the right to food remains underexamined, however, and existing legal and political structures have failed to adjust to the problems and opportunities presented by the ongoing transformation of the food industry.

Increased consolidation of retail chains simultaneously increases retailers' power over their supply chains and intensifies the competitive pressure to ensure reliable delivery of high-quality, low-cost foods. Modern procurement systems and economies of scale and scope have increased supermarkets' capacity to deliver more affordable high-quality foods.[1] However, critics claim that supermarket buying practices, which pressure suppliers to cut costs and produce on shorter notice, reduce job security, reinforce low wages and contribute to poverty at the bottom of the supply chain.[2]

---

[1] PR Kaufman, 'Consolidation in Food Retailing: Prospects for Consumers & Grocery Suppliers, Collateral Damage' [2000] *Agricultural Outlook* 18, available at www.ers.usda.gov/publications/agoutlook/aug2000/ao273g.pdf.

[2] ActionAid, 'Who Pays? How British Supermarkets Are Keeping Women in Poverty' (2007), available at www.actionaid.org.uk/doc_lib/actionaid_who_pays_report.pdf. See also Banana Link, 'Collateral Damage: How Price Wars between UK Supermarkets Helped Destroy Livelihoods in the Banana and Pineapple Supply Chains' (2006), available at www.bananalink.org.uk/images/stories/documents/2007/August/COLLATERALDAMAGEfinal.pdf (describing how price pressures from UK retailers have forced banana producers to cut wages, replace permanent labourers with temporary contract workers, and suppress trade union rights).

66 *Margaret Cowan Schmidt*

The transformation of food procurement and distribution networks has made fresh fruit and vegetable markets more lucrative. Smallholder farmers that have access to supermarket supply chains generally enjoy a higher standard of living. However, developing countries' comparative advantages over industrialised countries in respect of fresh fruit and vegetable production do not necessarily result in better opportunities for the smallholders within those developing countries.[3] Increased competition among suppliers, rigorous new product standards and the demand for flexible supply have exacerbated scale-based disadvantages and may limit smallholders' ability to participate in mainstream supermarket channels. At the same time, traditional food retail in the developing world is declining as supermarkets enter and dominate developing markets around the world.[4] Smallholders, who already have a high risk for poverty and hunger, have increasingly limited access to food supply streams. Without proper assistance and support, these farmers will be unable to effectively sell fresh produce in the global market and risk falling more deeply into poverty. Part I of this chapter documents the rise of supermarkets in industrialised and in developing countries respectively. Part II examines the modernisation of procurement systems and its consequences. Part III discusses antitrust and competition policy, particularly in the US and the EU, and explains how current antitrust and competition laws are inadequately tailored to modern food retailer practices. Part IV considers how to increase the competitiveness and security of smallholders.

---

[3] Comparative advantages are most likely in the fresh produce sectors, since they are relatively free of economies of scale present in staple crop cultivation, such as corn and wheat. O Brown and C Sander, 'Supermarket Buying Power: Global Supply Chains and Smallholder Farmers' (International Institute for Sustainable Development, 2007) 11.

[4] FAO, 'Special Feature: Globalization, Urbanization and Changing Food Systems in Developing Countries' (2004) 3 (reporting that FDI in food industries increased from $743 million to more than $2.1 billion from 1988 to 1997, far outpacing agricultural investments, and stating that '[t]he 30 largest supermarket chains now account for about one third of food sales worldwide'). See also World Bank, 'Horticultural Producers and Supermarket Development in Indonesia', Report No 38543-ID (2007) vi-vii ('Traditional retail loses about 2 percent of its share each year. Informed observers believe within a decade modern retail will dominate the majority of the food market in Indonesia.') But see D Tschirley, 'Supermarkets and Beyond: Literature Review on Farmer to Market Linkages in Sub-Saharan Africa and Asia', paper prepared for the AgInfo Project funded by the Bill and Melinda Gates Foundation (2007) (noting that expectations of supermarket growth in Africa and parts of Asia have cooled in last few years and that traditional markets continue to persist and thrive in parts of developing world); see also T Reardon and A Gulati, 'The Rise of Supermarkets and Their Development Implications: International Experience Relevant for India', Discussion Paper 00752 (IFPRI, 2008) (noting that rates of decline of traditional retail are widely varied and dependent upon product category and providing summaries of research from Indonesia, Chile, Argentina, and Hong Kong).

I. THE RISE OF SUPERMARKETS

A. From Traditional Food Retail to Chain Markets in Industrialised Countries: the US Experience

In the US, supermarkets became dominant over the traditional food retail system over the course of more than 100 years. As in the rest of the world, traditional food retail in the US included wet markets, 'mom and pop' stores offering full customer service, street vendors, and home delivery of milk and dry goods.[5] Modern chain food retail began in the late 1870s, when the A & P chain began operating small grocery stores. A & P opened its first 'supermarket' in 1936 and remained dominant through the 1950s, until it was outpaced by its competitors' procurement-system innovations.[6]

The transition from traditional to supermarket food retail in the US has been characterised by several key trends. One trend was the progression from non-food retail chains to dry-food chains and then to full-range chains offering fresh produce. Another trend was the general evolution of retail from full service to self-service, while grocery retail evolved from traditional outlets to chains and supermarkets. Although supermarkets initially diffused from large cities and economic boom areas to smaller cities and suburban areas,[7] once established, they further adapted to their locations. Retail food chains evolved into increasingly large supermarkets and hypermarkets in the suburbs and into convenience stores and neighbourhood shops in urban areas. Supermarket retail also expanded from primarily or entirely providing food products to offering a broader range of goods and services, including, for example, in-store credit systems, banks and health clinics.[8] As those changes were taking place, the modernisation of food procurement and logistics systems made increasingly aggressive cost cutting possible. The recent massive growth of the industry as a whole, and of individual retailers in particular, has dwarfed earlier cycles of grocery chain growth.[9]

Socioeconomic changes that altered consumer demand triggered this transformation.[10] First, there was a dramatic population shift from rural

---

[5] Reardon and Gulati, ibid, 17.
[6] Ibid, 3.
[7] Simultaneously, diffusion tends to extend from high to low-income areas.
[8] Reardon and Gulati, above n 4, 3. See also KW Stiegert and T Sharkey, 'Food Pricing, Competition, and the Emerging Supercenter Format' (2007) 23 *Agribusiness* 295, 296 (noting that 'hypermarkets' are now selling general merchandise and pharmaceuticals all under one roof).
[9] Reardon and Gulati, above n 4, 3–4.
[10] There has been, however, opposition to the proliferation of chain stores. For an analysis of the citizen movement to protect local economies from the 'absentee landlordism', represented by chains, see B Price, 'A Movement Diverted: How Corporations Bastardized Anti-Chain Store Campaigns of the 1920s and 1930s' (Community Environmental

to urban areas. In 1900, 60% of the US population was rural. By 1990, 75% of the population was urban. Secondly, women began working outside the home in large numbers. Relatively few women worked outside the home in 1900, but by 2000, 75% of American women held independent employment. Thirdly, per-capita income increased over the century.[11] As the distance between Americans and raw food production increased, fewer Americans grew their own foods. Instead, Americans relied more heavily on grocery foods. The movement of women from the home to the workforce increased the emphasis on convenience of 'one-stop shopping' and processed foods. Higher per-capita incomes funded this transition.

Although market demands spurred chain food retail and consolidation, until relatively recently, the top five retail firms controlled less than 20% of the market.[12] From 1997 to 2000, the top five US retail firms increased their market share from 24% to 42% of all retail sales. By 2003, those firms controlled over half of all grocery sales.[13] Much of this consolidation occurred through mergers and acquisitions, frequently pursued in an effort to compete with Wal-Mart Stores, Inc. Although the US has a history of strong anti-supermarket regulation and competition policy, underlying economic and social forces have resulted in market concentration similar to that in the UK, which has had much less stringent regulations.[14] Antitrust policy in the US has failed to prevent radical concentration of the food retail sector.

B. The Rise of Supermarkets in the Developing World

The proliferation of supermarkets in the developing world has transformed the food retail landscape at a faster pace than that at which similar changes occurred in the industrialised world. Smallholders in developing countries have had relatively little time or opportunity to adapt to the new opportunities and challenges presented by this trans-

---

Legal Defense Fund, 2005), available at www.celdf.org/downloads/A%20Movement%20Diverted.pdf.

[11] Reardon and Gulati, above n 4, 2.

[12] Those top five firms were Wal-mart, Kroger, Costco, Supervalu/Albertsons and Safeway. K Mamen, 'Facing Goliath: Challenging the Impacts of Supermarket Consolidation on our Local Economies, Communities, and Food Security'(2007) 1 *The Oakland Institute Policy Brief* 2, available at www.oaklandinstitute.org/pdfs/facing_goliath.pdf.

[13] Ibid. Similar consolidation has occurred in other industrialised markets. Between 1993 and 1999, the aggregate concentration of the 10 largest grocery retailers in the EU grew by 24.9%, while the 10 bottom companies declined by 72.9%. The Institute of Grocery Distribution, using historical growth rates in Europe, predicted that the 10 largest retailers will increase their market share to 60% by 2010. T Lang, 'Food Industrialisation and Food Power: Implications for Food Governance' (2003) 21 *Development Policy Review* 555, 558–60.

[14] Reardon and Gulati, above n 4, 4. Reardon notes, however, that the current levels of concentration were achieved over a longer period of time than in the UK.

formation. Some researchers have cautioned that projected supermarket market dominance in parts of the developing world is overstated,[15] but supermarket take-off has clearly had a tremendous impact on how farmers sell their goods and on how consumers shop.

As in industrialised countries, the proliferation of supermarkets in emerging economies coincides with shifts in consumer demand, proactive marketing and modernisation of procurement strategies.[16] Urbanisation, the entry of women into the workforce, rising incomes, increased demand for processed foods, and access to refrigeration and transportation all helped to set the stage for supermarket take-off.[17]

Diffusion patterns in developing countries largely mirror the progression in industrialised countries. The retail format utilised in a particular location reflects the needs of that area's consumers: discount and convenience stores are established in inner cities and small towns, and larger supermarkets and hypermarkets are established in suburban areas. Supermarket chains tend to begin in large cities, and then expand to reach smaller cities and rural areas. Diffusion and product selection are also tailored to consumer demographics. Retailers focus first on wealthier consumers, then middle-class consumers and finally the urban poor. Supermarkets initially provide processed foods, then semi-processed foods and eventually fresh produce. Although there are significant logistical challenges in providing high-quality fresh produce, there are also higher profit margins and competitive advantages over retailers with less diverse selections.

The liberalisation of retail foreign direct investment (FDI) and other early 1990s policy reforms have triggered rapid supermarket take-off in developing countries.[18] Economic liberalisation opened developing countries to foreign investment, including retail investment, which facilitated supermarket proliferation. Conversely, policies constraining retail FDI have constituted the primary cause of delayed take-off.[19] FDI in

---

[15] See, eg Tschirley, above n 4. See also J Humphrey, 'The Supermarket Revolution in Developing Countries, Tidal Wave or Tough Competitive Struggle?' [2007] 7 *Journal of Economic Geography* 433: '[T]he extent of transformation of retailing . . . as a consequence of [supermarket expansion] is overestimated'.

[16] T Reardon et al, '"Proactive Fast-Tracking" Diffusion of Supermarkets in Developing Countries: Implications for Market Institutions and Trade' (2007) 7 *Journal of Economic Geography* 399, 400: 'Indeed, these retailers have been extraordinarily proactive in both adapting to [as Dicken (2000) terms it, "placing the firm"] but also changing the environment [as Dicken terms it, "firming the place")'.

[17] Reardon and Gulati, above n 4, 8. See also International Food Policy Research Institute, *IFPRI Forum*, December 2003, available at http://ageconsearch.umn.edu/bitstream/16500/1/if030012.pdf.

[18] This liberalisation frequently occurred, least in part, through bilateral or multilateral trade agreements, although sometimes it occurred well after trade liberalisation, as in Indonesia, the Philippines and Thailand. Reardon and Gulati, above n 4, 8–9.

[19] Ibid, 5. For example, China (a so-called 'third-tier' country) had no supermarkets in 1989, and food retail at the time was completely controlled by the governments. From

food retail can take several forms,[20] one of the most common being the direct entry of a Western European or American global multinational into the developing market. Alternatively, FDI may come from regional multinationals or through the acquisition of a local chain by a foreign multinational. A supermarket chain may also form a joint venture either with a local grocery chain or with the government.[21]

Market liberalisation also resulted in the widespread abolition of marketing boards and commodity agreements. Marketing boards act as legal cartels by pooling produce and bargaining power. As the name suggests, they also market products, coordinate distribution of inputs, and often facilitate research and provide basic technologies to farmers.[22] Their collapse dramatically altered smallholders' prospects, flooded the market with newcomers eager to sell in global markets and undermined the incentive for collective action.[23]

Supermarkets enter developing countries with vast monetary, technological and infrastructure resources at their disposal, and may also have regulatory and policy advantages over traditional retailers. Supermarket chain diffusion has been facilitated by communication innovations,[24] technology and improved transportation that are frequently unavailable to traditional food retailers.

Evidence suggests that 'the regulatory balance appears to promote the net diffusion of supermarkets in developing countries'.[25] Some governments have proactively encouraged the modernisation of their food retail systems. In the 1960s and 1970s, the governments of Latin American countries, Malaysia and Hong Kong unsuccessfully promoted food retail

its beginning in 1990, the supermarket sector rose to about 15% of food retail nationally and up to 35% in some urban centres by 2003. Reardon notes that the driving forces for supermarket take-off (rising incomes and urbanisation) were in place prior to the take-off, but that privatisation of the retail market and the liberalisation of retail FDI that began in 1992 and culminated in 2004 in the WTO accession process were necessary for supermarkets to proliferate.

[20] For examples highlighting various structures for investment in supermarkets in China, Russia, Chile and Indonesia, see Reardon and Gulati, above n 4, 9–10.

[21] Ibid. FDI-based retail (sole and joint ventures involving transnational retailers) roughly accounts for only about 50% of modern retail sales in developing countries, but was an important trigger for domestic investment, whipped up to compete with or forestall foreign corporation. Substantial domestic and regional investment has also contributed to supermarket take-off. Reardon et al, above n 16, 404–05.

[22] Before this, commodity markets were regulated by multilateral agreements on price bands, production limits and export quotas designed to stabilise prices and keep them high.

[23] K Raworth, 'Trading Away Our Rights—Women in Global Supply Chains' (Oxfam, 2004) 67.

[24] Ibid, 33.

[25] Reardon et al, above n 16, 402. Policies favouring supermarkets over smaller retailers are, of course, not limited to emerging markets. For a report on the influence supermarkets exert over community planners and lawmakers in the UK, see Friends of the Earth, 'Shopping the Bullies: Why the Planning System for Retail Needs to be Strengthened, not Weakened' (2007).

modernisation as part of their development policies.[26] In the 1990s and 2000s, many governments supported the establishment and expansion of grocery chains more directly. For example, the Chinese government has invested directly in modern retail; state-sponsored groceries compete with private retailers, but have access to low-interest-rate credit, inexpensive real estate and other benefits.[27] Similar measures imposed elsewhere have generally been successful, and are often accompanied by simultaneous supermarket regulation and government support for traditional retailers.

Informal imbalances favouring organised modern retail may be more influential than direct regulatory support for modern groceries. National regulations that are facially neutral with respect to retailer size may discourage informal and traditional food retail in practice, by providing incentives that can be captured only by supermarkets. Government incentives are generally more accessible to formal, well-organised commercial operations,[28] while smaller businesses may find them difficult to understand or to apply. Supermarkets are also often better situated to avoid unfavourable regulations than smaller food retailers. Store format is surprisingly fluid among the grocery chains, and regulation based upon criteria related to size or store format is often unable to restrict supermarket expansion.[29]

Tax systems can, by design or inadvertently, subsidise chain stores. In extreme cases, tax incentives strongly favour modern retailers. For example, certain Russian municipalities and the South Korean government have offered tax exoneration to supermarkets.[30]

Policies restricting the operation of traditional forms of food retail also support supermarket diffusion. Some governments impose strict zoning limits[31] or other regulations on wet markets, citing the informal nature of such markets, the markets' potential to cause street congestion, their

---

[26] Reardon and Gulati, above n 4, 11 (citing A Goldman et al, 'The Persistent Competitive Advantage of Traditional Food Retailers in Asia: Wet Markets' Continued Dominance in Hong Kong' (1999) 19 *Journal of Macromarketing*; JH Lee and T Reardon, 'Forward Integration of an Agricultural Cooperative into the Supermarket Sector: The Case of Hanaro Club in Korea', Department of Industrial Economics, Chung-Ang University and Michigan State University Joint Working Paper (2005); L Dries and T Reardon, 'Central and Eastern Europe: Impact of Food Retail Investments on the Food Chain', Report Series No 6 (FAO Investment Center, 2005); and D Hu et al, 'The Emergence of Supermarkets with Chinese Characteristics: Challenges and Opportunities for China's Agricultural Development' (2004) 22 Development Policy Review 557.
[27] Hu et al, ibid.
[28] Reardon and Gulati, above n 4, 12.
[29] For example, Carrefour and Tesco have used small-format stores, kiosks, convenience stores and neighbourhood markets in Thailand to avoid regulations aimed at hypermarkets.
[30] Reardon and Gulati, above n 4.
[31] China has made particularly aggressive use of this strategy, actually converting wet markets into supermarkets.

sometimes unhygienic standards and vendors' frequent failure to pay taxes.[32] Despite domestic pressures on those markets, some researchers urge the continued importance of what they consider the 'dominant' role of traditional food retail in parts of the developing world.[33]

II. MODERNISATION OF PROCUREMENT SYSTEMS AND ITS CONSEQUENCES

Vertical integration of supermarket supply chains has been key to the success of the supermarket model,[34] and has transformed the way food is grown and sourced. The use of technology has radically shaped both agricultural production and quality standard enforcement.[35]

Although modernisation patterns vary according to product and from country to country, generalisations can be drawn. Procurement modernisation is expensive, and generally occurs first in the largest retail chains operating in a given region, usually large multinational or large domestic chains. Delays in procurement modernisation result in significant competitive disadvantages.[36]

As a particular retail chain grows, it typically shifts from a fragmented per-store procurement system to a model using a system of distribution centres (hubs) that serve several stores in a given zone (spokes). Hub and spoke centralisation increases procurement efficiency by reducing coordination and transaction costs.[37] Centralisation and technology enables retailers to track shifting supply and demand with greater accuracy, allowing them to reallocate associated risks. Efficiencies of global food supply have been captured through the use of bar-coding and product tracking for 'just in time' delivery and improved, inexpensive transportation. Indeed, the cost of sea freight fell nearly 70% between the early 1980s and the mid-1990s, and the use of airfreight jumped between 1993 and 2003.[38]

As procurement systems centralise, supermarkets channel purchases

---

[32] Reardon and Gulati, above n 4, 11.

[33] Tschirley, above n 4.

[34] For an overview of the general structure of supply chains and the factors influencing buying practices, see Insight Investment Management Ltd, 'Buying Your Way into Trouble? The Challenge of Responsible Supply Chain Management' (2004) (emphasising need for quick and well-timed production and delivery to satisfy consumer demand for year-round, high-quality produce).

[35] See, eg O De Schutter, UN Special Rapporteur on the Right to Food, 'Agribusiness and the Right to Food, Delivered to the Human Rights Council, 13th Session', UN document A/HRC/13/33 (22 December 2009) ¶¶ 6–9.

[36] Reardon et al, above n 16, 411.

[37] Integration of the market through centralised distribution is accompanied by lower cost by reduced congestion, lower quality monitoring and coordination costs, and reduced risk of supplier hold-ups. Increased transport costs partially offset these savings. Ibid, 412.

[38] Brown and Sander, above n 3, 2.

through specialised wholesalers that exhibit a preference for larger and more modern farming operations.[39] Supermarkets use specialised wholesalers to ensure consistent compliance with private and public quality and safety standards, and to reduce coordination costs by limiting the number of intermediaries with which they must interact. The accompanying shift toward large-scale, monoculture agriculture typically requires increased technological and chemical inputs[40] that are unavailable to smallholders in developing countries.

Traditionally, small and medium-sized farmers in most developing countries have brought their produce from the field to small local brokers, who then sell to zone-level brokers. In turn, those intermediaries sell to traditional wholesalers that ultimately source the traditional retail sector.[41] Based on changes in the supply chain structure, smallholder farmers now generally sell either to a field broker, who sells to the traditional channel only, or to a specialised wholesaler, who sources the supermarket channel.[42]

Despite modern global procurement practices, local and regional sourcing remain crucial to retailers operating in emerging economies and have arguably become more important. Supermarkets in developing regions source an estimated 90% of their food products from local sources rather than through imports,[43] particularly for fresh produce. Local

---

[39] Ibid, 6 (noting that in Kenya and other major horticultural exporting countries in Africa, the market share of smallholders—previously key to production—has declined as a few large exporters source predominately from large-scale production units). See also B Vorley and T Fox, 'Global Food Chains—Constraints and Opportunities for Smallholders', paper prepared for the OECD DAC POVNET Agriculture and Pro-Poor Growth Task Team Helsinki Workshop (2004) 20. But see R Hernández et al, 'Supermarkets, Wholesalers and Tomato Growers in Guatemala' (2007) 36 *Agricultural Economics* 281, 284, 289 (examining difference between farmers who provide to traditional markets through traditional channels versus farmers who provide tomatoes to supermarkets through modern wholesalers. Their study found that 'there is no significant difference in overall farm size between the groups'; that 'household size is about the same for the two groups', although rental share of supermarket-channel farmers' arable land is higher than traditional-channel farmers (40 v 20%); and that supermarket-channel farmers are far more specialised in tomato production than traditional-channel farmers. They concluded that supermarket-channel farmers tend to be 'upper-end' smallholder farmers, while traditional-channel farmers are 'lower-end').

[40] Mamen, above n 12, 3. This may be partially offset by the requirements imposed by EurepGap and other safety standards.

[41] Hernández et al, above n 39, 282 (describing marketing channel for small- and medium-sized farms producing tomatoes in Guatemala). See also Harilal et al, 'Power in Global Value Chains: Implications for Employment and Livelihoods in the Cashew Nut Industry in India' (International Institute for Environment and Development (IIED) and Madras Institute of Development Studies, 2007) 10–11 (describing supply chain in cashew industry).

[42] Reardon and Gulati, above n 4, 15.

[43] Reardon et al, above n 16, 413 (citing NM Coe and M Hess, 'The Internationalisation of Retailing: Implications for Supply Network Restructuring in East Asia and Eastern Europe' (2005) 5 *Journal of Economic Geography* 449).

production reduces transport- and time-related quality decline.[44] Farmers in developing countries enjoy relatively low land and labour costs, long growing seasons and, in some cases, relative proximity to importing industrialised markets.[45] Local fruits and vegetables may also be more appealing to consumers, in contrast to consumers' relative indifference to the origins of processed foods. Supermarkets in developing countries are also more likely to import produce from the same or other developing regions than from industrialised countries, thus spurring 'south–south' trade among countries[46] and intensifying competition among producers in developing regions.[47] Although supermarkets encourage 'fellow-sourcing' within a country or region, they are unlikely to rely on a developing country's relatively unsophisticated logistics sector, instead typically using large multinational logistics and wholesale companies.[48] This section examines several important aspects of modern global supply chains: flexible production and 'just in time' delivery, produce regulation and private standards, and 'preferred supplier' relationships. It also addresses the impact of modern procurement systems on consumers.

A. Flexible Production and 'Just in Time' Delivery

Procurement modernisation, along with rapid retailer consolidation and a growing number of suppliers, gives supermarkets sufficient bargaining power to demand 'flexible' production[49] in response to consumer demands for high-quality, year-round produce.[50] The result is a real-location of supply risk from retailers to producers. Flexible production requires producers to adjust to shifts in supply and demand by producing more when demand is high, and by absorbing surpluses when demand

---

[44] Ibid (citing T Reardon and J Berdegué, 'The Rapid Rise of Supermarkets in Latin American: Challenges and Opportunities for Development' (2002) 5 *Development Policy Review* 317).

[45] Brown and Sander, above n 3, iii.

[46] Reardon et al, above n 16, 414. For instance, Dairy Farm, Carrefour and national chains such as Matahari in Indonesia, Metro in Vietnam, Tesco in Thailand and E-Mark in South Korea source fruits and vegetable from China to sell in local stores. Reardon also lists several potential 'sourcing evolutions paths', reflecting supermarket responses to the variety of goods they source, maximising local sourcing for cost, freshness and 'local appeal' to consumers, and in response to evolution in packaging, process and storages innovations for food.

[47] Harilal et al, above n 41.

[48] Reardon et al, above n 16, 422; S Hertz and M Alfredsson, 'Strategic Development of Third Party Logistics Providers' (2003) 32 *Industrial Marketing Management* 139; T Reardon et al, 'The Rise of Supermarkets in Africa, Asia, and Latin America' (2003) 85 *American Journal of Agricultural Economics* 1140.

[49] Raworth, above n 23, 2–3.

[50] Insight Investment Management Ltd, above n 34.

is low. Flexible demand also requires 'just in time' product distribution[51] to ensure freshness and to diminish the risk that food spoils before sale.

Flexible production and 'just in time' delivery require producers to respond quickly to changes in supply and demand. Market information, access to communication networks and technology, and responding to sudden increases in demand require capital investments unavailable to many smallholders. As a result, many supermarkets are wary of supplying from smallholders due to perceived higher transaction costs, inconsistent performance, and apprehensions about quality, safety and compliance with environmental standards.[52] Despite advantages in labour and land costs, and, in some cases, proximity, small producers are frequently 'squeezed out' of supermarket supply chains[53] due to difficulty in meeting modern procurement requirements and quality standards.

Thus, although smallholders involved in a buyer's procurement system may enjoy increased access to fertilisers and seeds, credit, technology and market information,[54] and may have lower transaction costs,[55] smallholders also have difficulty entering supermarket procurement chains. Even if they succeed in doing so, other factors may diminish potential benefits.[56] To enter global supply chains, producers may have to shift production from traditional staple crops to higher-value crops that require different skills, inputs and technology, and that may be subject to different agricultural policies (for example, reduced subsidies or less favourable tax treatment).[57] Transportation is also frequently inadequate. Smallholder farms tend to be widely scattered and remote from centralised collection facilities.[58] Poor roads and unreliable access to transportation increase transportation costs and can result in inconsistent quality.[59] Local corruption may create additional difficulties. Educational disadvantages may make it more difficult for smallholders to effectively negotiate and create equitable business relationships with wholesalers.[60]

---

[51] Lang, above n 13, 557; Raworth, above n 23, 36.
[52] Brown and Sander, above n 3, 6.
[53] Ibid, iii. See also Raworth, above n 23, 34.
[54] Brown and Sander, above n 3, 2. See also Hernández et al, above n 39, 289 (reporting these advantages for tomato farmers in Guatemala who participated in supermarket supply channels as opposed to traditional retail supply channels, but concluding that, although supermarket-channel farmers earned higher gross incomes per hectare than traditional-channel growers and obtained greater credit and technical assistance, the increased cost of the higher input requirements left them with profit rates roughly similar to traditional-channel farmers). For the Indonesian case, see World Bank, above n 4, vi–vii.
[55] Hernández et al, above n 39, 289.
[56] See generally S Page and R Slater, 'Small Producer Participation in Global Food Systems: Policy Opportunities and Constraints' (2003) 21 *Development Policy Review* 641.
[57] *IFPRI Forum*, above n 17, 3.
[58] Brown and Sander, above n 3, 6.
[59] World Bank, above n 4, vii.
[60] Brown and Sander, above n 3, 6 (citing C Dolan and J Humphrey, 'Governance and

In addition, production technology and access to credit are key determinants of whether a producer will have access to supermarket supply chains.[61] Typically, producers need to invest in irrigation, greenhouses, trucks, cooling sheds and packing technologies. They must sort and grade their produce, document farming practices, and satisfy demanding timing and delivery deadlines.[62] These investments require either significant liquid assets or access to credit, as well as access to technological and business expertise.[63] Moreover, delayed payments by retailers, a consequence of modern billing systems, expose marginalised smallholders to further economic risk, particularly if they have assumed heavy up-front costs.[64]

Procurement requirements have also triggered changes in the agricultural workforces of participating farmers. Developed-world farms have shed permanent labour in favour of inexpensive (migrant) labour, often with increased pressure on employees to work around the clock at times of increased demand.[65] The costs of increased flexibility and precise timing are ultimately borne by agricultural workers in the developing world as well. Farm workers are frequently hired on temporary and precarious contracts[66] so that farm management can reduce their supply risks.[67]

B. Produce Regulation and Private Standards

Advances in food procurement systems have made certain regulations, private quality standards and 'tracing requirements' possible. These

---

Trade in Fresh Vegetables: The Impact of UK Supermarkets on the African Horticultural Industry' (2001) 37 *Journal of Development Studies* 147, 175).

[61] Hernández et al, above n 39, 282.

[62] Brown and Sander, above n 3, 7–8. See also D Boselie, S Henson and D Weatherspoon, 'Supermarket Procurement Practices in Developing Countries: Redefining the Roles of the Public and Private Sectors' 5 (2003) *American Journal of Agricultural Economics* 1158.

[63] For example, larger farmers have more leverage in negotiating with freight providers and are more able to finance such investments. Dolan and Humphrey, above n 60, 163. But see Hernández et al, above n 39, 285–86 (concluding there was no significant difference according to size of farm, but that supermarket-channel farmers obtain twice amount of credit per farm as traditional-channel farms).

[64] Brown and Sander, above n 3, 10.

[65] Lang, above n 13, 556. See also Insight Investment Management Ltd, above n 34, 27–28. A detailed review of the effects of supermarket globalisation on workers is beyond the scope of this chapter, but for an overview of the effects on agricultural and processing workers in the cashew industry as an example, see RN Harilal et al, above n 41, 4, 15 (emphasising that flexibility demands of supermarkets result in 'increasing informalisation of [employment] . . . [creating] insecure and hazardous working conditions'). See also Raworth, above n 23, 39, 42 (describing how the World Bank and the International Monetary Fund have contributed to precarious employment for workers).

[66] Raworth, above n 23, 3.

[67] See De Schutter, above n 35, paras 10–27.

changes can be difficult to understand and costly to implement, posing additional barriers to smallholder participation in modern food procurement systems.[68]

Both supermarkets and producers can be subject to product requirements and quality standards originating from governments and private groups in developed countries. For example, the 1990 Food Safety Act in the UK requires retailers to demonstrate that they have shown 'due diligence' in the manufacture, transportation, storage and preparation of food. Similarly, producer certification has been required by EurepGap, which was founded in 1997 by the Euro-Retailers Produce Working Group in order to harmonise supply chain standards worldwide for good agricultural practices. EurepGap produced a Protocol aimed at standardising food safety to assure consumers who were alarmed about pesticide use and food hygiene. As a result, participating growers must be independently certified by an approved certification body.[69]

In addition to standards imposed pursuant to government food and import regulations, supermarkets promulgate additional, and often more stringent, private safety, quality and cosmetic standards as a means to govern and coordinate their supply chains,[70] assure compliance with other standards, compete with other retailers while shifting the focus away from price, and substitute for missing or inadequate standards in underdeveloped regions.[71] Supermarkets may also impose 'tracing requirements' on their producers.[72] Tracing requirements impose additional burdens on products that require processing, such as nuts, particularly if raw produce is shipped from one region to another for centralised processing.[73] As retail chains regionalise and globalise their

---

[68] Brown and Sander, above n 3, 8; Raworth, above n 23, 36–37; see also Harilal et al, above n 41, 19–20 (describing effects of such measures in cashew industry).

[69] Secondarily, EurepGap was concerned with workers' rights and environmental issues. Brown and Sander, above n 3, 7, 9.

[70] Reardon et al, above n 16, 418–19 (citing T Reardon, J Berdegué and CP Timmer, 'Supermarkatization of the Emerging Markets of the Pacific Rim: Development and Trade Implications' (2001) 36 *Journal of Food Distribution Research* 3; S Henson and T Reardon, 'Private Agri-food Standards: Implications for Food Policy and the Agri-Food System' (2005) 30 *Food Policy* 241): 'Standards specify and harmonize product and delivery attributes thereby lowering transaction costs and, least in principle, improving the efficiency of food marketing systems in developing countries'. This trend mirrors a similar progression in industrialised nations. L Fulponi, 'Private Voluntary Standards in the Food System: The Perspective of Major Food Retailers in OECD Countries' (2006) 31 *Food Policy* 1 (stating that quality and cosmetic standards are strongly consumer-driven); see also Insight Investment Management Ltd, above n 34, 14: '[W]here once consumers perceived that they must pay more for a higher-quality product, this no longer appears to be the case, with retailers reporting that consumers search out the lowest price without compromising their quality expectations'.

[71] Brown and Sander, above n 3, 8.
[72] Dolan and Humphrey, above n 60, 17.
[73] Harilal et al, above n 41, 33.

operations, they also 'diffuse' those standards, possibly reducing trade-related costs.[74]

The costs of implementing such standards are generally pushed from the retailers onto wholesalers, who in turn shift the burden to producers, who either shift their costs to workers or absorb the additional costs. Standardisation thus provides another concrete example of how supermarkets remain competitive by 'pushing down the line' requirements, obligations and implementation of competitive strategies.

Because the monitoring and compliance costs are usually shifted to producers, producing crops according to strict quality standards is risky for smallholders. Compliance requires investment in up-front inputs, such as irrigation and fertilisation, that are particularly costly for smallholders. Those who have access to capital to purchase such inputs are gambling against the risk of losses in the event of sub-standard crops.[75] Farmers, unlike wholesalers, have limited opportunities to sell graded produce and capture profit difference,[76] and are acutely vulnerable to boom-and-bust years. In particular, cosmetic standards transfer nearly the entire risk of a sub-standard harvest to growers, even if safety and other quality requirements are met.[77]

C. 'Preferred Supplier' Relationships

Another development of global supply chains deserves to be highlighted because it, too, could have an impact on the ability of smallholders to enter these supply chains. As noted above, supermarkets are more closely tying their procurement to a small number of producers to reduce transaction costs, guarantee greater consistency and further integrate their operations. These relationships are often established through contracts. Large grocery chains and their wholesalers are increasingly entering into 'preferred' supplier relationships, establishing de facto contracts with their suppliers.[78]

As supermarkets become more dominant in a particular region, they tend to shift from product procurement through spot markets to preferred supplier lists, which emphasise quality and consistency. 'Preferred'

---

[74] Reardon et al, above n 16, 419.
[75] D Boselie et al, 'Supermarket Procurement Practices in Developing Countries: Redefining the Roles of the Public and Private Sectors' (2003) 5 *American Journal of Agricultural Economics* 1158.
[76] World Bank, above n 4, viii.
[77] Raworth, above n 23, 68–69.
[78] Reardon et al, above n 16, 419 (citing B Hueth et al, 'Incentive Instruments in Fruits and Vegetables Contracts: Input Control, Monitoring, Measurements and Price Risk' (1999) 21 *Review of Agricultural Economies* 374).

farmers and processors tend to be associated or individually large.[79] 'Preferred supplier' contracts are formed when the retailer, either directly or through a wholesaler intermediary, 'lists' a supplier. Although 'listing' is usually informal, it establishes an operational contract.[80] The contracts provide incentives for suppliers to commit to the buyer and, over the course of the relationship, invest in physical and human assets tailored to the retailer's operation.[81] As an extreme example, Wal-Mart nominates only one supplier per produce category in a mutually exclusive deal.[82] In some cases, such contracts provide assistance to producers making capital investments in order to meet retailers' demands.[83]

Research on the effects of these contracts on farmers is difficult to reconcile and generalise. Some researchers emphasise the dangers for farmers arising from unequal bargaining power and potentially opportunistic buyer behaviour that could lock farmers into pervasive indebtedness and food insecurity.[84] Others emphasise the potential benefits for farmers, such as risk sharing, marketing benefits, and cheaper access to technology and other inputs.[85]

Supermarkets often fix the volume of produce they expect in the contract, but may not provide any explicit agreement as to price, instead relying on price parameters. When this occurs, suppliers absorb price

---

[79] Ibid. For examples, see D Boselie, 'Business Case Descriptions: TOPS Supply Chain Project, Thailand' (Agrichain Competence Center, 2002) (describing relationships established by Ahold in Thailand); NM Manalili, 'The Changing Map of the Philippine Retail Food Sector: The Impact on Trade and the Structure of Agriculture and the Policy Response' (2005) 6 *Pacific Food System Outlook* 11 (describing Big R in the Philippines); Hu et al, above n 26 (describing fresh cuts for Lianhua chain in Shanghai); L Dries and T Reardon, 'Central and Eastern Europe: Impact of Food Retail Investments on the Food Chain', Report Series No 6 (FAO Investment Center, 2005).

[80] Reardon et al, above n 16, 420 (citing Hueth et al, above n 78); but see Raworth, above n 23, 38 (describing such contracts as 'verbal and easily broken if a better deal can be found; buying commitments often go no further than one season or just a few months').

[81] Reardon et al, above n 16, 420; Hueth, above n 78.

[82] Raworth, above n 23, 68–69 (stressing bargaining imbalance and enforcement difficulties for frequently verbal contracts).

[83] Reardon et al, above n 16, 420; World Bank, above n 4, vii.

[84] S Singh, 'Contracting Out Solutions, Political Economy of Contract Farming in the Indian Punjab' (2002) 30 *World Development* 1621; Watts, 'Life Under Contract: Contract Farming, Agrarian Restructuring and Flexible Accumulation' in PD Little and MJ Watts (eds), *Living Under Contract: Contract Farming and Agrarian Transformation in Sub-Saharan Africa* (Madison, WI, University of Wisconsin Press, 1994).

[85] J Govereh and T Jayne, Cash Cropping and Food Crop Productivity: Synergies or Trade-Offs? (2003) 28 *Agricultural Economics* 39; N Key and WD McBride, 'Production Contracts and Productivity in the US Hog Sector' (2003) 85 *American Journal of Agricultural Economics* 121; N Key and D Runsten, 'Farming, Smallholders and Rural Development in Latin America: The Organization of Agro-Processing Firms and the Scale of Outgrower Production' (1999) 27 *World Development* 381. For a brief overview of this literature and an examination of farmers' motivations in entering such contracts, see O Masakure and S Henson, 'Why Do Small-Scale Producers Choose to Produce Under Contract? Lessons from Nontraditional Vegetable Exports from Zimbabwe' (2005) 33 *World Development* 1721.

fluctuations, thus bearing the risk of volatile markets.[86] Additional fees and charges may be applied merely to be 'listed' and to enjoy shelf space in the supermarket.[87] Because such arrangements are often established on an informal, verbal basis, contract enforcement can be difficult. As a result, supermarkets may continue to shop for lower prices despite such commitments.

D. Consumers

Consumers, particularly urban and suburban consumers of fresh produce, have benefited from the price reductions achieved by modern supermarket procurement practices.[88] But while large supermarkets can produce tremendous cost savings, they have also been accused of limiting poor consumers' access to healthy, affordable foods by closing stores in lower-income areas and relocating to suburban areas with higher average incomes.[89] The trend toward larger 'hypercentres', which are frequently located beyond city boundaries, where property values are lower, may achieve substantially the same results as traditional redlining behaviour, because lower-income individuals may have reduced access to those stores.

There is debate over whether intense competition among retailers, combined with efficiencies in the 'supercentre' format, has resulted in consumer savings despite market concentration.[90] The 'warehouse' format introduced in the 1970s has been credited with price reductions,[91] but price reductions plateaued in the 1980s.[92] Using models of retail behaviour, researchers have concluded that increased supermarket concentration in the US will result in price increases. One study predicts that a ten-percentage-point increase in concentration would lead to a 0.12% increase in food prices, and that further consolidation could lead

---

[86] Raworth, above n 23, 69–70.
[87] Ibid, 71.
[88] World Bank, above n 4, vii.
[89] Mamen, above n 12, 5 (citing E Eisenhauer, 'In Poor Health: Supermarket Redlining and Urban Nutrition' (2001) 55(2) *Geo Journal* 125). See also D D'Rozario and JD Williams, 'Retail Redlining: Definition, Theory, Typology, and Measurement' (2005) *Journal of Macromarketing* 175, 177–181. See also SJ Goetz and H Swaminathan, 'Wal-Mart and County-Wide Poverty' (2006) 87(2) *Social Science Quarterly* 211.
[90] Stiegert and Sharkey, above n 8, 310.
[91] Ibid (citing BW Marion, K Heimforth and W Bailey, 'Strategic Groups, Competitions, and Retail Food Prices' in RW Cotterill (ed), *Competitive Strategy Analysis in the Food System* (Boulder, CO, Westview Press, 1993) 179).
[92] Ibid (citing BW Marion, 'Competition in Grocery Retailing: The Impact of a New Strategic Group on BLS Price Increases' (1998) 13 *Review of Industrial Organization* 381).

to dramatic price increases.[93] The study further noted that food pricing has become more sensitive in recent years. Although introduction of the supercentre format and related concentration in the mid-1990s did not influence pricing, concentration through mergers and a dramatic decline in the number of new entrants have made pricing more sensitive.[94]

In some cases, the presence of supermarkets has been linked to increased poverty levels. One study determined that the entry of new Wal-Mart stores in US counties directly increased county-wide family poverty levels, despite offering lower prices.[95] As retail formats shift from the presence of multiple stores in an area to fewer and larger stores in more suburban areas, where property costs are lower and more space is available, consumers have to travel further to obtain food, increasing their food-related costs.[96]

Emphasis on non-price marketing among major retailers may reflect that competition among these retailers has moved from price to convenience,[97] product variety and quality.[98] Consumers have failed to actively and rationally use price comparisons due to increasingly large selections, the continuous entry of new products, the introduction of barcoding and the removal of price stickers. Continuous price fluctuation also reduces the importance of price competition among retailers. Retailers rely more heavily on their reputation for lower prices, which is frequently achieved by significantly lowering prices on high-visibility products while increasing prices elsewhere.[99]

Finally, some researchers have suggested that, even if consumers enjoy savings at the outset, they will actually bear those costs later, in the form of farming subsidies, welfare benefits and other costs imposed upon the lowest links of the supply chain.[100]

---

[93] Ibid, 299, 306. Mergers from eight symmetric sized firms to four, over the course of 7 years, would lead to an 88% price increase and a $3.92 billion increase in operating profit to firms.
[94] Ibid, 307.
[95] Goetz and Swaminathan, above n 89, 211–26.
[96] Stiegert and Sharkey, above n 8, 306.
[97] Ibid, 310.
[98] RL Smith, 'The Australian Grocery Industry: A Competition Perspective' (2006) 50 *Australian Journal of Agricultural and Resource Economics* 33, 43.
[99] Ibid.
[100] WS Grimes, 'Buyer Power and Retail Gatekeeper Power: Protecting Competitions and the Atomistic Seller' (2005) 72 *Antitrust Law Journal* 563, 577. This concern may be most pointed in the case of local producers who would directly benefit from the social welfare systems that consumers support through taxes, but global poverty has also been garnering increased attention as a factor in global economic and security threats.

III. ANTITRUST AND COMPETITION POLICY

Current antitrust and competition laws are inadequately tailored to the realities of modern food retailer practices and their anticompetitive effects. Antitrust and competition analyses tend to focus on seller-side violations, giving short shrift to the anticompetitive effects of buyer power. Further, reliance on traditional metrics to define relevant antitrust markets[101] fails to capture accurately the scope of behaviours in which supermarkets engage. Incorporating business theory in addition to economic analysis in the evaluation of retailers' decisions regarding marketing and supplying might result in a more accurate assessment of their potentially anticompetitive motivations and effects.[102] One proposal to alleviate the inadequacies of current antitrust and competition laws is to coordinate international antitrust policy through the World Trade Organization (WTO), the Organisation for Economic Co-operation and Development (OECD), or some other international body. This coordination could overcome extraterritoriality problems, enhance understanding of the health of global competition, and more accurately assess the power of corporate actors, although many experts remain sceptical of this route for a variety of reasons.[103]

Determining the relevant market is a threshold inquiry in competition analysis. The relevant market for measurement of horizontal market power has two dimensions: product and geography. The US Federal Trade Commission (FTC) has determined that supermarket sales are the relevant product market for supermarkets, not some broader category of purchases. Thus, sales from hypermarkets are included, but sales from wholesale or club stores are not. The UK Competition Commission has used a similar product-market definition.[104] High barriers to entry, such as large sunk costs, infrastructure requirements and exclusive agreements with distributors, customers and wholesalers, limit the ability of new entrants to succeed in a given market. This is an important issue in supermarket retail, where sunk transportation, infrastructure and real

---

[101] RW Cotterill, 'Antitrust Analysis of Supermarkets: Global Concerns Playing Out in Local Markets' (2006) 50 *Australian Journal of Agricultural and Resource Economics* 17. This is in fact happening. Investigations have shown that, while inflation in the supermarket sector increased by 3.7%, prices paid to agricultural producers remained stable and low, while supermarket margins grew. While consumer prices continued to rise in 2004 and 2005, agricultural incomes declined to levels below those seen in 1990. Regoverning Markets Programme, 'The EU Retail Sector: When is a Market Not a Market?' (2007), available at www.regoverningmarkets.org/en/filemanager/active?fid=671 (citing 'Quien se queda lo que tu pagas?' (COAG, 2006)).

[102] S Weber Waller, 'What Should Antitrust Learn from the Business Schools? The Use of Business Theory, in Antitrust Litigation' (2003) 47 *New York Law School Law Review* 119.

[103] A Bradford, 'International Antitrust Negotiations and the False Hope of the WTO' (2007) 48 *Harvard International Law Journal* 383.

[104] Cotterill, above n 101, 19.

property costs, along with the difficulty and costs involved in establishing relationships with producers, constitute significant barriers to new entrants.

Determining the market power of a given retailer usually determines the extent of the firm's pricing power.[105] Market power arises when the seller can raise and sustain a price increase without losing so many sales that it has to lower the price again; when demand falls sharply, there is no profit to be made from higher prices.[106] The inverse is true for retailer buyer power.

Retailer buyer power is the ability of leading firms to obtain from suppliers more favourable terms than those available to competitors, or which would otherwise be expected under normal competitive conditions.[107] This power may arise from size differences among buyers (scale-based advantages) and can also arise if there are limited numbers of buyers of a particular scale (oligopsony).

Oligopsony can occur when a retailer has a substantial portion of purchases in the market, there are significant barriers to entry into the buyer's market and an upward sloping supply curve exists.[108] Thus, large retailers in concentrated retail markets likely have both relative and absolute ability to obtain low prices from suppliers.[109] If a retailer represents a significant percentage of the suppliers' sales, abusive exercises of retailers' gatekeeper power can occur even if the retailers'

---

[105] Ibid, 18.

[106] Department of Justice and the Federal Trade Commission, Horizontal Merger Guidelines (1997) §0.1.

[107] One proposed index for measuring market power would examine (i) the market share of the buyer, (ii) the elasticity of supply and (iii) the elasticity of fringe supply. Unless supply is relatively inelastic, significant power cannot be exercised over price. R Blair and J Harrison, *Monopsony: Antitrust Law and Economics* (Princeton, NJ, Princeton University Press, 1993) 52–53. The OECD has also proposed a definition of buyer power: '[A] retailer is defined to have buyer power if, in relation to at least one supplier, it can credibly threaten to impose a long-term opportunity cost (ie harmful or withheld benefit) which, were the threat carried out, would be significantly disproportionate to any resulting long term opportunity cost to itself. By disproportionate, we intend a difference in relative rather than absolute opportunity costs, eg Retailer A has buyer power over Supplier B if a decision to delist B's product could cause A's profits to decline by 0.1 percent and B's to decline by 10%.' OECD Background Paper by the Secretariat, 'Buying Power of Multiproduct Retailers', DAFFE/CLP (99)21 (1998). In addition, the FTC has defined buyer power in the retail context as 'the ability of a firm to influence significantly the terms on which it purchases its supply of inputs, for reasons not related to efficiency considerations but rather to the relative bargaining positions of buyer and supplier'. Federal Trade Commission, Workshop on Slotting Allowances and Other Marketing Practices in the Grocery Industry (2001) 55, 58, available at www.ftc.gov/os/2001/02/slottingallowancesreportfinal.pdf.

[108] PW Dobson et al, 'Buyer Power and Its Impact on Competition in the Food Retail Distribution Sector of the European Union'1 (2001) 1 *Journal of Industry, Competition & Trade* 247, 250.

[109] PW Dobson, 'Exploiting Buyer Power: Lessons from the British Grocery Trade' (2005) 72 *Antitrust Law Journal* 529, 532.

market share is 10% or less.[110] In the case of UK supermarkets, the major retailers typically account for between 10 and 30% of a supplier's total sales, while such purchases represent only a tiny fraction of the retailers' sales,[111] giving the supermarkets tremendous relative bargaining power over suppliers.

Food retail competition analysis usually arises in the context of a proposed merger between retailers. Mergers between already prominent retailers are justified based upon the efficiencies generated by the resulting firm. However, absent some major technological change that is merger specific, projected cost reductions following a merger are usually based on the acquisition of buyer power and the ability to exercise monopsony or oligopsony power to reduce input prices.

Current antitrust law strongly emphasises consumer welfare, even in the analysis of vertical restraints. Vertical relationships exist between upstream (input) suppliers and downstream (retail) firms. Some scholars argue that consumer welfare is the only justifiable antitrust consideration and that, absent lower quantities or quality or higher prices, regulation is unnecessary.[112] However, the assertion that consumers are unharmed by vertical restraints absent price increases or lower-quality goods or services has been criticised.[113] The effects of vertical restraints on consumers may be more accurately characterised as involving a series of trade-offs between short-term and long-term benefits and consumer costs versus overall costs to the public.[114]

Despite continuing debate, buyer power has increasingly been a concern of competition authorities.[115] Buyers may also have greater

---

[110] Grimes, above n 100, 563. Note that there is debate concerning what should be deemed 'abusive'. From a Chicago School point of view, buyer power abuses should only encompass conduct that reduces aggregate well-being or causes a wealth transfer loss. Research shows that buyer power frequently results in a wealth transfer injury without short-term reductions in input (the amount purchased by retailers). Wealth transfer losses may also result from external subsidies to compensate for buyer power in certain contexts, particularly with regard to food. Ibid, 566.

[111] Dobson, above n 109, 537.

[112] R Scheelings and JD Wright, '"*Sui Generis*"?: An Antitrust Analysis of Buyer Power in the United States and European Union' (2006) 39 *Akron Law Review* 207, 211.

[113] M Schwartz, 'Should Antitrust Assess Buyer Market Power Differently than Seller Market Power?', presented at DOJ/FTC Workshop on Merger Enforcement, 17 February 2004.

[114] For example, consumers may bear higher future prices if competition plateaus among heavily consolidated retailers. Further, they risk reduced choice among both retailers and products. Finally, some of the cost reductions achieved through vertical integration of supply chains can be characterised as externalised retail costs reallocated from supermarkets and ultimately borne by consumers in the form of taxes. Dobson et al, above n 108, 249–50.

[115] See UK Competition Commission, 'Supermarkets: A Report on the Supply of Groceries from Multiple Stores in the UK', CM 4842 (London, HMSO, 2000) (finding that while supermarket concentration in UK presented only limited potential for abuse with respect to consumers, there was cause for concern regarding suppliers, and highlighting 27 oligopsonistic practices).

incentives to collude than sellers because the nature of buying discourages defection. The exploitation of buyer power can lead either to price discrimination among buyers or exclusionary practices with respect to the competitors.[116] The pivotal market characteristic appears to be producers' need for access to outlets.

The exercise of buyer power can result in price discounts, but it may also be manifest in contracts requiring additional supplier payments or discounts, such as 'listing charges', 'slotting allowances', contributions to promotional expenses and retroactive discounts on goods already sold. Contracts may also include 'most favoured customer clauses' or clauses substantially shifting burdens of financial risk onto suppliers.[117]

Evidence suggests that small 'atomistic' sellers may be more vulnerable to buying power abuses, particularly in businesses that require significant 'sunk costs', such as agriculture. This is intensified by the perishable nature of the goods.[118] Smallholders are often required to absorb all of the risks and costs associated with buyers' demands and pricing because, unlike powerful agribusiness conglomerates, they have no one onto whom they can pass the costs.[119] Their costs are, in turn, frequently externalised to society.[120]

These behaviours also operate to the detriment of competing retailers—particularly if they are disadvantaged by economies of scale—by providing another form of horizontal competition and creating increased barriers to new entrants. A dominant firm extracting cost concessions from a supplier may effectively force the supplier to charge the retailer's competitors more in order to remain solvent, thus coalescing power into a pattern that has been observed in the New England milk market in the US.[121] These findings suggest that antitrust analysis needs to be refined.[122]

---

[116] PC Carstensen, 'Buyer Power and Merger Analysis—The Need for Different Metrics', prepared for the Workshop on Merger Enforcement held by the Antitrust Division and the Federal Trade Commission, 17 February 2004, available at www.justice.gov/atr/public/workshops/docs/202606.htm.

[117] Dobson, above n 109, 532–33.

[118] Grimes, above n 100, 568.

[119] Ibid.

[120] Ibid, 575.

[121] Cotterill, above n 101, 27. Buyer power can facilitate horizontal competition in another sense as well. In addition to their role as 'customers', supermarkets are 'competitors' in the sense that they often sell store-brand products directly competing with brand-name products. The retailers retain power to undermine supplier products by providing suboptimal shelving, raising retail prices or substituting them for store-brand products. See also 'Commission Green Paper on Vertical Restraints in EC Competition Law', COM(96) 721 (1997). In this sense, supermarkets are also 'suppliers' of retail and advertising space, allowing them to impose slotting fees and promotional support payments and to require discounted products. Grimes, above n 100, 568.

[122] Generally, when farm prices to supermarkets drop and retail prices do not also drop, concerns about non-competitive food marketing channels should surface. Traditional models for evaluating price transmission have found that the relationship between farm

Antitrust authorities in both the US and Europe have had difficulty addressing food retail consolidation, particularly with respect to monopsony power. In the US, the FTC and the Department of Justice (DOJ) have struggled to develop a coherent framework for antitrust analysis in the food retail sector, reflecting a more general failure to keep pace with transformations within the industry and among consumers. Antitrust law in the US generally focuses on seller power abuses and consumer welfare. Although there have been buyer power cases, relatively few merger cases have considered the issue of buyer power.[123]

The Sherman Antitrust Act was enacted in 1890, and requires the federal government of the US to investigate potential monopolies and cartels. The Clayton Antitrust Act was subsequently enacted in 1914 to specify prohibited conduct and provide a more detailed enforcement scheme. In 1936, in response to practices in which chain food retailers were able to purchase goods at lower prices than other retailers, the US Congress enacted the Robinson-Patman Act, which prohibits price discrimination. It provides a private right of action for injured parties. Unfortunately, proving a violation has proved 'complicated, time-consuming and expensive . . . Court decisions have made it an extremely difficult law for plaintiffs to use successfully'.[124] Initially, producers from poor countries for whom large US retailers act as gatekeepers could not rely on this legislation: the early case law limited the Sherman Act's application to the territorial jurisdiction of the US, and anticompetitive behaviour that took place overseas was not proscribed by the Act.[125] This view was later abandoned, allowing application of the Sherman Act to activities taking place abroad.[126]

Establishing horizontal competition violations nonetheless remains difficult. Enforcement agencies consider high concentrations with high barriers to entry necessary, but not sufficient, to establish collusion. Generally, to establish that a particular behaviour is anticompetitive, the agencies must find facilitating practices that are otherwise unjustifiable in a competitive market.[127]

---

and retail prices is unstable. It follows that price transmission is not an accurate indicator for anticompetitive behaviour. However, these models rely upon fundamentally unsound and inflexible assumptions that fail to consider actual non-competitive behaviour. See, eg T Lloyd et al, 'Buyer Power in UK Food Retailing: A "First-Pass" Test' (2009) 7 *Journal of Agricultural & Food Industrial Organization* Article 5, 21 (finding that foundational assumption of perfect competition in UK food industry can be rejected and that market is characterised by buyer power).

[123] Grimes, above n 100, 565.
[124] AA Foer, 'Food Retailing: The Two Faces of Supermarket Mergers' (American Antitrust Institute, 1999), available at www.antitrustinstitute.org/archives/37.ashx.
[125] *American Banana Co v United Fruit Co*, 213 US 347 (1909).
[126] *United States v Aluminum Co. of Am. (Alcoa)*, 148 F.2d 416 (2d Cir. 1945); *Hartford Fire Ins Co v California*, 509 US 764 (1993).
[127] Cotterill, above n 101, 20.

The FTC has had aggressive policies limiting chain acquisitions since the 1960s, usually by blocking mergers and requiring store divestitures. In some challenges, the FTC relied solely on evidence of the retailer's market concentration.[128] The FTC continued to aggressively challenge supermarket mergers through subsequent decades, although its approach varied regarding firms that merged in order to compete with the increasingly dominant Wal-Mart chain.[129] In 2000, the FTC challenged a targeted synergistic merger between Kroger and Winn-Dixie in Texas, arguing that high market shares and concentration created a presumption of illegality, and that new entrants would lack the scale needed to counteract anticompetitive effects. The merger faltered prior to any decision on those issues. Fundamental confusion remains in determining the product market[130] and geographic market for a given store, as well as the weight the FTC is willing to give to Wal-Mart's competitive strength.[131]

The Merger Guidelines, created jointly by the FTC and DOJ, provide a framework for determining whether an agency should challenge a particular merger.[132] The Merger Guidelines explicitly consider the effect of mergers on buyer power[133] and provide a flexible authority to evaluate the effects of buyer power within existing antitrust law related to mergers.[134] In practice, however, it is difficult to successfully apply the guidelines with respect to buyer power cases. Monopsony power has been evaluated in both upstream and downstream mergers under a consumer welfare standard, and courts have rejected arguments that

---

[128] DL Feinstein and MB Bernstein, 'All Over the Map: Grocery Store Enforcement From Von's to Whole Foods' (2007) 22 *Antitrust* 52.

[129] Ibid, 53.

[130] This is particularly difficult as supermarkets offer non-food services—including, but not limited to, clothing, pharmacies, banking services and photo studios—and stores differentiate themselves from competition based on format.

[131] Feinstein and Bernstein, above n 128, 54.

[132] These factors require officials to: (i) define the relevant market and calculate initial and post-merger concentration; (ii) analyse the competitive effects; (iii) assess entry considerations; (iv) determine whether any merger-specific efficiencies exist; and (v) determine whether either firm would likely fail without the merger. Horizontal Merger Guidelines, above n 106; see also FTC and US DOJ, Antitrust Guidelines for Collaborations Among Competitors (2000). Note that revised Merger Guidelines were released for public comment in 2010. In 1998, an FTC challenge based on a market concentration argument failed in a case in which one retailer's post-acquisition share of the market would be between 67 and 75%. The court cited the Department of Justice Merger Guidelines and FTC Statements Concerning Horizontal Mergers, and found that a showing of the retailer's likelihood to be able to exercise market power was required. Feinstein and Bernstein, above n 128, 57.

[133] Horizontal Merger Guidelines, above n 106, §0.1: 'Market power also encompasses the ability of a single buyer (a 'monopsonist'), a coordinating group of buyers, or a single buyer, not a monopsonist, to depress the price paid for a product to a level that is below the competitive price and thereby depress output. The exercise of market power by buyers ('monopsony power') has adverse effects comparable to those associated with the exercise of market power by sellers. In order to assess potential monopsony concerns, the Agency will apply an analytical framework analogous to the framework of these Guidelines.'

[134] Scheelings and Wright, above n 112, 231.

conduct that harms competitors while reducing consumer costs violates antitrust law.[135] Further, allegations of exclusionary buyer conduct must generally be supported by evidence that the defendant's conduct injured consumers.[136]

Competition law in the EU embodies similar limitations. EU competition law, as on the national level, is geographically limited. Two treaty articles prohibit anticompetitive behaviour. Article 101(1) of the Treaty on the Functioning of the EU (TFEU) (ex-Article 81(1) EC) prohibits horizontal and vertical agreements commonly known as cartels.[137] Article 102 TFUE (ex-Article 82 EC) prohibits the abuse of a dominant position. Evidence of dominance is no longer required to challenge a merger.[138]

Consideration of 'buyer power' as a general concept is not precluded under either Article 101 or 102, and European Commission institutions have addressed 'buyer power' in merger cases both as 'countervailing power' when assessing upstream mergers among suppliers and as an a priori concern when considering downstream mergers among buyers. Buyer cooperatives and upstream collusive activity are examined under Article 101.

'Abuse of dominance', under Article 102, requires: (i) determination of the relevant market definition; (ii) the firm's dominance; and (iii) abuse by the firm of its dominant position. 'Dominance' refers to the position of a firm that enjoys a level of market power sufficiently serious to warrant oversight. The European Court of Justice has defined 'dominance' as the ability 'to behave to an appreciable extent independently of its competitors and customers and ultimately of consumers'.[139] If a supplier's competitive behaviour is meaningfully constrained by consumers, then it cannot be dominant. Because *relative* dominance is not considered, it is difficult for suppliers to establish a retailer's market dominance.[140] For a supplier to successfully argue buyer dominance, it must prove that it has no other possible trading partner.[141]

Merger assessment generally involves three stages. First, the relevant market must be defined. In buyer power cases, this is the procurement

---

[135] *Kartell v Blue Shield of Mass, Inc*, 749 F.2d 922 (1st Cir 1984). See also SC Salop, 'Anticompetitive Overbuying by Power Buyers' (2005) 72 *Antitrust Law Journal* 505.

[136] Scheelings and Wright, above n 112, 225.

[137] Undertakings do not restrict trade under this Article if the aggregate market share does not exceed 15% of any of the relevant markets affected. Further, the agreement must 'influence trade among the member states', and exemptions for otherwise prohibited arrangements are provided if they do more good than harm. See UK Food Group, 'EU Competition Rules and Future Developments from the Perspective of Farmers and Small Suppliers', briefing (2005) 7.

[138] Ibid, 4.

[139] Case 27/76, *United Brands Co and United Brands Continental BV v Commission* [1978] ECR 207, (1978) 1 CMLR 429.

[140] UK Food Group, above n 137, 8.

[141] Ibid.

market. Secondly, the concentration of the properly defined procurement market is measured. Thirdly, the market behaviour of suppliers and customers within the relevant market is evaluated.

Although the European Commission has considered a number of cases involving buyer power with respect to supply-side mergers, it has considerably less experience with cases involving anticipatory concern about future buyer power of buyer-side mergers. The primary cases in this area are *Kesko/Tuko* and *Rewe/Meinl*. Those cases have informed subsequent merger cases, such as *Carrefour/Promodes*. The European Commission has adopted an 'unwarranted dependence upon the merging retailer' doctrine and has set a 'threat point', defined as the maximum revenue share that a supplier can lose without seriously risking bankruptcy.[142]

In the EU, harmonised regulation covering the entire European market and explicitly addressing the anticompetitive effects of buyer power is necessary.[143] Activists urge Members of Parliament to sign Written Declaration 88/2007, recognising supermarkets' gatekeeping function, their impact on farmers and their buying power, and calling for modernisation of regulations responding to these issues in food retail.[144]

Some European countries have tougher laws[145] and have even specifically enacted regimes focused on buyer power using a theory of 'dependence' to fill perceived gaps in EU law.[146] Unfortunately, the use of vaguely defined terms has stymied effective enforcement of these provisions.

IV. INCREASING THE COMPETITIVENESS AND SECURITY OF SMALLHOLDERS

Given the business and regulatory environment described above, improving smallholder access to global supply chains will require the coordinated efforts of public and private bodies. Smallholders need access to improved communication, technology, market knowledge, credit and inputs such as seeds and fertilisers. Improved domestic

---

[142] See L Venturini, 'The Food System in Transition: An EU Perspective', Working Paper WP03-1, prepared for the 8th Joint Conference on Food, Agricultue & the Environment (2003).

[143] Regoverning Markets Programme, above n 101.

[144] Ibid.

[145] See, eg ¶ 20(3) GWP (Germany), prohibiting firms from using their market position to pressure other undertakings to grant preferential terms unless objective justifications are offered; book IV of the Commercial Code of France, prohibiting sales below costs and provisions on unfair practice; and Ireland's Restrictive Practices (Groceries) Order 1987. Regoverning Markets Programme, above n 101.

[146] See, eg in France, the Galland Law (1996), which was retained in 2005. Scheelings and Wright, above n 112.

infrastructure in the form of better roads and market connectivity can reduce smallholders' costs and risks. Regional coordination of agricultural policies and marketing initiatives may also give smallholders greater leverage. Coordination and cooperation among growers can allow them to jointly negotiate, invest in capital improvements, meet quality and safety standards, and mitigate risks through insurance-like programmes. Homogenisation and clarification of these standards may also improve smallholders' compliance. Opportunities to use intercropped plots can also greatly mitigate risks for farmers. This section explores government policies that can increase smallholder security, and examines the role of the private sector and non-governmental organisations in supporting smallholders.

A. Government Policies to Ensure Smallholder Security

To increase smallholders' security, their governments, along with the supermarkets' governments, will need to engage in coordinated efforts to increase their access to the modern food retail system. Consistent with their obligations towards the right to food, governments in developing countries should facilitate access by creating an appropriate policy environment for trade and by providing infrastructure to gather and disseminate necessary inputs, technology and market information. In addition to improving smallholder access to the global retail system, domestic governments can protect and improve the operation of traditional food retail to protect alternative supply channels and provide 'buffers' for farmers attempting to enter supermarket supply chains.

There is no clear precedent for how governments should shape policies to help smallholder farmers, and it is clear that, to be effective, such policies should be tailored to the domestic context and to the types of crops being cultivated. Governments should do so carefully because, once in place, such policies may be difficult to adapt to changing circumstances or to remove.

Price stabilisation and marketing boards have exploited as well as helped smallholders, but they remain potentially powerful tools to pool resources and help increase the bargaining power of smaller players. Given market liberalisation in many developing countries, it may be difficult to reconstitute such organisations in their previous form, but similar collective bodies could be formed to focus specifically on the issues plaguing smallholders and to provide educational resources.

Domestic policy should also support cooperative and outgrower schemes to help farmers overcome economies of scale.[147] At the

---

[147] Brown and Sander, above n 3, 12.

same time, effective competition policy, frequently underdeveloped in emerging economies, can make a dramatic impact on the livelihoods of small and marginal farmers. Government subsidies, which typically tend to benefit larger farmers over smallholders, could be shaped with smallholders in mind.

More specifically targeted policies have been also effective. For example, Argentina passed a law requiring payments to all fresh produce growers within 30 days. Other policies promoting good business practices, such as commercial codes of practice, could be envisioned to respond to particular problems within a given country.

At the same time, retailers' 'home countries', where many of the largest supermarkets are based, should create policies limiting the ability of supermarkets to gain competitive advantages through the exercise of market power that allows them to engage in opportunistic behaviours. These governments need to recognise the globally interconnected nature of food supply and retailing to shape effective and coherent national policy with respect to those corporate behemoths.[148]

Additionally, international and intergovernmental organisations such as the WTO, the UN and the OECD could serve coordination functions among different countries and promulgate transnational policies that can reduce transaction costs for smallholders and facilitate their participation in global supply chains. Trade associations and dispute resolution bodies, such as the Association of Food Industries in the US, can help shape appropriate norms and fill an information-forcing role by gathering and publicising supermarket practices.

B. The Role of the Private Sector and Other Organisations in Supporting Smallholders

The evolution of the private retail sector and of agrifood systems more generally will be decisive for the future ability of smallholders to benefit from the development of global chains. Investors and commodity buyers can provide basic marketing and production functions, assist with transportation needs and facilitate access to the global markets.[149]

The institutional dimensions of supply chains are also of crucial importance. New organisations aimed at bridging information gaps between small producers and supermarket retailers may be necessary. If successful, such organisations could reduce transition and compliance costs borne by smallholders. If combined with outside expertise, these organisations can provide business information, including specifics

---

[148] Lang, above n 13, 562.
[149] Page and Slater, above n 56, 647.

about retailers, quality and safety standards, weather, technology such as cross-border payment systems, and agricultural innovation; they can also help small producers pool resources and share costs associated with compliance. Some groups have been successful in increasing financial services and assisting members to obtain credit.[150]

Such organisations can coordinate monitoring and compliance with quality and safety standards at a manageable cost to farmers. At the same time, they can help instil confidence in supermarkets that standards can and are being met. They can also reduce contracting costs to enable farmers to negotiate and enter into contracts.[151]

Some research has suggested that farmer-established cooperatives are more successful than NGO-initiated organisations. To be successful, however, 'soft' assets such as agricultural expertise and business experience are necessary, and uneducated farmers are unlikely to be equipped to manage such groups without outside support.[152] Further, the farmers involved in cooperatives must trust each other. The collapse of some cooperative arrangements has been directly linked to mistrust of peers and an inability to police agreements made within the group. For example, when an organisation contracts with a retailer and spot prices for produce exceed contract prices, it may be difficult to identify and address members who sell at higher spot rates. Fear of alienating other community members who fail to comply with organisation requirements can also create barriers to effective coordination. Additionally, some organisations have successfully diversified their members' production;[153] the costs of providing the technical and business expertise to do this, however, are often unsustainably high for the poorest farmers.[154]

Outgrower schemes are a related alternative. These schemes generally are managed by centralised agribusinesses. Typically, the growers provide land and labour in return for technical assistance, credit and infrastructure support. Although these relationships create additional potential for abuse by allowing agribusinesses to continue to allocate risks to growers, such arrangements have been effective in providing market knowledge and mitigating costs burdens for some African farmers.[155]

---

[150] Ibid, 648.
[151] C Narro et al, 'The Role of Public–Private Partnerships and Collective Action in Ensuring Smallholder Participation in High Value Fruit and Vegetable Supply Chains', Working Paper No 70 (CAPRi, 2007).
[152] J Hellin et al, 'Farmer Organization, Collective Action and Market Access in Meso-America', Working Paper No 67 (CAPRi, 2007).
[153] Ibid.
[154] Ibid (citing T Reardon and L Flores, 'Customized Competitiveness Strategies for Horticultural Exporters: Central American Focus with Lessons From and For Other Regions' (2006) 31 *Food Policy* 483).
[155] Brown and Sander, above n 3, 14 (noting that Homegrown, a Kenyan outgrower scheme, and Hortico, in Zimbabwe, have both played roles in shaping smallholder activity in Africa).

Supermarkets have also shown a willingness to participate in projects helping farmers upgrade their operations through public–private partnerships. In addition to investing in farmers, supermarkets can simplify their codes and standards, and facilitate fair partnerships with contract growers. For example, the French retailer Carrefour has used investments in farmers as a means to improve its competitive position in relation to other supermarkets, working with farmers and wholesalers to improve supply chains, upgrade production and enhance grower expertise.[156]

Contracts with supermarkets may provide farmers with regular orders, market information, technological advice and, in some cases, access to superior inputs, such as fertilisers and credit. Such schemes are particularly effective in reducing transaction costs with regard to perishable goods, such as produce. On the other hand, concerns remain regarding farmers' vastly unequal bargaining power, particularly with respect to small producers. Overall, research suggests that many contract farmers tend to enjoy higher incomes and greater economic security.

Supermarkets typically prefer contracting with larger producers, perhaps due to the high transaction costs of establishing contracts with large numbers of small output farmers. A possible remedy is greater coordination and collective action among small producers in contracting with supermarkets.[157] Studies have shown that selection of contract farmers is also frequently based upon location and labour availability rather than on farm size per se or the education levels of producers. The success of contract farming varies based on the commodity at issue.[158] Domestic policy can increase the security of contract farming by developing institutions capable of effectively enforcing contracts.

Because access to credit remains a fundamental barrier for many small producers, specially tailored lending programmes for smallholders may significantly improve the economic welfare of those producers. There is a great deal of debate over the efficacy of such programmes, but some studies have shown that the availability of microfinance credit can assist farmers transitioning from traditional crops to high-yield crops.[159] One example is Wal-Mart's 'Tierra Fértil' microfinance programme in Central America, which it started in 2006, and other similar initiatives in India.[160]

Finally, fair trade schemes should be further explored. Fair trade arrangements can help farmers access inputs, coordinate with other farmers and with buyers, and generate income. These initiatives, often tied to cooperatives or other grassroots organisations in the producing

---

[156] Reardon et al, above n 16, 424.
[157] Narro et al, above n 151.
[158] S Miyata et al, 'Impact of Contract Farming on Income, Linking Smallholders, Packers, and Supermarkets in China', Discussion Paper 00742 (IFPRI, 2007).
[159] S Rashid et al, 'Micro-lending for Smallholders in Bangladesh: Does it Affect Farm Households' Land Allocation Decision?', Discussion Paper No 45 (MSSD, 2002).
[160] Reardon et al, above n 16, 424.

country, can also empower farmers.[161] The most prominent examples of successful fair trade initiatives have involved coffee and cocoa growers. Any successful plan would have to be tailored to the particular crop, the domestic context and the capacities of the farmers involved.

V. CONCLUSION

As food security becomes a greater concern of national and international policymakers, the fundamental role of retailers in shaping the current retail and supply chain landscapes should not be overlooked. Rather than viewing the consolidation and growing market power of supermarkets as inevitable, domestic policies and trade regulations can play a significant role in shaping these developments.

Given the commitments to the right to food made in numerous legal instruments, the impact of retailers on rural poverty should be explicitly recognised, and actions should be taken to alleviate the burdens on farmers transitioning to modern procurement channels. This is not only an obligation imposed by international law, but also a forward-looking goal. The success of smallholders in developing countries will be crucial to ensuring global food security as the costs of foods soar. Achieving these goals will require coordinated efforts among national and international bodies, as well as private entities and organisations.

---

[161] A Redfern and P Snedker, 'Creating Market Opportunities for Small Enterprises: Experiences of the Fair Trade Movement', Working Paper No 30 (SEED, 2002).

4

Biofuels and the Right to Food: An uneasy partnership

ANN SOFIE CLOOTS[1]

BIOFUELS HAVE BEEN hailed as a key solution to the global climate change problem. As greenhouse gas (GHG) emissions from transport have been deemed to be a major contributor to climate change, an alternative to fossil fuels for transport has been sought for years. The environmental gains from biofuels are not as obvious as previously proclaimed, however, especially for current first-generation biofuels that use mainly food crops such as corn and sugar as feedstock. More importantly, although national governments worldwide have mainly supported their domestic biofuel policies in environmental terms, traditionally these biofuel policies have been introduced for completely different reasons. Part I of this chapter examines the reasons behind the biofuels boom and the debate it has provoked. Part II then seeks to contribute to this debate by examining the potential impacts of an expanded production of crops for fuel from the angle of the right to food. Such impacts may relate to food prices, shifts in land use, trade, increased use of water and other environmental impacts, but also to employment and local energy supply. Part III then relates these impacts to the obligations of states to respect, protect and fulfil the right to food, as well as to the responsibilities of companies regarding the right to food.[2] Part IV offers a brief conclusion.

---

[1] I would like to thank Lior Ziv, Dries Cools, Michael Merrigan and Carlos Barnard for their valuable comments and insights, both on this chapter and on human rights law and critical legal thinking in general.

[2] For a description and analysis of the right to food, please refer to the introduction of this book, which was written by the UN Special Rapporteur on the Right to Food, Olivier De Schutter, and Kaitlin Cordes. This chapter aims to analyse the impact of biofuels on the right to food as it is defined by the Special Rapporteur. The question as to the efficiency and desirability of framing the discussion (merely) in terms of human rights, though interesting, is outside the scope of this chapter.

I. THE BIOFUEL BOOM

A. The Drivers

The first main objective of domestic biofuel policies is energy independence. For example, Brazil, which has the longest experience with biofuels, imposed a 5% ethanol blend as early as 1938.[3] In light of the oil crisis of the 1970s, the country tried to ensure its energy independence by supporting a domestic ethanol policy, Proálcool, in 1975.[4] Energy security remains one of the main motives behind its domestic biofuel policies.[5] A second main objective of national biofuel policies is to support domestic farmers.[6] When agricultural commodity prices are low, a blending mandate for fuel can absorb part of the agricultural surplus, driving up prices for those products. This distorting practice has been a second major driver of biofuel policies.

In short, there are other motives behind biofuel policies than environmental concerns. This chapter explores whether current biofuel policies are an appropriate answer to those different concerns, and how those concerns can be reconciled with the right to food.

B. The Debate

Although current support for biofuels has, to a large extent, been framed in environmental terms, the effects on GHG emissions from the use of biofuels instead of traditional fossil fuels are not uniformly positive. Depending on the feedstock and the transportation and processing methods used, the net gains in environmental terms could turn out to be very limited or even negative.[7] This is especially the case with

---

[3] M Kojima, D Mitchell and W Ward, 'Considering Trade Policies for Liquid Biofuels', Energy Sector Management Assistance Program (ESMAP) (2007) 52. ESMAP was established in 1983 under the joint sponsorship of the World Bank and the UN Development Programme (UNDP); for more information, see www.esmap.org.

[4] Ibid. The ethanol story of Brazil has known ups and downs. The Proálcool initiative was supported by price guarantees, public loans, state-guaranteed private loans and price subsidies. In 1997–99, both gasoline and ethanol prices were liberalised, while flex-fuel vehicles allowed for a flexible switch between ethanol and petroleum, depending on oil prices. In 2006, high sugar prices made ethanol less attractive and forced the government to suspend the 20% ethanol import tariff and to lower the blending mandate from 25 to 20%, though the ethanol market has regained its competitiveness by enhancing production efficiency.

[5] J Ziegler, UN Special Rapporteur on the Right to Food, 'Interim Report of the Special Rapporteur on the Right to Food', UN document A/62/289 (August 2007) 24. The US passed a bill in 2007 that was originally called the 'Clean Energy Act', but was finally adopted as the 'Energy Independence and Security Act'.

[6] The Worldwatch Institute, *Biofuels for Transport: Global Potential and Implications for Sustainable Energy and Agriculture* (London, Earthscan, 2007) 9.

[7] See, eg E Gallagher, Chair of the UK Renewable Fuels Agency, 'The Gallagher Review

the current first-generation biofuels, which use mainly food crops such as corn or sugar as feedstock.[8] The energy used to cultivate and then process those crops into ethanol or biodiesel may be too high to make a meaningful contribution to GHG reduction.[9]

In addition, serious concerns have arisen regarding other impacts of the increasing production of biofuels.[10] Most relevant for our purposes is the 'food versus fuel' concern. As more food crops are used to produce biofuels, the supply of food may shrink, causing higher food prices. In addition, many other potentially negative effects have been noted. Some of those effects are directly linked to rising biofuel production, while others are linked thereto more indirectly. Those impacts are examined in part II of this chapter. First, however, it is necessary to clearly distinguish between the different types of biofuels, and to provide an overview of the current domestic policies that support the expanded production or consumption of biofuels.

The term 'bioenergy' comprises three sorts of energy sources: solid biomass, biogas and biofuel. Biofuel is the most common type and is the focus of this chapter. The generic term 'biofuels' comprises two subcategories: ethanol and biodiesel. Ethanol is currently the predominant form of biofuel; biodiesel only accounts for a small, albeit growing, share of total biofuel production. First-generation biofuels comprise ethanol and biodiesel produced mainly from food crops using existing technology. Ethanol is currently produced predominantly from starchy food crops, mostly corn and sugarcane, but it can also be produced from a variety of other feedstock, such as cassava, wheat, sweet sorghum and sugar beet. The main input for biodiesel consists of oily crops such as palm, rapeseed, jatropha and soybean oil.

As current first-generation biofuels are mostly made from food crops, they have the potential to endanger food security. Research currently is being undertaken into second-generation biofuels. Those advanced technologies would allow for the production of biofuels from a much wider variety of feedstock, such as agricultural, forest and industrial waste, rather than from food crops. Although not yet economically viable, much

---

of the Indirect Effects of Biofuels Production', July 2008, which concludes that the balance of evidence shows a significant risk that current policies will lead to net GHG emissions and a loss of biodiversity.

[8] Joint Research Center of the European Commission (JRC), 'Biofuels in the European Context: Facts and Uncertainties' (2008) 3.1.4.

[9] A comprehensive life-cycle calculation should include, among other things, GHG emissions from water and fertiliser use, (in)direct land-use change, and the energy used for transportation of feedstock and in the conversion process. Current lifecycle analysis fails to take account of indirect land change. See Gallagher, above n 7, 11.

[10] For an overview of the potential and risk of biofuels, see the Food and Agriculture Organization (FAO), 'The State of Food and Agriculture 2008—Biofuels: Prospects, Risks and Opportunities' (2008).

hope is vested in this second generation of biofuels, which holds the potential to avoid many of the detrimental effects of current first-generation biofuels. Nevertheless, second-generation biofuels may have their own disadvantages, such as more energy-intensive production processes, a higher cost, greater net land-use changes,[11] and the potential advantage of large agribusinesses over small-scale farms due to the potentially high cost of conversion technology and installations.[12] All of those potential advantages and disadvantages will need to be carefully balanced. In addition, a third generation of biofuels is also being developed, which would use renewable resources that do not compete for land with food and feed, such as algae. Those advanced technologies, however, are at least a decade away from commercial viability.

C. Current Domestic Biofuel Policies

The list of countries establishing pro-biofuel policies is increasing rapidly, and includes countries as diverse as Argentina, Australia, Canada, China, Colombia, Ecuador, India, Indonesia, Malawi, Malaysia, Mozambique, Mexico, the Philippines, South Africa, Thailand, the US and Zambia.[13] The EU has also elaborated a biofuel policy, which is discussed below. These policies will be almost exclusively fulfilled by industrial biofuels, rather than small-scale production.[14]

Presently, the biofuel market is dominated by Brazil and the US, and,

---

[11] First-generation biofuels generate co-products, which may be used in a variety of ways (as animal fodder, natural fertiliser or for local energy supply). If these co-products are used for fuel production, this means other crops generating such co-products may need to be cultivated on other land to meet the demand for these other uses. This is a potential risk, which depends on many factors, including the efficiency of advanced technologies and the demand for residues for other purposes. There is a large amount of uncertainty on this question, which requires more research. See Gallagher, above n 7, 13, 53.

[12] FAO, 'Jatropha: A Smallholder Bioenergy Crop—The Potential for Pro-Poor Development' (2010) 8 *Integrated Crop Management* 6 (hereinafter FAO Jatropha Report); D Bradley and D Cuypers, '2nd Generation Biofuels and Trade—An Exploratory Study', study for the International Energy Agency (IEA) Task 40 on Sustainable International Biofuel trade (14 December 2009) 25, 42; World Bank, 'World Development Report 2010—Development and Climate Change', 147. Conversion technology for second-generation biofuels is not only expensive, it also requires skilled labour. With the exception of certain countries such as Mexico, Brazil, China, India and South Africa, many developing countries do not have sufficient skilled labour for such conversion. This means that these countries would be limited to the cultivation of biofuel crops, missing out on the added value from the conversion process. The cultivation of biofuel crops also requires a decent infrastructure to transport the feedstock. See IEA, 'Sustainable Production of Second-Generation Biofuels. Potential and Perspectives in Major Economies and Developing Countries' (February 2010) 3.

[13] UN-Energy, 'Sustainable Energy: A Framework for Decision Makers' (15 April 2007) 3; World Bank, 'World Development Report 2008: Agriculture for Development' (2007) 70.

[14] ActionAid, 'Meals per Gallon—The Impact of Industrial Biofuels on People and Global Hunger' (January 2010) 2.

to a lesser extent, the EU for the smaller market of biodiesel.[15] The US[16] and Brazil focus on ethanol, made predominantly from corn in the US and from sugarcane in Brazil (the latter being much more efficient in terms of GHG savings).[17] The EU, on the other hand, focuses on biodiesel instead of ethanol, for which it is currently the market leader. This biodiesel is produced from oily crops grown within the EU (for example, rapeseed grown in Germany[18]) and from imported material such as palm oil from Malaysia.

Several other countries, including Malaysia, Indonesia, Colombia, India and China, are establishing or expanding biofuel production schemes. For the newcomers, technology transfer[19] and the sharing of experiences, as well as market access to the currently highly protectionist western markets, will be crucial for the success of their biofuels policies. As far as current production methods are concerned, technology transfers are taking place in all directions: from north to south, from south to south (eg Brazilian technology transfer to Kenya and Paraguay) and from south to north.[20] The International Energy Agency's Task 40 on Sustainable International Biofuel Trade deals specifically with biofuel trade and could enhance further technology transfer.[21] Moreover, the

---

[15] Around 90% of the global fuel ethanol production is located in the US and Brazil; 95% of biodiesel is produced in the EU. FAO Jatropha Report, above n 12, 6–7. Brazil is the largest exporter of ethanol, while the US and the EU are the largest importers. For biodiesel, the US and Argentina are the largest exporters; the EU is both the largest producer and consumer. See M Junginger et al, 'Opportunities and Barriers for International Bioenergy Trade', IEA Task 40: Sustainable International Bioenergy Trade (May 2010) 7–9.

[16] For an overview of the ethanol industry in the US, see eg C Ford Runge and B Senauer, 'How Biofuels Could Starve the Poor', *Foreign Affairs*, May–June 2007.

[17] Biofuels produced from corn in the US cause more GHG emissions than gasoline. See World Bank, above n 12, 147. The GHG emissions caused by indirect land-use change would negate any GHG savings for corn ethanol (as compared to petrol) for 167 years. Gallagher, above n 7, 19 (referring to research by Searchinger). GHG savings from ethanol produced from sugar cane in Brazil are potentially very high, on the condition that no land-use change occurs.

[18] Germany has the largest share of biofuels within the EU, amounting to 6% of transport fuels in the country in 2008. See European Commission, 'Commission Sets Up System for Certifying Sustainable Biofuels', MEMO/10/247 (10 June 2010) (hereinafter Commission Memo).

[19] Technology transfer will be even more important for second-generation biofuels, which require complex and expensive conversion technology.

[20] According to a report of the Clean Development Mechanism (CDM), over 70% of technology transfer originates from Japan, the US, Germany, France and Great Britain. Brazil, China, India, South Korea and Taiwan are the main providers of technology transfers for countries that did not undertake specific emission reduction targets (so-called 'non-Annex I countries', referring to the list of countries in Annex I of the UN Framework Convention on Climate Change (UNFCCC), New York, 9 May 1992). Currently, technology transfer is higher for agriculture than for biomass energy. See CDM 2008 Report, 'Analysis of Technology Transfer in CDM Projects' (December 2008) 18, 20.

[21] See generally Task 40, Sustainable International Bio-Energy Trade, available at www.bioenergytrade.org. The core objective of Task 40 is 'to support the development of a sustainable, international, bioenergy market, recognising the diversity in resources, biomass applications'.

UN Framework Convention on Climate Change already imposes the requirement that developed states facilitate transfer of environmentally sustainable technologies and know-how.[22] The Kyoto Protocol and its Clean Development Mechanism further encourage the transfer of green technology.[23] Technology transfer should also include training locals on advanced technological processes. If it does not, locals could only cultivate crops without being able to participate in the value-added processing activity.

Several countries have imposed blending mandates so far. For example, as stated above, Brazil imposed blending mandates as early as 1938.[24] At present, it mandates a blending of 20–25% of ethanol in gasoline, while imposing a 2% mandate for biodiesel, to be increased to 5% by 2013. Colombia mandates a 10% ethanol blend in cities with more than 500,000 inhabitants, while Argentina is imposing a mandate of 5% to be blended from both gasoline and diesel. India's national policy aims at 20% biofuels by 2017.[25] China expects to meet 15% of its transportation fuel needs through biofuels.[26] Japan is one of the most ambitious countries, with plans for biofuels to comprise 20% of gasoline by 2030. In addition, the EU's Renewable Energy Directive sets an overall target of 20% renewable energy for the total EU energy consumption by 2020. A 10% target is set for the transport sector.

The current US plan is to increase the use of biofuels for transportation to 36 billion gallons (136 billion litres) per year by 2022.[27] Approximately 200 kg of corn is needed to provide enough biofuel to fill an average SUV car tank once; it is also sufficient to feed one human being for a full year. Currently more than 20% of US corn production is used for only 2.5% of the country's fuel. The amount of grain used in the US to produce ethanol would be sufficient to feed around 330 million people for 1 year—or one-third of the global number of hungry people.[28] Moreover, even if all corn and soybean produced in the US in 2005 were

---

[22] See UNFCCC, Arts 4.1(c), 4.3, 4.5 and 11.1. An Expert Group on Technology Transfer has been established.

[23] See Arts 10(c) and 11.2(b) of the Kyoto Protocol to the UN Framework Convention on Climate Change, Kyoto, 11 December 1997. Facilitating technology transfer is not explicitly included in the mandate of the CDM (see 'Modalities and Procedures for a Clean Development Mechanism', annex to UN document FCCC/KP/CMP/2005/8/Add.1, 30 March 2006). It may, however, contribute to such technology transfer through the financing of emission reduction projects. See CDM 2008 Report, above n 20.

[24] Kojima, above n 3.

[25] ActionAid, above n 14.

[26] M Kraus, 'Fuelling New Problems—The Impact of China's Biodiesel Policies' (Brussels Institute of Contemporary China Studies) 3. See also China Climate Change Info-Net, available at www.ccchina.gov.cn/en.

[27] USDA, 'Biofuels Strategic Production Report—A USDA Regional Roadmap to Meeting the Biofuels Goals of the Renewable Fuels Standard by 2022' (23 June 2010) 1.

[28] Earth Policy Institute, 'Data Highlights: US Feeds One Quarter of its Grain to Cars while Hunger is on the Rise' (21 January 2010).

used for the production of biofuels, this would only replace 12% of the country's gasoline demand and 6% of its diesel demand.[29] In contrast, in Brazil, the country with the most efficient biofuel production, sugarcane ethanol provides 40% of the country's fuel for cars, accounting for about 54% of sugarcane production.

D. Land Availability

A sharp increase in biofuel production will be required if all of those blending mandates and national biofuel policies are to be put in place. Those ambitious targets will not be achieved by production in developed countries, which are currently the main consumers. Estimates suggest that the US would have to convert all the corn and soy it currently produces into biofuels in order to achieve its target, while the EU target would require 70% of its agricultural land.[30] The idea that energy independence could be achieved by the promotion of biofuels is therefore largely unrealistic.[31] The burden of ambitious biofuel targets will very likely be placed upon developing countries. Concerns regarding oil dependency and agribusiness interests, however, should not result in actions that harm populations in other countries.[32] The right to food imposes upon every country the duty to respect this right vis-à-vis the populations in other countries. This means that governments should carefully assess the impact of their biofuel targets on the countries where such fuel would be predominantly produced, in order to ensure that their national biofuel policies do not have negative impacts on the enjoyment of the right to food of the populations in those countries.

Presently, the global amount of cropland is around 1,500 million hectares. The World Bank estimates that it is unlikely that more land that is suitable for agricultural production will be obtained.[33] By 2020, there is estimated to be an additional land demand of around 200–500 million hectares;[34] this number includes anticipated yield improve-

---

[29] M Muller et al, 'Food Versus Fuel in the United States: Can Both Win in the Era of Ethanol?' (Institute for Agriculture and Trade Policy, 2007) 2.

[30] J Ziegler, 'Interim Report of the Special Rapporteur on the Right to Food, delivered to the General Assembly', UN document A/62/289 (22 August 2007); M Kojima and T Johnson, 'Potential for Biofuels for Transport in Developing Countries' (ESMAP, October 2005) xiii.

[31] The huge volume of biofuels required to substitute for fossil fuels is beyond the capacity of agriculture with present day technology. See FAO Jatropha Report, above n 12, 5.

[32] See available at www.srfood.org.

[33] See World Bank, above n 12, 148.

[34] According to a 2007 study by the UN Environment Programme, the additional land required for food, feed and pasture would amount to 200 to 700 million hectares by 2020. See ActionAid, above n 14, 33.

ments.[35] Currently, land use for biofuels is estimated at around 13.8 million hectares in the US, EU, Brazil and China combined, or around 1% of the total 1,500 million hectares currently estimated to be in use for cropland globally. If all major countries and regions were to attain their stated targets for 2020, the total land requirement for biofuel production would be between 56 and 166 million hectares.[36] Thus, biofuels could represent between 11 and 83% of the additional global agricultural land requirements.[37]

One of the main difficulties in measuring the impact of biofuel policies is the very large uncertainty concerning land availability.[38] Estimates of (i) currently used agricultural land, (ii) the total amount of land that could potentially be used for agriculture and (iii) the total amount of land required to implement current biofuel policies vary considerably. Undertaking efforts to remedy this information gap is therefore important. This could be done in three steps. A very useful first step would be a mapping exercise that illustrates the land that is currently used for agriculture. Such an overview of current agricultural land use is necessary to check whether sustainability criteria are being met: an EU Communication, for example, stipulates that land not yet used for agriculture should in principle not be used for the production of biofuels.[39]

Secondly, a similar mapping exercise that determines the available land for agriculture would allow for a better calculation of the potential impact of expanded biofuel production. Such an overview should not only provide an aggregate number of available hectares of land, but should also detail the current use (to determine the GHG stocking rate of the land), climate conditions, soil quality (to determine which crops could be grown efficiently), land ownership and other factors.

Finally, in a third step, the available land should be compared with the land required to meet current biofuel policies, taking into account the additional land required to accommodate and feed the growing global

---

[35] Gallagher, above n 7, 29.

[36] Of course, this depends on the use of by-products, second-generation technology, and other factors. Some predict that biofuel production will require around two billion hectares, compared to around 1.5 billion hectares currently used for cropland. The very large range of estimates reflects the high degree of uncertainty regarding the future land demands. See World Bank, above n 12, 147.

[37] See Gallagher, above n 7, 30.

[38] Ibid, 29. That review concludes that the balance of evidence indicates there is sufficient land available to satisfy demand until 2020, but that there is still a high degree of uncertainty in such forecasts, which needs to be clarified before significantly increasing global biofuel supply. Ibid, 33–35.

[39] European Commission, 'Communication from the Commission on the Practical Implementation of the EU Biofuels and Bioliquids Sustainability Scheme and on Counting Rules for Biofuels', C/2010 160/02 (10 June 2010) (hereinafter Commission Communication). More precisely, the Commission Communication stipulates that in principle only biofuels grown on existing agricultural land will count towards the 10% target and can receive financial support.

population. While many studies remain silent on the previous two steps, calculations for this third step are more common—even though a large degree of uncertainty remains. When calculating additional land demand, potential yield improvements should be taken into account to get a more nuanced picture,[40] although one should keep in mind that yield improvements may come at the price of more intensive use of fertilisers, which adds to GHG emissions. Currently, approximately one-third of global GHG emissions are estimated to result from intensive agriculture and associated land use.[41] If improving yields are achieved by intensifying production, this may attenuate land scarcity, but at the price of increased GHG emissions. Some studies estimate that yield improvements may to a large extent counterbalance the additional land needed for population growth and biofuel production. One report estimates that the impact of such yield improvements amounts to approximately 10% of total land demand for biofuel production.[42] One could argue that the best way to improve yields (without increasing the use of fertilisers) is to manually cultivate fields. Although the cost of such a labour-intensive production process may make it unrealistic on a large scale, it is a factor that should be taken into account when elaborating sustainability criteria.

E. Biofuels in International Trade

If environmental benefits were the only rationale behind biofuel policies, only a limited amount of market-distorting measures would be appropriate.[43] However, the current elaborate and protectionist trade system reflects the other crucial motives for states to promote biofuels. Measures in support of biofuels can be taken at different levels, and include import tariffs, low-interest loans for the construction of processing plants or other producer subsidies, funding for basic and applied research and development, blending mandates, and reduced taxes at the pump. Each of these supportive measures may benefit different players.[44]

---

[40] Yields may need to more than double over the next 50 years, according to one study. See World Bank, above n 12, 148.

[41] ActionAid, above n 14 (referring to International Panel on Climate Change (IPCC), 'Change 2007: Mitigation. Contribution of Working Group III to the 4th Assessment Report of the IPCC' (2007)).

[42] The FAO estimates that overall agricultural output will need to rise by 70% over the next 40 years in order to feed over nine billion people in 2050. See 'FAO Sees Demand, Biofuels, Oil Fuelling Food Prices', *Reuters*, 18 February 2010. See also Gallagher, above n 7, 29, Box 3.1.

[43] See, eg the joint OECD/IEA report, 'Biofuel Support Policies: An Economic Assessment', which concludes that the high level of policy support contributes little to GHG savings.

[44] Specific measures could benefit farmers, including both smallholders and large-scale farmers; individuals or entities involved in milling, refining, distribution; or end consumers.

Start-up incentives are necessary in order to convince both consumers and producers to switch to biofuels. So far, all countries with biodiesel[45] programmes have supported the biodiesel industry, sometimes very substantially. Incentives are also important in the ethanol industry.[46] Even Brazil still relies in part on government intervention, though its biofuel production has the longest history and is the most efficient in the world.[47]

Biofuels, especially ethanol, are subject to high import tariffs. The EU levies an import duty of €0.192 per litre on undenatured ethanol and €0.102 on denatured ethanol—although approximately 100 developing countries benefit from duty-free access to the EU market.[48] In the US,

---

[45] Biodiesel is mainly traded under HS codes 38249099 and 38249029 (Miscellaneous chemical products—Prepared binders for foundry moulds or cores; chemical products and preparations of the chemical or allied industries (including those consisting of mixtures of natural products), not elsewhere specified or included—Other). See Junginger et al, above n 15, 8.

[46] Ethanol is traded under HS code 2207 (Beverages, spirits and vinegar—Undenatured ethyl alcohol of an alcoholic strength by volume of 80% vol or higher; ethyl alcohol and other spirits, denatured, of any strength). As ethanol and biodiesel are traded under different codes, different tariffs apply. The import tariffs on biodiesel used to be much lower on biodiesel than on ethanol. Import tariffs for wood pellets are much less common. Ibid, 7, 15.

[47] There are many factors, however, that make Brazil's success difficult to replicate. The government support exists notwithstanding Brazil's fairly long history of ethanol production, its very favourable growing conditions for sugarcane, and the ability of sugar mills to switch easily between sugar and ethanol. In addition, Brazil has the advantage of an entirely rain-fed sugarcane industry and a greater capacity for arable land expansion—although this may come at the expense of serious deforestation or other land-use change. Moreover, some have argued that the highly efficient ethanol market of Brazil is predicated on the 'subsidy' of the very low wages for sugarcane cutters. In recent years, wages have gone down, yet productivity has doubled. That phenomenon can be explained by the system of paying workers only for the amount of sugarcane that they are able to cut. A FIAN fact-finding mission to the state of Piauí found that one farm in Brazil imposed an unrealistically high quota for cutters, which apparently no family was able to meet. As a result, cutters were punished through reduced payments, and consequently incurred high debts. The FIAN report concludes that the Brazilian success story can be explained by this trade-distorting exploitation. One other reason for Brazil's success could be its high investment in research and development, which has resulted in more than 500 varieties of sugarcane that are resistant to more than forty diseases. In addition, Brazilian refineries have used bagasse, a residue of sugarcane, to provide the plants' energy needs and to earn money by selling the surplus energy. The efficient use of this by-product has considerably increased the cost efficiency of Brazilian sugarcane refineries. The harvesting of sugarcane, however, has potentially adverse environmental and health consequences, as fields are often burned down before the actual harvesting. Field burning is only necessary for manual harvesting. FIAN, 'Agrofuels in Brazil: Fact-Finding Mission Report on the Impacts of the Agrofuels Expansion on the Enjoyment of Social Rights of Rural Workers, Indigenous Peoples and Peasants in Brazil' (2008). The Brazilian ZEA Cana legislation will gradually prohibit manual harvesting in areas suitable for mechanical harvesting. The potential ecological gains of mechanic harvesting are to be balanced against the negative impact on local employment.

[48] An ESMAP report assesses the impact of potential liberalization of trade in biofuels. The study predicts that efficient producers with an ability to expand their production will gain. Those countries presently benefiting from a preferential trade treatment, such as the Caribbean, however, could be traded off the market completely. See Kojima and Johnson, above n 30, xiv.

a tariff of $0.1427 has been levied per litre of ethanol, in addition to an ad valorem tariff of 2.5%.[49] Brazil levied a 20% ad valorem import tariff on ethanol, while India levied an import tariff of 182% on undenatured ethanol and a remarkably lower 30% on denatured ethanol. These high import tariffs can prohibit developing countries from producing biofuels even when they might be more efficient ethanol producers. This illustrates that environmental motives are not the major driver behind biofuel policies. As a result of these import tariffs, biofuels can also hardly be said to boost developing countries' economies.

Even if these import tariffs were removed, the question of domestic support for producers, including direct support, remains. The US, for example, spent $5 billion in ethanol subsidies in 2006, which was approximately 40% of the market price. If the current level of subsidies for the European biofuel industry continues, it would receive around €13.7 billion per year to meet the EU biofuel target by 2020.[50] Removing import barriers in the global market without removing subsidies would only worsen inequalities, as products originating from countries with high subsidies would have an even greater market in which to dump their subsidised products. Some commentators, however, have argued that the rising demand for biofuels may bring an end to the present dumping practices of agricultural products by developed countries.[51] If the surplus of highly subsidised agricultural products were used domestically for biofuel production, it would decrease the quantity of commodities dumped in developing countries. Because those dumping practices are one of the major impediments to equitable free trade and agro-economic stimulation in developing countries, biofuels could be one solution to the current unfair trade regime. A decrease in agricultural dumping, however, does not do anything to help farmers in developing countries export their biofuels to the EU or the US.

From the point of view of developing countries, it is not illogical to levy export taxes on the raw materials for biofuels while exempting biofuels themselves from taxes. This would create an incentive for producers to process raw materials into biofuels domestically, creating local added value. Argentina, for example, levied an export tax of 27.5% on soybeans and 24% tax on soybean oil, but low or no export taxes on biofuels.

Formal talks are underway within the WTO on so-called environmental goods and services (EGS), with an aim to diminish or abolish trade barriers to these products. This could certainly affect the biofuel market. Many European countries want to link EGS with certain production criteria, in order to ensure that they are produced in an environmentally

---

[49] See Junginger, above n 15.
[50] ActionAid, above n 14, 2.
[51] Obviously, not all products currently being dumped are suitable for biofuel production.

sustainable way. Other countries have raised concerns that such criteria may be designed as a disguised trade barrier.[52] When fairly implemented, however, such criteria could stimulate the production of biofuels that are actually produced in an environmentally and socially sustainable way and therefore deserve the label *bio*fuels. If criteria are established, these should not only require an equitable trading regime between nations, but should also reflect an equitable distribution of the biofuel profit within the state.

II. POSSIBLE IMPACTS OF BIOFUELS

A. Rising Food Prices

The most obvious concern in the food-versus-fuel debate is the fact that arable land would be used to produce fuel instead of food. This would intensify competition over land use, and lead to a higher risk of increased food prices. Clearly, this may have an impact on the urban poor, who buy all the food they consume. Moreover, although it is generally thought that higher commodity prices benefit farmers, the poorest farmers in developing countries in fact tend to be net food buyers. Thus, even if they were to receive higher prices for their crops, they would still suffer from higher food prices. The transmission of prices from the international markets to the domestic markets depends, of course, on a variety of factors, including the trade policies pursued by the governments concerned.

Food prices attained record heights in 2008. Although they subsequently dropped, food prices have again reached peak heights in 2011. Biofuel production, which very likely contributed to the higher food prices, was not the only cause. Other factors, such as poor harvests due to drought and high oil prices, also played a role. Those factors may again be important in the future: climate change may cause poor harvests more frequently in the future, and high oil prices may turn out to be structural. Notwithstanding those other factors, there is a general consensus that biofuel policies played an important role in the food

---

[52] One study identifies import tariffs and sustainability criteria as the major obstacles to international bioenergy trade (especially for ethanol) in the eyes of market actors. Technical standards, on the other hand, were seen as an opportunity rather than as a barrier. Certain technical barriers may, however, act as a trade barrier. For example, the EU established a standard for biodiesel, imposing the iodine level for the vegetable oil used for biodiesel production. The stated reason was that other types of vegetable oil might not have the viscosity characteristics needed for the cooler European climate. However, only rapeseed oil (which is predominantly produced in the EU) easily attains the iodine level fixed in the EU's standard (DIN EN 142124), while palm and soil oil have more difficulty complying with this standard. See Junginger, above n 15, 2, 19, 20, 25.

price surges, even though the precise extent remains subject to diverse estimates.[53] Estimates have been made that the achievement of all global biofuel targets would cause food prices to rise by an additional 76% by 2020.[54] It should be no surprise that such price hikes can lead to social unrest. In Indonesia, the government had to increase the export tax from 1.5 to 6.5% while halving the blending mandate from 5 to 2.5% after an 80% increase in palm oil prices resulted in social unrest.[55] Another example is the street protests in Mexico in the run-up to the 2008 peak food prices, when the price of tortillas in Mexico quadrupled. Increased ethanol production from corn in the US at least partially caused those price increases, especially since Mexico has become increasingly dependent on US corn exports after the introduction of the North American Free Trade Agreement (NAFTA). Worldwide, higher prices for corn had the greatest impact on increased poverty. As the US is the leading exporter of corn, accounting for around 40% of global corn trade, its biofuel policy is particularly prone to having an impact on the poor around the world. The question can be raised as to whether this imposes a greater responsibility on the US to monitor the impact of its biofuel policy. At present, the US maintains one of the highest levels of trade-distorting support for domestic ethanol producers.

The food crops currently used to produce ethanol are also the crops that form the largest part of the diets of poor people. Food expenditure already comprises a very large share of poor people's income, making them highly vulnerable to price increases in basic food products.[56] The Energy Sector Management Assistance Program (ESMAP) predicts that prices for food products imported by developing countries will rise more sharply than prices for products they export. Eritrea, Lesotho and Gambia are among the countries that would suffer from the most negative balance-of-payments impacts.[57]

In short, while higher commodity prices could benefit some farmers, it is not at all clear that small farmers in developing countries would gain any net benefit, since they are often net food buyers. In addition, urban

---

[53] Although debatable, one leading World Bank economist estimated that biofuels accounted for around 70–75% of the increase in world food prices. The remaining 20–25% of the price increases would have been caused by other factors such as higher energy and fertiliser costs, droughts in specific regions of the world, and currency fluctuations. D Mitchell, 'A Note on Rising Food Prices', Policy Research Working Paper No 4682 (World Bank Development Prospects Group, July 2008) 14. See also OECD/FAO, 'Agricultural Outlook 2008–2017' (2008) 11 (stating that biofuel demand is strong factor underpinning upward shift in agricultural commodity prices).

[54] ActionAid, above n 14, 3.

[55] R Naylor et al, 'The Ripple Effect: Biofuels, Food Security, and the Environment' (2007) 49 *Environment* 30, 34, 40.

[56] OECD/FAO, above n 53, 12.

[57] World Bank Development Committee, 'Rising Food Prices: Policy Options and World Bank Response' (2008) 2.

poor would suffer from increasing food prices. According to estimates, an extra 16 million people would suffer from undernourishment for each percentage point increase in the real price of staple food.[58] This would eradicate several years of poverty reduction efforts. Moreover, it is likely that only those farmers who own the land they cultivate could benefit from any higher income. Those who rent land will likely be confronted with higher rents once food prices go up due to land scarcity.

Many studies reflect a somewhat utilitarian cost–benefit analysis, calculating how many people will benefit and how many will be hurt, then simply offsetting the one by the other. A genuine right-to-food analysis, however, should be more nuanced. It should not only take into account whether the country in total would benefit, but should ask who would benefit and, more importantly, at the detriment of whom. Such analyses should distinguish, for example, between the impact on rural and urban poor; farmers, processing firms and distributors; large-scale producers and smallholders; and landowners and landless farmers. A right-to-food analysis requires protecting those most vulnerable, not simply ensuring that the gross domestic product or average incomes will increase.

In addition, studies often only take account of direct price impacts, which renders the picture incomplete. One example of an indirect consequence is the impact of the use of certain crops for fuel on the by-products of those crops[59] or on crops used as a substitute. In addition, higher prices for food crops could cause an increase in the price of meat and dairy, since the price of animal feed produced from crops and crop residues could also increase. Another indirect effect of increasing food prices is a possible reduction in the quantities of food aid. Some countries determine their food aid in terms of a certain value in dollars instead of a certain quantity. When food prices go up, this means the total quantity of food that can be bought with that fixed aid budget decreases, at the exact moment when the poorest will be most in need of aid because prices are high.[60] In Malawi or Zimbabwe, for example, where food aid provides around one-fifth of coarse grain consumption, this could have dramatic results.

Although studies have produced a vast amount of data and estimates, the concrete impact of biofuel policies on poverty remains unclear. Much depends on which factors are taken into account in calculations. Although

---

[58] Ziegler, above n 5, 35.

[59] The impact on the price for by-products of certain crops can vary. For example, if more corn is produced for both feed and fuel, then more waste material will be available, which lowers the price of by-products made from this waste. If by-products are also used for the production of biofuels, however, prices will rise.

[60] The modes of calculation of commitments to food aid under the Food Aid Convention are criticised for this very reason in the report of Olivier De Schutter, the UN Special Rapporteur on the Right to Food. O De Schutter, 'Food Aid and Development Cooperation, UN document A/HRC/10/5 (March 2009).

there are numerous factors that may play a role in the impact of biofuel policies, most studies select the most obvious ones. While this approach is understandable, it results in very few studies that actually provide a detailed and accurate view of the entire situation. Calculations that do not take into account inflation, employment opportunities, infrastructure, climatic conditions, soil quality, indirect land-use change,[61] land titles, gender differences,[62] local energy supply, and micro- and macroeconomic conditions, among other factors, cannot accurately assess the concrete impact that certain biofuel policies have on specific populations. The challenge therefore is to bring that data together while ensuring a right-to-food perspective.

Not only will food prices rise due to increased biofuels production, they will also become more volatile.[63] The market for biofuels will be inextricably linked to the market for crude oil, as high oil prices will provide an incentive to produce and consume more biofuels. The negative corollary of this link is that the biofuel market will be contaminated by the price volatility of the oil market. Such price volatility particularly hurts the poorest segments of society, which spend a large percentage of their income on food—around 75% for the poorest people—and therefore are less able to absorb sudden price increases. Such volatility goes against one main aspect of the right to food, namely the regular and permanent access to food.[64]

The so-called second-generation biofuels are often put forward as a possible solution to the problem of food-versus-fuel competition, because they are produced from waste materials and thereby avoid direct competition with food. There are, however, few waste materials that are really 'waste'. For example, if the stalks and leaves of certain crops that were previously used for animal feed are then used to produce biofuels, it might be necessary to grow other crops to produce such animal feed. This would not be helpful to mitigate the competition over land. Such practical impacts should guide the development and testing phase of second-generation biofuels. Other guiding questions,

---

[61] This includes change from both above ground carbon and below ground carbon.

[62] See, eg the key messages of the first FAO-BEFSCI Technical Consultation on Criteria and Indicators on Sustainable Production that Safeguards Food Security, held in Rome in November 2009, which mention potentially differentiated impacts that biofuel production may have on men and women, due for example to different access to land, credit and markets. The outcomes suggest providing, whenever possible, gender-disaggregated data.

[63] Price volatility may also be caused by speculation, even though studies differ as to the impact of speculation on world food prices. See OECD/FAO, above n 53; ActionAid, above n 14, 12; O De Schutter, 'Food Commodities Speculation and Food Price Crises', Briefing Note 2 (September 2010); Gallagher, above n 7, 61, Box 7.1.

[64] On the definition of the right to food, see FAO, 'Voluntary Guidelines to Support the Progressive Realization of the Right to Adequate Food in the Context of National Food Security' (2004) 15; see also the website of the Special Rapporteur, available at www.srfood.org.

from the perspective of the right to food, are, for example, whether these more advanced technologies are affordable, how they could be useful for small-scale (local energy supply) applications, what amounts of raw material and water are needed to produce a litre of second-generation biofuel, and, from an environmental point of view, how much GHGs are emitted through the production process.

B. Land Use, Deforestation and Biodiversity

The competition over land for biofuels and food makes agricultural land increasingly valuable. In the US, for example, prices for one hectare of farmland increased 74% between 2000 and 2007.[65] Increasing land prices risk favouring larger agribusinesses to the detriment of smaller farmers, not only in the US but also in developing countries, where large multinationals are buying increasing amounts of land in order to set up ambitious biofuel projects.[66] Those investments have been described as land grabs and have been characterised by some as a form of neo-colonial behaviour.[67] The battle for land may also drive both smallholders and agribusinesses to search for new agricultural land, which in turn risks ruining precious ecosystems. In the US, some areas of land previously protected by the Conservation Reserve Program have been made available for corn production, jeopardising biodiversity and wildlife habitat.[68] Serious concerns have arisen that rainforests and savannas in several countries will be converted into land for biofuels. Indonesia, for example, planned to convert 4 million hectares of the Borneo rainforest into oil plantations. After pressure from environmental groups including the World Wide Fund (WWF), however, the government decided to cancel the project. In Brazil,[69] 5.6 million hectares

[65] Naylor, above n 55, 35.
[66] Since mid-2008, around 180 such land transactions have been reported; between 2006 and mid-2009, foreign investors sought or secured between 15 and 20 million acres of farmland in the developing world. See The Oakland Institute, 'The Great Land Grab—Rush for World's Farmland Threatens Food Security for the Poor' (2009) 1. See also O De Schutter, 'Large-scale Land Acquisitions and Leases: A Set of Minimum Principles and Measures to Address the Human Rights Challenge', addendum to the 2008 Report, UN document A/HRC/13/33/Add.2 (28 December 2009). ActionAid states that it is no coincidence that companies buy land in countries that benefit from preferential import tariffs for the EU. However, if such preferential tariffs are granted to promote economic development in specific countries, these reductions should benefit not just international undertakings operating on the country's territory, but also the country's population. See ActionAid, above n 14, 11.
[67] T Molony and J Smith, 'Biofuels, Food Security and Africa, African Affairs Advance Access' (20 April 2010); ActionAid, above n 14, 3.
[68] Naylor, above n 55, 35.
[69] The UN Special Rapporteur on the Right to Food conducted a fact-finding mission to Brazil in 2009, the findings of which can be found in the addendum to the 2009 Report, UN document A/HRC/13/33/Add.6 (19 February 2009).

of cropland is currently being used for growing sugarcane, although this is estimated to almost double over the next 10 years, to roughly 10 million hectares.[70]

From an environmental point of view, this evolution does not make sense.[71] If one of the greatest merits of biofuels is a reduction in the emission of GHGs, as often claimed, it is absurd to clear rainforests in order to provide more land for fuel crops. Trees absorb carbon, and this is released once the trees are cut down. One hectare of mature rainforest contains about 200 tons of carbon and can absorb another 6 tons every year, while one hectare of industrial tree planting can store only approximately 28 tons of carbon dioxide. Deforestation in Southeast Asia causes annual carbon emissions that equal almost half of the total carbon emissions from fossil fuel combustion per year, while deforestation in general accounts for 20% of GHG emissions globally. Tropical forests around the world contain over 210 million tons of carbon, and an additional 500 million tons of carbon contained in the soil could be released due to changed land use. If no immediate measures are taken to reverse deforestation, 10 million tons of carbon dioxide could be released annually for the next 50–100 years. Each year, around 0.2–0.3 billion tons of carbon is released due to deforestation in the Brazilian part of the Amazon alone.[72] The Amazon forest itself contains 90–140 billion tons of carbon, which equals 9–14 years of the current annual global human-induced carbon emissions. In addition, deforestation in general would pose a serious threat to biodiversity.

It is also important to take into account the more indirect effects of deforestation on local populations. Forests provide a livelihood to many people, either in the form of fruits or hunting territory, or as a place to collect wood for cooking. If forests are cleared in favour of large-scale biofuel production, local communities will suffer twice, by losing their land and by facing higher food prices. A fact-finding mission led by a non-governmental organisation (NGO), FIAN, has documented how the expansion of sugarcane plantations has threatened indigenous people living in reservations in the state of Piauí, Brazil.[73] Competition over land is fuelling internal conflict and violence among them. Moreover, for people living in the vicinity of tropical rainforests such as the Amazon,

---

[70] Brazil introduced the Sugarcane Agroecological Zoning project (ZAE Cana), which is aimed at limiting the land that can be used for sugarcane production. Certain valuable areas, such as the Amazon biomes, cannot be used for sugarcane expansion. In addition, areas with native vegetation cannot be used for sugarcane expansion. For more information on the ZAE Cana legislation, see www.cnps.embrapa.br/zoneamento_cana_de_acucar/ZonCana.pdf (Portuguese).

[71] A lack of protection of biodiversity may also be a violation of a state's obligations under international environmental treaties.

[72] Worldwide Fund, 'The Amazon's Vicious Circles' (2007) 15.

[73] FIAN, above n 47.

increasing deforestation can lead to decreased rainfall, which in turn could jeopardise food security in the region.

Furthermore, as land becomes scarcer, farmers may try to maximise yields by more intensive farming and shorter crop rotations, as is already the case in the US. Such unsustainable practices lead to soil depletion, further jeopardising future food security. One way to combat this is to plant certain perennials at regular intervals in order to restore soil quality. Farmers, however, will only have the incentive to do so if it is mandatory, or if they receive an equal price for such perennials, either from the market or from subsidies.

There is, however, land that could be efficiently used for biofuel production without necessarily causing some of those detrimental environmental or social impacts. So-called marginal lands are unfit for agricultural use but may still be well suited for certain non-food crops that are used to produce biofuels. As discussed above, one such crop is *Jatropha curcas*, which is used for biodiesel production. It can be planted on arid lands, improving the soil quality and protecting against desertification; it can also be intercropped. Although initial studies on this plant were promising, experience has imposed a more realistic view. One of its pitfalls is that, although jatropha may be grown on low-quality soil, the harvest will be equally low. Other crops have also been put forward as potentially mitigating the food-versus-fuel competition. One example is sweet sorghum, which allows for a dual use: the seeds at the top of the crop can be harvested for food, while the sugars in the stalks can be converted into ethanol. Other experiments are taking place, for example with algae. Growing and converting algae into biofuel is still far from being commercially viable, however. The competition for land thus looks set to continue for at least a decade.

Estimates of available marginal land and unused agricultural land require great caution. These lands may contain important carbon stocks, which will be released once the land is cleared for biofuel production. Little land is actually 'unused'.[74] Calculations of available land should therefore be based on a precise definition of what constitutes marginal or unused land. Land not currently used for agriculture might already be used in another way: it may be used as pasture, or the local population may use the fruits of the plants that grow there. If this land is cleared for biofuels, those alternative uses may be relocated to other lands, such as forests, savannas or peatland.

This indirect land-use change has been overlooked for a long time. However, it can have a tremendous impact on both food security and climate change. Ignoring the growing evidence of this very important factor is no longer an option. The EU, for example, has come under

---

[74] See IEA, above n 12, 7.

increased attack for not taking account of indirect land-use changes that could be caused by its biofuel targets. The current evidence suggests that the EU target is unlikely to be met sustainably.[75] A recent communication from the European Commission[76] lays down certain conditions that biofuels for transport have to fulfil to be counted towards Member States' achievement of the EU target. One of the conditions is that, in principle, biofuels cannot be grown on land that is not currently used for agriculture. This ignores the fact that, if the biofuels needed to achieve the EU's targets are grown on existing agricultural land, agriculture will simply be relocated, be it to forest or peatlands that will need to be cleared. An earlier draft of this communication even went so far as to state that conversion of forests into palm oil plantations was not considered to be a land-use change,[77] although such conversion would obviously lead to very high GHG emissions.[78] Fortunately, that was amended in the final communication. However, there is still no mechanism to ensure that the biofuels needed to attain the EU's target will not lead to deforestation and other unacceptable land-use changes.

At present, the European Commission seems to underestimate these indirect land-use changes. It estimates that its 10% target would require around 2–5 million hectares of land[79]—a number that does not take into account indirect land-use changes and the potentially substantial GHG emissions resulting from such change.[80] Other estimates predict that the EU's 10% target may directly require 17.5 million hectares of land to produce industrial biofuels, without even taking into account indirect land requirements.[81] Still other estimates predict 20–30 million hectares.[82]

---

[75] Gallagher, above n 7, 10.
[76] Commission Communication, above n 39. The communication describes how Member States and economic operators should implement the sustainability criteria laid out in the Renewable Energy Directive (Directive 2009/28/EC) for biofuels and bioliquids and in the Fuel Quality Directive (Directive 98/70/EC as amended by Directive 2009/30/EC) for biofuels. The Commission submitted a progress report in January 2011 (SEC(2011) 130 Final, 31 January 2011).
[77] Draft Communication from the Commission to the Council and the European Parliament on the practical implementation of the EU biofuels and bioliquids sustainability scheme and on counting rules for biofuels, draft 2009, BI (10) 381 Art 4.2.1.
[78] See also Commission Decision on guidelines for the calculation of land carbon stocks for the purpose of Annex V of Directive 2009/28/EC (10 June 2010).
[79] The Commission estimates that the EU could produce all biofuels on land within the EU that are no longer in arable use. It also points to a few million hectares of land in Indonesia that have been deforested in the past. The Commission envisages that these could be used for biofuel production. It would make sense, from an environmental point of view, to restore the forests on those lands instead of using it for biofuel production. This could potentially save more GHG emissions than producing biofuels. See Commission Memo, above n 18.
[80] Ibid. The payback time for biofuel feedstock causing land-use change can amount to several decades. See Gallagher, above n 7, 26, Table 2.1.
[81] ActionAid, above n 14, 4.
[82] Dutch Environment Assessment Agency, 'Local and Global Consequences of the EU Renewable Directive for Biofuels' (2008), as cited in ActionAid, above n 14, 35. See also

Regardless, the GHG emissions of indirect land-use changes need to be taken into account when calculating whether biofuels really attain the 35% GHG savings as compared to petrol and diesel, as required by the EU Renewable Energy Directive.[83] Compliance with the sustainability criteria will be audited as in the financial sector. This type of auditing will require a different type of expertise and tools for the auditor than, for example, the auditing of a company's annual accounts. Auditors will need to verify that biofuels produced in developing countries, such as Malawi and Indonesia, have not replaced forests or other valuable land. This assumes that it is (already) possible to know for each part of land in the world what the current use is.

The European Commission prefers to rely on voluntary schemes that it monitors.[84] Alternatively, economic operators could use default values to prove compliance with the sustainability criteria.[85] Unfortunately, those values are not differentiated according to the geographical origin of the feedstock. The European Commission allows for such voluntary schemes to be incorporated in bilateral or multilateral treaties concluded by the EU (not Member States).[86] This leaves room to include sustainability criteria in bilateral investment treaties or even in international agreements. It might be useful to follow the suggestion of the European Commissioner for Energy, Mr Oettinger, to establish a logo that could assure consumers at the pump that the biofuels they buy fulfil all the sustainability criteria set at the EU level.[87] Member States, however, are not allowed to impose additional sustainability criteria,[88] which gives the

Gallagher, above n 7, 32 (estimating that EU 10% target would require between 22 and 31.5 million hectares of gross land).

[83] Renewable Energy Directive, Art 17 (2). As of 2017, this percentage will be increased to 50% GHG savings.

[84] Art 18(4), second subparagraph and Art 18(7) of the Renewable Energy Directive; 'Communication from the Commission on Voluntary Schemes and Default Values in the EU Biofuels and Bioliquids Sustainability scheme', 2010/C 160/01 (10 June 2010) 2.5.

[85] These default values are, according to the Commission, set at conservative levels to make it unlikely for economic actors to claim default values that are better than their actual value. Typical values derived from scientific data and the methodology used in the Renewable Energy Directive are transformed into default values by applying a factor +40% to the emissions from the 'processing' element to transform typical values into conservative values. However, no such factor is applied to the 'transport and distribution' element, because, in the view of the Commission, its contribution to overall emissions is small. This might be a rather optimistic view. Moreover, the Commission does not intend to introduce default values for specific pathways according to the geographical origin of where the feedstock or biofuel are produced, but rather related to specific practices, technologies and other factors. The pathway for a specific crop, however, can vary substantially, depending on where the feedstock is grown. See 'Communication from the Commission on Voluntary Schemes', ibid, 3.

[86] Art 18(4), first subparagraph, and Art 18(7) of the Renewable Energy Directive; 'Communication from the Commission on Voluntary Schemes', ibid 2.6. The Commission has to recognise the agreement, in the same as voluntary schemes.

[87] IP/10/711 (10 June 2010).

[88] Commission Communication, above n 39, Art 2.4.

EU an even greater responsibility to fine-tune its norms. A first step in fine-tuning the EU policy is to differentiate between types of feedstock and types of land, as these factors will substantially affect potential GHG emissions.

C. Concentration of Economic Power through Intellectual Property Rights

As one paper by the Institute for Agriculture and Trade Policy reveals, few studies on biofuels focus in detail on the issue of patents. According to one study, however, patents granted in the biotechnology industry increased from 6,000 in 2000 to 22,000 in 2005, predominantly for biofuel production.[89]

As land becomes scarcer, there will be a huge incentive to increase crop yields for biofuels by developing improved seeds. Inevitably, debate over genetically modified (GM) crops will come to the forefront again. It remains to be seen whether countries reluctant to allow GM crops for food into their territories will be less suspicious vis-à-vis GM crops for biofuels. Brazil, a long-time opponent of GM crops, has recently given permission for field experiments with GM sugarcane biofuels.

The highly concentrated seed market could impede small-scale farmers' ability to compete in the production of crops for biofuels. If only a few companies dominate the seed market, the lack of genuine competition may lead to artificially high prices for seeds, so that they become affordable only for large agribusinesses. Small-scale farmers may not be able to afford the more productive seeds. They might also encounter legal problems from seed companies that aggressively monitor the use of their seeds. If developed countries provide substantial protective measures for their domestic biofuel producers, and if only larger firms are able to afford the most productive seeds and to buy the most fertile land, then it is questionable whether biofuels could empower the poor, as is often claimed.

While the issue of patents is most relevant to the seed industry, it is also likely that enhanced processing technologies could also be strictly protected by patents. Research on second-generation biofuels is underway, although it will take time and money to fully develop the appropriate technology. Guarantees should be put in place to ensure that it is not only large agribusinesses that are able to afford the processing technology.

---

[89] Institute for Agriculture and Trade Policy (IATP), 'Patents: Taken for Granted in Plans for a Global Biofuels Market' (2007) 2.

D. Water

The water requirements of different fuel crops vary substantially. The cultivation of soybeans and sugarcane requires large quantities of water, while sorghum is much less demanding.[90] An additional concern is that, as feedstock prices rise, farmers might be encouraged to use more water in order to maximise yields. A potential increase in water usage would be problematic, especially because agriculture currently uses 70% of the global fresh water supply, and up to 85% of the water in the developing world.[91]

Biofuel conversion is also water intensive, especially for ethanol production.[92] In the US, most plants consume about 3.5–6 gallons (13–23 litres) of water per gallon of ethanol produced,[93] as compared to 1.5 gallons of water for petroleum.[94] Put differently, a typical ethanol plant that produces 50 million gallons (around 190 million litres) of biofuel per year would require around 500 gallons (around 1900 litres) of water per minute.[95] In addition, some experts predict that second-generation biofuels, which have many potential benefits, might actually require much more water for conversion than the current conversion of corn into ethanol.[96]

Moreover, biofuel production can pollute waterways. For example, reports warn that the effluents of palm oil mills pollute waterways, further jeopardising local food security.[97] In addition, sugar mills have to be flushed each year, which also causes the pollution of local waterways.[98] Water pollution by processing plants is not, of course, a phenomenon limited only to biofuel production, but increased biofuel production will add to the existing problem.

As the former UN Special Rapporteur on the right to food noted in his 2007 Interim Report, few studies have examined the impact of increased biofuel production on water resources.[99] If increased land demand leads to an expansion of the total land used for crop production, more water will be required to irrigate those lands, even where marginal lands are

---

[90] UN-Energy, above n 13, 26.
[91] Kojima and Johnson, above n 30, 207; UN-Energy, above n 13, 45.
[92] Kojima and Johnson, above n 30, 219.
[93] D Keeny and M Muller, 'Water Use by Ethanol Plants: Potential Challenges' (IATP, 2006) 4.
[94] National Research Council, Committee on Water Implications of Biofuels Production in the United States, *Water Implications of Biofuel Production in the United States* (The National Academies Press, 2008) 46.
[95] Keeny and Muller, above n 93.
[96] Naylor, above n 55, 34.
[97] Naylor, above n 55, 39.
[98] Kojima and Johnson, above n 30, 218.
[99] Ziegler, above n 5. One example is the OECD/FAO, above n 53, 14, which does not include water shortages in its calculations.

used for less demanding crops such as jatropha. It is important to be mindful of the risk that large-scale companies will be able to afford the water needed for their plantations while small-scale farmers will be confronted with either an insufficient water supply or increasing water prices that they cannot afford.[100]

E. Fertilisers and Pesticides

Increasing land and food prices create the incentive to use more fertilisers and pesticides in order to ensure a maximum yield on limited land. Some fuel crops require larger quantities of fertiliser than others to produce good yields. Corn and rapeseed require very fertile soil, while jatropha can flourish on much less fertile soil—although this comes at the price of low yields. The increased use of fertilisers for biofuel production could lead to more GHG pollution.[101] It can also seriously jeopardise local water quality and the local population's health. One solution would be to use natural fertilisers, for example, by leaving certain crop residues on the fields. Once second-generation biofuels made from crop residues become more commercially viable, however, it could be hard to convince farmers to leave part of this potential biofuel feedstock on the fields.

Biofuel production can also contribute to air pollution. For example, some ethanol plants in the US emit cancer-causing chemicals such as toluene and formaldehyde. The production of biodiesel requires the use of methanol,[102] which is highly toxic and has an environmental impact similar to that of petroleum production. These impacts should, at the very least, be included in calculations of GHG savings for biofuels and other impact assessments.

F. Employment Opportunities

An expanding biofuel industry has the potential to create more employment opportunities. A job can generate the income needed to buy food. The growing and harvesting of certain fuel crops is labour intensive. For example, the seeds of jatropha currently have to be harvested by hand. Sugarcane is also largely harvested by hand, though mechanisation of the process, which prevents field burning prior to harvesting, is

---

[100] Ziegler, above n 5.
[101] Nitrogen fertiliser results in N_2O emissions. The global warming potential of N_2O is almost 300 times as much as the same mass of CO_2. See JRC, above n 8, 3.1.3.
[102] Methanol, also known as wood spirits, is a highly toxic chemical (CH_3OH). Even a small dose can lead to permanent blindness or death.

being promoted.[103] Biofuel production, especially biodiesel production, is much more labour intensive than traditional oil extraction. A World Bank study estimates that biofuels require around 100 times more workers to produce the same amount of energy than fossil fuel. Of course, the more viable the biofuel market becomes, the more research and development efforts will focus on the mechanisation of crop production.

In addition to harvesting the crops, the biofuel production process may create other employment opportunities. Since biomass is very bulky, transporting the material could create additional jobs in the transport sector. From an environmental point of view, however, the net advantages of biofuels would be seriously decreased if the transportation of biomass requires a heavy energy input. Transportation is also limited for certain feedstocks that need to be processed within a short time span. One example is sugarcane, which needs to be processed within 24–48 hours. This means that the processing plant cannot be too far away from the fields.[104] On the other hand, the required proximity of processing plants is positive both in environmental terms and because it creates an opportunity for local employment. Unlike crude oil, which may be transported and refined abroad, biomass feedstock would be converted locally, creating added value at the local level. However, as described above, the current import tariffs of some developed countries risk undermining this potential by imposing higher tariffs on biofuels than on basic feedstock. Despite this, positive examples exist. For example, a UN-Energy paper reports that a Dutch–Nepalese programme has constructed more than 120,000 biogas plants in Nepal, and a Dutch–Vietnamese undertaking has led to the construction of 25,000 biogas plants.[105] Those large numbers suggest an important amount of local processing. The paper does not mention what the ownership structure is of those plants, however, so it remains unclear who benefits the most from the local processing. If local employees are trained for processing jobs, they could obtain valuable skills, which in turn could be a way out of poverty by enhancing personal and community-level development.

The employment potential at local processing firms could also create additional indirect job opportunities. People working in processing plants should in theory earn a better wage. This would enhance their buying power and could therefore stimulate the local economy to the extent that they buy their food and other products locally. Even local farmers who are not net food buyers could gain, since their income would be expected to rise: as the competition between food and fuel intensifies, that will drive up local prices, which could potentially reverse

---

[103] See Brazil's ZEA Cana legislation, above n 47.
[104] For this reason, producing states do not need to impose export tariffs in order to encourage local processing, as this is necessary in any case.
[105] UN-Energy, above n 13, 14.

the current trend of decreasing prices for agricultural products. This microeconomic evolution could ensure that local farmers receive a better price for their products.

However, there are some caveats. First, it is not at all clear that higher commodity prices would necessarily lead to higher incomes for farmers. If the biofuel market follows the example of the agricultural market, it will tend to privilege concentration in the hands of large multinational agribusinesses. As noted above, that tendency for centralisation already seems to be suggested by the ethanol markets in Brazil and the US. Some estimates predict that the Brazilian ethanol market may be dominated by just six or seven larger groups over the next few years, as compared to approximately 250 millers today.[106] The risk exists that, in a concentrated market, farmers would not benefit from increased prices because they are price takers. This risk exists especially when feedstock has to be processed within a short time span and farmers consequently only have a limited choice of wholesale buyers. One solution could be for farmers to establish cooperatives in order to have the resources to buy processing equipment.

In addition, as land for both food and fuel crops becomes scarcer and land prices increase steadily, local farmers risk being driven off their land. Especially in countries without clear land titles and registries, this is a tangible threat. In this scenario, the potential for increased employment opportunities and the profits of the biofuel boom could completely bypass those who are most in need of economic development.

Moreover, the current highly protectionist trade measures in industrialised countries threaten market access for biofuel products from developing countries, which further diminishes the prospects of employment gains. Even if biofuels were predominantly produced in developing countries, the local processing plants could still be owned by large agribusiness companies, which could render local farmers vulnerable as price takers.

As mentioned above, one solution could be to set up cooperatives of local farmers, which could give them a stronger negotiating position vis-à-vis agribusiness companies and enhance mutual information sharing. Some governments have already attempted to support such cooperatives. One example is the Brazilian Selo Combustíve Social, which aims at promoting family cooperatives.[107] Biofuel producers can receive certification if they purchase a percentage of their feedstock from

---

[106] Kojima and Johnson, above n 30, 133.
[107] 'Selo Combustíve Social', Instrução Normativa N°1 Dispõe sobre os critérios e procedimentos relativos à concessão, manutenção e uso do selo combustível social—Social Fuel Seal, Normative Instruction N°1 relating to the criteria and procedures for the concession, maintenance and use of the Social Fuel Seal of 19 February 2009. A useful summary of this legislation is provided in M Ismail and A Rossi, 'A Compilation of Bioenergy Sustainability Initiatives' (FAO, 2010); see also FAO, Bioenergy and Food Security Criteria and Indicators (BEFSCI) Project, available at www.fao.org/bioenergy/foodsecurity/befsci.

smallholder farmers.[108] The contract concluded with these farmers must fulfil detailed conditions. Collective contracts have to be concluded with all farmers involved, though they must exclude co-responsibility between those farmers. Such contracts need to include the quantity of contracted raw material and specification of the equivalent areas in hectares, the conditions for cases of bad harvest and instances of *force majeure*, and identification of the representative of the family farmers who participated in the commercial negotiations and consented to the contract by way of a notarised letter. Biofuel producers have to provide services of technical assistance and training to all family farmers, and the collective contract must explain the producer's responsibility in this respect. This system has the great advantage of allowing farmers to become fully fledged players in the biofuel chain, rather than mere employees on large-scale plantations.

Decentralised biofuel production could come at the expense of economic efficiency and also, as some suggest, of quality. A UN-Energy report points to negative consumer experiences due to quality problems in Colombia, Costa Rica and Australia, and warns that such negative experiences may discourage customers from buying biofuels.[109] This argument does not hold when countries impose blending mandates. Some commentators have already suggested that some form of international certification system will be necessary. It is important, however, that this should not be allowed to serve as a cover for disguised trade restrictions. National standards have already been established in certain countries, while several NGOs are attempting to design transnational criteria for sustainable biofuels. It seems unrealistic to expect that one international logo, comparable to the Fairtrade logo, could sufficiently reflect the necessary sustainability criteria. However, the most important biofuel-consuming countries could spell out the minimum criteria that certification schemes have to meet in order to be recognised.[110] This

---

[108] Biofuel producers as well as family cooperatives have to keep records of the purchase and sale of raw materials for 5 years. The documentation kept by the producer needs to include the prices received by the farmers and proof of amounts spent on technical assistance. The producer has to submit a final report to the authorities at the end of each season, summarising all activities undertaken with the family farmers, the occurrence of accidents resulting in reduced yields and crop productivity, and other crop-related problems for each community. However, the obligation to purchase a certain percentage of feedstock from a specific type of buyer may need to be reconciled with trade rules such as those imposed by the WTO, NAFTA and the EU.

[109] UN-Energy, above n 13, 17.

[110] Inspiration can be drawn from the Bioenergy and Food Security Criteria and Indicators (BEFSCI), a project of the FAO. BEFSCI analyses certification schemes in light of certain benchmarks, which include environmental, socio-economic, governance and food security parameters. The BEFSCI project has conducted assessments of, among others, the EU Renewable Energy Directive, the World Bank/World Wildlife Fund Biofuels Environmental Sustainability Scorecard, and the voluntary standards of the Roundtable on Sustainable Biofuels and the Roundtable on Sustainable Palm Oil. The results of these

could be a first quality filter in the plethora of voluntary schemes. As the UN Special Rapporteur on the right to food has remarked, a code of conduct that does not move beyond those minimum requirements is a source of confusion, not progress.[111] The Special Rapporteur adds that companies that proclaim to adhere to codes of conduct but do not implement them could be considered guilty of misleading advertising.[112] The same reasoning could be applied to companies signing up to voluntary certification schemes. The disadvantage of certification schemes, however, is that they may be too costly for smallholders to pay for the necessary auditing if the burden of the certification procedure is imposed on them.[113]

Increased employment may benefit those directly involved to the extent that decent wages are provided. Others who cannot benefit directly from the biofuel boom may be disadvantaged. The enhanced income of the former category of locals could drive up prices for food and other products at the local level. Moreover, as mentioned above, most farmers in poor countries are net buyers of food, which means that higher food prices would also not benefit them. Nonetheless, one could argue that this gap within local communities is unavoidable and will be an inherent consequence of any form of economic development. Whatever the new technology or improved employment opportunities may be, there will always be 'haves' and 'have nots' in such processes. The micro- and macroeconomic dynamics of enhanced biofuel production should nevertheless be included in impact assessments, to get a nuanced view of who benefits or loses in the immediate vicinity of biofuel production areas or in the wider surroundings.

Even for those involved in biofuel production, the creation of employment opportunities is not all that matters. Concerns have arisen regarding the working conditions in fuel crop production. Especially with respect to the sugarcane plantations in Brazil, claims of degrading working conditions have surfaced. This problem is of course not limited

---

analyses can be found at www.fao.org/bioenergy/foodsecurity/befsci/62379/en/. A similar analysis has been undertaken by IEA's Task 40 on Sustainable International Bio-Energy Trade. See 'Update: Initiatives in the Field of Biomass and Bioenergy Certification' (April 2010). The substance of the benchmarks can be assessed against the FAO's Voluntary Guidelines, above n 64. The UN Special Rapporteur on the Right to Food has suggested that lessons can be drawn from the Kimberly Process Certification Scheme in the diamond sector. See O De Schutter, 'Building Resilience: a Human Rights Framework for World Food and Nutrition Security, delivered to the Human Rights Council, 9th session', UN document A/HRC/9/23 (8 September 2008) n 36.

[111] O De Schutter, 'Agribusiness and the Right to Food, delivered to the Human Rights Council, 13th session', UN document A/HRC/13/33 (22 December 2009) 23. See also Gallagher, above n 7, 18–19 (concluding that effectiveness of voluntary biofuels certification schemes in improving sustainability of biofuels remains to be proven).

[112] Ibid.
[113] Ibid, 39.

to the biofuels industry, but applies to the agricultural industry in general. Such situations should not be pointed to as a reason to promote more mechanical harvesting, as some agribusinesses have done—except where mechanisation results in clear environmental gains, for example. Rather, policymakers should address the poor working conditions. An even better protection against inhumane working conditions is to promote production schemes where farmers own the land they till and can sell their products at fair prices. The farmer cooperatives mentioned above could make people less vulnerable to the power of agribusinesses and large plantation owners, giving them a more active role in the production chain. Such schemes in which farmers own the land they cultivate, rather than being employees on plantations, could better promote the realisation of the right to food. In the words of the Special Rapporteur, 'the right to food is not primarily about being fed. It is about being guaranteed the right to feed oneself.'[114] Such cooperatives would allow for economies-of-scale advantages, while ensuring that this does not lead to a marginal and vulnerable role of small farmers vis-à-vis agribusiness companies. Cooperatives that have processing equipment can give farmers a stake further up the supply chain. This would make farmers less vulnerable to price volatilities, as they could compensate for lower feedstock prices with the additional prices for the biofuel produced.

G. Local Energy Supply

Currently, around 3 billion people still rely on traditional biomass for cooking and other energy needs, while 1.6 billion have no access to electricity whatsoever.[115] This lack of reliable and sufficient energy supply is a serious impediment to development and economic growth. From this perspective, biofuels could become an important driver of development for people who currently cannot afford the high oil prices for their energy needs. Liquid biofuels, such as biodiesel made from vegetable oils, have the advantage that they can be produced on a small scale.[116]

[114] 'Right to Food', available at www.srfood.org/index.php/en/right-to-food.
[115] FAO, 'Key Messages on "How to Design, Implement and Replicate Sustainable Small-Scale Livelihood-Oriented Bioenergy Initiatives"', based on the Technical Consultation held in October 2009 in Rome, with reference to UNDP/WHO, 'The Energy Access Situation in Developing Countries—A Review Focusing on the Least Developed Countries and Sub-Saharan Africa' (2009); IEA, 'World Energy Outlook' (2002), Chapter 13.
[116] Palm oil can create good opportunities for smallholders. Currently, smallholders manage 35-40% of the land under palm oil cultivation in Malaysia and Indonesia. A disadvantage of palm oil production is that palm nuts need to be processed within 24 hours of harvesting. If there is only one mill in the vicinity of smallholders' land, it should be ensured that the smallholders, as price takers, receive a fair price from the milling facility. Moreover, if a substantial amount of land in the vicinity of the milling facility is used for palm oil production, this might have important microeconomic effects for the local

This can enable poor people in agrarian or remote areas to plant some of the land with certain fuel crops or trees with oily seeds, such as jatropha. Locally produced biofuels could provide enough energy for a relatively small electricity grid in a village or community. While such small-scale local production may perhaps not be the most economically efficient (in the sense that more working hours are needed per litre biofuel), it could at least increase local communities' energy supply.[117] It may prove especially useful for more remote villages, where oil prices are even higher because of substantial transportation costs. This would have the added advantage of a more reliable, less volatile energy supply than with traditional oil.

In many developing countries, women and girls have the burden of gathering wood for cooking and heating. Local biofuel production made of agricultural waste could save them much time and possibly dangerous trips to woodlands. The shift to local biofuel production could decrease the absence of young girls at school, as they no longer would have to help find dead wood. It could also result in women having more time for personal development or for earning a partial income, for example, by allowing them to grow a fuel crop, mill it and sell it to nearby plants. Moreover, it would seriously reduce the health risks related to indoor pollution from burning traditional biomass. Cooking and heating with dead wood is one of the major causes of sickness or death in many poor households, causing more fatalities than malaria.[118]

A crucial condition for promoting local energy supply from biofuels is that the mills needed for the conversion of biomass into fuel must be affordable. These machines should also be easily available, and easy to use and maintain. Machines for which spare parts are hard to find or very costly will not be very effective.

---

population (both for the price of palm oil used as cooking oil and the impact on the prices for other food crops). See World Bank, above n 12, 148, Box 3.4.

[117] For example, a project in a village in the south of Mali aims to plant 1,000 hectares of jatropha in order to fuel a power plant that would ensure the energy needs of more than 10,000 citizens. Another project in that country aims at encouraging the growing of jatropha near villages, in order to provide an alternative to expensive fossil fuels. Women have converted the oily seeds into biofuels, increasing their income and social standing. Such initiatives clearly reflect a large development potential for underdeveloped areas. See UN-Energy, above n 13, 8; see also Kojima and Johnson, above n 30, 130–31.

[118] See, eg WHO, 'Indoor Pollution and Health', Fact Sheet No 292 (June 2005); KR Smith, 'Health Impacts of Household Fuelwood Use in Developing Countries' (FAO, 2006), available at http://www.fao.org/docrep/009/a0789e/a0789e09.html.

III. EVALUATING BIOFUELS FROM THE PERSPECTIVE OF THE RIGHT TO FOOD

It is clear that biofuels could be either a blessing or a curse. It all depends on the broader policy frameworks that are implemented, which must ensure that the biofuel boom fully realises its potential advantages while mitigating or neutralising the potentially severe consequences. As phrased in one study: 'it is important for policymakers to keep in mind that there are really two different biofuel "worlds": large-scale, high-tech production, and smaller-scale, low-tech biofuel production focused primarily on poverty alleviation through rural energy provision and local agro-industry development'.[119] The Food and Agriculture Organization of the UN (FAO) has remarked that 'if biofuels are to deliver on the huge promises in terms of rural development and the environment, there is a pressing need for transparent and internationally agreed governance'.[120] The FAO has further stressed the importance of human-rights-based bioenergy governance. This section explores which measures states could take in order to comply with their obligations to respect the right to food and which responsibilities may be imposed on private companies.

A. States' Obligations Towards the Right to Food

In the context of biofuel production, states' obligations concerning the right to food encompass two levels. First, a state has to ensure that its biofuel policy does not infringe on the right to food of the people under its jurisdiction. Secondly, a state has the additional duty to not jeopardise the right to food of people in other countries.

On the first level, that of a state's jurisdiction, the traditional triple duty rests upon a state to respect, protect and fulfil the right to food. This means that each state should undertake a comprehensive and participatory assessment of its biofuel policies. Such assessment should, first, provide a detailed feasibility study for biofuel production, including an examination of available land and water resources and the expected yields for specific crops. Secondly, it should evaluate the range of potential impacts of a biofuel-promoting policy. Thirdly, it should assess the capacity and resources available to mitigate the negative consequences of such policy, in order to ensure not only that the overall impact of a biofuel policy is positive, but also that those most vulnerable in society do not bear the burden of the policy.

---

[119] The Worldwatch Institute, above n 6, 311.
[120] FAO, 'Right to Food and Bioenergy, FOCUS ON' (2007).

The definition of the right to food, as formulated by the Special Rapporteur, comprises different aspects.[121] It is defined as the right to have regular, permanent and unrestricted access, either directly or by means of financial purchases, to quantitatively and qualitatively adequate and sufficient food corresponding to the cultural traditions of the people to which the consumer belongs, and which ensure a physical and mental, individual and collective, fulfilling and dignified life free of fear.

Biofuel production has the potential to affect some of these aspects of the right to food.

The food-versus-fuel competition touches on the availability, ie the physical accessibility, of food. Depending on various factors—including how much land will be used for fuel crops, the progress in technology, crop yields and national blending mandates—the question could arise as to whether enough food can be produced to feed the world's growing population. At present, the global food supply is more than sufficient to feed every single human being, and the global hunger problem is due to the inequitable distribution of food to those most in need. In other words, the greatest imminent threat to the right to food is not the physical availability of food, but the economic accessibility of sufficient and qualitatively satisfactory food. The World Bank estimates that cereal production will need to be increased by 50% and meat production by 85% by 2030 in order to satisfy projected demand; this does not take into account the demand for land for biofuel production, or the fact that climate change may cause lower crop yields.[122] This could change the current situation in which there is, theoretically at least, sufficient food for everyone.

The use of marginal lands for biofuel production is not a sufficient guarantee that arable land will not be diverted from food production. Even when the use of marginal lands increases the total land available for both food and fuel crops, the growing demand for both will probably continue to lead to rising land prices. Large agribusiness and investors would still be able to buy up the most fertile lands, though, resulting in the highest yields and hence fortifying their market strength relative to smaller farmers, who would be relegated to less fertile lands. Consequently, states should implement policies that limit arable land from being used for fuel production, in order not to widen the poverty gap.

Small-scale farming is preferable in respect of its environmental impact, as well as its implications for employment and empowerment of the local poor.[123] Small farmers, however, are generally more risk averse than larger companies, because any failure in experimenting

---

[121] See also FAO, Voluntary Guidelines, above n 64, 15.
[122] See World Bank, above n 12, 148.
[123] See, eg FAO, 'Making Sustainable Biofuels Work for Smallholder Farmers and Rural Households' (2009).

will lead to substantial income loss. States should launch information campaigns and knowledge-sharing platforms to encourage small farmers to produce biofuels on part of their land for consumption at the family or community level. An additional problem that small-scale farmers face is their lack of access to credit at affordable terms. Responsible microcredit systems could be encouraged to tackle this problem.[124]

By developing a framework that enhances employment opportunities for its poorest citizens, a state can help to meet its obligation to fulfil the right to food by ensuring its citizens' 'economic accessibility' to food. To prevent a violation of the right to food, it is critical that states ensure that the biofuel market does not follow the example of the present, highly monopolised agricultural market. Policies should be put in place to ensure that small-scale farmers have a substantial role to play in the production chain, and that they are not merely price takers. Such policies could take the form of a supportive framework for decentralised production. Potential policies could include imposing highly reduced taxes up to a certain quantity of production, facilitating microcredit, organising cooperatives of small-scale farmers and promoting local small-scale use of biofuels. Another option is to promote contract farming to provide small farmers with assured market access on fair terms. Further, the Special Rapporteur has looked into the question of whether competition law could be used to prevent the concentration of economic power in the hands of a few players. As the Special Rapporteur remarks, existing competition laws focus on protecting consumers from abusive practices of dominant players, rather than protecting producers from dominant buyers. States could analyse how to amend existing competition rules accordingly.[125] Competition law should also allow national competition authorities to investigate the abuse of dominant positions of middle men vis-à-vis producers located abroad.

As to the choice of crops to be grown for biofuels, states could favour those crops that allow for intercropping. Jatropha can once more be cited as an example. Even though this tree has not produced the expected yields under suboptimal soil and water conditions, it could be planted together with food crops. Jatropha has the advantage of providing a natural hedge against animals, preventing soil erosion and improving soil quality. Intercropping could allow families to grow food and biofuel feedstock at the same time, which mitigates food-versus-fuel competition. Its physical and chemical properties make it very suitable for

---

[124] Examples of other solutions are found in India, where poor families have been given a piece of degraded land to plant jatropha, and in Honduras, where small farmers were given loans to plant jatropha that could be repaid in the form of a certain weight of the trees' fruits (if the yields are sufficient to repay the loan and make a decent living). See Regional Hunger and Vulnerability Programme (RHVP), 'Biofuel Production and the Threat to South Africa's Food Security', Wahenga Brief 11 (April 2007).

[125] De Schutter, above n 111, 35.

processing into biodiesel. Seeds can be stored, so that processing can be delayed. The oil can also be used directly in lamps and cooking stoves, as well as in certain adapted diesel engines.[126] A state should also diligently assess whether its biofuel policy creates employment opportunities, while ensuring that the jobs created will provide decent working conditions and fair wages. Where possible, states could promote biofuels from more labour-intensive crops. This could include favouring biodiesel production over ethanol, as harvesting the oily seeds used for biodiesel is often more labour-intensive and less susceptible to mechanisation than ethanol.[127] Presently, the biodiesel market is still much smaller than the ethanol market, although quite a few countries are experimenting with oily crops and trees for biodiesel, such as India with jatropha or Malaysia and Indonesia with palm oil. Another advantage of biodiesel made from oilseed crops is that the processing is easier than for ethanol. This could ensure that even those communities with less technology or capital could have a role to play in biofuel processing.[128]

It is somewhat surprising that so many commentators discuss the question of whether public policy should favour small-scale bioenergy production merely in terms of costs and benefits. Certainly, a biofuel policy favouring local small-scale farmers may be economically less efficient, in the sense that it may require more labour input. However, this discussion should not be exclusively framed in economic terms. In light of states' obligations under the right to food, the question should not merely be whether supportive policies for small-scale farmers are more costly than allowing large companies to take over the market. On the contrary, every decision should be guided by a state's obligation to ensure the right to food for its entire population, and especially those most vulnerable. As a general rule, a state should ensure that, when public money is used to subsidise green energy, safeguards are put in place in order to guarantee that this public money does not primarily end up in the pockets of large agribusinesses instead of local farmers. Indeed, a people-centred approach can be more efficient than a profit-centred one, if it prevents people from falling into poverty, which in turn prevents the need for public social expenditures.

In short, domestic frameworks should be based on a comprehensive analysis to ensure that domestic policies take into account the entire complexity of the biofuel question. This means that, at the domestic level, different government departments should be involved in drafting

---

[126] FAO Jatropha Report, above n 12, 24–25 (provides overview of strengths and weaknesses of jatropha).

[127] This can make biodiesel more expensive than ethanol, a handicap that will need to be mitigated in other ways, for example by levying lower taxes.

[128] Small-scale production of straight vegetable oil requires the least economies of scale; it thus has the greatest potential to benefit small farmers and rural development, according to the FAO. FAO Jatropha Report, above n 12, 6.

the national biofuel policy, including the departments of energy, agriculture, economy, rural development, trade and international development. In addition to a variety of actors, the process should address a variety of issues. Those should include, among others: a detailed assessment of the availability of land and water; climatic conditions; the economic, social and environmental advantages and disadvantages of the different feasible crops; land titles; economic access to land; infrastructure;[129] food availability; deforestation and involuntary resettlement; biodiversity; soil depletion and pollution; and the optimal use of by-products.

An adequate policy framework should start with identifying the most food-insecure segments of the population, then determining whether they have clear land titles, how they make their living and what the consequences of potential biofuel policies would be on their economic, social and environmental living conditions. This assessment should be undertaken through a participatory process, as the local population is likely to have the best insights in the economic, social and environmental dynamics of their surroundings. Secondly, cross-department policy framing should take place. The importance of the department that is selected to coordinate research on biofuels should not be underestimated. Departments of energy, trade or agriculture each have their own angle from which to interpret information. However, in light of the right to food, the information generated by this cross-departmental dialogue should be human rights oriented. One obvious way to do this would be to put the national human rights department in charge (where such an entity exists). If there is no such department, the state should guarantee that human rights experts are consulted, in order to ensure that the assessment of information is human rights based. Such an assessment should include demarcating how much and which land can be used for biofuels and how much land is needed to secure the food supply. In addition, the policy framework should unequivocally prohibit clearing forests or other vital ecosystems, to prevent biofuels from generating more GHG emissions than savings. Moreover, it should ensure that the local population can retain the land they need for subsistence activities and ensure that these lands are protected by clear land titles. The phenomenon of land grabbing, which intensifies due to increasing food prices, makes the need for clear and fair land titles even more urgent.[130] Thirdly, clear benchmarks or 'danger signals' should be formulated in order to monitor whether the biofuel policy stays on track.

---

[129] The need for infrastructure includes the availability of non-exclusive upstream channels through which farmers can receive a fair price for their products. The availability of computer kiosks in villages is one way to ensure that farmers are aware of the market price for their products.

[130] On this phenomenon, refer to De Schutter, above n 66.

It would help to designate specific departments or people in charge of the monitoring progress.

At the international level, states should not infringe on the right to food of people outside their territory. Over one billion people suffering from hunger is already a scandalously unacceptable number, and even worse is the fact that the number has continued to increase since 1996. In a world where hunger kills 25,000 humans per day—more than malaria, AIDS and tuberculosis combined—the duty of states not to violate the right to food of populations abroad should be at the centre of international attention.[131]

The international dimension of the problem is illustrated by the statement of the former Special Rapporteur that the biofuel hype can be labelled a 'crime against humanity'.[132] If the international community reserves the right to intervene in internal conflicts when serious human rights violations occur, there is no reason to be less vociferous when the basic human right to food—and hence the very right to life—is being jeopardised not simply in one country but all over the world. This is all the more true if those basic human rights violations are, in large part, a direct result of the developed world's biofuel targets. Taken together, these factors make a coordinated international reaction to current biofuel policies even more urgent. As at the national level, any attempts for 'global governance' on biofuel policies should integrate different issues, such as trade, the environment, rural development and patents.

The extraterritorial obligation of states to respect the right to food in other countries also holds true for their participation in international institutions. For example, member states of the World Bank should use their leverage to ensure that any project supported by the World Bank Group has undertaken a genuine impact assessment regarding the right to food. This currently does not always happen.[133]

States should also assess whether there are more efficient ways to combat GHG emissions than by promoting biofuels, and whether such alternatives would be less likely to jeopardise the right to food. Some examples could be to make more efficient or electric-powered cars, to promote good insulation of buildings, to discourage excess plastic packaging of products and the consumption of products with a high carbon footprint due to long transportation routes, and to further develop wind and solar energy. Another effective tool may be to reward those countries that protect the integrity of their forests and other land that is

---

[131] UN-Energy, above n 13, 32.
[132] R Domingo, 'Biofuels Drive Threatening Food Security', *Consumer Watchdog, Inquirer*, 11 April 2007.
[133] For example, the Norwegian government was criticised by an NGO report for supporting projects through the World Bank, IMF or WTO that violate the right to food. FIAN International, 'The Right to Adequate Food and the Compliance of Norway with its Extraterritorial Obligations', FIAN document No D43e (2 May 2005).

stocking high amounts of carbon. For example, countries can earn carbon credits for a commitment not to clear forests. However, the value of such carbon certificates would need to equal or outweigh possible gains by expanded biofuel production. Climate change negotiations could aim at improving the financial incentive for states to preserve the 'lungs' of the world.

B. The Responsibilities of Private Actors

This chapter has so far focused on state policies and obligations, because they are the direct holders of the duties under the right to food. However, they are not the only players: companies hold a dominant role in the biofuel boom too. This chapter has largely ignored their role, however, because it is unclear to what extent duties arising out of the right to food can be imposed on such non-state actors. This does not mean that companies do not have obligations, though. As the former Special Rapporteur has noted, 'all corporations involved in the production in biofuels should avoid complicity in these violations'.[134] Moreover, companies could still be held responsible for their involvement in more specific human rights violations linked to biofuel production, such as illegal land acquisitions or forced evictions to make way for plantations. In this respect, they face the same legal and reputational risks as any other business.

Some companies, especially transnational ones in the extractive industry, have realised the value of undertaking human rights and assessing social and environmental impacts prior to the implementation of projects. Perhaps it is time for agricultural companies to follow that example. It may be difficult to convince companies to undertake and abide by such human rights impact assessments; nevertheless, many western companies are investing in biofuel plantations in developing countries. For those companies active abroad, there is a strong argument that they have a due diligence requirement to undertake an impact assessment on local food security. This concept of due diligence has been promoted by the Special Representative of the Secretary-General on human rights and transnational corporations and other business enterprises. National corporate law could facilitate the use of concepts such as due diligence to hold companies within their jurisdiction accountable for violations of the right to food and other human rights abroad, even if those violations are committed by subsidiaries.

In addition to companies, NGOs have an important role to play, by documenting the impact of biofuel policies on the right to food, including

---

[134] Ziegler, above n 5, 38.

instances of forced resettlement; measurable price increases of land, food and water; and deforestation or other environmental impacts. NGOs can also assist local communities and other groups in legal and advocacy efforts. For example, the Center for International Environmental Law has assisted over 700 community members and ex-sugarcane workers from Nicaragua to file a complaint with the International Finance Corporation (IFC) for health and environmental damages caused by a sugarcane company.[135]

IV. CONCLUSION: BAN BIOFUELS?

An unconditional and general ban on biofuels seems unrealistic and probably undesirable. Biofuels seem to have at least the potential to produce an overall positive outcome. Rather than throwing away the baby with the bathwater, it seems more useful to invest in research to fully realise their potential. Nevertheless, first-generation biofuels should be regarded with necessary suspicion. The former Special Rapporteur called for a five-year moratorium on existing first-generation biofuels production until second-generation biofuels are commercially viable. It is not very realistic, however, to expect that all ongoing production and expansion would be halted—even though the industry could be slowed down by revising current ambitious targets. At the same time, such statements are useful to frame the debate and ensure that the discussion on green energy incorporates a human rights perspective. Instead of calling for a general ban, it is better to be more nuanced. For example, a moratorium on industrial fuels could be implemented until the necessary mapping exercises have been undertaken to assess to what extent current technologies could be used sustainably on available land without displacing or endangering food production and accessibility. At the same time, small-scale biofuel production facilitating local energy supply could be promoted with a view to assisting local economic development. Policies that encourage intercropping could help promote local energy supply without endangering local food production.

Research into second-generation biofuels should be continued in order to make them commercially viable as quickly as possible. In this scenario, more efficient (meaning both economically efficient and environmentally and socially sustainable) technology could be developed, which would

---

[135] The IFC had granted the company a $55 million loan in 2006 to expand its sugarcane production and build an ethanol plant. The complaint raises concerns about the health consequences of field burning and the chemicals used on the plantation, as well as the substantial volume of water used to process the ethanol. The negotiations that were conducted as a result of the complaint resulted in certain commitments from the company concerned. See Office of the Compliance Officer/Ombudsman (CAO) of the IFC, available at www.cao-ombudsman.org/cases/case_detail.aspx?id=82.

give companies a commercial incentive to shift to those more sustainable second-generation biofuels. Second-generation biofuels may nevertheless have their own negative effects. Even if only crop residues and other waste material were used for second-generation biofuels, prices for these products would still increase. Moreover, if research leads to the development of certain crops that have higher yields of waste material (for example, sugarcane with more leaves and stalks), those plants may require increased inputs, such as fertiliser. In addition, as waste products become commercially valuable, it will be more difficult to convince farmers to leave their waste materials on the fields as natural fertilisers. The use of waste materials for fuel production could make animal feed produced from such waste more expensive. In short, even the successful development of commercially viable second-generation biofuels will need a sound policy framework to mitigate negative effects.

The large amount of research that still needs to be undertaken will require at least partial public funding. That should be preceded by a clear policy on the relationship between public funding and private patents. It is unacceptable that public funding is used to support research that leads to highly protective private patents. The purpose of patents is to ensure that companies are rewarded for their research. Such incentives should not be necessary when most of the funding comes from public sources.

In short, biofuels could be an impetus for innovative and progressive rethinking of agricultural trade and patents, which could have broader ripple effects on other industries that face similar problems. On the other hand, biofuel production could continue as just more business as usual. In that case, it will aggravate existing inequities and further widen the poverty gap. The current agricultural market, with its subsidies and protectionist measures, will destroy a large part of the potential benefit to poor countries that biofuels offer. The negative effects would be further aggravated by the lack of domestic measures to protect the environment against the increasing expansion of agricultural land, as well as against increased monoculture, water shortages and pollution. Without the indispensable regulatory framework, the biofuel boom may indeed come close to what the former Special Rapporteur described as a crime against humanity. States and companies can no longer use ignorance as an excuse: the thirty-year experience in Brazil and the growing body of scientific evidence leaves no doubt as to the potential destructive consequences of the current biofuel boom.

Although domestic policies are important, it is clear that the biofuel issue cannot be resolved by countries in isolation. Rather, a transnational framework must be set up, analogous to the Kyoto Protocol. Some transnational, multi-stakeholder initiatives are already surfacing. One such initiative is the Roundtable on Sustainable Palm Oil, set up in August 2003, which comprises international and local organisations as well as major producers; it is unfortunately underrepresented by small-scale farmers. South–south cooperation is also on the rise. Brazil, as an experienced major ethanol producer, can share its valuable experiences with developing countries seeking to reap the fruits of the biofuel boom.[136] The UN Environment Programme's REED (Rural Energy Enterprise Development) Programme offers start-up financing to bioenergy enterprises in Brazil, China and five African countries. In 2005, the UN Conference on Trade and Development (UNCTAD) launched its Biofuels Initiative, while another initiative, the Global Bioenergy Partnership,[137] grew out of the G-8 commitment of 2005.

Other promising signs are, for example, the mounting pressure on the EU to constantly fine-tune its biofuel policies in accordance with scientific findings, and the cooperation agreement recently signed between the Netherlands and Brazil to produce biofuels in a sustainable way. During the negotiations, the Dutch insisted on independent monitoring in order to ensure that no forests were cleared for biofuel production. The Brazilian government, on the other hand, called for lifting import duties for ethanol in the EU. Such compromises increase efficiency—in the broad sense—for both parties.

At present, several international bodies are involved in assessing the impact of biofuels. This fragmentation of research could lead to overlaps and gaps, duplication of efforts, and uncoordinated approaches, consequently making it harder to efficiently collect all the available information. On the other hand, the fact that different institutes are delving into the matter, each with a different focus, ensures that a number of bodies are integrating the biofuel dilemma into their respective policies. The more entities that take up the issue, the more the biofuel debate is stimulated.

In short, a plethora of fora seems to be a good thing for scientific purposes. Studies on the economic, environmental and—to a lesser extent—social impacts of biofuels are plentiful. There are, however, few studies that collect all the information in order to assess it specifically in light of the right to food. This should be remedied. On the international level, the Human Rights Council is perhaps the best placed to fulfil this role. The Council would not only be able to collect the relevant information, but could also act upon it, by issuing recommendations or asking for further studies on specific aspects. As the FAO states, 'as the missing link, the rights-based approach can establish credible and legally binding inter-sectoral umbrella principles'.[138]

The aim of this chapter was not to provide another study containing numbers and formulas; rather, it was to bring together the main findings

---

[136] For examples of such cooperation, see ActionAid, above n 14, 11.
[137] See Global Bioenergy Partnership, available at www.globalbioenergy.org.
[138] FAO, above n 120.

of such studies in light of the right to food. It has sought to clarify that biofuel policies can have an impact on the right to food through a variety of direct and indirect factors. No accurate assessment of the concrete impact of biofuels can be given in studies that do not take account of these various factors, however complex the different dynamics may be to analyse. It is, of course, easier to show the open questions than to provide an answer. Nevertheless, knowing what the questions are is the first step in providing the answers.

Part II

Trade and Aid: An Enabling International Environment

5

International Trade in Agriculture and the Right to Food

OLIVIER DE SCHUTTER

THIS CHAPTER EXPLORES the relationship between the Agreements of the World Trade Organization (WTO) and the obligation of the members of the WTO to respect the human right to adequate food, as recognised under international law.[1] The most important achievement of the General Agreement on Tariffs and Trade (GATT) and, since 1994, the WTO has been to provide states with a rule-based, predictable international trade system, now backed by the threat and imposition of economic sanctions under the Dispute Settlement Understanding of the WTO. Here, I ask what impact the multilateral trading system thus set up has on the ability of the WTO members to comply with their obligations towards the right to adequate food. I explore, in particular, what incentives trade liberalisation in agricultural commodities creates for governments, and whether such incentives are conducive to the full realisation of the right to adequate food.[2]

The background of this discussion is as follows. Since the 2007–08 food prices crisis, there has been renewed interest in using international trade rules to support a more enabling environment for food security.

---

[1] See Art 25 of the Universal Declaration on Human Rights (GA Res 217 A (III), UN document A/810, 71 (1948)) and Art 11 of the International Covenant on Economic, Social and Cultural Rights (adopted on 16 December 1966, GA Res 2200(XXII), UN GAOR, 21st sess, Supp No 16, UN Doc A/6316 (1966), 993 UNTS 3). The right to adequate food is also referred to in the Convention on the Rights of the Child (Art 24(2)(c)) and in the International Convention on the Elimination of All Forms of Discrimination Against Women (Art 12(2)).

[2] This chapter is based on the report the author presented to the Human Rights Council following his mission to the World Trade Organization in June 2008. See O De Schutter, UN Special Rapporteur on the Right to Food, 'Mission to the World Trade Organization', delivered to the Human Rights Council', UN document A/HRC/10/005/Add.2 (March 2009), an expanded version of which was published in the Dialogue on Globalization—Occasional Papers series of the Friedrich-Ebert Stiftung (No 46, November 2009).

The international community has reiterated its support for conclusion of the WTO Doha Round trade negotiations on agriculture as a long-term response to the food crisis. Statements to this effect were made repeatedly at the highest level. In the L'Aquila Joint Statement on Global Food Security of July 2009, the leaders of the G-8 and of 19 other states, joined by the major international agencies both within and outside the UN, committed to 'reduce trade distortions and refrain from raising new barriers to trade and investment and from implementing WTO-inconsistent measures to stimulate exports'. 'To this end,' they added, 'we aim at an ambitious, comprehensive and balanced conclusion of the Doha Development Round and call for renewed, determined efforts to bring it to a timely and successful conclusion' (at paragraph 7). A similar pledge was made at the World Summit on Food Security convened in Rome on 16–18 November 2009.[3] At the same time, however, WTO members remain deeply divided over the future direction of agricultural trade policy, and the Doha Round negotiations have been at a virtual standstill since the middle of 2008. The existing divergences go beyond disagreements about the level of concessions each WTO member is prepared to make for the sake of achieving an agreement; they increasingly reflect a conflict between two views about how to ensure food security at the domestic level.[4]

One view sees the lowering of obstacles to trade in agricultural commodities as an important contribution to food security. At the risk of oversimplification, there seem to be two major arguments in favour of this view. The first argument follows the classic theory of comparative advantage: whether the comparative advantage of each country is defined according to its labour productivity, as in the original model of Ricardo, or, as in the Heckscher–Ohlin theorem, according to its endowment in factors of production such as land, water and labour, all countries will gain if food is produced in the locations that are comparatively better at doing so. That view was particularly convincing during the 1980s and 1990s, when the current international trade regime for agriculture was created. At the time, overproduction and declining prices dominated the agenda. The presumption that this would continue dominated the

---

[3] See the Declaration of the World Summit on Food Security, document WSFS 2009/2, para 22.

[4] The reference to 'food security' in the context of international discussions is of course not innocuous: it implies a focus on the objective of ensuring that each person can be fed, wherever the food originates from and whomever produces the food available. In contrast, a reference to food sovereignty—the paradigm opposite to that of food security—draws our attention to the questions of who produces, for whom and under what conditions. Finally, an approach defined by reference to the right to food emphasises issues of accountability, transparency and participation, and the obligations of states that correspond to the right to food of the individual. For a comparison between the 'food security' paradigm and the right-to-food based approach, see K Mechlem, 'Food Security and the Right to Food in the Discourse of the UN' (2004) 10 *European Law Journal* 631.

international trade regime that was agreed upon following the Uruguay round of negotiations of the GATT. Against this background of declining prices, many poor countries considered it less costly to import food than to produce it locally, and a shift to greater food imports thus appeared as a secure and low-cost means of food provision. Developing countries were encouraged to restructure their domestic agricultural sectors away from food production for local consumption to specialised commodity production for export. While the liberalisation programme included in the Agreement of Agriculture was expected to lead to a rise in the prices of food commodities—compensating in part for the structural decline in prices—it was considered that the resulting balance-of-payments problems could be easily met through temporary support measures granted to the net food-importing least-developed countries (LDCs).

More recently, a second argument has emerged. It is based on the threats that many regions are facing regarding their ability to produce enough food to meet their consumption needs. Climate change, which translates as more frequent and extreme weather events such as droughts or floods and less predictable rainfall, is already having a severe impact on the ability of certain regions and communities to feed themselves, and it is destabilising markets. The acidification of oceans, a result of the greater carbon dioxide concentration in the atmosphere, is destroying coral reefs, leading to a decrease in fish stocks. The change in average temperatures is threatening the ability of entire regions, particularly those living from rainfed agriculture, to maintain actual levels of agricultural production.[5] Less fresh water will be available for agricultural production, and the rise in sea levels is already causing the salinisation of water in certain coastal areas, making water sources improper for irrigation purposes. By 2080, 600 million additional people could be at risk of hunger as a direct result of climate change.[6] In sub-Saharan Africa, arid and semi-arid areas are projected to increase by 60–90 million hectares, and the Intergovernmental Panel on Climate Change estimated in 2007 that in Southern Africa yields from rainfed agriculture could be reduced by up to 50% between 2000 and 2020.[7] Losses in agricultural production in a number of developing countries, particularly in sub-Saharan Africa, could be partially compensated by gains in

---

[5] *Stern Review Report on the Economics of Climate Change* (Cambridge, Cambridge University Press, 2007) 67.

[6] UNDP, 'Human Development Report 2007/2008. Fighting Climate Change: Human Solidarity in a Divided World' (2007) 90 (citing R Warren, N Arnell, R Nicholls, P Levy and J Price, 'Understanding the Regional Impacts of Climate Change: Research Report prepared for the Stern Review on the Economic of Climate Change', Research Working Paper No 90 (Tyndall Centre for Climate Change).

[7] IPCC, *Climate Change 2007: Climate Change Impacts, Adaptation and Vulnerability. Working Group II Contribution to the Fourth Assessment Report of the Intergovernmental Panel on Climate Change* (Cambridge, Cambridge University Press, 2007) ch 9.

other regions, but the overall result would be a decrease of at least 3% in productive capacity by the 2080s, and up to 16% if the anticipated carbon fertilisation effects[8] fail to materialise.[9] The losses would be particularly important in Africa and Latin America, with 17 and 13% average losses, respectively, if the carbon fertilisation effects materialise, and 28 and 24%, respectively, in the absence of carbon materialisation effects.[10]

Against this changing background, food security is said to be achievable by improved trade: the more the most fragile regions will lose their ability to produce enough food to feed their population, the more international trade may be required in order to satisfy the increased needs of net food-importing countries. The volumes of food traded are predicted to more than double between 2000 and 2030 under a business-as-usual scenario, that is, if we do not invest massively in improving agriculture in Africa and if we do not improve the capacity of the countries concerned to cope with climate change.[11] Indeed, Article 11(2) of the International Covenant on Economic, Social and Cultural Rights alludes to the fact that, while certain regions may be producing too little food to feed their population, other regions may have surpluses: the free flow of food commodities would therefore be desirable, in that it enables the supply from food-surplus regions to be linked to food-deficit regions.[12]

There are also powerful counter-arguments to the view that facilitating international trade in agricultural commodities would contribute to the realisation of the right to food. First, we are witnessing the end of the era of cheap food. Population growth, the switch to more protein-rich diets in the large portion of developing countries that are succeeding in their fight against poverty, and the increased competition for the

---

[8] These consist in the incorporation of carbon dioxide in the process of photosynthesis, which uses solar energy to combine water and carbon dioxide to produce carbohydrates, with oxygen as a by-product (definition adapted from WR Cline, 'Global Warming and Agriculture. Impact Estimates by Country' (Center for Global Development and the Peterson Institute for International Economics, 2007) 24).

[9] Ibid, 96.

[10] Ibid. See also, confirming these views, DB Lobell et al, 'Prioritizing Climate Change Adaptation Needs for Food Security in 2030' (2008) 319 *Science* 607 (showing, on the basis of analysis of climate risks for crops in 12 food-insecure regions, that South Asia and Southern Africa are two regions that, without sufficient adaptation measures, will likely suffer negative impacts on several crops that are important to large food-insecure human populations).

[11] MW Rosegrant, S Msangui, T Sulser and C Ringler, 'Future Scenarios for Agriculture: Plausible Futures to 2030 and Key Trends in Agricultural Growth', background paper prepared for the World Development Report 2008.

[12] Art 11(2) of the Covenant, which recognises the 'fundamental right of everyone to be free from hunger', also requires states to adopt, 'individually and through international cooperation, the measures, including specific programmes, which are needed, *taking into account the problems of both food-importing and food-exporting countries, to ensure an equitable distribution of world food supplies in relation to need*' (emphasis added). It thus refers to food imports (and the corresponding exports) as a means to ensure the fundamental right to be free from hunger.

use of farmland between production of crops for food and for fuel all increase the pressure on the supply side of the global equation.[13] In the future, prices of food commodities on international markets will be more volatile, and they will be higher. By remaining dependent on imports to cover their food needs, therefore, poor countries are in a vulnerable situation, and this vulnerability is far more problematic now than it was 15 years ago, when the Uruguay round of trade negotiations was finalised.

Secondly, in this alternative view, the challenges posed by climate change are a reason to favour regimes that deconcentrate food production, and that encourage each region to satisfy its own needs to the largest extent possible. Indeed, it is where food production is concentrated in certain regions that the markets are most vulnerable to price shocks, as a result of those regions being affected by certain weather-related events. It is precisely because climate change is putting such a stress on food production that each region should strive towards being less dependent on international markets, which will be less reliable in the future.

Thirdly, the presumption that trade permits the efficient transfer of food supplies from surplus to deficit regions fails to take into account the wide differences in purchasing power of different regions, and the fact that hunger and malnutrition are generally not the result of the lack of food availability but, rather, of the inability for the poorest segments of the population to have access to food at an affordable price. Under a hypothetical fully liberalised trade regime, in the absence of transaction costs, food commodities would flow not from surplus to deficit regions, but from regions where food is produced at the most competitive prices to regions where there is a solvent demand, ie where the purchasing power of the populations is sufficient, in comparison to other markets, including the domestic markets of the source country. It should come as no surprise, therefore, if certain countries are net exporters of food while at the same time having a large segment of their population that is hungry. Also, among the net food-importing countries, a heavy dependence on food imports may not be a problem for some, since their revenues from exports are largely sufficient to make this solution sustainable. In contrast, for other countries, whose trade balance is negative or almost negative, being net importers may not be sustainable.

Fourth and finally, food availability, while certainly a necessary condition for the right to adequate food, is not a sufficient condition. The most pressing challenge today is to ensure accessibility of food for the poor and the marginalised. Trading more food will not help them if they are excluded from production and have no means to buy the food

---

[13] On these factors see O De Schutter, 'Background Note: Analysis of the World Food Crisis' (2 May 2008). See also A Evans, 'The Feeding of the Nine Billion: Global Food Security for the 21st Century', Chatham House Report (January 2009).

that arrives on the markets; and producing more food will not assist them in purchasing food if their incomes remain too low. The majority of hungry people in the developing world depend directly or indirectly on agriculture for their livelihoods.[14] They are hungry because they are poor: they are mostly net buyers of food,[15] and their incomes, which, on average, are significantly lower than those of the non-rural populations,[16] are insufficient to buy the food that they do not produce themselves. Any trade regime that does not benefit this group, by allowing them to raise their incomes through improved productivity levels, is bound to create more hunger rather than less.

This chapter seeks to contribute to the current debate about the relationship between trade in agricultural commodities and the realisation of the right to food, which has been sketched above. It is premised on the idea that our challenge today is not simply to produce more food and ensure that it flows as freely as possible from food-surplus to food-deficits regions, but is to organise such production so that it raises the incomes of those who are, today, most food insecure—small-scale farmers and agricultural labourers in developing countries—and to encourage modes of food production that are resource-conserving and that do not accelerate climate change. However, there is a conflict between the short-term objective of acquiring cheap food from abroad in order to supply the local markets and thus make food affordable for the poor, particularly the urban poor (or the important proportion of the rural poor that are net food buyers), and the long-term objective of allowing local producers to improve their productivity and serve the local markets without being subjected to the dumping of imported food commodities on these markets. The main difficulty that poor net food-importing countries are facing today is how to ensure this transition, towards a relocalisation of the food systems, that can lead to better

---

[14] Of the total of approximately one billion people who are hungry, 50% are among the 2.1 billion smallholders who currently are living off 2 hectares of cropland or less; 20% are landless labourers;10% of the hungry are pastoralists, fisherfolk and forest users; finally, the remaining 20% are the urban poor. See UN Millennium Project, *Halving Hunger: It Can be Done, Summary Version of the Report of the Task Force on Hunger* (New York: The Earth Institute at Columbia University, 2005) 6.

[15] The World Bank, 'World Development Report 2008—Agriculture for Development' (November 2007) 109 (box 4.7) (comparing representation among poor smallholders of net buyers of food, self-sufficient or net sellers: in all seven countries surveyed (Bolivia, Ethiopia, Bangladesh, Zambia, Cambodia, Madagascar, and Vietnam), the two first categories are a strong majority among poor smallholders).

[16] MA Aksoy, 'The Evolution of Agricultural Trade Flows' in MA Aksoy and JC Beghin (eds), *Global Agricultural Trade and Developing Countries* (Washington, DC, The World Bank, 2005) 17–19 (noting that '[o]n average, farmers are poorer than nonfarmers in developing countries . . . In all developing countries, rural households have lower average incomes than nonrural households. The ratio of rural incomes to nonrural incomes ranges from 40 to 75 percent, a relationship that remains consistent across groups of developing countries').

incomes in the rural areas and limit the dependency on the international markets.

The question is whether the project on which the WTO framework was built—gradually lowering the barriers to trade, whether in the form of tariffs or non-tariff barriers—contributes to these objectives or whether it makes them more difficult to achieve. If the latter, the question then becomes which measures can be taken to channel international trade in a direction that is more conducive to the realisation of the right to adequate food. This chapter addresses these questions. No position is adopted on whether, in comparison to the existing regime, the proposals made in the Doha Development Round of trade negotiations will bring about a significant improvement. This author shares the conviction of many that the current regime is severely distorted in favour of industrialised countries, and that it should be mended urgently. First, however, we must ask the more fundamental question of whether more trade is a desirable objective or whether the incentives it creates for states to invest in an export-oriented model of agricultural development do more damage than the benefits they bring about.

This chapter is divided into six sections. The first section briefly reviews the disciplines imposed on the WTO members under the Agreement on Agriculture concluded as part of the Agreements establishing the WTO.[17] Section II recalls why the current trade regime is considered unsatisfactory and inequitable towards developing countries, despite the 'special and differential treatment' provisions it includes. However, from the fact that current distortions are an obstacle to developing countries reaping the benefits from international trade in agriculture,

---

[17] See also the Report prepared on this issue by the High Commissioner for Human Rights, submitted in accordance with the Commission on Human Rights resolution 2001/32, E/CN.4/2002/54 (15 January 2002). In addition, see MG Desta, 'Food Security and International Trade Law: An Appraisal of the World Trade Organization Approach' (2001) 35 *Journal of World Trade* 449; C Downes, 'Must the Losers of Free Trade Go Hungry? Reconciling WTO Obligations and the Right to Food' (2007) 47 *Virginia Journal of International Law* 619; CG Gonzales, 'Institutionalizing Inequality: The WTO Agreement on Agriculture, Food Security, and Developing Countries' (2002), 27 *Columbia Journal of Environmental Law* 433; K Mechlem, 'Harmonizing Trade in Agriculture and Human Rights: Options for the Integration of the Right to Food into the Agreement on Agriculture' (2006) 10 *Max Planck Yearbook of UN Law* 127; M Ritchie and K Dawkins, 'WTO Food and Agricultural Rules: Sustainable Agriculture and the Human Right to Food' (2000) 9 *Minnesota Journal of Global Trade* 9; B Karapinar and C Häberli (eds), *Food Crises and the WTO* (Cambridge, Cambridge University Press, 2010). While other WTO agreements, particularly the General Agreement on Trade in Services (GATS) and the Agreement on Trade-Related Intellectual Property Rights (TRIPS), may have an impact on the right to adequate food—since they affect access to productive resources by food producers—the Agreement on Agriculture (AoA) constitutes the most important of the WTO agreements in the context of this paper, which focuses on the impact of trade liberalisation in agricultural commodities on the enjoyment of the right to adequate food. The discussion in this paper is therefore limited to this Agreement.

it does not follow that the pathway of reform premised on the need for more liberalisation shall benefit all developing countries equally, or even that it shall be beneficial to all. In order to illustrate this, section III discusses the ambiguous notion of establishing a 'level playing field' between countries, and considers whether the removal of existing 'distortions' to international trade would serve the needs of poor farmers in least-developed countries or, more generally, in poor food-deficit countries where hunger and malnutrition are currently concentrated. Section IV then examines the impacts of the removal of barriers to trade in agriculture on the right to food, focusing successively on the macroeconomic level and the position of countries in the international division of labour; on the microeconomic level and the shape of global supply chains; and on the non-economic dimensions of trade liberalisation, ie the impacts on the environment, as well as on nutrition and health. The conclusion of that section is that greater trade liberalisation is not necessarily a tool for improved food security or for the further realisation of the right to food. Rather, the priority for states should be to strengthen their own agricultural sector, thereby allowing the poorest segment of their populations to benefit from an increased income and additional source of employment. Section V lists a set of procedural recommendations that favour the reconciliation between the commitments of states under trade negotiations and their obligation towards the right to food of their populations. Finally, section VI concludes that the key challenge facing states is how to reconcile their short-term interest in buying food where it is produced at a lower cost, even if this means placing their less efficient producers in a perilous position, and their long-term interest in avoiding an excessive dependence on international markets for their food supplies and regaining a certain degree of self-sufficiency.

I. THE DISCIPLINES OF THE AGREEMENT ON AGRICULTURE: FROM MARRAKECH TO DOHA

Although agriculture was never formally exempted from the GATT disciplines, agriculture did occupy a highly specific position until the successful completion of the Uruguay Round of trade negotiations (1986–94), which put an end to its insulation from the trade liberalisation process. The Agreement on Agriculture (AoA) was adopted as part of this round of negotiations following the insistence of large agriculture-based developing countries. It imposed on WTO members, essentially, three sets of obligations.

(1) First, they were to increase market access for agricultural products. Under the AoA, all quantitative restrictions or other non-tariff measures

except those justified by health and safety reasons should be replaced by tariffs (Article 4.2), and members should subsequently bind themselves to reduce these tariffs (Article 4.1).[18] Products that are the predominant staple in the traditional diet of a developing country may be exempted from the tariffication obligation, however (Article 5).

Despite its promises, the process of tariffication and subsequent lowering of tariffs did not work equally for the benefit of all developing countries. Some developing countries, particularly in sub-Saharan Africa, rely more on agricultural products than on manufactured goods for their export revenues, yet average agricultural tariffs remain much higher than tariffs for non-agricultural products. Moreover, despite the special advantages given to least-developed countries[19] in initiatives such as the 'Everything But Arms' initiative of the EU,[20] high tariffs were maintained on developing country export products such as cotton, sugar, cereals and horticulture. Tariff peaks were maintained, and the tariffs on tropical products remain higher and more complex than those on temperate zone products. In addition, tariff escalation, which protects the processing industries of importing countries, creates an obstacle to the diversification of exports and the export by developing countries of higher-value-added products. This perverse structure of tariffs—which systematically disadvantages developing countries and works against, rather than in favour of, those countries climbing up the ladder of devel-

---

[18] Developed countries were to cut their tariffs by an average of 36% over 6 years; developing countries were to reduce their tariffs by an average of 24% over 10 years; least-developed countries did not have any reduction commitments imposed (see AoA, Art 15.2).

[19] There are altogether 49 least-developed countries (LDCs). The African LDCs are: Angola, Benin, Burkina Faso, Burundi, Cape Verde, Central African Republic, Chad, Comoros, Democratic Republic of Congo, Djibouti, Equatorial Guinea, Eritrea, Ethiopia, The Gambia, Guinea, Guinea-Bissau, Lesotho, Liberia, Madagascar, Malawi, Mali, Mauritania, Mozambique, Niger, Rwanda, Sao Tome and Principe, Senegal, Sierra Leone, Somalia, Sudan, Tanzania, Togo, Uganda and Zambia. The LDCs in the Asia-Pacific region are: Afghanistan, Bangladesh, Bhutan, Cambodia, Kiribati, Lao People's Democratic Republic, Maldives, Myanmar, Nepal, Samoa, Solomon Islands, Timor-Lesté, Tuvalu, and Vanuatu.

[20] This refers to a special arrangement benefiting the 49 LDCs, under which these countries are guaranteed duty-free and quota-free access to the EU market for all products except those listed under Chapter 93 of the Common Customs Tariff, which concerns arms and ammunition. The 'Everything-but-arms' initiative is part of the EU's Generalized System of Preferences initiated in 1971, and currently defined under a 2008 Regulation for 2009–11 (see Council Regulation (EC) No 732/2008 of 22 July 2008, applying a scheme of generalised tariff preferences for the period from 1 January 2009 to 31 December 2011 and amending Regulations (EC) No 552/97, (EC) No 1933/2006 and Commission Regulations (EC) No 1100/2006 and (EC) No 964/2007, [2008] OJ L211, 1). In addition to the EBA initiative for the LDCs, the GSP scheme comprises a general arrangement granted to all beneficiary countries that are not classified by the World Bank as high-income countries and that are not sufficiently diversified in their exports (176 countries currently benefit from this scheme); and a special incentive ('GSP+') arrangement for sustainable development and good governance, which benefits vulnerable countries that have ratified a number of conventions in the areas of human rights, labour rights, and the protection of the environment.

opment—is one of the major sources of discontent with the current multilateral trading regime.

(2) Secondly, the members were to reduce the level of domestic support (calculated through the concept of 'Aggregate Measure of Support' (AMS)[21]). But these subsidies are treated differently, depending on how much they are considered to distort trade. Three different categories were established. The first, residual category is referred to as the 'Amber Box' subsidies. All members may provide product-specific support up to a *de minimis* threshold (5% of the total value of production of the good concerned per year for developed countries; 10% for developing countries), and non-specific support for the same percentage, for instance to provide seeds or fertilisers to producers. Few of the developing countries in fact have the financial means required to reach those levels of support. Beyond the *de minimis* threshold, members must refrain from the introduction of new forms of support. In addition, they must reduce the existing domestic support they provide to their agricultural producers by 20% from the base period of 1986–88 for developed countries and by 13.3% for developing countries (LDCs are not under any obligation to reduce domestic support, although they are to bind support levels). Since these percentages are calculated on the basis of the Base Total Aggregate Measurement of Support in the base period, the arrangement is most beneficial to countries that already had high levels of support during the base period, since their advantage can be to a certain extent maintained. In that sense, the AoA maintains and legitimises imbalances between countries, based on their respective ability to support their agricultural producers.

Some forms of support to domestic agricultural producers do not fall under the undertakings described above. 'Blue Box' measures are direct payments made against production-reducing commitments, a system that is particularly important to the EU under the Common Agricultural Policy. These payments are considered to be less trade distorting, because they do not encourage overproduction and dumping of surpluses on the international markets. These measures are therefore exempted from reduction commitments under the AoA. Again, however, these are not forms of support that developing countries can afford for their farmers. Thus, this exemption in practice only benefits producers in the north, and there is no prohibition to export to developing countries the products that are thus indirectly subsidised. Finally, 'Green Box' measures are

[21] This refers to the levels of support received for each product, as calculated under the complex rules set out in annexes 3 and 4 of the Agreement on Agriculture. AMS includes (i) 'price support', measured by multiplying the difference between the applied administered price and the world market price by the quantity of production eligible to receive the administered price; (ii) product-specific subsidies; and (iii) non-product-specific subsidies. Whether they are product-specific or non-product-specific, subsidies are included in the calculation of the current total AMS only if they exceed the relevant *de minimis* level.

considered not to distort trade or to distort trade only minimally; they too are exempt. Domestic support measures may be placed in this category (i) if they are 'provided through a publicly-funded government programme (including government revenue foregone) not involving transfers from consumers'; and (ii) if they do not have the effect of providing price support to producers (AoA, Annex 2, 1). Such measures are, for example, investments in research, marketing or promotion, or they may consist in the provision of rural infrastructure (although the 'subsidized provision of on-farm facilities other than for the reticulation of generally available public utilities' and 'subsidies to inputs or operating costs' are explicitly excluded). This also includes public stockholding for food security purposes or domestic food aid, provided that it is distributed 'subject to clearly defined criteria related to nutritional objectives'.

(3) Thirdly, the members must reduce existing export subsidies, and they may not introduce new export subsidies not already in operation in the 1986–90 base period. Under the AoA, developed countries must reduce their export subsidies by 36% in value terms and by 21% in terms of the volumes benefiting from subsidies over a period of 6 years, as compared to the base period. Developing countries are subjected to fewer obligations in this regard, and they have longer implementation periods. The LDCs are under no obligation to reduce whichever export subsidies they may have. However, since the introduction of any new export subsidies is prohibited, the system has in fact been advantageous to developed countries, as they were the only category of states to have significant export subsidies in place prior to the entry into force of the AoA.

Export subsidies are the most harmful form of subsidies for developing countries. They lead to subsidised products arriving on domestic markets and displacing local production, which typically cannot benefit from levels of support that would allow it to remain competitive. In the short term, this means that the groups of the population in developing countries that are not producers competing with imported products will benefit from cheaper prices. This has led certain commentators to note that developing countries that are net food-importing countries and their populations would, in general, be hurt by the inflationary impact of the removal of subsidies, aggravating the impact on food security of the current peak in prices.[22] But, as noted already in chapter 1 above, this

[22] See A Panagariya, 'Agricultural Liberalisation and the Least Developed Countries: Six Fallacies' [2005] *World Economy: Global Trade Policy* 1277; J Stiglitz and A Charlton, *Fair Trade for All. How Trade can promote Development* (Oxford, Oxford University Press, 2005) 233: '[developed countries'] domestic production support for price-sensitive necessities that are widely consumed in developing countries should be reduced gradually, with some of the savings in developed country subsidy budgets being directed at ameliorating the adjustment costs of those in the developing world. Many developing countries

also leads to a form of addiction to low-priced foods on the international markets that is not sustainable. In the long term, subsidies, particularly export subsidies, discourage local production in the importing countries, and create a dependency on international markets that represents a major source of vulnerability, particularly as the prices on international markets will be increasingly volatile.

A number of provisions sought to accommodate what the preamble of the AoA refers to as 'non-trade concerns', among which 'food security and the need to protect the environment' are explicitly mentioned. In particular, measures adopted by developing countries that seek to encourage agricultural and rural development, investment subsidies in agriculture, and agricultural input subsidies generally available to low-income or resource-poor producers in those countries are exempted from domestic support reduction commitments that would otherwise be applicable to such measures (Article 6.2). Other provisions aim at ensuring special and differential treatment for developing countries, in the form of longer implementation periods and reduced commitments (Article 15).[23] Yet, overall, the obligations established under the AoA clearly fit under a programme of trade liberalisation in agricultural products. The expectation, when the Uruguay Round was completed, was therefore that this programme would lead to increased food prices, particularly as the result of the phasing out or lowering of existing subsidies.[24] Article 16 of the AoA therefore provides that, in order to counteract the negative impacts this might produce on net food-importing developing countries, developed country members shall take the measures provided for under the Decision on Measures Concerning the Possible Negative Effects of the Reform Programme on Least-Developed and Net Food-Importing

in North Africa, sub-Saharan Africa and Latin America (though not Brazil, Argentina, or Mexico) rely on imports of subsidised grains and oilseeds from OECD producers. [These] countries are particularly exposed to agricultural reforms which might increase the price of some commodities'.

[23] See generally, on the provisions ensuring a special and differential treatment to developing countries, C Thomas and JP Trachtman (eds), *Developing Countries in the WTO Legal System* (Oxford, Oxford University Press, 2009). The idea, of course, is not a new one: for a history of the concept see JH Jackson, *World Trade and the Law of the GATT: A Legal Analysis of the General Agreement on Tariffs and Trade* (Indianapolis, IN, Bobbs-Merrill, 1969) 625–71; RE Hudec, *Developing Countries in the GATT Legal System* (Aldershot, Gower, 1987).

[24] More recent analyses have sought to estimate the increases of real international commodity prices following complete trade liberalisation: for example, increases are estimated to be 20.8% for cotton, 15.1% for oilseeds, 11.9% for dairy products, 7.0% for coarse grains and 5.0% for wheat (The World Bank, above n 15, 107 (fig 4.6)). It is not clear which methodology has been followed to arrive at these estimates. It is important to note, however, that the level of prices on international markets will not be determined by the production costs of farmers from OECD countries minus the subsidies from which they currently benefit; instead, since a relatively small percentage of the total food produced is in fact traded internationally, those prices will be close to the marginal cost of the most competitive producers from countries such as Brazil, Uruguay and Argentina, which combine a high degree of mechanisation with very low wages for agricultural workers.

Developing Countries (the Marrakesh Decision). In sum, while food security was recognised as a legitimate objective, it was to be achieved in principle not by retreating from the programme of trade liberalisation in agriculture, but by supporting countries through the reform programme, including, where necessary, by the delivery of food aid. This is the core philosophy underlying the system of the AoA. It is one that is premised on the ability of international markets to provide food security and, consistent with the idea that trade shall lead to allocative efficiency, it is one that considers that, far from having to achieve a certain degree of self-sufficiency in food, countries should specialise in the production of whatever they have a comparative advantage in, as this would suffice to bring them sufficient export revenues to buy food from abroad.

This was the framework existing when the Doha Development Round of trade negotiations was launched in November 2001. In the Ministerial Declaration adopted on 14 November 2001 at the Sixth Ministerial Summit held in Doha, the WTO members committed themselves to 'comprehensive negotiations aimed at: substantial improvements in market access; reductions of, with a view to phasing out, all forms of export subsidies; and substantial reductions in trade-distorting domestic support'. They also agreed to make special and differential treatment for developing countries 'an integral part of all elements of the negotiations', and to review the provisions relating to special and differential treatment in order to make them more precise, effective and operational.[25] At the Sixth WTO Ministerial Conference held in Hong Kong in December 2005, it was agreed that 'all forms of export subsidies and disciplines on all export measures with equivalent effect' would be eliminated by the end of 2013, with a substantial part of the elimination to be realised by the end of the first half of the implementation period; that developing countries could themselves designate some products as 'special products' for which tariff reductions will not be very stringent; and that developing countries could retain their permissible *de minimis* level of domestic subsidy.

Finally, the 2008 Draft Modalities presented to the negotiators within the WTO[26] show advances on several of the issues that have hitherto delayed the conclusion of an agreement. Those Draft Modalities anticipate cuts to the overall domestic subsidies that are trade distorting (including the 'Amber Box' Aggregate Measure of Support, the support under the *de minimis* threshold under this category of subsidies and the direct payments made against production-reducing commitments placed under the 'Blue Box' category), as well as a capping of per product

[25] See the Ministerial Declaration adopted on 14 November 2001 (WT/MIN(01)/DEC/1), paras 13 and 44.
[26] See Revised Draft Modalities for Agriculture, Committee on Agriculture, Special Session (TN/AG/W/4/Rev.4 (19 May 2008)).

Amber Box support. The Modalities also provide a tightening of Green Box provisions, particularly on income support, in order to ensure that they are really decoupled from production levels, as well as stricter rules for monitoring and surveillance. In order to improve market access for agricultural products, tariffs would be cut according to a formula that imposes deeper cuts on higher tariffs.[27] However, developing country members would have the right to designate up to one-third more tariff lines as 'Sensitive Products', allowing them to deviate from the otherwise applicable tiered reduction formula in final bound tariffs on products designated as sensitive.[28] The Special Agricultural Safeguard (SSG) would be eliminated in 7 years. Tariff escalation would also be reduced, and tariffs and tariff quotas should be simplified, while their administration would be better monitored. The liberalisation of tropical products would also be accelerated. Least developed countries would have duty-free and quota-free market access for at least 97% of products. Export subsidies granted by industrialised countries would be eliminated over a transition period of 5 years (with half of the elimination happening by the end of the second year). There would also be tighter provisions on export credit, guarantees and insurance, international food aid, and exports from state-owned trading enterprises. Finally, the Draft Modalities propose to modify Article 12 of the AoA in order to restrict export prohibitions or restrictions. When such prohibitions or restrictions are imposed, they should be notified to the Committee on Agriculture within 90 days of the adoption of the measure, and notice should be given of the reasons for introducing and maintaining such measures. In addition, existing export prohibitions and restrictions in foodstuffs and feeds under Article XI.2 (a) of GATT 1994 should be eliminated by the end of the first year of implementation, and any new export prohibitions or restrictions should not normally be longer than 12 months, and should only be longer than 18 months with the agreement of the affected importing members.

At the time of writing, the Doha Round of world trade negotiations still has not been concluded. It is stumbling particularly on the discussions surrounding the trade-distorting impacts of various forms of domestic support provided by developed countries to their farmers, and on the specifics of the special safeguard measure. The purpose of this chapter, however, is not to offer any detailed commentary of these negotiations; rather, it is to identify whether the general direction in which trade liberalisation is moving under the framework of the AoA, thus summarised, is compatible with the members' obligations towards the right to food. With this aim in mind, the next sections examine why the current regime is not benefiting the countries that need most to be

---

[27] See the tiered formula proposed under para 61 of the Revised Draft Modalities for Agriculture, and the other proposals in paras 62–65.
[28] Ibid, paras 71–78.

supported—poor developing countries—and in which directions it could be reformed.

II. THE DISCONTENTS OF THE CURRENT REGIME

There is general agreement that the current regime of international trade is not a satisfactory one. In particular, it has not worked for the benefit of smallholders in developing countries, who form the majority of those who are hungry in the world today. On their own domestic markets, agricultural producers from developing countries have often faced unfair competition from highly subsidised products exported by farmers from OECD countries. Government support to farmers in OECD countries was 258 billion USD in 2007, representing 23% of total farm receipts in these countries.[29] This is the lowest level of support since 1986 (when the estimates first were available) in proportion of the production value, but it still represents a very high level of support, against which developing countries are unable to compete.

In addition, agricultural producers from developing countries have faced important obstacles when seeking access to the high-value markets of industrialised countries. They have failed to benefit even from preferential schemes such as the African Growth and Opportunity Act or the Caribbean Basin Initiative of the US, the Everything But Arms initiative adopted by the EU in favour of least-developed countries referred to above, or the Cotonou Agreement between the European Commission and the African, Caribbean and Pacific countries.[30] This failure may be attributed, in part, to the complexity of the rules involved—particularly the requirements resulting from rules of origin—and to the non-tariff barriers that potential exporters face, linked in particular to standards requirements, including not only standards adopted under the Agreement on the Application of Sanitary and Phytosanitary Measures and the Agreement on Technical Barriers to Trade, but also standards set by private buyers.[31]

---

[29] 'Agricultural Policies in OECD Countries: At a Glance' (Paris, OECD, June 2008).
[30] For Africa, see UNCTAD, *Economic Development in Africa 2008—Export Performance Following Trade Liberalization: Some Patterns and Policy Perspectives* (Geneva, UNCTAD, 2008) ch. 2.
[31] M Garcia Martinez and P Poole, 'The Development of Private Fresh Produce Safety Standards: Implications for Developing and Mediterranean Exporting Countries' (2004) 29(3) *Food Policy* 229; LJ Unnevehr, 'Food Safety Issues and Fresh Food Product Export from LDCs' (2000) 23(3) *Agricultural Economics* 231. For a less pessimistic view, see SM Jaffee and S Henson, 'Agro-Food Exports from Developing Countries: The Challenges of Standards' in Ataman Aksoy and Beghin, above n 16, ch 6 (showing that in countries where private sector is well organised and in which public sector supports efforts of exporters, producers have been able to enter markets such as for seafood and fresh fruits and vegetables). In their study of the vegetable export chain in Senegal, Johan Swinnen and Miet Maertens conclude

Finally, as already mentioned, many agricultural products currently confront tariff peaks and tariff escalation (higher tariffs on processed products), which discourages diversification into higher value-added products, leading developing countries to an excessive dependence on an often limited number of primary commodities.[32] This is a point that I return to later, because it is key to understanding not only the current discontent with the existing system, but also why further trade liberalisation may not be the best way forward, if we replace trade within the broader framework of development.

As a result of a regime that is heavily biased against the interests of developing countries, the domestic agricultural sector in these countries has been unable to attract investment over the past 30 years. This has led to a vicious cycle in which this sector, because it faces unfair competition, further loses competitiveness. Indeed, not only did private investment not flow into this sector; it is also one which governments have for many years neglected.[33] The World Bank's Independent Evaluation Group (IEG) recognises that this failure is one not of developing countries alone, but of the international community as a whole, including of the World Bank itself.[34] Specifically, according to the IEG, too little has been done to support irrigation; to take into account the challenges posed by the great diversity of agro-ecological conditions in Africa; to devise effective strategies for countries to maintain their own food security; and to expand small farmers' access to credit and to markets by improvements in transport infrastructure. The percentage of official development assistance going to agriculture has declined significantly between 1980 and 2005, moving from 18% to only 4% of total official development assistance.[35] While the prices of agricultural inputs rose, farmers were not supported to cope with these cost increases, and their productivity suffered as a result. In addition, structural adjustment policies imposed on many developing countries as a condition for access to loans led to

that exports grew despite tightening standards: such tightening, they conclude, led to a shift from smallholder contract farming to integrated estate production, leading poorest households to benefit through being employed on such estates rather than by producing themselves for the global markets. M Maertens and JFM Swinnen, 'Trade, Standards and Poverty: Evidence from Senegal' (LICOS Centre for Institutions and Economic Performance & Department of Economics, KUL, 2008).

[32] AF McCalla and J Nash, *Reforming Agricultural Trade for Developing Countries. Key Issues for a Pro-Development Outcome of the Doha Round*, vol I (Washington, DC, World Bank, 2007).

[33] The World Bank, above n 15, 7 (noting low percentage of public budgets that developing countries dedicate to agriculture).

[34] Independent Evaluation Group of the World Bank, 'The World Bank's Assistance to Agriculture in Sub-Saharan Africa: An IEG Review' (October 2007).

[35] This calculation of the author is based on the figures collected by the OECD Development Assistance Committee (DAC). See also D Resnick, 'Smallholder African Agriculture: Progress and Problems in Confronting Hunger and Poverty', DGSD Discussion Paper No 9 (IFPRI, July 2004).

dismantling whichever public support schemes existed in the past in favour of the agricultural sector, both in order to reduce public deficits and in order not to distort the price signals. In the process, a number of sub-Saharan African countries became net food importers.

III. THE ILLUSORY NOTION OF A 'LEVEL PLAYING FIELD'

The negative impacts of the current distortions are real. It does not follow, however, that the solution consists simply in the removal of the existing distortions. One reason for this is that improved access to export markets for farmers from developing countries will benefit only some of these, and not the most vulnerable, unless affirmative action is taken to support the latter. Another reason is that, if trade is to work for development and to contribute to the realisation of the right to adequate food, it needs to allow more flexibilities to developing countries and to ensure that those flexibilities are more operational, particularly in order to shield their agricultural producers from competition from industrialised countries' farmers—thus providing more protection rather than less.

The reason for this is obvious, and it is at the heart of what justifies special and differential treatment for developing countries: even after the removal of existing trade-distorting measures, which currently are disproportionately benefiting developed countries, the productivity per active labourer in agriculture will remain much lower in developing countries, on average, than in developed countries. In 2006, agricultural labour productivity in LDCs was just 46% of the level in other developing countries and below 1% of the level in developed countries. In addition, these massive differences in productivity are increasing: labour productivity grew by only 18% in LDCs between 1983 and 2003, but it grew by 41% in other developing countries and by 62% in developed countries.[36] Depending on the kind of equipment available to farmers in LDCs or in developing countries, some estimates suggest that the differences in productivity per active agricultural labourer between the most efficient and the least efficient producers amount to 1:1000 or more.[37]

In this context, the idea of establishing a 'level playing field' is meaningless. The reform programme under the AoA anticipates improved market access, limits on domestic support and the phasing out of export subsidies, all issues that are also components of the 2008 Draft Modalities

---

[36] UNCTAD, *The Least Developed Countries Report, 2006—Developing Productive Capacities* (Geneva, UNCTAD/LDC, 2006) 137.

[37] M Mazoyer, 'Pauvreté paysanne, sous-alimentation et avenir de l'humanité' in S Desgain and O Zé (eds), *Nourrir la planète* (éd Luc Pire, 2008) 10–29, esp 20.

on Agriculture that represent the current state of negotiations within the Doha Development Agenda. This programme alone, however, will not result in agricultural producers from most developing countries being able to compete on equal terms with producers from industrialised countries or from the most competitive and highly mechanised producers of certain other developing countries, unless the wages in the least competitive chains are repressed at very low levels to compensate for the much lower productivity per active labourer. Certain developing countries have a highly mechanised agricultural sector and, particularly since the wages in the agricultural sector remain low in comparison to those in OECD countries, have a strong comparative advantage in agriculture; they would clearly benefit from the removal, or at least the lowering, of the trade-distorting subsidies of developed countries.[38] In other developing countries, though—particularly LDCs—agriculture remains a fragile sector, as a result of the lack of investment in agriculture over a number of years. Encouraging these countries to open up their agricultural sector to competition by binding themselves to low rates of import tariffs would therefore be entirely inappropriate, particularly if we take into account that food insecurity is mostly concentrated in the rural areas. Moreover, a large portion of the population in the countries that are most vulnerable depends on agriculture for their livelihoods: in 2000–03, 70% of the economically active population was engaged in agriculture in the LDCs, as against 52% in other developing countries and 3% in developed countries.[39]

It should be emphasised that neither the failure of many developing countries to invest sufficiently in agriculture nor the damage caused to their agricultural sector by the lowering of import tariffs on agricultural products can be attributed to the WTO rules. The main responsibility for this situation lies with the international financial institutions, particularly with the structural adjustment programmes imposed on states in the 1980s as a condition for their access to loans.[40] As noted by Howard

---

[38] This is the case, in particular, for countries in the Cairns Group (Argentina, Brazil, Chile, Colombia, Costa Rica, Indonesia, Malaysia, Philippines, South Africa, Thailand and Uruguay).

[39] UNCTAD, above n 36, 137. It is however difficult to generalise across LDCs, because international comparable data are scarce. Only five LDCs (three in Africa and two in Asia and the Pacific) report data on employment, including three (Bangladesh, Tanzania and Uganda) that have trend data. See UN Economic and Social Council, ;Meeting the Challenges of Employment Creation and Productivity Growth in Africa and the Least Developed Countries' (Geneva, 5 July 2006).

[40] On the impact of structural adjustment programmes on economic growth and on the ability of the countries concerned to fulfil social and economic rights, see, among many others, A Przeworski and JR Vreeland, 'The Effects of IMF Programs on Economic Growth' (2000) 62 *The Journal of Development Economics* 385. MR Abouharb and DL Cingranelli, *Human Rights and Structural Adjustment* (Cambridge. Cambridge University Press, 2007) conclude that 'World Bank and IMF structural adjustment agreements lowered levels of government respect for economic and social rights, contributing to a deterioration in the

Stein on the basis of a systematic review of the impacts of structural adjustment on the agricultural sector in African countries, the efforts to retract state intervention during that period 'contributed to increasing poverty and income inequality in African countries'.[41] Trade liberalisation—the lowering of import tariffs—and the devaluation of local currencies in order to boost the competitiveness of exports encouraged export-led agriculture, undermining the livelihoods of the least competitive (small-scale) farmers while at the same time increasing the competition for land and land concentration.

Domestic policies too may often be faulted for having paid too little attention to agriculture, and for having sacrificed the long-term interest of the country in strengthening their agricultural sector to the short-term interest of governments in the arrival of food at low prices on local markets. Conversely, adequate domestic policies can be a condition for any opportunities created by improved market access to materialise, for example by removing supply-side constraints facing producers or by helping to meet adjustment costs. But, just as the current distortions and inequities in the international trade regime have discouraged investment in agriculture, the deepening of trade liberalisation and the increased specialisation of each country in the international division of labour may not significantly contribute to the reduction in rural poverty, because small-scale farmers in many developing countries are still not in a position to benefit from the opportunities that will result from such reforms. In fact, these farmers may lose twice. First, if their country loses the possibility of imposing certain restrictions, they may be further exposed to competition from imported products on their local markets. Secondly, as a result of the progress of export-led agriculture, inequalities may increase in the rural areas between the better-off and larger farmers, who have access to global supply chains, and the small-scale farmers, who risk gradually being forced to exit from agriculture as they will be priced out of land markets and be unable to compete.

We must assess the impact of trade liberalisation by taking into account the reality of the constraints developing countries are currently

---

situation for the mass of the population in these countries. The impacts of these agreements have been detrimental to those countries entering into them, even accounting for the selection effects of these institutions . . . Instead of promoting high-quality or equitable economic growth that lifts the poor out of poverty and social misery, the consequences of these programs have been to perpetuate these conditions' (149). Others have demonstrated that the adverse impact of IMF-led programmes on economic growth (confirmed also by A Dreher, 'IMF and Economic Growth: The Effects of Programs, Loans, and Compliance with Conditionality' (2006) 34 *World Development* 769) are concentrated on labour, while benefiting capital whose share of income increases (JR Vreeland, 'The Effects of IMF Programs on Labor' (2002) 30 *World Development* 121).

[41] H Stein, 'World Bank Agricultural Policies, Poverty and Income Inequality in Sub-Saharan Africa' [2010] *Cambridge Journal of Regions, Economy and Society* 1.

facing. In many cases, these constraints make it difficult or impossible for them to implement policies at domestic level that would allow them to maximise the benefits from trade while minimising the negative impacts, particularly by fully using the flexibilities they are allowed. It would be irresponsible to simply presume that such complementary domestic policies can be implemented adequately in the countries concerned, with a speed commensurate to the impact of trade liberalisation itself. Indeed, to a large extent, as a result of the wide differences between the applied and the bound tariff rates in agriculture, the current applied regime of agricultural trade is not far removed from what would result from any further commitments that should result from the successful conclusion of the Doha Round of negotiations. Yet, with few exceptions, developing countries' governments have been unable to take the measures which would alleviate the problems referred to above—insufficient market access for producers from developing countries and the vulnerability of these producers to import surges on their own domestic markets. The lesson is that we should not presume too lightly that these countries have the ability to adapt to the context shaped by international trade: while governments may be unable to take all appropriate measures to do so—in sub-Saharan Africa in particular, as a result of the removal of state institutions (such as crop marketing boards) which supported agricultural producers until the early 1980s[42]—there may be no private sector robust enough to adjust and seize what some describe as the opportunities of trade liberalisation.

IV. TRADE LIBERALISATION IN AGRICULTURE AND THE RIGHT TO FOOD

The impacts of the removal of barriers to trade in agriculture on the right to food are examined at three levels. At the macroeconomic level, trade liberalisation may constitute an obstacle to diversification and lock countries into development patterns which are not sustainable; and it may increase the vulnerability of countries as a result of their dependency on international trade, at the same time rendering vulnerable the situation of agricultural producers in certain developing countries (A). At the microeconomic level, trade liberalisation contributes to reshaping the global food supply chains in a way that favours transnational corporations, whose freedom to act is broadened at the same time as the regulatory tools that states may resort to are being limited (B). But the economic impacts are not all that matters. International trade in

---

[42] UNCTAD, *Economic Development in Africa 2008—Export Performance Following Trade Liberalization: Some Patterns and Policy Perspectives* (Geneva, 2008) ch 2, 37–47.

agricultural commodities also has profound impacts on the environment, and on nutrition and health, which states cannot ignore (C).

A. The Macroeconomic Impacts of Trade Liberalisation: the International Division of Labour and Increased Dependency on International Trade

(i) The International Division of Labour

Trade liberalisation encourages each country to specialise into the production in which it has a comparative advantage. The promise of trade liberalisation is that, by creating incentives for producers from different states to specialise in the products or services in which they have a comparative advantage, it will benefit all the trading partners, since it will lead to efficiency gains within each country and to increased overall levels of world production. Extensions of the classical 'static' theory of comparative advantage suggest that economic growth and poverty alleviation may result.

There are a number of problems with this view. First, the standard theory is based on assumptions that may be questionable. It assumes that there exists in the states concerned a private sector at once sufficiently robust and sufficiently flexible to act on price signals from the market. It also presupposes that economic growth will result in poverty alleviation through a 'trickle-down' effect. However, the agricultural sector in sub-Saharan Africa, for instance, was in such a state in 2000, at the end of two decades of structural adjustment programmes, that is was in fact unable to respond to the price signals; in many cases, it has been so neglected that it is unable to move beyond subsistence agriculture. As to the automatic existence of a 'trickle-down' effect, it remains contentious among economists: it has been demonstrated instead that in certain cases—depending on how trade is managed—inequalities and poverty could increase as a result of trade liberalisation.[43] As Stiglitz writes:

> The theory of trade liberalization (under the assumption of perfect markets, and under the hypothesis that the liberalization is fair) only promises that the country as a whole will benefit. Theory predicts that there will be losers. In principle, the winners could compensate the losers; in practice, this almost never happens.[44]

---

[43] See, for a critique of the standard view that trade will lead to poverty alleviation through a 'trickle-down' effect, SG Reddy and HLM Nye, 'Making Trade Policy Work for the Poor: Shifting From Dogma to Detail' (August 2002). For the standard view, see D Dollar and A Kraay, *Growth is Good for the Poor* (Washington, DC, World Bank, 2000).
[44] JE Stiglitz, *Making Globalization Work* (New York, WW Norton & Co, 2006) 63. See also, reiterating this point, Stiglitz and Charlton, above n 22, 28–29.

But the idea of specialisation of countries through international trade is problematic for other reasons, once it is put forward as a prescription applicable throughout all countries and for all sectors. Whether or not a country is competitive in agriculture depends heavily on political choices: how much is invested in rural infrastructure, in irrigation or in developing access to microcredit, or how much support is given to farmers to compensate for insufficiently remunerative prices. Although countries are naturally constrained in what they may produce by natural factors, these policy choices are decisive, in agriculture as in other sectors, in defining the position of a country in the international division of labour. We must therefore ask which incentives result from the lowering of barriers to trade in the definition of these policy choices. Is there a risk that countries will have an incentive to specialise in the production of raw commodities only, after they realise that other countries have already achieved important economies of scale in certain lines of production? Is this conducive of long-term development?

Reliance on comparative advantage should not be a pretext for impeding the climb of developing countries up the ladder of development, including in the agricultural sector, by moving towards the export of more value-added goods, for instance processed foods.[45] But it is precisely this prospect which is made more distant by trade liberalisation, when it transforms itself from a means to ensure development to an end to be pursued for its own sake. As a result of past history, while industrialised countries have been able to build a comparative advantage in manufactured products or in services, most developing countries, particularly the least-developed ones, have been relegated to the production of raw materials, particularly agricultural commodities. As Galeano has written, the result is that these countries have been specialising in losing while industrialised countries have been specialising in winning:[46] because returns are decreasing in agriculture while they are increasing in the production of manufactured goods or services, the current international division of labour is systematically working against the interests of developing countries. These countries were advised to open themselves to international trade before their industries were ready to compete—indeed, in many cases, before they had any industrial sector at all. It has been highlighted by a number of economists that the result of this would be that the terms of trade would further deteriorate for countries forced to open up to international trade too early, and who were not able to prepare themselves for international competition behind

---

[45] See H-J Chang, *Kicking Away the Ladder: Development Strategy in Historical Perspective* (London, Anthem Press, 2002).

[46] E Galeano, *Las venas abiertas de América Latina* (Editores XXI Siglo Veintuno De Espana, 1971).

trade barriers.[47] Yet we seem to insist on building international trade on a wrong premise: on a fictitious Ricardian world, in which all values are reduced to labour and in which neither qualitative differences between various kinds of production nor the dynamic perspective are integrated. It is therefore a profound mistake to search for a solution in more specialisation in the production of commodities with the least added value rather than in providing developing countries with the ability to diversify into various lines of production. This basic point is missed by those who insist that the real problem is that trade is currently distorted in the sector which matters most to developing countries—agriculture—and that the solution is therefore to remove these distortions.

(ii) The Incentive to Specialise in Export Crops and the Resulting Dependency

Because comparative advantage is constructed rather than determined by natural factors, it is crucial to ask which incentives result for states, in the construction of their comparative advantage, from the opening of international trade. States may of course seek to improve the ability of their producers to benefit from the opportunities of international trade, and particularly, for developing countries, from better access to the high-value markets of industrialised countries. At the same time, states may find that importing certain goods, such as processed foods, may be cheaper than producing them locally, and they may therefore increase their dependence on imports for feeding their population. Specialisation according to comparative advantage thus leads to two forms of dependency: first, for the acquisition of foreign currency, on the value of exports; secondly, for the ability of countries to feed their population, on the price of imports.

The example of sub-Saharan African countries is illustrative. Due in part to the highly penalising structure of tariffs in OECD countries through tariff peaks and tariff escalation, and in part to the presence on international markets of highly subsidised foods produced in industrial countries, sub-Saharan Africa has remained dependent on traditional non-fuel primary commodity exports such as coffee, cotton, cocoa, tobacco, tea and sugar, and was essentially unable to develop into an

---

[47] See in particular ES Reinert, *How Rich Countries Got Rich and Why Poor Countries Stay Poor* (London, Constable, 2007); Chang, above n 45. Globalisation has benefited those countries—such as Brazil, China, South Korea or India—that carefully sequenced trade liberalisation, and that built an industry and a services sector behind trade barriers before opening up to trade. See also Stiglitz and Charlton, above n 22, 17: 'To date, not one successful developing country has pursued a purely free market approach to development. In this context it is inappropriate for the world trading system to be implementing rules which circumscribe the ability of developing countries to use both trade and industry policies to promote industrialization'.

exporter of processed food (South Africa, the largest African exporter of processed food, had a global market share of only 1% in the period 2000–05).[48] At the same time, while many African countries were net food-exporting countries until the 1970s, they have become for the most part net food-importing countries since the 1980s. As we have seen, this was due partly to the lack of investment in agriculture and partly to the agricultural subsidies in developed market economies, which itself discouraged agricultural investment.[49] The result is well known: it has led to increased vulnerability of these countries both to worsening terms of trade and to fluctuations in commodity prices—fluctuations which are particularly important in the agricultural sector due to the sensitivity of this sector to weather-related events and the low elasticity of both supply and demand. More precisely, the dependency on international trade may lead to three consequences: to the loss of export revenues when the prices of export commodities go down; to threats to local producers when cheap imports arrive on the domestic markets, against which these producers are unable to compete; and to balance-of-payments problems for the net food-importing countries when the prices of food commodities go up. The WTO agreements sought to address the latter two problems; since the phasing out of the commodity stabilisation agreements of the 1960s and 1970s, the first problem has not been addressed at all.

The volatility of prices on the international markets of commodities makes states which are most dependent on international trade most vulnerable to shocks, such as overproduction or harvest failures in other states, leading to brutal price drops or increases in prices. Indeed, compared to other goods, the prices of agricultural commodities are particularly volatile. Is more trade liberalisation an answer? In general, volatility can be lessened by spreading the supply and demand across a larger number of producers and consumers—the thinner the market, the greater the risk that sudden increases or decreases of prices will occur as the result of a few important producers not serving the market or oversupplying it. That, in general, is seen as a strong argument in favour of the development of international markets in agricultural commodities; it is one lesson which many international agencies have learnt, for example, from the impact of export restrictions imposed during the spring of 2008 by some major exporters of rice.

This reasoning is premised on the idea that shifts in production (towards significantly lower levels or, conversely, higher levels) are attributable primarily to exogenous factors—for example, to weather-related

---

[48] OECD, *Business for Development 2008, Promoting Commercial Agriculture in Africa: A Development Centre Perspective* (Paris, OECD, 2008).
[49] UNCTAD, 'The Changing Face of Commodities in the Twenty-first Century', TD/428, note prepared by the UNCTAD secretariat, UNCTAD XII, Accra, Ghana, 20–25 April 2008.

events—so that the bad harvests in one country will be compensated by higher production in another, resulting in an insurance effect for the buyers of the product concerned. In fact, however, the levels of production of agricultural commodities are mainly dependent on choices made by the producers: the factors explaining shifts in production are endogenous for the large part, rather than exogenous. As is well known, these choices are made during the planting season, 4–6 months before the harvests, on the basis of the expectations of the producers about the prices they will eventually receive. This results in what has been called the 'cobweb effect': the producers plant more of the crops whose prices are highest during the planting season, and they plant comparatively less of the crops whose prices are low. This results in a structural volatility, since high prices are an incentive to overproduce (thus leading to lower prices), while low prices are an incentive to produce less (leading to higher prices). The important point is that, in the absence of supply management schemes— ie if producers simply seek to respond to the price signals—all producers, wherever they are located, will behave according to the same predictions. In this case, far from neutralising each others' failures to produce enough or overproduction, all the actions converge: since price signals are the same for all producers once markets are globalised, the reactions of all suppliers will be in the same direction. The lack of insulation of domestic markets from the prices of international markets thus leads to more instability, not less. Hoarding practices by private traders or by public bodies can further worsen this volatility, as was clearly illustrated between February and April 2008 in rice, for instance.

In the future, more attention should be paid to the need to develop tools to limit this volatility, which results in shocks that, for many developing countries, are particularly difficult to cope with. The fundamental issue, however, is the dependency of countries on food imports for the food security of their population, and the impacts this can have on the right to adequate food. In order to assess these impacts, we must compare two opposite scenarios, one in which the prices of food commodities on international markets are low (the slump scenario)—and this has been the historical tendency—and another in which the prices increase suddenly (the boost scenario)—as we may see more frequently in the future.

In the slump scenario, oversupply on international markets, particularly by heavily subsidised producers from OECD countries, leads to a decrease in prices on international markets. In the absence of strong tariff protections, this results in import surges, which may threaten the ability of the local producers in net food-importing countries to live from their crops if these surges lead to such low prices on the domestic markets that they are driven out of business. Such surges have been a frequent occurrence, both before and after the entry into force of the

Agreement on Agriculture. The FAO documented some 12,000 cases of import surges in a survey covering 102 developing countries over the period 1980–2003. Using the definitions contained in Article 5 AoA, it found that the frequency of import surges exceeded 20% (ie one every 5 years) for all basic food commodities, with particularly high frequencies for rice (40.1%), sugar (40.4%), palm oil (36.6%), cheese (36.4%) and wheat (35.9%). These frequencies have increased for most commodities in the post-1994 period, except for wheat, rice, maize and palm oil. The countries most affected were India and Bangladesh in Asia, Zimbabwe, Kenya, Nigeria, Ghana and Malawi in Africa, and Ecuador and Honduras in Latin America.[50]

Such import surges threaten the livelihoods of farmers and agricultural labourers living off these crops.[51] For instance, in Ghana, rice imports increased from 250,000 tonnes in 1998 to 415,150 tonnes in 2003. Domestic rice, which had accounted for 43% of the domestic market in 2000, captured only 29% of the domestic market in 2003. As a result, 66% of rice producers recorded negative returns.[52] In the same country, tomato paste imports increased by 650% from 3,300 tons in 1998 to 24,740 tons in 2003, a significant proportion (36%) coming from Italy. Local producers—which are mostly small-scale farmers, suffering from a lack of competitiveness and investment—lost 35% of the share of the domestic market. In Cameroon, poultry imports increased nearly 300% between 1999 and 2004, and 92% of poultry farmers dropped out of the sector. Some 110,000 rural jobs were lost each year from 1994 to 2003. In Côte d'Ivoire, poultry imports increased 650% between 2001 and 2003, causing domestic production to fall by 23%. The falling prices forced 1,500 producers to cease production and led to the loss of 15,000 jobs. In Mozambique, vegetable oil imports (palm, soy and sunflower) saw a fivefold increase between 2000 and 2004, as local production was unable to supply the rapidly increasing local demand. In the context of declining prices, with the domestically refined oils following the price movements of imported refined oil, the margins of local producers shrank drastically, leading to plant closures and to an overall reduction in the volumes of locally produced oil.

These import surges experienced by developing countries are the result of the lowering of import tariff barriers to levels significantly below the tariffs bound under the AoA, which these countries consented

---

[50] FAO Brief on Import Surges—Issues.

[51] See, for a series of case studies, the FAO Briefs on Import Surges. See also R Sharma, 'Overview of Reported Cases of Import Surges from the Standpoint of the Analytical Content', FAO Import Surge Project Working Paper No 1, Commodities and Trade Division (Rome, 2005).

[52] See also A Paasch et al (eds), 'Trade Policies & Hunger. The Impact of Trade Liberalisation on the Right to Food of Rice Farming Communities in Ghana, Honduras and Indonesia' (FIAN and the Ecumenical Advocacy Alliance, October 2007).

to as part of the structural adjustment programmes imposed on them as a conditionality to receive loans. Combined with the declining prices on the international markets, partly attributable to subsidies provided to their agricultural producers by OECD countries and the resulting overproduction, this led to the arrival of cheap commodities on domestic markets with which the local producers in developing countries were unable to compete. The supply-side constraints facing these producers vary from country to country, but they include low productivity due to reliance on low agricultural technology, lack of access to credit and agricultural inputs, lack of training and technical assistance, and lack of rural infrastructural services. While these constraints could be partly removed by increased investments in agriculture and public policies supporting farmers, this represents a medium- to long-term perspective that does not constitute a response, in the short term, to the inability of farmers affected to increase supply in response to demand, and to improve their competitiveness in the face of competition from imports.

The provisions contained in the current version of the AoA are insufficient to allow countries to react to the disruptions caused by import surges. Under the AoA, members which resorted to tariffication of their non-trade barriers may impose an SSG in the form of additional tariffs when confronted with import surges of certain products—ie imports exceeding a specified trigger level, or whose price falls below a specified trigger price (Article 5). However, most developing countries did not use tariffication. Thirty-nine WTO members, including 22 developing countries, have reserved the right to resort to the special safeguard option on hundreds of products. But the SSG mechanism was triggered by only 10 members, including six developing countries, between 1995 and 2001; and between 1995 and 2004, developing countries triggered the SSG in only 1% of the cases in which they could have applied it.[53] As a protection against import surges, the current SSG mechanism is thus largely ineffective. Because they did not undertake tariffication, most developing countries could not reserve their right to invoke the SSG. Of those who did reserve that right, only six of the 22 did make use of this possibility, either because of their limited capacity to collect data or because of the complexity of the safeguard process, making it difficult to use.[54]

The right to food is impacted very differently as a result of developing countries' dependency on food imports when, in the 'boost'

---

[53] See FAO, 'A Special Safeguard Mechanism for Developing Countries', Trade Policy Briefs on Issues Related to the WTO Negotiations on Agriculture, No 9.

[54] See South Centre, Controversial Points in the Discussion on Special Safeguard Mechanism (SSM) in the Doha Round, Analytical Note SC/AN/TDP/AG/7, November 2008.

scenario, prices undergo increases on international markets. In such circumstances, net food-importing countries may experience balance-of-payments problems. The difficulties these countries encountered through the period of 2007–08, when these prices rose significantly, provide a vivid illustration of this risk. The Marrakesh Decision, which is part of the WTO agreements, was intended to provide an answer to such a situation. In this Decision, the members note that, as a result of the reform programme, LDCs and net food-importing developing countries (NFIDCs) 'may experience negative effects in terms of the availability of adequate supplies of basic foodstuffs from external sources on reasonable terms and conditions, including short-term difficulties in financing normal levels of commercial imports of basic foodstuffs'. Four response mechanisms are provided. These are: (i) the provision of food aid at a level which is sufficient to continue to provide assistance in meeting the food needs of developing countries; (ii) the provision of technical and financial assistance to lLDCs and NFIDCs to improve their agricultural productivity and infrastructure; (iii) favourable terms for agricultural export credits; and (iv) short-term financing facilities benefiting developing countries in order to allow them to maintain normal levels of commercial imports.

However, WTO members have failed to implement the Marrakesh Decision adequately. There is no mechanism within the WTO that systematically monitors the impact of the AoA reform process on the NFIDCs, which means that only in the most extreme circumstances could any mechanisms established under the Marrakesh Decision be triggered.[55] Furthermore, the notion of 'adequate supplies' of basic foodstuffs –which NFIDCs should be able to obtain from external sources 'on reasonable terms and conditions' throughout the reform process— remains undefined, although it is this notion that should trigger the mechanisms provided for under the Decision. Finally, there are major difficulties with each of the four mechanisms that the Marrakesh Decision establishes:

(1) The Marrakesh Decision refers to the need to review the level of food aid established periodically by the Committee on Food Aid under the Food Aid Convention 1986 and to 'initiate negotiations in the appropriate forum to establish a level of food aid commitments sufficient to meet the legitimate needs of developing countries during the reform programme'. The 1995 and 1999 Food Aid Conventions (FACs), revising

---

[55] UNCTAD, 'Impact of the Reform Process in Agriculture on LDCs and Net Food-Importing Developing Countries and Ways to Address Their Concerns in Multilateral Trade Negotiations', UN document TD/B/COM.1/EM.11/2 and Corr.1 of 23 June 2000, paras 25ff.

the initial FAC of 1967,[56] were a result of this proclaimed objective. The Marrakesh Decision also included a commitment to

> adopt guidelines to ensure that an increasing proportion of basic foodstuffs is provided to least-developed and net food-importing developing countries in fully grant form and/or on appropriate concessional terms in line with Article IV of the Food Aid Convention 1986.

However, Article VII(a) of the Food Aid Convention provides that food aid under the Convention may be provided to least-developed countries and low-income countries, as well as to

> lower middle-income countries, and other countries included in the WTO list of Net Food-Importing Developing Countries at the time of negotiation of this Convention, *when experiencing food emergencies or internationally recognised financial crises leading to food shortage emergencies, or when food aid operations are targeted on vulnerable groups* [emphasis added].

Thus, as regards the NFIDCs which are neither LDCs nor low-income countries, more restrictive conditions are stipulated under the FAC than would be required in order to ensure an adequate implementation of the Marrakesh Decision.[57] The FAC could be amended in order to put an end to this discrepancy. In addition, the guidelines referred to in the Marrakesh Decision could be adopted in order to impose an obligation on the states that are party to the FAC to provide food aid at levels which ensure that NFIDCs will at all times be able to ensure an adequate protection of the right to food under their jurisdiction.

(2) The provision of assistance to LDCs and NFIDCs in order to allow them to improve their agricultural productivity and infrastructure has been insufficient over the last two decades. As we have seen, both the proportion of official development assistance dedicated to agriculture and the proportion of national budgets going to agriculture have declined significantly since the early 1980s. While commitments have been made at various fora to reverse this trend, it remains to be seen whether there will be sufficient political will to implement these resolutions.

(3) The Marrakesh Decision provides that appropriate provision should be made in any agreement on agricultural export credits for differential treatment of LDCs and NFIDCs. For the moment, the shares of these countries in total agricultural exports remain small, yet little progress has been achieved on this point.

---

[56] The Food Aid Convention was initially adopted in 1967 as one component of the International Grains Agreement. It is specific in that it contains commitments by its state parties to provide certain quantities of food as food aid. The parties to the Food Aid Convention are Argentina, Australia, Canada, Japan, Norway, Switzerland and the US, as well as the European Community (now the European Union) and its Member States. The present version of the FAC entered into force on 1 July 1999.

[57] The countries concerned are Barbados, Mauritius, St Lucia, Trinidad and Tobago.

(4) Paragraph 5 of the Marrakesh Decision provides for the possibility for NFIDCs experiencing balance-of-payments difficulties to draw on 'existing facilities, or such facilities as may be established' in order to enable them to address their financing difficulties. The main facility which has been considered to satisfy this requirement is the IMF Compensatory Financing Facility (CFF), initially established in 1963. The CFF was expanded in 1981 to cover excess cereal import costs, following requests of the World Food Council and the UN Food and Agriculture Organization (FAO), and in consideration of the high volatility of food prices in the 1970s. In fact, this facility has been of little use to NFIDCs.[58] Access to the CFF is restricted to countries experiencing temporary balance-of-payments difficulties linked to factors largely beyond the control of the authorities, such as a rise in cereal import costs. However, this is a condition which very few countries have been considered to meet. In addition, access to loans is subject to conditionality, which the Marrakesh Decision recognises explicitly by referring to facilities extended 'in the context of adjustment programmes'. Finally, here, too, there is a discrepancy between the CFF and the Marrakesh Decision: the CFF is limited to cereals only, whereas the Decision covers all basic foods.

On 25 April 2001, a group of 16 developing country members of the WTO submitted a proposal which called for, inter alia, the establishment of an inter-agency revolving fund[59] under which, in addition to technical and financial assistance to LDCs and NFIDCs for specific projects linked to improving agricultural productivity and related infrastructure, financing would be provided at concessional terms without requiring any justification other than evidence that import bills were excessive. This system was conceived as self-financing: borrowing countries would assume the obligation to repay their loans, for instance within a period of 2 years. The UN Conference on Trade and Development (UNCTAD) later elaborated on this proposal, which was included by the WTO Doha Ministerial Conference among the implementation issues[60] and led to an inter-agency panel being established to examine the issue.[61] There has been no follow-up, at yet, to the proposal for a revolving fund. It is

---

[58] It is significant that, in order to assist countries to face the balance-of-payments difficulties in 2008 as a result of the brutal increases in prices of food commodities on international markets, the International Monetary Fund provided additional balance-of-payments support by augmented access to 12 countries under Poverty Reduction Growth Facility (PRGF) arrangements.

[59] 'Proposal to Implement the Marrakesh Ministerial Decision in Favour of LDCs and NFIDCS', G/AG/W/49, 19 March 2001, and Add.1 (23 May 2001), and Add.1/Corr.1 (27 June 2001).

[60] 'Decision on Implementation-Related Issues and Concerns', WTO document WT/MIN(01)/17 of 20 November 2001, para 2.2.

[61] 'Inter-Agency Panel on Short-Term Difficulties in Financing Normal Levels of Commercial Imports of Basic Foodstuffs', Report of the Inter-Agency Panel, WTO document WT/GC/62 G/AG/13 of 28 June 2002.

therefore to be welcomed that the Exogenous Shocks Facility was revised in September 2008 in order to allow the IMF to help its members cope with events such as commodity price changes, by including a rapid-access component in the facility and by providing concessional terms of financing, focused on the adjustment to the underlying shock but with less emphasis than previously on broader structural adjustments.

B. The Microeconomic Impacts of Trade Liberalisation: the Impact on the Shape of the Global Food Supply Chain and the Dualisation of the Farming Sector

Increased cross-border trade in agricultural products implies that, as the production of food is reoriented towards serving the foreign markets rather than the domestic markets, the role of transnational corporations—commodity traders, food processors and global retailers—increases. These corporations serve an indispensable function in linking producers, particularly from developing countries, to markets, particularly to the high-value markets of industrialised countries. However, since these corporations have activities in different countries and can choose the country from which they source, they may be difficult to regulate, particularly as regards their buying policies. This constitutes a source of dependency for the farmers who supply them. It also encourages the segmentation of the farming sector, increasingly divided between one segment which has access to high-value markets and, as a result, to the best technologies, inputs (including land, water and state support), credit and political influence, and another segment which is left to serve only the low-value, domestic markets, and is comparatively neglected and marginalised.

Concentration in the food system is significant. This results in widening the spread between world and domestic prices in commodity prices for wheat, rice and sugar, for instance, which more than doubled between 1974 and 1994; since most large commodity buyers are based in the OECD countries, this limits the portion of the value captured by developing countries. In other words, an increasing portion of the end value of agricultural products goes to the large transnational corporations in the agrifood system—commodity buyers, food processors and retailers—who now have come to occupy a dominant position as a result of concentration in different segments of the chain. In its World Development Report 2008, the World Bank highlights high concentration rates in coffee, tea and cocoa:

> Coffee is produced by an estimated 25 million farmers and farm workers, yet international traders have a CR4 of 40 percent, and coffee roasters have a CR4 [the share of market of the 4 dominant actors] of 45 percent. There

are an estimated 500 million consumers. The share of the retail price retained by coffee-producing countries—Brazil, Colombia, Indonesia, and Vietnam account for 64 percent of global production—declined from a third in the early 1990s to 10 percent in 2002 while the value of retail sales doubled. Similar concentrations are observed in the tea value chain where three companies control more than 80 percent of the world market. Cocoa has a CR4 of 40 percent for international traders, 51 percent for cocoa grinders, and 50 percent for confectionary manufacturers. Developing countries' claim on value added declined from around 60 percent in 1970–72 to around 28 percent in 1998–2000.[62]

Farmers in industrialised countries face the same constraints, resulting from the need to go through commodity traders which a have a dominant position: for example, two companies control 40% of the grain exports from the US.[63] Similar trends towards increased concentration occur in the retail sector,[64] although the speed of concentration here seems to have decreased in recent years.[65]

The results of the expansion of global supply chains are ambiguous. On the one hand, it creates opportunities, by giving farmers from developing countries access to high-value markets, particularly where these farmers have certain comparative advantages, such as lower land and labour costs and longer growing seasons, and where they are relatively close to those markets—as are sub-Saharan producers to European markets. On the other hand, global sourcing increases the number of suppliers and, thus, the competition between them, leading to pricing policies by buyers which reduce the share of the final value of the product which goes to the producers—the farm gate price as opposed to the retail price. Given the increased concentration of market power in the agricultural commodities system, in the hands of commodity buyers and large retailers, these actors impose their prices on producers; they impose standards which many small-scale farmers are unable to meet; particularly for crops like wheat or soybean, for which economies of scale represent important productivity gains, small-scale farmers are unable to compete, and they are relegated to the low-value, local markets, which puts them at a strong disadvantage in the competition for land, water or

---

[62] World Bank, above n 15, 136.

[63] S Murphy, 'Concentrated Market Power and Agricultural Trade', EcoFair Trade Dialogue Discussion Papers No 1 (August 2006) 14.

[64] See FAO, 'Special Feature: Globalization, Urbanization and Changing Food Systems in Developing Countries' (2004) (reporting that FDI in food industries increased from $743 million to more than $2.1 billion from 1988 to 1997, far outpacing agricultural investments, and noting that 30 largest supermarket chains now account for about one-third of food sales worldwide). See also 'Horticultural Producers and Supermarket Development in Indonesia', World Bank Report No 38543-ID (2007) vi and vii (noting that traditional retail loses about 2% of its share each year in Indonesia).

[65] T Reardon and A Gulati, 'The Rise of Supermarkets and Their Development Implications: International Experience Relevant for India', Discussion Paper 00752 (IFPRI, 2008) 17.

other productive resources, unless they end up working as badly paid agricultural labourers.

Certain strategies could be developed to avoid small-scale farmers being squeezed out by the development of global supply chains. These include cooperatives, outgrower schemes, public–private initiatives and regional initiatives.[66] However, these strategies are sometimes ambiguous in their effects. For instance, outgrower schemes and contract farming may be means to shift the risks to the independent producer, since that producer is not guaranteed a stable income and will have to cope with severe losses if the harvests fail, or if the prices undergo sudden decreases. In addition, these strategies aiming at integrating small-scale farmers into global supply schemes are still underdeveloped and clearly not sufficient, at present, to counteract the trend towards more concentration and increased dualisation of the farming sector. This is particularly the case since large buyers seek to minimise transactions costs, which are high when they seek to source from small-scale farmers who are dispersed geographically and are far removed from centralised collection facilities. Further, large agricultural producers are better equipped to adapt to shifting demand and to comply with volume and traceability requirements, as well as with the environmental and food safety standards that global retailers increasingly seek to monitor compliance with.[67]

It has been written about the global food system that

> it has a dualistic structure. The The vast majority of farms (85 percent) remain operations of less than two hectares. But the 0.5 per cent of farms that exceed 100 hectares capture a disproportionate share of global farm income, enjoy privilege access to policy makers and, particularly in developed countries, receive generous subsidies. Outside of farming, buying power is increasingly concentrated in the hands of supermarkets and other powerful corporate actors. Preferences of affluent consumers in high- and middle-income countries are shaping global food and agricultural systems, offering smallholders opportunities and niche markets. However, they may face difficulties in being able to produce up to the standards of the buying agents.[68]

Far from counteracting this, the expansion of global supply chains will reinforce this unequal structure, and increase the gap between these different worlds of farming.

---

[66] See, highlighting the measures which could facilitate cooperation between supermarkets and smallholder farmers, O Brown and C Sander, 'Supermarket Buying Power: Global Supply Chains and Smallholder Farmers' (International Institute for Sustainable Development, March 2007) 11.

[67] C. Dolan and J. Humphrey, 'Governance and Trade in Fresh Vegetables: The Impact of UK Supermarkets on the African Horticultural Industry' (2001) 37(2) *Journal of Development Studies* 175.

[68] MJ Cohen et al, 'Impact of Climate Change and Bioenergy on Nutrition' (IFPRI and FAO, 2008) 3.

C. The Non-economic Impacts of Trade Liberalisation: Environmental and Health Dimensions

The reliance on international trade to achieve food security cannot ignore its impact on the environment and on nutrition. Until recently, these elements were mostly ignored in discussions on international trade. They are nevertheless crucial. As mentioned earlier in this chapter, climate change constitutes the single most important threat to the future ability of the planet to feed its population; any measure that contributes to further global warming should be therefore avoided. Also, the right to food cannot be equated with just a sufficient daily intake of calories: it is the right to *adequate* food, which requires that the diet as a whole contains a mix of nutrients for physical and mental growth, development and maintenance, and physical activity, requiring that states maintain, adapt or strengthen dietary diversity and appropriate consumption and feeding patterns.[69]

(i) Environmental Dimensions

The lowering of barriers to international trade leads to increased competition between producers located in different countries, each with their own policies aimed at controlling emissions of greenhouse gases (GHGs) and the depletion of soils, particularly through the use of chemical fertilisers. This leads to the fear that investors and buyers may turn to jurisdictions which impose fewer constraints, and whose producers are therefore put at a competitive advantage. While this concern has been mainly expressed as regards the relocation of industries, it may also be relevant to agricultural production, since agriculture produces significant effects on climate change, not only through the production and release of GHGs such as carbon dioxide, methane and nitrous oxide, but also by altering the earth's land cover: land use change such as deforestation and desertification is a major anthropogenic source of carbon dioxide. For the moment, there seems to be no evidence that countries are discouraged from imposing restrictions on agricultural practices, with a view to limiting their GHG effects or their impact on soils, because of the potential impact of such restrictions on the productivity of their producers.

But there is more to the relationship between trade liberalisation and the environment. Consider three major potential impacts of the expansion of international trade on the environment. First, long production chains imply long distances of transport. It has been stated that

---

[69] UN Committee on Economic, Social and Cultural Rights, General Comment No 12, 'The Right to Adequate Food (Art 11)', ¶ 9, UN document E/C.12/1999/5 (1999).

about three quarters of the energy consumption in the food system takes place beyond the farm gate, and energy used to transport foods to rich country markets from around the globe, 365 days a year, regardless of seasons, accounts for a significant part of total energy consumption in the food system.[70]

General conclusions are difficult to draw, since the impact of the transportation of food over long distances, as encouraged by the globalisation of supply chains, depends on the mode of transportation used, and may be offset to some extent if food imported to an area has been produced in an environmentally more sustainable way than the food available locally. For example, one case study has shown that it can be more sustainable (at least in energy efficiency terms) to import tomatoes from Spain than to produce them in heated greenhouses in the UK outside the summer months.[71] What is clear, however, is that road transport and air transport (representing respectively 74 and 12% of the GHG emissions produced by transport, which itself is responsible for 23% of the world energy-related GHG emissions),[72] which are typically used for the transportation of fresh food, both have a serious impact on climate change. This impact is increasing as consumers in developed countries now expect all foods to be available at all times of the year. A study done on the 'food miles' of food consumed in the UK, for instance, highlighted that airfreight is the fastest growing mode of food transport, accounting for 11% of the food industry's transport emissions despite only carrying 1% of the food and making up just 0.1% of the food miles.[73] Such modes of food consumption are not sustainable in the long term.

A potentially far more important impact of trade on the environment stems from the fact that the various modes of agricultural production may have widely different impacts on global warming. If clearing forest to create farmland is included, agriculture is estimated to be responsible for 32–33% of total global man-made emissions of GHGs.[74] The

---

[70] W Sachs and T Santarius, 'Slow Trade—Sound Farming' in *Ecofair Trade Dialogue* (Heinrich Böll Stiftung, Misereor and Wuppertal Institut, 2008) 24.

[71] Ibid, v.

[72] These are figures from the International Energy Agency for 2004.

[73] DEFRA, 'The Validity of Food Miles as an Indicator of Sustainable Development: Final Report' (July 2005) ii.

[74] FAO, 'World Agriculture: Towards 2015' (2003). Agriculture currently accounts for about 13–15% of global man-made GHG emissions, and it is especially GHG-intensive in the developed countries, where agriculture is more highly mechanised and relies heavily on synthetic fertilisers. Although some of these emissions are from energy-related carbon dioxide (CO_2) (9% of GHG emissions from agriculture), most are from methane (CH_4), which is emitted by rice paddies, livestock digestion and manure handling (45%), and nitrous oxide (N_2O), from nitrogen-based fertilisers and manure applications to soils (46%). CH_4 and N_2O represent respectively 14.3 and 7.2% of total GHG emissions, and they are particularly potent in trapping heat: CH_4 traps 21 times and N_2O traps 260 times more heat than CO_2. Deforestation for the expansion of crop areas and pastures produce an additional 19% of global GHG emissions. See A Kasterine and D Vanzetti, 'The

conversion of tropical forests to agricultural land, the expansion of rice and livestock production (31%), and the increased use of nitrogen fertilisers (38%) have all been significant contributors to GHG emissions, in the form of methane and nitrous oxide. While both of these gases are released in much smaller quantities than carbon dioxide, they have a much greater global warming potential: one tonne of nitrous oxide or methane will have a far greater impact on climate change than one tonne of carbon dioxide.[75] While the gradual switch to more intensive forms of agricultural production, with the attendant environmental impacts and negative consequences for global warming, cannot be attributed directly to the increase of global trade in agricultural commodities, this is nevertheless a trend which is encouraged by the specialisation of countries in cash crops for export. The future regulation of international trade in agricultural commodities should take into account the impact of various modes of agricultural production on climate change, in order to allow countries to provide incentives in favour of forms of production which better respect the environment. Agro-industrial forms of agricultural production are also unsustainable because of their dependence on cheap oil. Reversing the trend towards a generalisation of these forms of production is important if we aim at food security, considering the threat of climate change on our ability to maintain current levels of agricultural productivity in many regions.[76]

The relationship between trade and environment was examined in 2009 in a joint report of the WTO and the UN Environment Program (UNEP).[77] The report essentially concludes that international trade and the adoption of mitigation measures to combat climate change can be mutually supportive. Increased international trade would facilitate the transfer of clean technologies, the report notes; and trade opening would lead to rising incomes, thus leading both the populations benefiting and the rich countries to demand higher environmental standards, including those for GHG emissions. These conclusions remain debatable. First, one of the main obstacles to the transfer of clean technologies is the insistence of certain WTO members, among the industrialised countries, on full compliance with the TRIPS Agreement, also as regards such technologies. Secondly, the assertion that the lowering of barriers to international trade and more global supply chains increases incomes depends on the population group concerned: the evidence is overwhelming that it does

Effectiveness, Efficiency and Equity of Market-based and Voluntary Measures to Mitigate Greenhouse Gas Emissions from the Agri-food Sector' in *Trade and Environment Review 2009/2010* (Geneva, UNCTAD, 2010) 87–111.

[75] For details, see ibid; Friends of the Earth, 'Food and Climate Change—Briefing' (October 2007).
[76] See in particular Lobell et al, above n 10.
[77] *Trade and Climate Change* (WTO-UNEP, Geneva, 2009).

not do so per necessity and that, on the contrary, inequalities may grow as a result of the opening of trade. Thirdly, what the report essentially omits is any discussion of the impact of the development of exports on farming practices.[78] However, it is clear that different types of farming have different levels of emission of GHGs, and in most cases export-led agriculture has been the most damaging to the environment, due to its high level of mechanisation and its intensive use of external, petroleum-based inputs. Fourthly, while the WTO-UNEP report does consider the 'technology effect' of international trade, noting that in many cases trade favours the spread of cleaner technologies which, once taken up, can lead to less carbon-intensive types of growth in the importing country, such an effect should be balanced against what might be called the 'scale effect' of international trade: as trade favours increased economic growth and levels of consumption, resources are freed up from their less productive uses to be reinvested or spent elsewhere. Studies are now converging to show that the 'scale effects' of international trade outweigh 'technology effects'.[79]

Finally, it is vital for food security in the future that we protect the genetic diversity of crops. For thousands of years, reasonable levels of production were achieved by the management by farming communities of a vast portfolio of genetic diversity. Stability in the level of protection to specific diseases, drought and variations in temperature was achieved through the coexistence of an array of plants presenting different traits that made them resistant. This genetic diversity is now under severe threat. As a result of the pressure towards more uniform crops, efforts have concentrated on the development of a limited number of standard, high-yielding varieties, so that barely more than 150 species are now cultivated; most of mankind now lives off no more than 12 plant species.[80]

---

[78] While the report does refer at length to agriculture, it essentially focuses on the threat climate change represents to agricultural productivity, on the need for countries where agriculture will suffer most to import more food, and on the benefit from importing new technologies. See 19–20.

[79] See M Heil and T Selden, 'International Trade Intensity and Carbon Emissions: A Cross-Country Econometric Analysis' (2001) No 10(1) *Journal of Environment and Development* 35; M Cole and R Elliott, 'Determining the Trade–Environment Composition Effect: the Role of Capital, Labor and Environmental Regulations' (2003) No 46(3) *Journal of Environmental Economics and Management* 363. For an excellent overview, see T Santarius, 'Climate and Trade. Why Climate Change Calls for Fundamental Reforms in World Trade Policies', German NGO Forum on Environment and Development and Heinrich Böll Foundation (2009).

[80] J Esquinas-Alcázar, 'Protection Crop Genetic Diversity for Food Security: Political, Ethical and Technical Challenges' (2005) 6 *Nature* 946. See also PC Mangelsdorf, 'Genetic Potentials for Increasing Yields of Food Crops and Animals' (1966) 56 *Proceedings of the National Academy of Sciences USA* 370.

This is an extremely worrying prospect. Genetic erosion increases our vulnerability to sudden changes in climate, and to the appearance of new pests and diseases. For example, after the fungus *Helminthosporium maydis* destroyed much of the standing maize crop in the southern part of the US in 1970, leading to losses to consumers and farmers totalling some 2 billion USD,[81] it was necessary to breed a variety resistant to this pest by using genetic resources borrowed from other parts of the world. A number of varieties had been ignored for a long time due to their negative agricultural characteristics, before it was found that they could contribute to agricultural developments due to their specific traits, such as their resistance to certain pests or their higher nitrogen-fixing capacity. Preserving those varieties is thus vital. However, the emphasis put on the production of cash crops for export—a result of the greater opportunities created by international trade—encourages the development of homogenisation in agriculture, and the substitution of monocropping for polycropping.

(ii) Nutrition and Health Dimensions

Partly as a result of tariff escalation in developed countries and partly as a result of comparative advantage, developing countries mostly export commodities, including fresh fruit and vegetables, and import processed foods from developed countries. This has led to shifts in dietary habits in developing countries, whose populations increasingly consume 'western' diets that are rich in salt, sugar and fat. Higher rates of obesity have resulted, as well as diseases such as heart disease and type 2 diabetes. Overweight is now 'among the top five risk factors for loss of disability-adjusted life years (DALYs) in both developed countries and low-mortality developing countries (although underweight still ranks higher)'.[82] Urbanisation and increased employment of women, which leads to heavier reliance on foods prepared outside the home, including foods available from supermarkets, have played a significant role in this evolution; but reliance on imported foods has also been a factor, and governments should take this into account in their trade policy decisions.

---

[81] J Kloppenburg, *First the Seed: The Political Economy of Plant Biotechnology* (Cambridge, Cambridge University Press, 1988) 93.

[82] K Rideout, 'Food and Trade—An Ecological Public Health Perspective' (Oxfam Canada, 27 February 2005) 12 (referring to Chopra M, Galbraith S, Darnton-Hill I, 'A Global Response to a Global Problem: the Epidemic of Overnutrition' (2002) 80 *Bulletin of the World Health Organization* 952).

D. Conclusion

The impacts listed above cannot be attributed to the implementation of the WTO's AoA considered in isolation, nor, indeed, in many cases, to trade liberalisation alone; and many of these impacts can be mitigated even within the framework set by the AoA. However, it cannot be ignored that the WTO Agreements are implemented in a specific context, which is such that, all too often, developing countries have been unable to gain from the opportunities these agreements created, while suffering from the consequences of trade liberalisation on their economies. The pillars of the AoA—improved market access, and reduction in domestic support and export subsidies—are also not matched by corresponding obligations imposed on states to act cooperatively to limit the volatility of prices of commodities on international markets; to put in place safety nets and redistributive social policies in order to compensate those who lose out as a result of trade liberalisation; to regulate the commercial practices of transnational corporations along the global food supply chain; or to take into account environmental and health dimensions in their trade policies. It is this mismatch that is the source of the concerns raised by trade liberalisation; governments should pay as much attention to the need to develop trade sustainably as they do to remove existing distortions to trade.

A double-track strategy may therefore be recommended. First, states should strengthen their own agricultural sector, and thereby allow the poorest segment of the population to benefit from increased income and an additional source of employment. In the long term, due to the unavoidable rise in transport costs, there is no other way to achieve sustainable food security. That is not to say that there is no role for international trade, particularly for tropical products which can only be produced under certain climates; but where global supply chains do develop, they should work for the benefit of those who, today, are most food insecure, and they should be made more environmentally sustainable. This will not happen by chance; it can only happen by design. This should form a second part of the strategy: to the extent more trade is encouraged for certain products where it is justified, this should be accompanied by measures aimed at ensuring that their benefits are maximised, and that the potential negative impacts are minimised.

V. RECONCILING TRADE WITH THE RIGHT TO FOOD

A. The Challenge of Fragmentation

The previous section identified a number of potential impacts of trade liberalisation on the ability of states to comply with their obligation towards the human right to adequate food, as required in particular by Article 25 of the Universal Declaration of Human Rights and Article 11 of the International Covenant on Economic, Social and Cultural Rights. Yet their human rights obligations and the commitments they make through the conclusion of agreements under the WTO framework remain uncoordinated. At the international level, this lack of coordination is just one example of the problem of fragmentation of international law into a number of self-contained regimes, each with its own norms and dispute-settlement mechanisms, and each relatively autonomous vis-à-vis each other and vis-à-vis general international law.[83] All too often, this failure of global governance mechanisms to ensure an adequate coordination between the obligations imposed on states under these different regimes is replicated at domestic level: trade negotiators either are not aware of the human rights obligations of the governments they represent or do not identify the implications for their position in trade negotiations.[84] Even when they are well informed about the potential intersections, they routinely express the view that any potential incompatibility should be addressed through appropriate policies at domestic level, where the two sets of commitments should be reconciled.

This approach thus leaves it to each state to ensure, in its domestic policies, a consistency which is not sought after in the international legal process. This is not satisfactory. It amounts to treating obligations incurred under trade agreements as equivalent in normative force to human rights obligations. This not only fails to recognise that, both as a result of Article 103 of the UN Charter[85] and because human rights

---

[83] Report of the Study Group of the International Law Commission, 'Fragmentation of International Law: Difficulties Arising from the Diversification and Expansion of International law', UN document A/CN.4/L.702 (18 July 2006) para 8; B Simma, 'Self-contained Regimes' (1985) 16 *Netherlands Yearbook of International Law* 111.

[84] Only seldom have WTO members referred to the right to food in the context of trade negotiations within the WTO: this was done by Mauritius and Norway (Committee on Agriculture, Special Session, 'Note on Non-Trade Concerns', WTO document G/AG/NG/W/36/Rev.1 (9 November 2000) paras 44 and 57; WTO document G/AG/NG/W/101 (16 January 2001) paras 6ff); and by Burkina Faso (WTO document TN/AG/R/10 (9 September 2003) para 35).

[85] As members of the organisation of the UN, all states have pledged under Art 56 of the UN Charter to 'take joint and separate action in cooperation with the Organization for the achievement of the purposes' of the Charter, which include 'universal respect for, and observance of, human rights and fundamental freedoms for all without distinction as to race, sex, language or religion'. It follows from Art 103 of the Charter that this obligation prevails over any other international agreement.

norms have the status of peremptory norms of international law—no court could recognise as valid and apply a treaty adopted in violation of internationally recognised human rights—human rights should prevail over any other international commitments. It also creates the risk that, faced with situations of conflict, states will opt for compliance with their obligations under trade agreements: since these agreements are commonly backed by the threat of economic sanctions—as is the case within the WTO, under the Dispute Settlement Understanding—setting aside their human rights obligations will appear to governments less costly economically and even, often, politically.

The belief that compatibility between trade law and human rights law is best assured at the level of implementation in national policies also overestimates the ability of domestic political processes to compensate for the fragmentation of international law at the same time that it underestimates the contribution an enabling international environment can make to the fulfilment of human rights at national level. The imbalance created at international level between trade commitments backed by the threat of economic sanctions, on the one hand, and human rights treaties which are not enforced through similar means, on the other hand, cannot be easily rescued in national political processes: self-determination is illusory when it is exercised in such an incentives structure. Human rights require progressive implementation: apart from their immediate obligations to respect and protect human rights, states must fulfil human rights through measures which may require time to be fully implemented. For the adoption of such measures, states must have a certain policy space available, and they may need resources; certain trade policies adopted in implementation of trade agreements, however, may limit both, without this being always possible to predict in advance.

One safeguard does exist: under the so-called principle of 'integrity', commitments under the WTO framework must be interpreted, to the fullest extent possible, so as to be compatible with general international law, as well as with the rules of any treaty applicable in the relationships between the parties to the dispute giving rise to the question of interpretation, as such rules may develop, in particular, through adjudication.[86]

---

[86] The Appellate Body of the WTO takes the view that commitments under the WTO framework cannot be treated 'in clinical isolation' from general international law (Appellate Body Report of 20 May 1996, *United States—Standards for Reformulated and Conventional Gasoline (United States v Brazil and Venezuela)*, WT/DS2/AB/R). Art 3.2 of the Dispute Settlement Understanding confirms that WTO norms may be 'clarified . . . in accordance with customary rules of interpretation of international law', which the Vienna Convention codifies. Art 31, para 3(c) of the Vienna Convention on the Law of Treaties stipulates that the interpretation of treaties must take into account 'any relevant rules of international law applicable in the relations between the parties'. The 'relevant rules of international law' referred to by Art 31 para 3(c) of the Vienna Convention on the Law of Treaties are not deemed to be static, but may evolve, particularly, as a result of legal interpretation.

In the system of the WTO, the requirement that the agreements be interpreted in accordance with the other international obligations of the members is further strengthened by the fact that the authoritative interpretation of the agreements lies in the hands of the members themselves, within the Ministerial Conference or the General Council,[87] and the members cannot ignore their human rights obligations in providing such interpretations. Yet this does not provide a satisfactory answer to situations of real conflict which no conform interpretation could avoid. Such a principle of integrity in the interpretation of WTO agreements also does not address the 'chilling effect' that the norms established in these agreements may cause, when the members do not know whether or not any particular measure they take, in order to comply with their human rights obligations, will be considered acceptable by the other members or will instead expose them to retaliation, particularly when they seek to adopt measures which, although not strictly required by human rights treaties, nevertheless would contribute to the progressive realisation of human rights.

We therefore must ensure that the human rights obligations of the parties are taken into consideration at the negotiation stage of trade agreements: later may be too late. Unless adequately regulated and carefully sequenced, increased liberalisation may lead to further import surges, threatening the livelihoods of the local producers in the importing country, or alternatively to sudden increases in the prices of food commodities, against which the poorest food buyers are not adequately protected. It may lead to the expansion of global supply chains, which will benefit some but may marginalise many others who are already the most vulnerable. It will increase competition between, on the one hand, farmers from OECD countries and well-equipped, highly mechanised farmers from certain developing countries, and on the other hand, farmers in many other developing countries whose productivity per active labourer is 100 times lower. It may encourage forms of agricultural production and the lengthening of supply chains, at the risk of further damages to the environment in the form of increased GHG emissions and biodiversity erosion. In a world in which those who are

---

See *Legal Consequences for States of the Continued Presence of South Africa in Namibia (South-West Africa) notwithstanding Security Council Resolution 276 (1970)*, Advisory Opinion, ICJ Reports 1971, 16, 31, para 53; *Case concerning the Gabčíkovo-Nagymaros Project (Hungary/Slovakia)*, ICJ Reports 1997, 76–80, paras 132–47. On the need for an evolutionary interpretation, see Appellate Body Report, 12 October 1998, *United States—Import Prohibition of Certain Shrimp and Shrimp Products (United States v India, Malaysia, Pakistan, Thailand)*, WT/DS58/AB/R, para 129.

[87] See Art IX(2) of the WTO Agreement, also referred to in Art 3.9. DSU. And see C-D Ehlermann and L Ehring, 'The Authoritative Interpretation Under Article IX:2 of the Agreement Establishing the World Trade Organization: Current Law, Practice and Possible Improvements' (2005) 8 *Journal of International Economic Law* 814.

hungry are small-scale farmers and other food producers, including agricultural labourers, as well as urban poor, and in which climate change constitutes the single most important threat to food security in the future, pursuing the route of trade liberalisation while ignoring these potential consequences would be unacceptable. On the basis of the findings made above, the following proposals seek to assist states in better taking into account their human rights obligations in the negotiation and implementation of their commitments under the framework of the WTO. The first set of proposals are procedural in nature: they seek to ensure that trade negotiations are conducted in conditions which facilitate taking into consideration the right to food. The second set of proposals are substantive: they explore solutions to the impacts identified in section IV. Together, these proposals should promote the right of peoples to democratically determine their own agricultural and food policies, without these choices being dictated by the international trade regime. Moreover, they should channel this regime towards one that contributes not only to increased production and allocative efficiency, but also to the realisation of the right to food.

B. The Procedural Dimensions: Guiding Trade Negotiations Towards the Full Realisation of the Right to Food

(i) Assessing the Impact of Trade Agreements on the Right to Food

States should not accept undertakings under the WTO framework without ensuring that these commitments are fully compatible with their obligation to respect the right to food. This requires that they assess the impact on the right to food of these commitments.[88] It also requires that any commitments they make be limited in time, and subsequently re-evaluated, since the impacts of trade liberalisation on the ability of states to respect the right to food may be difficult to predict in advance, and may become visible only after a number of years of implementation. For instance, whatever the results of the current round of negotiations launched in Doha in November 2001, these results should be explicitly treated as provisional, and a sunset clause should be appended to the

---

[88] See Committee on Economic, Social and Cultural Rights, Concluding Observations regarding Ecuador, 7 July 2004, E/C.12/1/Add.100, para 56; Committee on the Rights of the Child, Concluding Observations regarding El Salvador, 30 June 2004, CRC/C/15/Add.232, para 48; Committee on the Elimination of Discrimination Against Women, Concluding Observations regarding Colombia, 2 February 2007, CEDAW/C/COL/CO/6, para 29; Committee on the Elimination of Discrimination against Women, Concluding Observations regarding Philippines, 25 October 2006, CEDAW/C/PHI/CO/6, para 26; Committee on the Elimination of Discrimination Against Women, Concluding Observations regarding Guatemala, 2 June 2006, CEDAW/C/GUA/CO/6, para 32.

outcome in order to allow for a renegotiation, following a period of a few years of implementation, on the basis of an independent review of the impact on the enjoyment of the right to adequate food.[89]

Impact assessments are a useful tool in order to help a state understand the implications of the agreements it enters into.[90] They have a powerful democratising effect, since they should provide an opportunity for civil society to participate in the evaluation of trade policies,[91] and allow national parliaments and civil society organisations to rely on their results in their dialogue with governments.[92] To the extent that impact assessments are based on the normative requirements of the human right to adequate food, and the corresponding indicators,[93] they can strengthen the negotiating position of governments in trade negotiations, particularly since the reference to the right to food is to an obligation imposed on all states under international law, which they cannot ignore in the context of trade negotiations.

In order to provide guidance to states in the preparation of such human rights impact assessments, this author has presented a draft set of guiding principles on human rights impact assessments of trade and investment agreements, in his official capacity of UN Special Rapporteur on the right to food. The draft guiding principles—still under discussion at the time of writing—define the preparation of human rights impact assessments as an obligation of states, which are bound by pre-existing human rights treaty obligations and therefore are prohibited from concluding any agreements that would impose on them inconsistent obligations: this, the guiding principles argue, imposes on states a duty to identify any potential inconsistency between pre-existing human rights treaties and subsequent trade or investment agreements, and to remove any inconsistency which has been found to exist. The draft guiding principles also refer to the right of every citizen to take part in the conduct of public affairs, recognised under the International Covenant on Civil and Political Rights:[94] the implication is that no trade or investment agreement should be concluded in the absence of a public

---

[89] See Art 20 AoA, which partially fulfils this objective in the current agreement.

[90] See generally J Harrisson and A Goller, 'Trade and Human Rights: What Does 'Impact Assessment' Have to Offer?' (2008) 8 *Human Rights Law Review* 587.

[91] OHCHR, Analytical study of the High Commissioner for Human Rights on the fundamental principle of participation and its application in the context of globalization, 23 December 2004, E/CN.4/2005/41.

[92] See Office of the High Commissioner for Human Rights, 'Report on Indicators for Monitoring Compliance with International Human Rights Instruments: a Conceptual and Methodological Framework', HRI/MC/2006/7 (11 May 2006) para 3.

[93] See, for a table of indicators based on the normative content of the right to food, Office of the High Commissioner for Human Rights, 'Report on Indicators for Monitoring Compliance with International Human Rights Instruments', HRI/MC/2008/3 (16 May 2008) 24.

[94] International Covenant on Civil and Political Rights, GA res 2200A (XXI), 21 UN GAOR Supp (No 16), 52, UN document A/6316 (1966), 999 UNT S 171, Art 25 (a).

debate, which human rights impact assessments precisely should serve to inform.

Yet, important though they are, impact assessments remain reactive—or defensive—in nature: they are tools to measure the consequences of the decisions which are taken, but they do not indicate, in and by themselves, which trade policies should be implemented in order to further the realisation of the right to food. Mechanisms should be set up to allow for the adoption of such policies, in addition to—and not as a substitute for—a regular monitoring of the impact of trade agreements and their implementation on the right to food.

(ii) International Trade as a Component of National Strategies for the Realisation of the Right to Food

States should ensure that the positions they take in trade negotiations—for example, as to which special products to protect, which schedules of commitments to accept or which services to open up to foreign competition—will not result in obstacles to the realisation of the right to food. To this end, they should define their positions in trade negotiations in accordance with national strategies for the realisation of the right to food. The adoption of such strategies is recommended by the Committee on Economic, Social and Cultural Rights,[95] and their content is further clarified by the Voluntary Guidelines to Support the Progressive Realization of the Right to Adequate Food in the Context of National Food Security adopted by member states of the Council of the FAO on 23 November 2004. Such strategies should also be seen as tools to guide trade negotiations: only by mapping food insecurity and identifying which actions should be taken to combat hunger will it be possible for those negotiating trade agreements to ensure that the commitments they make in trade negotiations will facilitate, rather than impede, efforts towards the fulfilment of the right to food of their population. Indeed, the usefulness of adopting such national strategies, based on a reliable mapping of food insecurity and vulnerability, goes far beyond the assistance it would provide negotiators in the WTO context. These strategies also should support the position of governments in their discussions with international financial institutions or with donors, or in bilateral trade negotiations. It is a particular source of concern that, in a large number of cases, states have been unable to use flexibilities allowed under the WTO agreements—or to apply certain tariffs remaining under their bound tariffs—because of prescriptions from such institutions or because of bilateral free trade agreements that deny them the flexibilities they are otherwise allowed under multilateral agreements. Adopting a

---

[95] UN Committee on Economic, Social and Cultural Rights, above n 69, para 21.

national strategy for the realisation of the right to food would strengthen the position of states in their discussions with these partners, at the same time that it would improve the accountability of governments to the rights-holders.

(iii) Transparency and Participation in Trade Negotiations

Right to food impact assessments and the adoption of national strategies for the realisation of the right to food are tools which should support negotiators in ensuring that they will not adopt positions at the international level which, at the national level, would impede the realisation of the right to food for all. In addition, however, it is essential that national parliaments and civil society are provided opportunities to monitor the positions adopted by governments in trade negotiations. They should not be presented, at the very final stage of the negotiation process—once agreement has been reached—with a set of commitments made by the Executive from which, at that stage, it would be politically very difficult or impossible to retreat from. National parliaments should regularly hold hearings about the positions adopted by the government in trade negotiations, and all groups affected, including in particular farmers' organisations, should have an opportunity to take part. The democratising potential of right to food impact assessments will only fully materialise if such procedures are put in place at the domestic level, in order to avoid a disconnection between commitments made at the international level and efforts developed at the national level for the realisation of the right to food. This is particularly important in the context of trade agreements relating to agriculture, given the risks of an increased dualisation of the farming system as a result of policies favouring the export sector, which is partly the result of disproportionate political influence being exercised in some countries by a relatively small number of very large agricultural producers—whereas small-scale farmers, in contrast, are poorly organised politically, and often unable to mobilise due to their geographical dispersion.[96]

C. The Substantive Dimensions: Taking into Account the Right to Food in the Multilateral Trade Regime

(i) Limiting the Dependency on International Trade

States should avoid excessive reliance on international trade in the pursuit of food security. 'Excessive' in this context should be understood

---

[96] See The World Bank, above n 15, 43.

as a situation in which, due to balance-of-payments difficulties or the lack of sufficient revenues from exports in other sectors, being dependent on the international markets to feed their population does not represent a sustainable option for states, in a context of increased price volatility and in which, most probably, the long-term trend towards declining prices of agricultural commodities is coming to an end. The short-term interest of states in procuring from international markets the food they cannot produce locally at lower prices should not lead them to sacrifice their long-term interest in building their capacity to produce the food they need to meet their consumption needs. There are two reasons for this. First, while rationales promoting allocative efficiency on the basis of specialisation according to comparative advantage emphasise the aggregate benefits, at the national level, of trade liberalisation, a perspective based on the right to food requires that we examine the impacts on the most vulnerable. Throughout the developing world, agriculture accounts for around 9% of GDP and over 50% of total employment. In those countries where more than 34% of the population are undernourished, agriculture represents 30% of GDP and 70% of employment.[97] Across all countries, the incomes of agricultural workers are significantly lower than in non-rural areas.[98] Therefore, for the realisation of the right to food, there is no alternative but to increase the productivity of the agricultural sector, with an emphasis on small-scale farmers. Where the agricultural sector is fragile—ie where it is not competitive against the most competitive farmers in the world—we cannot run the risk of limiting the policy space of governments by prohibiting them from maintaining tariff barriers, or from raising those barriers in the face of import surges. Such surges have in the past had disastrous effects on many producers in developing countries, impoverishing further the poorest in the rural areas. This may not be allowed to continue.

Secondly, by developing their capacity to feed their populations, states limit the vulnerability which results from the volatility of prices on international markets. As noted by the World Bank, 'managing grain price risk is a fundamental requirement in a world characterised by more volatile international grain prices and recurring supply shocks that will likely result from global warming'.[99] Consultations should be led on the needs to re-establish commodity-stabilising agreements for tropical products, cereals and oilseeds, sugar and cotton, all of which are of particular importance to developing countries, and on measures which could avoid the negative impacts of non-commercial speculation on the

---

[97] FAO, *The State of the Food Insecurity in the World 2003*, 16.
[98] See above n 16.
[99] Framework Document for proposed loans, credits, and grants in the amount of US$ 1.2 billion equivalent for a Global Food Crisis Response Program (GFRP), 29 May 2008, 6.

futures markets of those commodities. In the short term, we have to draw the consequences from the volatility of prices on international markets: each state should decide whether or not it is resilient enough to take the risk of increased vulnerability to external shocks, by maintaining or increasing its reliance on international markets to achieve food security at home—but it must do so in full awareness of the implications.

(ii) Maintaining Flexibilities

At present, a relatively small proportion of the food produced, estimated at 15%, is traded internationally. The percentages are 6.5% for rice, 12% for corn, 18% for wheat and 35% for soybeans.[100] Yet the prices fixed on international markets have an important impact on the ability of farmers in the world to make a decent living, since, as a result of trade liberalisation, there is a tendency for domestic and world prices to converge, insofar as imported goods compete with domestically produced goods on local markets. States, particularly developing states, in accordance with the principle of special and differential treatment, must therefore retain the freedom to take measures which insulate domestic markets from the volatility of prices on international markets. Unless the trade agreements they conclude provide for the necessary flexibilities, states may find themselves bound by certain disciplines which will make them vulnerable to variations in prices on the international markets.

One risk is that local producers will be driven out by import surges. It is this that the establishment of a special safeguard measure seeks to avoid. Indeed, the measures states may take in order to strengthen their agricultural sector, including the measures that fall under the 'Green Box' of allowable forms of domestic support to agriculture, will remain ineffective in the absence of such flexibility. Certain countries have supply management schemes in place. Such schemes guarantee a remunerative price to producers while at the same ensuring stable prices to consumers and a regularity of supply for processors and retailers. Countries should be encouraged to study such systems for management supply; they should be allowed to maintain or establish such schemes, although this may require that they be allowed to maintain import tariffs at levels allowing them to protect the products concerned from the impact of the arrival on domestic markets of low-priced products. It is particularly perplexing that certain management supply schemes, which seek to adapt production to demand and shield both producers and consumers from sudden shifts in prices, while at the same time ensuring processors a reasonable profit margin, would be threatened by proposals to reduce over-quota tariffs, even for products designated as sensitive because they

---

[100] Aksoy and Beghin, above n 16, 177–79.

are placed under such management schemes. Such schemes insure both producers and consumers against the fluctuations of prices on international markets, and, in an era of increased volatility, their stabilising function takes on a particular importance.

Another risk is that the net food buyers are made vulnerable to increases in prices, particularly since many developing states have little or no safety nets with which to protect the poorest segments of the population from such impacts. The Marrakesh Decision should insure net food importing developing countries against this risk, but as we have seen, the answer it provides remains deeply unsatisfactory. For this Decision to be fully effective, it would need to include a mechanism to systematically monitor the impact of the AoA reform process on the NFIDCs. It would also need to define the notion of 'adequate supplies' of basic foodstuffs (which, under the Decision, NFIDCs should be able to obtain from external sources 'on reasonable terms and conditions' throughout the reform process) by reference to the need to ensure that each individual has access at all times to adequate food or to means for its procurement, which is simply to say that the increased prices that may result from the reform process should not result in violations of the right to food. Finally, the Marrakesh Decision would need to be fully implemented, which it is not for the moment.

Implementing the Marrakesh Decision adequately would be consistent with the obligation of the WTO members to respect the right to food, not only towards their own populations, but also towards populations in other states, including those commercial partners that are impacted negatively by the reform programme resulting from commitments under the AoA. Yet, even with an improved operationalisation of the Marrakesh Decision, the problems of vulnerability of countries as a result of their dependency on international trade, and of the hidden costs of trade as a solution to achieving food security, remain real. More food aid and more easily accessible and less conditional financing facilities to meet balance-of-payments problems are no substitutes for the strengthening within all countries of the agricultural sector, both in order to enhance their food security and as a means to reduce poverty and, thus, hunger.

The measures suggested above seek to ensure that reliance on international trade will not have adverse consequences on the realisation of the right to food at domestic level. In negotiating trade agreements, all states should refrain from imposing on their trading partners the requirement to make concessions that could run counter to their obligation to guarantee the human right to adequate food. Instead, the international trade regime should be designed to facilitate and support national strategies for the realisation of the right to food. The Committee on Economic, Social and Cultural Rights has identified 'the failure of a State to take into account its international legal obligations regarding the right to food when entering into agreements with other states or with international organisations' as a specific instance of violation of the right to food.[101] Indeed, their obligations towards the right to food are imposed on states not only towards persons found on their national territory, but also towards persons situated outside the national borders, taking into account the sovereign rights of the territorial state. For instance, where a state heavily subsidies agricultural products that are exported by economic actors based under its jurisdiction, thus crowding out the local producers in the receiving markets, this should be treated as a violation of the right to food by the exporting state, since it constitutes a threat to food security in the importing country.[102] This is also the spirit of the General Comment that the Committee on Economic, Social and Cultural Rights adopted on the relationship between economic sanctions and respect for economic, social and cultural rights, in which the Committee noted that states imposing sanctions should not, in doing so, jeopardise the economic, social and cultural rights of the population in the targeted state.[103] All member states of the UN have committed themselves to cooperate internationally for the fulfilment of human rights, as stipulated in Article 56 of the UN Charter. The Universal Declaration of Human Rights refers to the right of everyone to an international social order that is conducive to the full realisation of human rights. States are therefore under a duty to cooperate in the establishment of a multilateral regime of international trade that supports the right to food.

(iii) Controlling Market Power in the Global Supply Chains and Counteracting the Risk of Increased Dualisation of the Farming System

One major imbalance in the current multilateral trade regime is that, while disciplines are imposed on states, transnational corporations, whose freedom to act has been significantly increased as a result, are not subject to any obligations as regards the exercise of their power on the market. This is an important gap in global governance. In the medium- to

---

[101] UN Committee on Economic, Social and Cultural Rights, above n 69, para 19. See also para 36: 'States parties should, in international agreements whenever relevant, ensure that the right to adequate food is given due attention and consider the development of further international legal instruments to that end'.

[102] See, *mutatis mutandis*, as regards the appropriate provision of food aid, UN Committee on Economic, Social and Cultural Rights, above n 69, para 39: 'Food aid should, as far as possible, be provided in ways which do not adversely affect local producers and local markets, and should be organized in ways that facilitate the return to food self-reliance of the beneficiaries'.

[103] UN Committee on Economic, Social and Cultural Rights, General Comment No 8 (1997), 'The Relationship between Economic Sanctions and Respect for Economic, Social and Cultural Rights', UN document E/1998/22.

long term, a multilateral framework may have to be established to ensure a more adequate control of these actors. In the short term, states should act in accordance with their responsibility to protect human rights by adequately regulating actors on which they may exercise an influence, including in situations where these actors operate outside the national territory of the states concerned.[104] While the exercise of extraterritorial jurisdiction constitutes one option in this regard, other initiatives could be taken by states, such as the imposition of transparency or reporting requirements, or the imposition of conditions for access to export credits, in order to ensure that commodity buyers, food processors and global retailers contribute to the realisation of the right to food and abstain from practices which might threaten its enjoyment. The best practices identified in the global food supply chain could be identified and, once identified, scaled up. Particular attention could be paid to the possibility of using competition law in order to protect not only end consumers, but also farmers selling their crops, from excessive concentration or abuse of dominant positions on the market.[105]

Another risk which trade liberalisation in agriculture entails is that the largest agricultural producers, which will benefit more easily from the opportunities resulting from improved market access, will crowd out smaller farms, for the reasons stated above. In many countries, small-scale farmers are among the most vulnerable segments of the population. States therefore owe them a special responsibility to counteract this tendency by supporting small-scale agriculture, in particular as regards access to land, water, genetic resources and credit; and by investing in, and improving their access to, rural infrastructures.

---

[104] See, eg UN Committee on Economic, Social and Cultural Rights, General Comment No 14 (2000), 'The Right to the Highest Attainable Standard of Health (Article 12 of the International Covenant on Economic, Social and Cultural Rights)', UN document E/C.12/2000/4 (2000), para 39; or UN Committee on Economic, Social and Cultural Rights, General Comment No 15 (2002), 'The Right to Water (arts 11 and 12 of the International Covenant on Economic, Social and Cultural Rights)', UN document E/C.12/2002/11 (26 November 2002), para 31. In these general comments, the Committee affirms that states parties should 'prevent third parties from violating the right [protected under the International Covenant on Economic, Social and Cultural Rights] in other countries, if they are able to influence these third parties by way of legal or political means, in accordance with the Charter of the UN and applicable international law'. Similarly, in 2007 the Committee on the Elimination of Racial Discrimination called on Canada to 'take appropriate legislative or administrative measures to prevent acts of transnational corporations registered in Canada which negatively impact on the enjoyment of rights of indigenous peoples in territories outside Canada. In particular, the Committee recommends that the State party explore ways to hold transnational corporations registered in Canada accountable' (CERD/C/CAN/CO/18, paragraph 17 (Concluding Observations/Comments, 25 May 2007)).

[105] See, for a more detailed exposition of the potential of a more systematic use of competition law in this context, 'Addressing Concentration in Food Supply Chains. The Role of Competition Law in Tackling the Abuse of Buyer Power', briefing note of the Special Rapporteur on the right to food (prepared with A Ganesh) (December 2010), available at http://available at www.srfood.org/index.php/en/areas-of-work/agribusiness.

D. Towards Socially and Environmentally Sustainable Trade

In addition to its obvious costs on the least competitive producers or on certain vulnerable segments of the population, the expansion of international trade in agricultural products may have hidden costs for the environment and for human health and nutrition; it may result in the smallest producers being offered prices so low for their crops that their revenues will hardly be sufficient to feed themselves and their families; and it may depress the wages of agricultural workers, as a result of increased international competition. The future regulation of international trade in agricultural commodities should take into account the impact of various modes of agricultural production on climate change, in order to allow countries to provide incentives in favour of forms of production, like organic farming or agroecological practices, which better respect the environment, while at the same time contributing to food security.[106]

In the future, the experience of Fairtrade schemes and other incentives-based initiatives should be studied in order to determine whether they should be expanded and, if so, how, in order to encourage socially and environmentally more sustainable trade. It may be asked, for example, whether inspiration could be sought from guidelines such as the Ethical Trading Initiative's smallholder guidelines, in order to promote sourcing practices that are more sustainable and that, instead of contributing to the dualisation of the farming system, strengthen the capacities and increase the incomes of small-scale farmers.

VI. CONCLUSION

For the poor, net food importing developing countries—where food insecurity is most widespread—the key challenge is how to reconcile

---

[106] See UNCTAD and UNEP, *Organic Agriculture and Food Security in Africa*, UNEP–UNCTAD Capacity Building Task Force on Trade, Environment and Development (UNCTAD/DITC/TED/2007/15) (New York and Geneva, UN, 2008) (showing the potential of organic agriculture in increasing agricultural productivity and raising incomes through reliance on low-cost, locally available technologies, without causing environmental damage, but also highlighting need for enabling policy and institutional support in order to scale-up organic agriculture and its associated positive side-effects). This study is only the latest in a series of studies whose conclusions converge on this point. See in particular J Pretty et al, 'Resource Conserving Agriculture Increases Yields in Developing Countries' (2006) 40(4) *Environmental Science & Technology* (reviewing 286 agricultural projects in 57 countries and concluding that low external input agriculture improves food crop productivity by average of 79%); J Pretty et al, 'Sustainable Intensification in African Agriculture' (2011) 9(1) *International Journal of Agricultural Sustainability* (forthcoming). For a systematic review of experiences, see O De Schutter, 'Agroecology and the Right to Food, presented to the 16th session of the Human Rights Council', UN document A/HRC/16/49 (March 2011).

their short-term interest in buying food where it is produced at a lower cost, even if this means rendering vulnerable the position of their less efficient producers, and their long-term interest in avoiding an excessive dependence on international markets for their food supplies and regaining a certain degree of self-sufficiency. The importation of cheap food onto their local markets can certainly bring relief to the poor urban consumers, as well as to the significant part of the rural poor that are net food buyers, but it is a strategy that may not be sustainable in the long run. The prices on international markets will be increasingly volatile and high in the future, and climate change will bring about more disruptions, particularly if food production is concentrated in a smaller number of areas: the more dependent countries are on imports for their food security, the more they risk being unable to face these shocks. In addition, for the poor countries whose agricultural sector is not sufficiently competitive, to deepen trade liberalisation before this sector is strengthened means to abandon the prospect of a broad-based rural development based on rising incomes among the rural households: in effect, it will mean little else than the continuation of the policies of the past three decades, which so lamentably failed. A number of recommendations follow:

1. It is axiomatic, first of all, that WTO members should ensure that their undertakings under the WTO framework are fully compatible with their obligation to respect, protect and fulfil the right to food. This requires that they perform transparent, independent and participatory human rights impact assessments before the conclusion of trade agreements. National parliaments should be encouraged to hold regular hearings about the positions adopted by the government in trade negotiations, with the inclusion of all groups affected, including in particular farmers' organisations. Only through such participatory mechanisms can it be ensured that trade liberalisation will not result in bringing about benefits for the export sectors, without compensations for the sectors that will suffer the most from foreign competition; and that trade liberalisation will be carefully sequenced, aligned with the ability of the state concerned to adapt to the restructuring to which it will lead. Most importantly, states should define their positions in trade negotiations in accordance with national strategies for the implementation of the right to food. National strategies are of particular relevance here because they are a tool to manage the conflict between short-term fixes and long-term visions: they ensure that policy decisions will not be myopic and discount the future costs of present decisions.
2. Improved transparency and participation in the negotiation of trade agreements should also ensure that each state will choose

democratically whether or not it can take the risk of becoming increasingly reliant on the international markets to achieve food security. This chapter has identified the reasons why states should avoid excessive dependence on international trade in the pursuit of food security, and why they should instead build their capacity to produce the food needed to meet consumption needs, with an emphasis on small-scale farmers. It has also provided arguments in favour of maintaining the necessary flexibilities and instruments, like supply management schemes, to insulate domestic markets from the volatility of prices on international markets. Collectively, states should explore means of limiting the volatility of prices on the international markets of commodities, particularly of tropical products, oilseeds, sugar and cotton, for instance through commodity stabilisation agreements. For poor countries, neither food aid nor the purchase of food commodities on the international markets is a substitute for strengthening their ability to feed their population by a robust agricultural sector serving the domestic market: although cheap food has been available from international markets and although prices have been declining for many years, this trend is now coming to a close, and the volatility of prices will be greater in the future, particularly as a result of the merger between the food and energy markets. However, where states do choose to increase their dependence on international trade—whether for the acquisition of export revenues or in order to achieve food security by buying food on the international markets—this choice would be much more acceptable in a context where mechanisms would be put in place in order to limit the volatility of prices on the international markets of commodities.
3. WTO members should also fully implement the Marrakesh Decision. In order for this Decision to be fully effective, a mechanism should be established to systematically monitor the impact of the AoA reform process on the NFIDCs. WTO members should agree on a definition of the notion of 'adequate supplies' of basic foodstuffs that refers to the need to ensure that each individual has access at all times to adequate food or to means for its procurement—ie that the increased prices which may result from the reform process will not result in violations of the right to food.
4. Trade liberalisation leads to strengthening the position of transnational corporations in the global supply chains without imposing on them corresponding obligations. It should be the duty of states to adequately regulate private actors over which they may exercise an influence, in order to discharge their obligation to protect the right to food. They should also explore ways to redirect trade towards products and modes of production that better respect the environment and do not lead to violations of the right to food. The international community

could support these efforts by moving towards the development of a multilateral framework regulating the activities of commodity buyers, processors and retailers in the global food supply chain, including the setting of standards for these actors and their buying policies. This is one reason why the strengthening of the architecture of the global governance of food security, with the reform in 2009 of the Committee on World Food Security,[107] is so encouraging: it not only signals the willingness of the international community to move together and to improve coordination of efforts in tackling global hunger and malnutrition; it should also ensure that the trade regime of international law should in the future develop less in isolation from other regimes that have an impact on food security. It is high time indeed that we overcome the current dispersion of efforts and fragmentation of international governance.

[107] The Committee on World Food Security (CFS) is an FAO intergovernmental committee that was transformed at the end of 2009 into an inclusive forum. Although governments are the only voting members on any decisions to be adopted, UN agencies working in the area of food security, international financial institutions including the WTO, civil society organisations and the private sector participate in reaching an international consensus on the measures that are desirable in order to improve global food security. Committee on World Food Security, Reform of the Committee on World Food Security, document CFS:2009/2Rev 2 (October 2009), available at ftp://ftp.fao.org/docrep/fao/meeting/018/k7197e.pdf. It has been described as 'the foremost inclusive international and intergovernmental platform for a broad range of committed stakeholders to work together in a coordinated manner and in support of country-led processes towards the elimination of hunger and ensuring food security and nutrition for all human beings' (ibid, ¶ 4).

6

How to Phase Out Rich Country Agricultural Subsidies Without Increasing Hunger in the Developing World

JENNIFER MERSING

IN JANUARY 2007, tens of thousands of people took to the streets of Mexico City to protest the rapidly rising price of tortillas. The price of tortillas, the main source of food for many poor Mexicans, had rapidly risen by over 400%.[1] Poor Mexican families were being forced to spend up to a third of their income on tortillas—or to switch to cheaper and less nutritious alternatives or to simply eat less.[2] As food prices increased dramatically all over the world, Mexico was not the only country to face a crisis over the higher price of food. Countries as diverse as India, Venezuela, Burkina Faso and even Italy also experienced food protests during the 2007–08 food price crisis. The Food and Agriculture Organization of the UN (FAO) calculated that the 2007–08 aggregate cereal import bill, which includes such vital products as wheat and maize, had increased by 62% from the previous season for Low-Income Food Deficit Countries.[3] Even with decreased global food prices in 2009, food prices have remained high in developing countries; all signs point to the end of the era of cheap food.

Simultaneous with the rise in food prices, a group of developing countries, the G-20, has been pressing for a reduction in agricultural

---

[1] 'Mexicans Stage Tortilla Protest', *BBC News*, 1 February 2007.
[2] M Roig-Franzia, 'A Culinary and Cultural Staple in Crisis', *Washington Post*, 27 January 2007, A1.
[3] FAO, 'Low-Income Food-Deficit Countries' Food Situation Overview' (April 2009) No 2 *Crop Prospects and Food Situation*, available at www.fao.org/docrep/011/ai481e/ai481e05.htm.

subsidies in rich countries. The G-20 emerged in August 2003, ahead of the Fifth World Trade Organization (WTO) Ministerial Conference in Cancun, Mexico, as an alliance of developing countries interested in forming a common position on key issues in the WTO agricultural negotiations.[4] Since the establishment of the current multilateral framework for international trade, rich countries have been allowed to continue to greatly subsidise their agricultural sectors. Many of those subsidies have lowered the price of rich country agricultural exports—thereby lowering the global price of agricultural commodities and often undercutting producers in poor countries. Viewing agriculture as one of their comparative advantages compared to rich countries, the G-20 has been demanding fewer rich country agricultural subsidies and a more level playing field in the agricultural context.

But phasing out rich country agricultural subsidies will not benefit all developing countries. In an era of already record high food prices, the reduction in rich country subsidies will further push up the cost of food. For those poor families that are already struggling to afford basic necessities, that increase will be extremely difficult to manage. Especially in poor countries that are net food importers, safeguard measures must be enacted to protect vulnerable populations from an increased incidence of hunger.

Part I of this chapter describes the food price crisis of 2007–08 and the increased vulnerability of hunger in developing countries. It contends that, although global food prices have dropped since 2008, the underlying factors for the crisis remain and are likely to contribute to another sharp increase in prices in the near future. Part II discusses rich country agricultural subsidies and the WTO. It argues that, while there has been some change in the composition of rich country agricultural subsidies, they continue to have a distorting impact on the global agricultural market. Moreover, while developing countries have pressed their case to the WTO, progress on reform remains slow. Part III discusses how to develop safeguards against hunger. It describes global efforts to respond to worldwide food insecurity and provides recommendations on actions that developing governments and rich country governments should take—including reducing rich country agricultural subsidies, strengthening the agricultural sector in developing countries and undertaking specific measures to protect against food insecurity.

---

[4] See US Department of Agriculture, Economic Research Service, 'WTO: Glossary', available at www.ers.usda.gov/Briefing/wto/glossary.htm. The G-20 is currently composed of 21 countries: Argentina, Bolivia, Brazil, Chile, China, Cuba, Egypt, Guatemala, India, Indonesia, Mexico, Nigeria, Pakistan, Paraguay, the Philippines, South Africa, Tanzania, Thailand, Uruguay, Venezuela and Zimbabwe. This group of countries is different from the G-20 that is composed of Finance Ministers and Central Bank Governors from key developed and developing countries.

I. GLOBAL FOOD PRICES AND THE THREAT OF INCREASED HUNGER IN DEVELOPING COUNTRIES

A. The Food Price Crisis of 2007–08

During 2007 and 2008, food prices were at record levels, leaving some staple foods in short supply in numerous countries. Although food prices decreased at the end of 2008, the threat of further food crises has not passed, since the underlying structural issues that contributed to the 2007–08 food crisis remain. This combination of agriculture and inflation has been given its own term—'agflation'.[5] In 2007, the FAO Food Price Index (which is the average of commodity group price indexes for meat, dairy, cereals, oils and fats, and sugar weighted against the average export share of each of the commodity groups) averaged 157. This was a 23% increase from 2006 and a 34% increase from 2005. By March 2008, the Food Price Index reached nearly 220—the highest recorded monthly average since the start of the Index in 1990.[6] In 2007, grain reserves had fallen to their lowest levels in decades.[7] Developing countries as a whole spent $50 billion importing cereals in 2007, which was a 10% increase from 2006.[8] Although global food prices decreased in 2009, many observers believe that food prices will indeed increase again in the near future.

The rapid rise in agricultural prices was driven by several factors. Although some countries had poor agricultural harvests leading up to the food price crisis, the main reasons for the rise in agricultural prices were due more to changes in demand rather than to a scarcity in supply. In fact, the total cereal crop in 2007 was 1.66 billion tons, which was a record amount and 89 million more than the cereal crop in 2006. Demand, however, has been growing faster than supply. Greater wealth in India and China has increased global demand for meat. For example, over the past 20 years, meat consumption in China has increased from an average of 44 pounds of meat per person per year to over 110 pounds per person per year. In developing countries as a whole, demand for meat has doubled while consumption of cereals has remained flat since the 1980s. The rising demand for meat has an enormous impact on grain prices, because, during the production cycle, meat requires much more wheat than bread does. Farmers have thus responded to the shift in consumption habits by feeding more grain to their animals, using 200–250

---

[5] D Howden, 'The Fight for the World's Food', *The Independent*, 23 June 2007.
[6] FAO, 'FAO Food Price Indices' (April 2008) No 2 *Crop Prospects and Food Situation*, available at www.fao.org/docrep/010/ai465e/ai465e06.htm.
[7] Howden, above n 5.
[8] 'Cheap No More', *The Economist*, 8 December 2007, 81–83.

million more tons of grain to feed their animals than they did 20 years ago.[9]

While this change in diet in the developing world has been gradual, another important factor in the huge price increase in food has arisen more rapidly: the substantial growth of ethanol fuel in the US. The impact of biofuels on the right to food is addressed in much more detail in chapter 4, by Ann Sofie Cloots, but, for the sake of completeness, it is important to note briefly the impact of increased ethanol production. Ethanol fuel can be produced from maize. In 2000, around 15 million tons of American maize was used for ethanol. In 2007, that quantity had multiplied to 85 million tons. The US is the world's largest maize exporter, but now more of its maize crop is destined for ethanol than for export. It is therefore arguable that the US government's expansion of its ethanol programme in 2005 helped to precipitate the 2007–08 food crisis. To take advantage of the expansion of the US biofuels programme, many American farmers shifted to more maize production at the expense of other crops, such as wheat and soybeans. The US's maize harvest in 2007 was 335 million tons, which was a quarter more than it was in 2006. Because ethanol production requires a tremendous amount of maize, the elimination of the ethanol programme in the US would satisfy over half of the world's unmet need for cereal. Since the US exports more grain than Canada, Australia and Argentina combined, changes in the US market have a profound effect on world prices—as has become very obvious.[10] Biofuels production in other countries also has an impact on the use of food crops.

The record high prices of oil also contributed to the 2007–08 soaring food prices. With oil trading for over $100 a barrel in 2008, food producers faced higher transportation costs.[11] There are signs that the food economy is merging with the fuel economy, as prices in the two sectors rise together.[12] In addition, high fertiliser prices have contributed to increased food prices. The inflation of fertiliser prices is being driven by the same factors that have resulted in the rapid increase in food prices, including increased demand for grains and higher energy prices.[13] Fertiliser prices increased by more than 200% in 2007, significantly raising farmers' costs of production. There is also debate concerning the impact of commodity price speculation in contributing

---

[9] Ibid.
[10] 'We Have to Accept that the Era of Cheap Food is Coming to an End', *The Independent*, 23 June 2007.
[11] Tami Luhby, 'Pain in the Pocketbook', *CNNMoney.com*, 28 February 2008, available at http://money.cnn.com/2008/02/27/news/economy/fuelandfood/index.htm?postversion=2008022807.
[12] Howden, above n 5.
[13] 'World Fertilizer Prices Surge 200% in 2007', *Mongabay.com*, 20 February 2008, available at http://news.mongabay.com/2008/0220-fertilizers.html.

to the 2007–08 food price crisis.[14] Further, although food prices decreased at the end of 2008, all of the factors that led to the 2007–08 food crisis show no signs of abating in the long term, signifying that high food prices will be a reality in the future.

B. The Threat of Greater Hunger in Developing Countries

Food insecurity plagues large parts of the developing world. The FAO classifies 77 countries as Low-Income Food-Deficit Countries. While almost half of those countries are in Africa, the classification encompasses a wide variety of developing countries—from behemoths like China to small islands like Haiti to landlocked countries like Pakistan, and from countries in tropical climates like Equatorial Guinea to colder countries such as Mongolia.[15] Even though there were bumper cereal harvests in many Low-Income Food-Deficit Countries in 2009, the FAO determined that food difficulties remained in 29 countries (with 19 of those in Africa) during 2010, designating them as 'countries in crisis requiring external assistance for food'.[16] Those countries face many problems, including drought and other weather problems, shortfalls in food production and supplies, lack of infrastructure, inadequate access to food markets, conflict and slow post-conflict recovery, and economic crises.

The UN World Food Programme (WFP), which is the main provider of emergency food aid, has issued warnings about food aid rationing. During the recent food crisis, the agency's budget requirements increased by several million dollars a week due to the rising food prices. The WFP's ability to mitigate the impact of rising prices has decreased during the past 5 years because of the decline in contributions of 'in-kind food aid', which is food produced abroad that is then delivered to vulnerable people in emergencies. The US, which is the world's largest food aid donor, was primarily responsible for this change, as it began to shift from 'in-kind food aid' to monetary donations due to the elimination of its large surpluses and low cereal prices. In addition to this crisis in

---

[14] See, eg O De Schutter, UN Special Rapporteur on the Right to Food, 'Food Commodities Speculation and Food Price Crises', Briefing Note 2 (September 2010) (arguing that significant part of food price increase was due to commodity price speculation).

[15] FAO, Country Profiles, 'Low-Income Food Deficit Countries (LIFDC)—List for 2010', available at www.fao.org/countryprofiles/lifdc.asp?lang=en.

[16] FAO, 'Countries in Crisis Requiring External Assistance for Food' (May 2010) No 2 *Crop Prospects and Food Situation*, available at www.fao.org/docrep/012/ak347e/ak347e00.pdf. As of May 2010, the 'countries in crisis requiring external assistance for food' are Mauritania, Niger, Zimbabwe, Eritrea, Liberia, Sierra Leone, Somalia, Burundi, Central African Republic, Chad, Congo, Côte d'Ivoire, Democratic Republic of Congo, Ethiopia, Guinea, Kenya, Madagascar, Sudan, Uganda, Iraq, North Korea, Mongolia, Afghanistan, Nepal, Pakistan, Philippines, Sri Lanka, Yemen and Haiti.

supply, the WFP is also facing new demands from countries like Afghanistan, where increasing numbers of people are newly unable to afford food. The shortages encountered by the WFP are particularly damaging because it is the only source of food for some people.[17]

The precise amount that food prices increased during the 2007–08 food crisis, and decreased in 2009, varied widely among countries. For example, while the FAO estimated that poor countries as a whole would see their cereal import bill rise by more than a third in 2008, Africa was expected to face a 49% increase. In some developing countries, prices increased by up to 80% for staple foods, pricing many of the poor out of the market. Even before the food crisis, people in extreme poverty, who were living on 50 cents a day, already had to allocate 80–90% of their budget to food—a situation that was only worsened during the food crisis, which priced some people out of the food market altogether.[18] According to estimates by economists, a one-third increase in food prices, while only decreasing living standards in rich countries by 3%, would cause an over 20% drop in living standards in very poor countries. The most vulnerable group is the urban poor, who are completely dependent on food from abroad. Consumers who rely on food that is not traded much across borders (such as potatoes in the Andes) are much more shielded from global price fluctuations.[19]

The rapid increase in food prices in 2007–08 has made poor consumers even more vulnerable to the prospect of facing hunger. Unless appropriate remedial measures are taken, the reduction in rich country agricultural subsidies, which would further raise global food prices, threatens to increase this risk of hunger.

II. RICH COUNTRY AGRICULTURAL SUBSIDIES AND THE WORLD TRADE ORGANIZATION

A. US and European Agricultural Subsidies

Although the US and European countries were founded as agrarian societies, their economies have long since been transformed from agriculture-based into industrial, and then later post-industrial, service-based economies. Despite those dramatic changes, agriculture remains an

---

[17] 'UN Warns Over Food Aid Rationing', *BBC News*, 25 February 2008, available at http://news.bbc.co.uk/2/hi/in_depth/7262830.stm. More than any other continent, Africa is beset by economic crises, civil conflict, and adverse weather conditions such as drought. All of these factors serve to further drive up the price of food. For example, of the 29 countries currently on the FAO's list of countries in crisis requiring external assistance, 19 of them are in Africa. See FAO, above n 16.

[18] 'UN Warns Over Food Aid Rationing', above n 17.

[19] 'Cheap No More', above n 8.

important force in the US and the EU. Both the US and the EU provide billions of dollars of subsidies to their domestic farmers.[20] In contrast, many developing countries, which have populations that are much more dependent on rural areas and agriculture, cannot provide their farmers with the same level of support. As a result of the rich country subsidies, those developing countries have therefore been losing out in the global agricultural export market. In addition, farmers in developing countries can be negatively affected by the importation of artificially cheap food.

According to the 2010 Organisation for Economic Co-operation and Development (OECD) Agricultural Policies report, OECD countries provided an estimated $252.522 billion in agricultural producer support in 2009. This actually represented a slight increase in support from 2008, when support had decreased due to the above-discussed high commodity prices. The EU was responsible for $120.840 billion of that figure and the US accounted for $30.598 billion. Agricultural support thus remains very high among rich countries, accounting for the equivalent of 22% of the aggregate gross farm receipts. The level of agricultural producer support in 2007–09, as measured by the percentage of producer revenue, in the US and the EU was 9 and 23%, respectively.[21]

While the most trade-distorting forms of subsides—such as market price support, output payments and payments linked to purchased inputs—continue to be widely prevalent, there has already been some success in changing the composition of rich country agricultural support.[22] For example, even though government support tied to the amount of commodity produced continues to be the single largest component of producer support in rich countries, this type of support has decreased from 30% of gross farm receipts in 1986–88 (representing approximately 85% of support) to just over 10% of gross farm receipts in 2007–09 (representing approximately 50% of support). In addition, government support that is not linked to the production of commodities represented 23% of

---

[20] See Organisation for Economic Co-operation and Development (OECD), 'Agricultural Policies in OECD Countries: At a Glance 2010'. The US and the EU are not the only rich countries that provide agricultural subsidies. For example, Japan, Switzerland, Norway, Australia and New Zealand all provide support for their agricultural producers. This chapter only focuses on subsidies from the US and the EU, however, as they are the two largest providers of agricultural subsidies.

[21] Ibid, 5–6, 17, 19.

[22] Market price support occurs when a government keeps the domestic price of an agricultural commodity relatively fixed, despite changes in world price, and pays agricultural producers based on the difference between the artificial domestic price and the world price. Output payments commit the government to paying agricultural producers based on the production level of a certain agricultural commodity. Payments based on input use offer financial incentives to agricultural producers to use certain variable inputs (such as a specific fuel or fertiliser) or certain fixed capital formations (for example, to undertake specific on-farm investments). Governments also have agricultural payment programmes based on area, animal numbers, farm receipts or income (with some based on commodity production and others not based on commodity production). See ibid, 20–32.

total agricultural support in 2007–09, whereas it represented less than 1% of agricultural producer support in 1986–88.[23]

As part of this change in the composition of agricultural producer support, rich countries have begun shifting towards programmes based on historical entitlements, areas planted, animal numbers and environmental conservation. At the same time, rich countries have increased budgetary support for general services for agriculture, including inspection, infrastructure, marketing and research. This represents a shift in agriculture assistance from support that is focused on the individual producer to government support that is provided to the agricultural sector as a whole.[24]

In addition to the demands from large parts of the developing world to phase out agricultural subsidies, many rich countries face tremendous internal pressures on their agricultural programmes. With the accession of 10 new member states to the EU in 2004, the Common Agricultural Policy (CAP) was confronted with huge new demands for support. In anticipation of that expansion, the EU reformed the CAP in 2003 to provide for a single payment scheme (SPS) that decoupled aid from production. By 2006, many EU member countries had started to apply this new system of direct payments, which distributed a unified payment based on historical levels of support or the number of eligible hectares farmed during the first year of the scheme. The EU expects practically all aid to be decoupled by 2012. The aim of the programme is to allow farmers to decide what to produce while still receiving the same amount of aid, thereby better aligning production with demand. But farmers may receive aid under other specific support schemes as well. For the new EU member states, a national ceiling for agricultural payments was established in the Accession Agreement.[25]

The US has not faced the same internal pressures to reform agricultural subsidies as the EU. In June 2008, the US Congress passed, over President George W. Bush's veto, the Food, Conservation, and Energy Act of 2008 ('2008 Farm Bill'), which governs the bulk of US federal agricultural programmes, as well as other related programmes, for the subsequent 5 years. The bill's fifteen titles include provisions, inter alia, on administrative and funding authorities for programmes on income and commodity price support, farm credit, conservation through land retirement, food assistance, agricultural development abroad, promotion of international access to US farm products, rural community and economic development initiatives, and research regarding certain areas of the agricultural

---

[23] Ibid, 19–20.
[24] Ibid, 32.
[25] European Commission, 'Agricultural and Rural Development, Direct Payments', available at http://ec.europa.eu/agriculture/markets/sfp/index_en.htm.

and food sector.[26] The 2008 Farm Bill authorised the spending of up to $307 billion, with $209 billion scheduled for nutrition programmes, such as domestic food aid or food stamps. Furthermore, the 2008 Farm Bill largely preserved the US agricultural support programmes already in existence. However, projected spending on commodities, conservation and trade programmes under the 2008 Farm Bill is between $72 billion and $74 billion, which is considerably less than the actual spending on those programmes under the 2002 Farm Bill, which ended up amounting to $95 billion over 5 years. In addition, the 2008 Farm Bill introduced a new optional insurance programme for farmers, the Average Crop Revenue Election, which is designed to protect US farmers against both low yields and drops in commodity prices.[27]

While there has been some reform, agricultural subsidies remain entrenched in rich countries. Especially when this support has been concentrated in trade-distorting measures, agriculture in developing countries has been losing out. Even though it will bring about a greater risk of hunger in some poor countries, rich countries should continue to be urged to phase out their most trade-distorting agricultural subsidies for the benefit of developing country farmers. And because reform at the domestic level has happened at too slow a pace, developing countries seeking a level playing field for agriculture have pressed their case for a reduction in subsidies in multilateral trade talks.

B. World Trade Organization Negotiations

Although trade-distorting subsidies are generally prohibited under the WTO, the Agreement on Agriculture carves out an exception to allow rich countries to continue to subsidise their agricultural sectors.[28] In the current Doha Development Round of WTO negotiations, however, developing countries are targeting the current imbalance and demanding a phase-out of rich country agricultural subsidies. Although the rich countries have been shifting the composition of their agricultural subsidy programmes away from the most trade-distorting measures, their progress has not been fast enough for many in the developing

---

[26] US Department of Agriculture, Economic Research Service, 'The 2008 Farm Bill Side-By-Side', available at www.ers.usda.gov/FarmBill/2008/2008FarmBillSideBySide041509.pdf.

[27] S Murphy and S Suppan, 'The 2008 Farm Bill and the Doha Agenda', Institute for Agriculture and Trade Policy (25 June 2008), available at www.iatp.org/iatp/commentaries.cfm?refID=103103.

[28] See The Agreement on Agriculture, 15 April 1994, Marrakesh Agreement Establishing the World Trade Organization, Annex 1A, 1867 UNTS 410, 33 ILM 1144 (1994). See also Agreement on Subsidies and Countervailing Measures, 15 April 1994, Marrakesh Agreement Establishing the World Trade Organization, Annex 1A, 1867 UNTS 154, 33 ILM 1144 (1994).

world. In fact, Brazil has already taken more aggressive measures and successfully challenged the US's cotton subsidy programmes using the WTO dispute settlement mechanisms.[29] Despite differences in agricultural situations, most developing countries have worked to develop a common front on agricultural issues, with a negotiating position of only offering small concessions on issues important to rich countries—such as market access for industrial goods—until their demands are met.[30]

Although the US and the EU agreed on a broad framework for agricultural reform before the 2003 WTO Ministerial Meeting in Cancun, their agreement was vague on details and the negotiations collapsed after demands from developing countries.[31] While the negotiations have since been revived and states have made more moves towards compromise, there nevertheless remains a high risk of failure. The parties still need to reach an agreement on, among other issues, elimination of export subsidies, cuts in trade-distorting agricultural subsidies, treatment of sensitive agricultural products and cuts in agricultural tariffs. As developing countries have made agriculture a pivotal issue to the successful conclusion of Doha negotiations, talks on non-agricultural market access have also been suffering from this impasse in the agricultural negotiations.[32]

Staking an assertive position to advance the situation of poor countries in international trade, the G-20 has made its advocacy for the phasing out of rich country agricultural subsidies a principal part of its agenda, even though many developing countries are currently food importers. An end to rich country subsidies, especially the benefits tied to exports, will very likely lead to a further increase in global agricultural prices, because there will be a decrease in the subsidised supply of food from rich countries that currently fills the market. For developing countries that are agricultural exporters and in direct competition with products from rich countries (such as Mali with the US over cotton), a reduction in rich country subsidies will be a boon to farmers and to the country as a whole through increased foreign earnings. In contrast, developing countries that are already suffering from high food prices will find themselves in an even more perilous position.

---

[29] See Appellate Body Report, *United States—Upland Cotton*, WT/DS267/AB/R (3 March 2005). The case was brought by Brazil against the US.

[30] See 'WTO Negotiators Look to 2008, Though Doha Deal Prospects Remain Slim' (2007) 11 *ICTSD Bridges Weekly Trade Digest* No 42, available at http://ictsd.org/i/news/bridgesweekly/7643/; S Cho, 'The Troubled Status of WTO Doha Round Negotiations', *American Society of International Law Insights*, 25 August 2005, available at www.asil.org/insights/2005/08/insights050825.html.

[31] Guy de Jonquières, 'Crushed at Cancun', *Financial Times*, 15 September 2003.

[32] See 'WTO NAMA Chair Defends Draft Text Against Charges of Backsliding in Talks' (2008) 25 *International Trade Reporter* No 9. See WTO, 'Doha Development Agenda: Negotiations, Implementation and Development', available at www.wto.org/english/tratop_e/dda_e/dda_e.htm.

Many poor countries have a comparative advantage in the production of agricultural products and they should be able to exploit this benefit. Reducing trade-distorting rich country agricultural subsidies, as well as promoting and strengthening the agricultural sector in poor countries, could lead to a number of positive outcomes for those countries. The countries could use the money from their increased international trade in agricultural goods to improve conditions in the country as a whole, such as by investing in infrastructure, education and social welfare programmes. Moreover, a global agricultural market that is not unfairly tilted in favour of rich countries would boost a vital sector of the economy on which much of the population in poor countries depends. Countries that are on the margins between being food importers and food exporters would be more likely to become at least self-sufficient in food under these circumstances. In addition, a vibrant rural economy could help to stem the population flow in developing countries to already overburdened cities. Policies and safeguards do need to be put in place, however, to protect the developing countries that will not be able to enjoy those benefits immediately but instead will be facing an increased risk of hunger.

III. DEVELOPING SAFEGUARDS AGAINST HUNGER

A. Responses to Food Insecurity

As part of the Millennium Development Goals, countries have committed to reducing by half the proportion of people who suffer from hunger by 2015.[33] Furthermore, in November 2009, the FAO hosted a World Summit on Food Security, which produced a declaration calling for increased agriculture funding and investment, improved governance regarding global food issues, efforts to confront the challenges posed by climate change and a renewed commitment to eradicate hunger.[34] In addition, rich countries, acting through various fora, have vowed continually to increase world food security. For example, at the 2009 meeting of the G-8 in L'Aquila, Italy, world leaders and international organisations launched the Aquila Food Security Initiative, committing US $20 billion over the course of 3 years for the development of sustainable agriculture and safety nets for vulnerable populations. The Aquila Food Security Initiative is being headed by the FAO Investment Center, in cooperation with other organs of the FAO, beneficiary countries, bilateral

---

[33] UN Millennium Declaration, 18 September 2000, A/Res/55/2, 'See We Can End Poverty 2015: Millennium Development Goals', available at www.un.org/millenniumgoals.
[34] World Summit on Food Security, Rome, Italy, 16–18 November 2009, Declaration of the World Summit on Food Security.

donors, international financial institutions and the aid community. The FAO Investment Center also supports the Global Agriculture and Food Security Program, a World Bank-managed, multi-donor trust fund designed to promote increased agricultural investment. Pledges to the Global Agricultural and Food Security Program have totalled US $813 million.[35]

B. Recommended Government Responses

To meet the targets of the Millennium Development Goals and fulfil their financing commitments, rich countries should contribute to easing hunger among the poor that is caused by high food prices. To finance that aid, rich countries could use some of the money that they will save from their reform of agricultural subsidies to provide food aid in food-importing developing countries. Food aid should be split between 'in kind food aid', which would allow the WFP to mitigate rises in food prices by delivering emergency food aid, and money transfers to poor countries that are earmarked for food subsidies or agricultural development. Those money transfers should be based on hunger risk and targeted towards countries where there are reasonable guarantees that the money will actually make it to the hands of the hungry or be invested in agricultural development (and not be lost to government corruption). Donors should focus particularly on the developing countries that are on the FAO's warning list. If a country misallocates this food aid, the resources should be withdrawn and given to another needy country; the former recipient country will then have to rely on international food aid from the WFP or other international organisations. Because the vast majority of rich countries are far below the target for the financing of official development assistance, this would be an efficient and productive way for rich countries to satisfy their obligations to help poor countries.

---

[35] FAO Investment Centre, 'Role of the Investment Centre in the Aquila Food Security Initiative', available at www.fao.org/tc/tci/othercollaboration/the-aquila-food-security-initiative/en. See also 'L'Aquila' Joint Statement on Global Food Security, available at www.g8italia2009.it/static/G8_Allegato/LAquila_Joint_Statement_on_Global_Food_Security[1],0.pdf. The G-8 group of developed countries consists of Canada, France, Germany, Italy, Japan, Russia, the UK and the US. In addition to the G-8, the Aquila Food Security Initiative was endorsed by Algeria, Angola, Australia, Brazil, Denmark, Egypt, Ethiopia, India, Indonesia, Libya, Mexico, the Netherlands, Nigeria, China, South Korea, Senegal, Spain, South Africa, Turkey, the Commission of the African Union, the FAO, the International Energy Agency, the International Fund for Agricultural Development, the International Labour Organization, the International Monetary Fund, the OECD, the Secretary General's UN High-Level Task Force on the Global Food Security Crisis, the WFP, the World Bank, the WTO, the Alliance for a Green Revolution in Africa, the Biodiversity/Consultative Group on International Agricultural Research, the Global Donor Platform for Rural Development and the Global Forum on Agricultural Research.

When confronted with high food prices, developing country governments, with the help of rich countries, need to take immediate action to alleviate food insecurity. And no matter what the current food prices are, developing country governments must also undertake long-term planning and investment in the agricultural sector in order to improve food self-sufficiency. Where possible, developing countries should provide staple foods or food subsidies to those parts of its population that are facing hunger, as well as those who are at severe risk of facing hunger. That should be done in conjunction with rich country assistance and the WFP. Countries also need to improve distribution networks to vulnerable areas to ensure that food aid actually arrives where it is intended. In addition, countries should eliminate import tariffs on staple foods in order for those necessities to enter the country as cheaply as possible. Countries should also develop food stockpiles to prepare for food emergencies. If the food in the stockpiles is in danger of perishing, the government can donate the food to the poor parts of the population that are most in danger of hunger.

To combat hunger, countries should try to import staple food as cheaply as possible.[36] In most circumstances, though, they should avoid imposing price and export controls on food. Export controls, by limiting the market, push farmers into growing different crops and can lead to increased global prices.[37] Price controls often exacerbate shortages and encourage the development of a black market within countries, making it even harder for the hungry to procure food. By setting prices artificially low, producers do not have an incentive to rush food to the official market (or, in the case of food-importing nations, foreign producers will likely not send a sufficient amount of food to that country). For example, when Russia imposed price controls on staples such as milk, eggs and bread, those foods disappeared from the shelves. In contrast, Morocco was able to more successfully manage the price of food. During Ramadan, a holy month of fasting under Islam, the Moroccan government fixed bread prices, which is the food of the poor, and cut import tariffs on food.[38] Those contrasting examples show that, if price controls are going to be used successfully, governments should try to target them narrowly towards the staple crops on which the poor depend, and should not use them indiscriminately for the benefit of the population as a whole.

Another way in which countries can reduce the price of food for the

---

[36] Although importing staple foods as cheaply as possible could potentially harm small-scale farmers in food-importing developing countries (especially in countries that have the potential to be food-exporters in the absence of rich country agricultural subsidies), it is a necessary step to reduce the threat of hunger. To assist these small-scale farmers, developing country governments can provide direct payments to small-scale farmers to compensate for the effect of rich country agricultural subsidies.
[37] 'Cereal Offenders', *The Economist*, 29 March 2008, 98.
[38] 'Cheap No More', above n 8.

poor is by acting as a purchasing agent. By coordinating the food demands for thousands, or even millions, of people, government purchasing agents can negotiate to receive bulk discounts by buying food in large volumes. The savings could then be passed along to the neediest consumers by allowing them to purchase the food at reduced prices at government distribution centres. The philanthropic Clinton Foundation has already pioneered a similar type of approach for securing more HIV/AIDS drugs for poor countries.[39] By executing a bulk purchasing contract, governments will be able to lock in the lower prices and provide some security to vulnerable parts of its population against future increases in prices. Otherwise, if the government decides to enter into voluntary agreements with producers, it runs the risk that producers will later choose to ignore the agreement and charge additional price increases.[40]

Food-importing developing countries should also work to encourage small-scale and subsistence agriculture among vulnerable parts of their populations and to promote more productive agriculture in general. Many countries that are food importers still have a large agricultural sector; some at-risk countries, such as Zimbabwe, were even food exporters until relatively recently.[41] Especially among the poorest countries, agriculture is the basis for food security, export earnings and rural development. According to World Bank estimates, 2.5 billion people are involved in farming (out of 3 billion living in rural areas, and with rural residents comprising three-quarters of the world's poorest people).[42] Despite the importance of agriculture in most developing countries, producer support estimates generally remain well below the level of rich countries. Developing country farmers are also confronted with problems such as slow land reform progress, water scarcity and deforestation, and a general lack of infrastructure and support. In addition, most poor countries lack the requisite policy coherence in their agricultural programmes that could foster economic growth and adjustment.[43]

Some developing country agricultural support is dominated by payments based on commodity output (such as market price support and payments based on output) and input use subsidies.[44] However, a more targeted support programme that focused on raising the incomes of poor farm households and promoting rural development would have

[39] J Raunch, 'This Is Not Charity', *Atlantic Monthly*, October 2007, 64–76.

[40] See, eg 'Mexicans Stage Tortilla Protest', above n 1. Although Mexican president Calderón negotiated a non-binding agreement with a number of agribusiness groups to cap the price of tortillas at 8.5 pesos (77 US cents) per kilogram, many producers chose to ignore this agreement and continued to charge ever increasing prices.

[41] 'Cheap No More', above n 8.

[42] Ibid.

[43] See, eg OECD, 'Agricultural Policies in Emerging Economies: Monitoring and Evaluation 2009'. The OECD report analyses policy developments in Brazil, Chile, China, India, Russia, South Africa and Ukraine.

[44] Ibid, 15–16.

a more beneficial impact on the rural poor. More specifically, developing countries should aim to improve the small-scale agricultural sector through the following measures: providing farmers with seeds for staple food crops, improving rural infrastructure, supplying insurance for crop failures, holding information sessions on effective farming techniques, guaranteeing a water source, sponsoring loans for small farms, ensuring some technology transfers, and providing general support through social service programmes, including for health and education. Such programmes, focused on small-scale and subsistence agriculture, would not be designed primarily to produce food for export, but rather to ensure a steady food supply for the part of the population that is most at risk of hunger. The problems in the agricultural sector will not be solved by any quick fixes; corrective and supportive measures should form the foundation of a long-term programme of rural outreach and agricultural development. In addition to alleviating hunger, improved small-scale agriculture will have the added benefit of reducing poverty and reducing the rural–urban divide. Over time, these efforts can help a country that is currently a food importer to become more self-sufficient in food and therefore less vulnerable to changes in the market.

Besides improving small-scale agriculture, many developing countries, especially the poorest ones, greatly need to improve the general efficiency of their agricultural sector. Many developing countries' agricultural sectors are characterised by slow production growth and drastic fluctuations in output, which is a leading cause of their persistent poverty and rising food insecurity. Developing country governments need to adopt coherent policy frameworks for improving domestic agriculture with an emphasis on investment in social and economic infrastructure. Those resources should be directed towards financing agricultural research, improving rural access to financial services, providing investment incentives, and increasing access of the poor to support services and productive resources. These measures, especially if accompanied by product diversification, might even eventually allow many of the poorest countries to overcome their marginalised position in the international trade system.[45] In addition, general services support has been shown to improve productivity and expand production capacity without much market distortion.[46]

As a transitional measure on the way to becoming food self-sufficient, poor food-importing countries should attempt to enter into agreements with food-exporting countries in the region. This would give food-importing countries a guaranteed close supply at a locked-in price.

---

[45] Third UN Conference on Least Developed Countries, Brussels, Belgium, 14–20 May 2001, 'The Role of Agriculture in the Development of LDCs and Their Integration into the World Economy', A/CONF.191/BP/6 (20 April 2001) v–vii.

[46] See OECD, above n 20, 32–33.

Under the agreement, when hunger levels in a member country reach critical levels, other countries involved in the arrangement would send food to that country on a priority basis. By sourcing from countries in the region, importers should reduce transportation costs and be able to access food relatively quickly in a food emergency. A designated supply source could also possibly lessen the threat of hunger and reduce some of the price volatility in the market, since countries would be able to access food rapidly, at a fixed price, during times of food crisis.[47]

C. Rich Country Reforms

In addition to transferring money to poor countries facing the prospect of malnourished populations, rich countries can take other actions to reduce the risk of hunger. First, one major step that the US could undertake to combat the threat of another food price crisis is to reform its ethanol programme by eliminating the generous subsidies provided to the ethanol industry. While the US should continue programmes to promote energy independence and environmental conservation, it should end its overwhelming emphasis on maize-based ethanol, which has a distortionary impact on the agricultural market. If the US continues to focus on biofuels production, it should support more research and development on non-maize-based biofuels, such as grasses, wood chips and algae, which have the potential to have stronger environmental benefits and less of a negative impact on food security.

The US should also be more receptive to ethanol produced abroad. Even though sugar-based ethanol from Brazil can be produced more efficiently than US maize-based ethanol, the US levies a 54 cents per gallon tariff on ethanol imports, which directly benefits US producers. At times of record production and demand, that tariff only serves to keep prices artificially high and should be eliminated immediately. If the US and other countries do not change their policies on biofuels, the International Food Policy Research Institute estimates that the increase in global biofuels production will push maize prices up by 41% by 2020.[48] From

---

[47] If a particular country did not have enough funds available to pay for the food when needed, it could attempt to negotiate with the other countries in the arrangement to develop a payment plan or to receive the food aid as a donation.

[48] See CF Runge and B Senauer, 'How Biofuels Could Starve the Poor', *Foreign Affairs*, May/June 2007. The US is not the only country producing biofuels. In some of the most impoverished parts of Africa, Asia and Latin America, ethanol demand is expected to increase the price of the staple crop cassava by 135% by 2020. Cassava, a high-starch potato-like food, already provides one-third of the caloric needs and is the primary staple for over 200 million Africans. The same qualities that make cassava a good food source also make it an excellent source for ethanol. As the technology for converting cassava into ethanol improves and the price of ethanol continues to increase, many countries, including China, Nigeria and Thailand, are considering using more cassava for the production of

a right-to-food perspective, a shift in the US away from maize-based ethanol, which places upward pressure on maize prices, and toward other biofuels would put far less pressure on agricultural markets and would not contribute to increased food prices.

Secondly, rich countries must make drastic changes in their agricultural subsidies programmes. The recent high prices present a good opportunity to reform the system, by making changes to the subsidy systems more politically palatable. Although a reduction in rich country subsidies will further increase the price of food, it will be a huge benefit to developing country farmers. Because most of the poor in developing countries live in rural areas, such reductions would have a positive impact on poor countries as a whole. Especially with improvements in their domestic agricultural sectors, developing country governments can take actions, as described above, to combat the threat of hunger. Despite the growing chorus of demands from many developing countries and other experts, there are many vested interests that do not want to see the rich country entitlement programmes reformed.[49] However, those vested interests can be accommodated to some extent, as correcting the distortions in the global agricultural market does not require that agricultural subsidies be eliminated entirely, and farmers can still receive support from governments through less trade-distorting methods.

The US and the EU have already made gradual moves towards reform by decreasing the amount they spend on trade-distorting subsidies. But much more can be done. In a period of food insecurity, the practice of paying farmers not to grow crops, which was started when overproduction was a problem, should be stopped immediately. Recognising that supply needs to be boosted and not depressed, the EU has suspended this 'set aside' part of its agricultural subsidies.[50] Also, pure income support payments can be used to prop up segments of the US and EU populations, such as struggling family farmers, without disadvantaging developing country producers. Pure income support payments, not tied to commodity production, would not have a distortionary impact on global agricultural markets. If accompanied by resource transfers and safeguard programmes to help the hungry, a reform of rich country agricultural subsidies will benefit developing countries by placing their poor farmers in a better competitive position.

---

ethanol. That increased demand for cassava could put the price of this vital staple out of reach of many of the poor who are already at risk for hunger. Ibid.

[49] There has also been pressure for reform within the rich countries. For example, in September 2010, the EU Budget Chief argued that European farm aid should be reduced to the level of one-third of all EU outlays (as compared to the current situation in which agricultural subsidies account for more than 40% of the EU budget). S Castle, 'EU Chief's Comments Likely to Spark Farm Aid Debate', *New York Times*, 6 September 2010.

[50] 'Cheap No More', above n 8.

IV. CONCLUSION

For too long, rich countries have used their subsidies to agricultural producers to distort the global market in agriculture. Because many developing countries hold a comparative advantage in agricultural production, reform of rich country agricultural subsidies has become a critical issue in the current round of WTO negotiations. However, the elimination of rich countries' agricultural subsidies, which will decrease rich country overproduction, coupled with high food prices, will hit food-importing developing countries very hard. The resulting situation could be especially grim for those countries' vulnerable populations that are most at risk for hunger.

Thus, even in advance of the elimination of rich country agricultural subsidies, food-importing developing countries need to implement a variety of short- and long-term measures, as discussed above, to reduce potential negative impacts of rich country reforms on the hungry and to promote food security. The governments first need to increase food aid to the poor to enable them to buy enough food when confronted with higher prices. Also immediately, the governments should undertake efforts to make staple foods cheaper, such as eliminating import tariffs. As a longer-term measure, the governments need to invest in sustainable small-scale agriculture to make that sector more viable and thereby decrease the risk of hunger for farmers and their families within the country. In addition, rich countries have an obligation to ensure that the change in agricultural subsidy policies does not have a negative impact on the hungry in other countries. One of the simplest ways through which rich countries could do this is to reallocate the money that they will save by reducing agricultural subsidies to international food aid and assistance for developing country agriculture. The global agricultural market should be reformed to reflect competitive realities, but measures must be taken simultaneously to protect the vulnerable populations in poor countries against the risk of increased hunger.

7

Invoking the Right to Food in the WTO Dispute Settlement Process: The Relevance of the Right to Food to the Law of the WTO

BOYAN KONSTANTINOV

THE WORLD TRADE Organization (WTO) is often criticised for failing to address human rights in its practices. There is a good reason for this criticism, as the impact of international trade on human rights issues is tremendous. Of special concern is the right to food. Negotiations on the new Agreement on Agriculture have stalled. Simultaneously, the practices of countries with big markets negatively influence the food sector in small economies, often seriously endangering the access of rural communities to food and jeopardising their food security. Even if the WTO wished to address right-to-food issues, its ability to do so is limited. Despite being called an 'organisation', the WTO does not have independent decision-making power. Rather, the adoption of decisions by the organisation is the result of complex and slow multilateral negotiation processes. Thus, even theoretically possible opportunities for raising human rights issues within the WTO system remain, for the most part, unproven.

There is one exception in which the WTO itself is the decisionmaker and its conclusions are binding—the WTO's Dispute Settlement Procedures (DSP). This chapter explores the prospects of invoking the right to food in dispute settlements. The potential opportunity to do so is explored in combination with important broader questions (what is the relationship between the right to food and trade liberalisation? Are disputes before the WTO the right fora in which to decide human rights issues?), as well as the newer query of whether the understanding that the WTO refrains from addressing human rights issues is still as true today as it was in the recent past. Part I discusses the right to food, the history of trade liberalisation and the WTO. Part II addresses the debates regarding whether human rights should ever be addressed by the WTO. Part III briefly considers potential opportunities for invoking human rights at the WTO. Part IV examines dispute settlement procedures and explores the possibility of invoking the right to food in dispute settlements.

I. THE DEVELOPMENT OF THE CONTEMPORARY DEFINITION OF THE RIGHT TO FOOD AND THE HISTORY OF TRADE LIBERALISATION AND THE WTO

A. Evolution of the Modern Understanding of Right to Food

The concept of the human right to food and the modern understanding of trade liberalisation started developing around the same time, at the end of World War II. The incorporation of both concepts in international documents was a result of lessons learned by world leaders during the war, and was part of the leaders' efforts to avoid yet another global catastrophe. In 1941, in his 'Four Freedoms Address', US President Franklin Delano Roosevelt described his vision of a world with 'freedom from want'[1] that would ensure economic well-being for each nation. That vision was later espoused in the preamble of the Charter of the UN when the organisation was founded in 1945, as well as in the Universal Declaration of Human Rights (UDHR) when it was adopted in 1948.

The UDHR is the first public international law document from which the concept of the right to food can be derived: Article 25 proclaims the right to an adequate standard of living for people's health and well-being, including food. Moreover, other rights within the UDHR can also be linked to the right to food, including the right to life, liberty and security of person (Article 3); the right to social security (Article 22); the right to adequate remuneration for work (Article 23); and the right to own property (Article 17). Those linkages are especially true in the contemporary understanding of the right to food as the right to have access to food or to means for its procurement, as well as the right to enjoy food security. Subsequent to the adoption of the UDHR, an explicit reference to the right to food was made in the International Covenant on Economic, Social and Cultural Rights (ICESCR), which was conceived as a continuation of the UDHR and adopted in 1966. As opposed to the UDHR, which is a 'soft law' document, the ICESCR is a binding inter-

---

[1] FD Roosevelt, US President, 'The Four Freedoms', Address to the US Congress (6 January 1941), available at www.americanrhetoric.com/speeches/fdrthefourfreedoms.htm.

national treaty that encompasses a system of positive rights and obliges the contracting parties to ensure their fulfilment.[2]

Article 11 of the ICESCR explicitly refers to the right to adequate food as one of the components of an adequate standard of living. In its General Comment 12, the Committee on Economic, Social and Cultural Rights (CESCR) further defines the right to food to include

> the availability of food in a quantity and quality sufficient to satisfy the dietary needs of individuals, free from adverse substances, and acceptable within a given culture . . . accessible to all, implying an obligation to provide special programs for the vulnerable.[3]

General Comment 12, which was issued in 1999, reflects the new understanding of the right to food that was developed at the 1993 World Conference on Human Rights in Vienna and the 1998 World Food Summit.[4] It includes a broader interpretation of the right to food than that featured in the texts of international instruments, such as the UDHR and the ICESCR, and focuses on the economic accessibility of food and resources to secure it.

The CESCR, in General Comment 12, stated that 'the right to adequate food is realized when every man, woman and child, alone *or in community with others*, have the *physical and economic access* at all times to adequate food *or means for its procurement*'.[5] The CESCR thus expressed an understanding of the right to food not only as the right of an individual but also as the right of communities and populations of entire states to access food or to have the means to procure it. This understanding is in harmony with the global efforts to combat poverty, eradicate famine and promote sustainable development that were proclaimed in the Millennium Development Goals.[6] The definition adopted by the former UN Special Rapporteur on the right to food summarises this more comprehensive contemporary definition:

Right to adequate food is a human right, inherent in all people, to have regular, permanent and unrestricted access, either directly or by means of financial purchases, to quantitatively and qualitatively adequate and sufficient food corresponding to the cultural traditions of people to

---

[2] It should be noted that the ICESCR has not been ratified by the US, despite the signature of President Jimmy Carter over 30 years ago.

[3] UN Economic and Social Council (ECOSOC), Committee on Economic, Social and Cultural Rights, 'General Comment 12 (Art 11), Right to Adequate Food', ¶ 8, UN document E/C.12/1999/5 (12 May 1999).

[4] See FAO, 'The World Food Summit and Its Follow Up', available at www.fao.org/docrep/X2051e/X2051e00.htm#P83_5958.

[5] General Comment 12, above n 3, 6 (emphasis added).

[6] UN Millennium Declaration, GA Res 55/2, UN GAOR, 55th Sess, Supp No 49, 4, UN document A/55/49 (8 September 2000). See also The UN, 'UN Millennium Development Goals', available at www.un.org/millenniumgoals.

which the consumer belongs, and which ensures a physical and mental, individual and collective fulfilling and dignified life free of fear.[7]

This modern understanding of the right to food brings it very close to the matter of trade liberalisation and the global impact that free trade has on human rights. In order to reveal this relationship, the next section briefly examines the history of trade liberalisation and the WTO, with an emphasis on the ever-growing impact that both have on the right to food and food security. The section also considers the specific significance that agriculture has in the multilateral negotiating process and in bilateral and regional trade agreements and practices.

B. Trade Liberalisation and the Creation of the WTO

The contemporary concept of trade liberalisation emerged a little after the modern concept of the right to food. Similar to his leading role in promoting 'freedom from want', Franklin Delano Roosevelt was one of the first world leaders to articulate the idea of modern trade liberalisation. In 1944, when representatives of the allied nations were meeting at the Bretton Woods Conference to discuss the post-World War II monetary and financial order, Roosevelt stated in his opening speech that '[t]he economic health of every country is a proper matter of concern to all its neighbors, near and far'.[8] The summit at Bretton Woods established the need to set rules and regulations for international trade, and participants suggested founding the International Trade Organization. Roosevelt, who died in April 1945, never lived to see the desired outcome of those negotiations on trade liberalisation—but neither did the other participants at the Bretton Woods forum. Despite the agreement at the 1948 UN Havana Conference on Trade and Employment to establish the International Trade Organization, the agreement was not ratified by the US Senate. As a result, the idea of having an independent specialised agency on free trade failed; an interim solution was achieved through the General Agreements on Tariffs and Trade (GATT).

From 1948 to 1994, the GATT, an incomplete contract, provided the rules for much of the world's trade. Despite its modifications throughout nearly half a century, the basic legal principles of the GATT remained more or less unchanged. Under the GATT's auspices, multilateral negotiations—'trade rounds'—were held in order to liberalise international trade. In the 1950s and 1960s, the success in tariff reduction was

---

[7] J Ziegler, UN Special Rapporteur on the Right to Food, 'Report by the Special Rapporteur on the Right to Food, delivered to the Commission on Human Rights', UN document E/CN.4/2001/53 (7 February 2001).

[8] FD Roosevelt, 'Opening Remarks at the Bretton Woods Conference' (29 June 1944), available at www.millercenter.org/scripps/archive/speeches.

noticeable, trade growth was constantly surpassing growth in production, and more and more countries strove to become members of the GATT. At the same time, however, the world economy was rapidly globalising, with the relative share of services, which were not covered by the GATT, continuing to increase.

The Tokyo Round in the 1970s brought down the average tariff on industrial products to an unprecedented low level, but also confirmed suspicions that the GATT 1947 would not last for much longer. Among many other issues, the Tokyo Round revealed the GATT's failure to address rising problems in agriculture and farm trade, as well as the increasing number of non-trade protectionist measures imposed by industrialised countries. In addition, the GATT's dispute settlement system was flawed: it had discordant practices, no clear procedural rules and no binding force of decisions made by the dispute settlement bodies unless consensus was achieved. In many cases, those problems paralysed the dispute resolution process. Thus, during the Uruguay Round between 1986 and 1994, the GATT members agreed on the need to reform the multilateral system. As a result of that round, the Marrakesh Agreement was signed and the World Trade Organization was created.

The 1994 Marrakesh Agreement establishing the WTO was signed 1 year after the Vienna World Conference on Human Rights and approximately 5 years before the CESCR adopted General Comment 12 and the UN member states adopted the Millennium Development Goals. Since those developments occurred in parallel, it should not come as a surprise that the text of the Marrakesh Agreement presents a high level of consistency with international human rights terminology. In the preamble of the Marrakesh Agreement, the WTO members recognise that:

> their relations in the field of trade and economic endeavor should be conducted with a view to raising standards of living, ensuring full employment and a large and steadily growing volume of real income and effective demand, and expanding the production of and trade in goods and services, while allowing for the optimal use of the world's resources *in accordance with the objective of sustainable development,* seeking both to protect and preserve the environment and to enhance the means for doing so in a manner consistent with their respective needs and concerns at different levels of economic development . . .[9]

The Marrakesh Agreement does not include a definition of 'sustainable development', but this definition can be derived through *lex specialis*. International documents that are more or less contemporaneous to the agreement, such as the UN General Assembly Resolution

---

[9] Marrakesh Agreement Establishing the World Trade Organization, The Legal Texts: Results of the Uruguay Round of Multilateral Trade Negotiations 4 (1999), 1867 UNT.S 154, 33 ILM 1144 (1994) (emphasis added).

on Sustainable Development, the Millennium Development Goals, and the World Food Declaration and Plan of Action, define and construe the term.

In addition, the Marrakesh Ministerial Declaration, which was adopted simultaneously to the Agreement, states that '[m]inisters confirm their resolution to strive for greater global coherence of policies in the fields of trade, money and finance, including cooperation between the WTO, the IMF and the World Bank for that purpose'.[10] On the surface, this text suggests cooperation in trade and finance fields only. The World Bank and the International Monetary Fund (IMF), however, play important roles in development issues, and human-rights-based approaches are increasingly mainstreamed into their programming and policies. The pledge to cooperate with those institutions is therefore significant. The Marrakesh Ministerial Declaration, similarly to the Millennium Development Goals, is a 'soft law' document, and does not have binding force. However, the Marrakesh Agreement is a binding international agreement. Read together with the Marrakesh Ministerial Declaration, the Agreement provides arguments in favour of the interpretation that, although not explicitly included, human rights are not entirely out of place in the WTO system. The case, however, is far from clear-cut. Many people and organisations either oppose raising human rights issues before the WTO or argue that it is not allowed. Some of those opinions are explored further in this chapter.

C. The Agreement on Agriculture, the Marrakesh Decision and the Doha Development Round

As agriculture plays an essential role for the development of most countries, many consider the Agreement on Agriculture (AoA) to be a key feature in the negotiations within the WTO. The AoA was negotiated during the Uruguay Round; it entered into force with the establishment of the WTO in 1995. Its main purpose was to make markets as accessible as possible for agricultural products and to increase the flow of commodities. The preamble of the AoA also refers to food security and takes into account 'the possible negative effects of the implementation of the reform programme on least developed and net food importing developing countries'.[11] In addition, Article 20(b) of the AoA stipulates

---

[10] Robert Howse and Makau Mutua elaborate on the pitiable record of cooperation between the WTO and other international institutions and emphasise the need to end its isolationism. See R Howse and M Mutua, 'Protecting Human Rights in a Global Economy: Challenges for the World Trade Organization' (Rights and Democracy, 2000), available at www.ichrdd.ca/english/commdoc/publications/globalization/wtoRightsGlob.html.

[11] Agreement on Agriculture, 14 April 1994, The Legal Texts: The Results of the Uruguay

that WTO members were committed to continuing their efforts for fundamental reform in agricultural trade while taking into consideration, among other factors, 'non-trade concerns' (NTCs). Those concerns include food security, rural development and environmental protection. At a later stage, the EU proposed—unsuccessfully—to add animal welfare and eco-labelling to the list of NTCs.

Most WTO members agree that agriculture, apart from producing food and raw materials, serves social objectives as well. For this reason, the AoA allows WTO members (including developed countries) to maintain some support measures in order to meet those social objectives, including food security. The support measures should be government-funded and should have no impact or only minimal impact on trade; they are included in Annex 2 of the AoA, called 'the Green Box'. WTO members, however, disagree as to which measures should be included in the Green Box. A number of countries argue that some of the subsidies in the Green Box cause more than just minimal distortion of trade. These include, for instance, large amounts in direct payments to agricultural producers (paragraph 5), income support for farmers (paragraph 6), and support for income insurance and safety (paragraph 7). While developed countries can typically afford such subsidies, most developing countries cannot.

The International Institute for Sustainable Development notes that the set of measures under the Green Box 'would seem to give governments a fair amount of policy space for pursuing NTCs such as rural development, environmental protection and food security. However, a summary of the various negotiating positions shows that the debate is far from straightforward.'[12]

In practice, the AoA has not managed to address successfully the role that agriculture plays in food security and development. Indeed, many countries have sharply criticised the effect of the AoA. One frequently raised criticism is the contradiction between the NTCs expressed in the AoA preamble and Article 20, on the one hand, and the overall agenda of the Agreement, on the other. As pointed out by analysts of the Institute for Agriculture and Trade Policies, as a whole the AoA adopts an export-oriented approach that benefits mostly large-scale food producers and

---

Round of Multilateral Trade Negotiations 33 (1999), 1867 UNT.S 410 (not reproduced in ILM), pmbl.

[12] International Institute for Sustainable Development (IISD), 'Non-Trade Concerns in the Agricultural Negotiations of the World Trade Organization', Trade and Development Brief (2003), available at www.iisd.org/pdf/2003/investment_sdc_may_2003_1.pdf. IISD distinguishes three groups of countries based on their position on how to address NTC such as food security. Essentially, the groups consist of proponents of additional measures related to food securities, opponents of such measures (advocates for free trade flow) and advocates to allow non-trade measures but only to developing countries.

traders.[13] In the past, another reason for concern was the so-called 'Peace Clause' (Article 13 of the AoA), which expired in January 2004. The Peace Clause essentially prohibited, for a 10 year period, challenges through certain WTO agreements to dumping and export subsidies that were legal under the AoA. Since the clause expired, countries have been allowed to challenge export subsidies—yet the practice has not really changed. As described further, the US and the EU continue to subsidise and dump agricultural products. The dependency of developing countries on the huge markets of these trading partners is so strong, however, that they prefer not to challenge such practices.[14]

During the conclusion of the Uruguay Round negotiations in 1994, representatives of the WTO Member States signed a document providing for the special treatment of least developed countries (LDCs) and net food importing developing countries (NFIDCs). This document, known as the Marrakesh Decision,[15] was signed in recognition that trade liberalisation under the WTO AoA is likely to cause an increase in the world market price of food, thereby putting LDCs and NFIDCs in danger of food shortages and in need of assistance to maintain their food security.

The Marrakesh Decision refers to the Food Aid Convention 1986,[16] which aimed to ensure that LDCs and NFIDCs received sufficient amounts of food aid while trade liberalisation in agriculture was taking place. As ActionAid points out, for years almost nothing was done to implement the Marrakesh Decision.[17] Export subsidies of agricultural products in developed countries continued. Food aid efforts, especially in the US, were often reduced to shipping domestic overproduction to needy countries. The WTO disregarded the recommendations provided by the IMF and the World Bank on the need to implement the Marrakesh Decision.[18] Those recommendations included, among others, the introduction of a 'food security box'. A food security box is a list of measures that are exempt from the requirement not to distort trade, because of

[13] Institute for Agriculture and Trade Policies (IATP), 'Planting the Rights Seed: a Human Rights Perspective on Agriculture Trade and the WTO', Background Paper (2005), 8–11, available at www.fao.org/righttofood/KC/downloads/vl/en/details/215216.htm.

[14] IATP, 'WTO Agreement on Agriculture: a Decade of Dumping: United States Dumping on Agricultural Markets' (2005), available at www.tradeobservatory.org/library.cfm?refid=48532.

[15] Decision on Measures Concerning the Possible Negative Effects of the Reform Program on Least-Developed Countries and Net Food-Importing Developing Countries, 14 April 1994, Agreement on Agriculture, Annex 1A, The Legal Texts: The Results of the Uruguay Round of Multilateral Trade Negotiations 33 (1999), 1867 UNT.S. 410 (not reproduced in ILM), available at www.wto.org/english/docs_e/legal_e/35-dag_e.htm.

[16] Food Aid Convention, 1 July 1986, S Treaty document No 101-1 (replaced by the Food Aid Convention 1999 under the International Grains Agreement).

[17] The Food Rights Campaign, ActionAid, 'The Marrakesh Decision', available at www.actionaid.org.uk/_content/documents/marrakesh2_3132004_122452.pdf.

[18] S Murphy, 'WTO Agricultural Deregulation and Food Security' (1999) 4(No 34) *Foreign Policy In Focus* 1–4, available at www.fpif.org/pdf/vol4/34ifag.pdf.

their important social objective. Subsequent to those recommendations, the EU and the US set forth proposals to reform the AoA; according to food security expert Sophia Murphy, only the EU proposal addressed food security issues.[19] Those proposals did not succeed.

In late 1996, at the Singapore Ministerial Conference, representatives of the WTO member states adopted the Recommendations in respect of LDCs and NFIDCs. This was consistent with the Declaration on World Food Security and the Plan of Action that was adopted by the World Food Summit that same year.[20]

Members of the WTO realise the necessity of addressing development issues. At the Doha Ministerial Conference in 2001, they announced their commitment to hold a 'development' round in order to address the needs of developing countries and renegotiate the AoA. In the Ministerial Declaration adopted during the conference (the Doha Declaration), WTO members reconfirmed their commitment to:

> establish a fair and market-oriented trading system through a programme of fundamental reform encompassing strengthened rules and specific commitments on support and protection in order to correct and prevent restrictions and distortions in world agricultural markets . . . [They committed themselves to] comprehensive negotiations aimed at: substantial improvements in market access; reductions of, with a view to phasing out, all forms of export subsidies; and substantial reductions in trade-distorting domestic support. [They agreed] that special and differential treatment for developing countries [shall be negotiated in an effective manner so as to] enable developing countries to effectively take account of their development needs, including food security and rural development.[21]

It has to be noted, however, that the Doha Development Agenda was adopted only after several ministerial delegations from developing countries left the negotiations. Those countries criticised the unfair system of trade rules that invades the domestic policy space of WTO members and pointed out that this system may inhibit development.

In 2003, the Ministerial Conference organised in Cancún, Mexico aimed to develop a specific agreement based on the objectives that were set during the Doha Ministerial Conference. It failed due to disagreements among members regarding farm subsidies and market access. At that point, opposition against the EU Common Agricultural Policy, as well

---

[19] Murphy points out the US proposal circumvented the real issues and diverted the debate. See S Murphy, 'Food Aid: What is the Role of the WTO' (National Institute of Agriculture and Policy, 2006), available at www.iatp.org/iatp/publications.cfm?accountID=451&refID=77567.
[20] International Grains Council, available at www.igc.org.uk/en/aboutus/default.aspx.
[21] World Trade Organization, Ministerial Declaration, 14 November 2001, Art 13, WT/MIN(01)/DEC/1, 41 ILM 746 (2001), available at www.wto.org/English/thewto_e/minist_e/min01_e/mindecl_e.htm.

as against the US agricultural support policies and subsidies (including the then-new Farm Bill of 2002), became even more acute. During the attempt to renew discussions in Geneva in 2004, the big markets of the US, the EU, Japan and Brazil agreed to cease export subsidies and to reduce agricultural domestic subsidies. After relatively fruitless discussions in Paris in 2005, the Sixth WTO Ministerial Conference opened in Hong Kong in 2005. At this conference, a deadline for eliminating export subsidies by 2013 was set. At the time, this was considered an important breakthrough to open the markets of developed countries for products from the world's poorest economies. Unfortunately, representatives failed to agree on reducing farming subsidies and lowering import taxes.

In June 2007, another attempt to renew negotiations within the Doha Round led to a conference in Potsdam, Germany—and failed again, because of similar disagreements. While those international summits were taking place, the broad Trade Promotion Authority granted by the US Congress to the President to take executive, 'fast track' decisions on trade matters expired in June 2007 and has not been renewed. Now, every new agreement under the WTO must be approved by the US Congress in order to bind the US. This unfortunate development is the reason for some pessimistic prognoses on reaching an agreement in the area of agriculture; it is also a major disincentive for countries to participate in the process of negotiating an agreement. When suspending the 2006 Geneva negotiations, the WTO Director-General, Pascal Lamy, concluded:

> [F]ailure of this Round would be a blow to the development prospects of the more vulnerable Members, for whom integration in international trade represents the best hope for growth and poverty alleviation. This is why it is called 'the development round': it is intended to be a contribution to the Millennium Development Goals . . . If the political will really exists, there must be a way. But it is not here today. And let me be clear: there are no winners and losers in this assembly. Today, there are only losers.[22]

D. The Rise of Free Trade and Bilateral Trade Agreements and Their Impact on Agriculture and Food Security

Circumvention of multilateralism through Free Trade Agreements (FTAs)[23] and other bilateral trade instruments is a process that develops together

---

[22] P Lamy, Director-General, World Trade Organization, 'Introductory Remarks to the Trade Negotiations Committee Meeting' (24 July 2006), available at www.wto.org/english/news_e/news06_e/tnc_dg_stat_24july06_e.htm.

[23] Sometimes the more general reference 'Preferential Trade Agreements' is used to describe all subcategories.

with—and to a certain extent because of—the lack of political consensus on development issues. Not only does this process threaten the multilateral system; it can also have a tremendous negative impact on food and food security issues. As explained by Peter Sutherland, former WTO Director-General, big markets such as the US and the EU have a 'bullying opportunity' when signing free trade and investment agreements with less powerful countries, especially developing economies.[24] Indeed, the negotiations of these documents are so non-transparent that even statistical data about their number is approximate. They appear to be proliferating rapidly, however; according to law professor and human rights adviser David Kinley, there are currently more than 2,500 bilateral investment treaties worldwide.[25]

Many bilateral trade agreements include protective provisions for investors. Their critics point out that bilateral agreements seem to infringe on the spirit of the most favoured nation (MFN) principle of the WTO;[26] critics further argue that bilateral agreements are essentially tactics of major trade powers to obtain concessions that they could not get under the WTO multilateral system due to the joint opposition of developing countries. Preferential trade agreements do not violate 'the letter of the law' of the WTO[27] but obviously threaten the multilateral system and other WTO values.[28] Instead of following the principle of comparative advantage and free competition among providers, FTAs discriminate against efficient, low-cost suppliers that are not part of the agreement and favour less efficient and costlier suppliers that originate from parties of the FTA. This leads to increased costs of products for the final consumer.[29] As Petros Mavroidis points out, the considerations for entering into a preferential trade agreement are actually quite often not trade related but politically motivated.[30]

---

[24] Oxfam Interarntional, 'Signing Away the Future: How Trade and Investment Agreements between Rich and Poor Countries Undermine Development', Briefing Paper (2007) 3–8, available at www.oxfam.org/sites/available at www.oxfam.org/files/Signing%20Away%20the%20Future.pdf.
[25] D Kinley, *Civilising Globalisation: Human Rights and the Global Economy* (Cambridge, Cambridge University Press, 2009) 91.
[26] In his lectures, Professor Jagdish Bhagwati aphoristically calls the MFN principle 'a principle of the least favored nation'.
[27] Art XXIV.4 of the GATT states: 'The contracting parties recognize the desirability of increasing freedom of trade by the development, through voluntary agreements, of closer integration between the economies of the countries parties to such agreements. They also recognize that the purpose of a customs union or of a free-trade area should be to facilitate trade between the constituent territories and not to raise barriers to the trade of other contracting parties with such territories.'
[28] Art XXIV includes the requirements that a Preferential Trade Agreement (PTA) has to meet in order to be WTO-consistent. Among these requirements is notification of the PTA to the WTO. However, practice shows that not all PTAs are notified. See WorldTradeLaw, available at www.worldtradelaw.net (listing notified bilateral trade agreements).
[29] Oxfam, above n 24, 15.
[30] PC Mavroidis, *Trade in Goods* (Oxford, Oxford University Press, 2007) 149, 151.

Intellectual property issues negotiated in FTAs, especially with the US, have a substantial impact on agriculture. The US and the EU persistently seek the adoption of regulations on patent protection for agricultural plants and seeds. Often these large trading partners require developing countries to implement, as a precondition for signing an FTA, international standards on protections of plant and seed patents that prohibit the selling or exchange of protected seeds. In some cases, the protections even prohibit farmers from using seeds from plants that they have grown themselves.[31] Some authors stress that the effect of those restrictions on small farmers and rural communities is extremely negative.[32] A counterargument to this criticism is that the farming of patented plants ensures production that is consistent with the requirements of big food retailers, and that doing so ultimately provides small farmers with access to retailers' supply chains. Oxfam experts, however, object to this counterargument, arguing that the effect is quite the opposite: as seed prices increase, small farmers lose their competitiveness and the relative share of large agribusiness grows.[33]

The US and the EU have a long history of subsidising their agricultural products and engaging in dumping practices.[34] Subsidies are strongly discouraged by the WTO; export subsidies are prohibited by Part II, Article 3 of the Agreement on Subsidies and Countervailing Measures (SCM). Although there used to be an exception under Article 3 of the SCM for goods under the AoA, it has not applied since 2004, when the AoA Peace Clause expired. Under the SCM, if illegal subsidies are established, affected countries can impose countervailing duties. Dumping is 'condemned' and recognised by a WTO Appellate Body as an unfair practice; however, it is not outlawed.[35] Instead, dumping is supposed to be regulated by the imposition of anti-dumping duties under procedures set forth in the Antidumping Agreement. In other words, both subsidising and dumping allow countries to recourse to counter-mechanisms.

Nevertheless, the US and the EU, as well as some other developed countries, persistently subsidise and dump their export agricultural products. Those practices make the problem of poverty and food security in developing countries even worse. Countermeasures and complaints before the WTO are infrequent, especially compared to the scale of

---

[31] UPOV 1991, which provides a framework of regulations on plant variety protection, is one of these standards.

[32] GRAIN (in cooperation with S Rodrigues-Cervantes), 'FTAs: Trading Away Traditional Knowledge' (2006), available at www.grain.org/briefings/?id=196.

[33] Oxfam, above n 24, 124.

[34] 'Dumping' in this context means exporting agricultural products to other countries at prices that are either below the prices on the domestic market or below the costs of production. See IATP, above n 13, 3.

[35] Panel Report, 'United States—Final Dumping Determination on Softwood Lumber from Canada', WT/ DS264 (11 August 2004).

dumping and subsidising. The reason for that is the imbalance that exists in developing countries' trade with big markets and their dependence on those markets. WTO values and regulations therefore are frequently violated.

FTAs exacerbate those problems. Some FTAs prohibit developing countries from enacting agricultural safeguard mechanisms that limit imports in the case of a rapid decrease of prices, despite the provisions of the AoA, under which such mechanisms are allowed. Other FTAs limit the situations in which safeguard measures can be enacted to such an extent that the clauses are rendered practically non-operational. In addition, tariff liberalisation under most FTAs is not a reciprocal process; the US and the EU liberalise only those sectors in agriculture in which they do not compete, or those that do not otherwise endanger their domestic production. In all other cases, the concessions are minimal. One example is Lebanese olive oil, which is virtually unavailable in the European market. Another example is the restrictions imposed on the import of various agricultural products from Jordan that are competitive to similar products from the EU.[36] Examples of such malpractices, as well as cases of endangering food security, are plentiful; the conclusion is that circumventing multilateralism, combined with the ever-growing imbalance in trade liberalisation, has the most negative effect on small farmers and producers in developing countries. These practices appear to perpetuate poverty rather than contribute to economic growth; in doing so, they also detrimentally affect the right to food of small farmers and producers in developing countries.

Interestingly, those infringements on the right to food and food security through FTAs seem to align the interests of the proponents of multilaterism and right-to-food advocates. Invoking the right to food before the WTO could serve as a way not only to protect the interests of developing countries and the food security of their citizens, but also to strengthen the multilateral model and discourage unfair trade negotiations in bilateral or regional settings. Whether invoking the right to food in the WTO is likely to actually happen is another matter, which will be examined further in the next section.

II. HUMAN RIGHTS AND THE WTO: THE HISTORY AND THE DEBATE

WTO agreements do not discuss human rights. The reason for this can be found in the history of the WTO, as well as in the very nature of the organisation. Negotiating the GATT was a lengthy, complicated and

---

[36] Oxfam, above n 24, 33.

often endangered process. Therefore, the unwillingness of the GATT bureaucracy and the 'high contracting parties' to add human rights considerations to the negotiations was understandable—consensus was difficult to achieve and much was at stake. The decision to not refer to human rights in the WTO Agreement probably had a similar rationale, although it was made in a different time and context.

When the WTO was established, human rights had already been mainstreamed into treaties such as the Treaty on EU, as well as in the work of international organisations, including the UN. The WTO did not follow course. Some countries tried to include labour and environmental rights in the Marrakesh Agreement. Their efforts were opposed by developing countries and ultimately failed.[37] One reason for that opposition was that countries were concerned that their own human rights record could lead to complications and justify the adoption of protectionist measures by other parties. Another reason was that the agreements under the WTO are agreements between member states, not within them. The agreements do not govern the behaviour of persons, entities or institutions in those states. In his critical comparison between international trade law and international human rights law, Steve Charnovtiz points out that '[w]hereas international human rights law aims to transmit norms from international law to domestic law . . . international trade law takes as a given that the responsibilities of a government . . . is a matter to be determined by each government, not by the international community'.[38] Thus, by that rationale, it does not make sense for WTO law to discuss human rights.

Some scholars argue that the WTO has no authority to address human rights. Jagdish Bhagwati, for example, strongly opposes the inclusion of human rights in WTO proceedings and agreements, arguing, among other reasons, that governments will use this as an opportunity to introduce masked protectionist practices.[39] Given the sad history of masked protectionism in international trade and related disputes, this is a viable scenario. Other scholars[40] suggest that the WTO system should be modified to be more responsive to human rights. Regardless of whether human rights issues should be included in WTO proceedings, others argue that simply being a part of the WTO can advance human rights in a member country. Despite the various theories on the relationship

---

[37] See The Doha Ministerial Briefing Notes, 'Trade and Labor Standards: A Difficult Issue for Many WTO Member Governments' (2001), available at www.wto.org/english/theWTO_e/minist_e/min01_e/brief_e/brief16_e.htm.
[38] S Charnovitz, 'The Globalization of Economic Human Rights' (1999) 25 *Brooklyn Journal of International Law* 113.
[39] J Bhagwati and R Hudec, *Fair Trade and Harmonization* (Cambridge, MA, The MIT Press, 1996) 1.
[40] T Cottier, J Pauwelyn and E Bürgi Bonanomi (eds), *Human Rights and International Trade* (Oxford, Oxford University Press, 2005).

between the WTO and human rights, however, a clear link between membership in the WTO and democratisation or rights cannot be established. Political scientist Mary Comerford Cooper has investigated the relationship between GATT/WTO membership and democratisation for the period of 1947–99 without any conclusive results.[41] Similarly, Susan Ariel Aaronson and Jamie Zimmerman compared WTO membership and political rights using a global assessment on countries provided by Freedom House. In 2005, the percentage of 'free' countries (with civil and political freedoms) in the WTO was 51.68%, or 77 out of 149, compared to 44.53%, or 57 out of 128, in 1994.[42]

While accepting that there is no clear connection between WTO membership and the human rights situation in member countries, and acknowledging that there are various theories on the admissibility of human rights issues in WTO proceedings, it is still possible to outline which theoretical opportunities exist for invoking human rights within the WTO system *de lege lata*. The next section discusses those opportunities.

III. POTENTIAL OPPORTUNITIES, ASIDE FROM DISPUTE SETTLEMENT PROCEDURES, FOR INVOKING HUMAN RIGHTS WITHIN THE WTO SYSTEM

One of the first points at which human rights issues can be invoked in WTO proceedings is during accession negotiations. For example, during the accession process of the People's Republic of China, human rights issues were raised—for the first time—as a precondition for accession to the WTO, although the concern was driven by the non-application of certain labour rights in China's export processing zones. Ultimately, however, the inclusion of human rights language in the process did not have a substantial positive impact on the human rights record of the country.[43] Requirements to adhere to the rule of law have been imposed on Albania, Cambodia, Saudi Arabia and other recent WTO members.[44] Abiding by rule-of-law principles is certainly beneficial for human rights.

---

[41] M Comerford Cooper, *International Organizations and Democratization: Testing the Effect of GATT/WTO Membership* (Stanford, CA, FSI Stanford Publications 2003).

[42] SA Aaronson and JM Zimmerman, *Trade Imbalance: The Struggle to Weigh Human Rights Concerns in Trade Policymaking* (Cambridge, Cambridge University Press, 2007) 35–37. The most recent accessions to the WTO of Albania, Cambodia, Macedonia, Nepal, Saudi Arabia and Vietnam—countries that have poor human rights records—have reduced the percentage to 50.99%. With the May 2008 accession of Ukraine, which Freedom House considers a 'free country' (I disagree with its position), the relative share of the 'free' WTO members has increased again.

[43] China was requested to introduce the rule of law in all of its territories, including Export Processing Zones (EPZ).

[44] See Aaronson and Zimmerman, above n 42, 41.

However, the requirements were formulated based strictly on trade-related concerns.

In addition to raising human rights issues at accession, another potential practice for sanctioning members for a poor human rights record is the non-extension of trading rights and privileges. In practice, however, non-extension has been used only by El Salvador and Peru against Israel and by the US against Romania, which was then a communist country. The reasons not to extend trading rights and privileges were political, not human rights driven.

Scholars frequently suggest recourse to the General Exceptions in Article XX of the WTO, or the National Security Exception in Article XXI of the GATT, as a good way to invoke human rights before the WTO. Unfortunately, there are no practical examples of countries invoking human rights using either of these theoretical concepts. Furthermore, many general exceptions in Article XX are defined either broadly (such as 'public morals') or quite narrowly (such as 'prison labour'). Human rights concerns thus could be introduced to those exceptions only by broadening their interpretation, which is not supported by the *travaux préparatoires* of the GATT. Mavroidis, however, suggests that reading Article XXa GATT together with Article XIV General Agreement on Trade in Services (GATS)[45] supports the theory that WTO members could deviate from their obligations under WTO law if such deviation could be justified on public order grounds.[46]

Recourse to the General Exceptions is additionally complicated because of the two-prong test that is used when a measure is contested. For example, in a 'public morals' hypothesis, if a measure is contested by the country against which the measure was used, the defendant member has to prove that the measure derogating from its obligations is necessary to protect morals, as well as that the measure does not constitute an 'arbitrary or unjustifiable discrimination between countries where the same conditions prevail, or a disguised restriction on international trade'.[47] Thus, even if one assumes that 'public morals' under WTO law includes human rights, member countries can always raise the argument that the measure is discriminatory or not necessary. For instance, if country A restricts trade in certain goods from country B on the grounds that they are produced with child labour and therefore violate public morals, country A then has to impose the same restrictions against all other countries that produce similar goods with child

---

[45] Art XIV GATS 'General Exceptions' essentially replicates the exceptions listed under Art XX GATT but adds 'public order' to 'public morals'.

[46] PC Mavroidis, 'Human Rights, Developing Countries and the WTO Constraint: the Very Thing That Makes You Rich Makes Me Poor?' in E Benvenisti and M Hirsch (eds), *The Impact of International Law on International Cooperation: Theoretical Perspective* (Cambridge, Cambridge University Press 2004) 244.

[47] Art XX GATT, 20 October 1947, 61 Stat A-11, 55 UNT.S 194.

labour. It is unlikely that country A would be able to gather accurate information on this matter or that it would decide to worsen its trade relations with all implicated countries. In addition, if the necessity of the measure is contested in a dispute, country A has to be able to prove that the measure is necessary, ie that there is no other less restrictive measure than limiting trade with country B through which it could achieve the same results.[48]

The broad drafting of the General Exceptions Clause (especially of Article XXa) and the two-prong test that applies when the clause is used impede the opportunities of countries to deviate from GATT-consistent behaviour for human rights considerations. Regardless, some scholars assert that doing so is possible: Professor Sarah Cleveland argues that, as long as the measure is non-discriminatory, a human rights-driven trade sanction can be introduced through Article XX GATT. She admits, however, that the *chapeau* requirement[49] makes the article 'less hospitable' for human rights sanctions than the National Security Exception.[50] There is one way in which the deficiencies of the General Exceptions could turn into an advantage in a WTO dispute settlement: it can protect against a state trying to justify its measures (such as trade sanctions) with disingenuous human rights concerns under Article XX. Considering the burden-of-proof and burden-of-persuasion system within the WTO DSP, which is described below, once the complainant establishes a prima facie case, it is very difficult for the defendant to rebut the presumption and justify its protectionist measure under Article XX GATT. In that way, the broad drafting could act as a 'safeguard' against protectionist measures masked as human rights concerns.

Similarly, the National Security Exception of Article XXI GATT is also not the most suitable human rights protection tool. It cannot be invoked for national security problems (including human rights violations) within a given WTO member country unless those problems threaten the national security of another WTO member or unless there is a relevant decision of the UN Security Council.

Waivers are a new opportunity under WTO law. They are permissions granted by WTO members allowing a WTO member, or a group of members (for instance LDCs), not to comply with certain commitments under WTO law for a certain period of time. Waivers have already been used to address social concerns. For example, the Kimberley Waiver

---

[48] This is the interpretation of the necessity requirement provided by the Appellate Body in *EC-Asbestos*. See Appellate Body Report, 'European Communities Measures Affecting Asbestos-Containing Products', WT/DS135/AB/R (12 March 2001).

[49] The *chapeau* requires that measures under Art XX shall not be applied as a means for arbitrary or unjustifiable discrimination between countries in which the same conditions prevail, or as 'a disguised restriction on international trade'.

[50] SH Cleveland, 'Human Rights Sanctions and International Trade: A Theory of Compatibility' (2002) 5 *Journal of International Economic Law* 133.

was used to limit trade in conflict diamonds. In 2002, the WTO General Council approved a waiver under the Trade-Related Aspects of Intellectual Property Rights (TRIPS) Agreement that exempts LDCs from the obligation to implement patent protection for pharmaceutical products. Another waiver, implemented under a 20 August 2003 Decision, allowed for compulsory licensing of patented medicines for export to certain developing countries.[51] The approval of waivers by the WTO on human rights grounds has set a precedent, which is one reason why some scholars speak about human rights 'seeping' into the WTO law.[52] All these waivers, however, arose through particular sets of factors. The Kimberley Waiver was a response to a UN General Assembly resolution to ban trade in conflict diamonds, as well as the initiation of the Kimberley Process Certification Scheme. The waivers from 2002 and 30 August 2003 were motivated by the efforts of WTO members to ensure that intellectual property protection does not violate the right to health and does not endanger access to medicines in developing countries that face serious public health problems, such as the HIV/AIDS pandemic. They did contribute, however, to the assumptions that human rights are slowly penetrating the WTO system.

Another avenue through which WTO member countries may raise human rights concerns is under the Trade Policy Reviews (TPRs). A TPR provides the opportunity to debate a country's trade conduct and related issues, including its relation to human rights. Aaronson and Zimmermann have examined several TPRs prepared by various countries and discovered that many of them have linked economic growth to human rights and the rule of law.[53] In theory, the reviews could encourage countries to apply self-discipline regarding human rights; they could also be used for 'naming and shaming' human rights violators. In practice, this has not happened. It is especially not likely that smaller economies would criticise at an official level the trade policies of countries with big markets on which they depend.

Some countries have sought to introduce rights issues through round

[51] Under Art 31(f) of the WTO TRIPS Agreement, compulsory licenses are authorised 'predominantly for the supply of the domestic market'. Para 6 of the Doha Declaration recognised that countries with insufficient pharmaceutical manufacturing capacity could not effectively use compulsory licensing and instructed the Council for TRIPS to find 'an expeditious solution'. On 30 August 2003, based on those findings, the WTO General Council adopted a decision on the implementation of para 6, which allowed compulsory licensing of patented medicines for export by WTO member states to LDCs, or other countries, that do not have sufficient manufacturing capacity. The 30 August Decision has so far been used only once, for the export of an AIDS drug from Canada to Rwanda in 2007, arguably because of its complicated procedure. The 30 August Decision was supposed to become permanent, as an amendment to the TRIPS Agreement, but so far has not been ratified by the required majority of two-thirds of WTO member states.

[52] SA Aaronson, 'Seeping in Slowly: How Human Rights Concerns Are Penetrating the WTO' (2007) 6 *World Trade Review* 413.

[53] Aaronson and Zimmerman, above n 42, 48–49.

negotiations. One example is the effort to include labour and environmental rights in the Marrakesh Agreement. Those attempts have failed so far, even though during round negotiations members have discussed non-trade issues such as the right to food and food security. Inserting human rights issues in round negotiations, however, seems like a viable option, despite the difficulties that would arise in achieving consensus. A similarly suitable option would be to introduce amendments to the existing WTO laws or to clarify provisions in the laws in a human rights-consistent manner. For example, a recent clarification on the public health exceptions to the TRIPS Agreement presented the opportunity for members to discuss human rights and the WTO. Again, the history of round negotiations thus far does not suggest that achieving consensus on such amendments would be an easy task.[54]

The opportunities described above, even if deemed valid under WTO law, require the decision-making power of the member states, and—in the cases of negotiations, amendments and waivers—a consensus among them. The opportunities under the dispute settlement procedures are substantially different. The next section examines the WTO DSP and explores the possibility of invoking the right to food in dispute settlements.

IV. WTO DSP AND THE RIGHT TO FOOD

A. Raising Human Rights Concerns in Dispute Settlement Procedures

Under WTO DSP, the adjudicating bodies can make independent decisions that will bind the parties concerned. No consensus by the parties is required. Mavroidis calls the Dispute Settlement Understanding (DSU), which is the main WTO agreement on settling disputes, 'the crown jewel of the WTO system'; he points out that this agreement was the result of a long period of practice development and did not emerge overnight.[55] In the early GATT years, dispute settlements required consensus by the parties to the dispute, including the defendant. Subsequent additions and amendments of the GATT system gradually added to the procedural rules and led to the binding effect of the dispute settlement reports. Nowadays, WTO dispute settlement has an established procedure described in the DSU, as well as in the reports of the panels and the

---

[54] WTO General Council, 'Least-Developed Country Members: Obligations Under Article 70.9 of the TRIPS Agreement with Respect to Pharmaceutical Products', WT/L/478 (12 July 2002), available at www.wto.org/english/tratop_e/trips_e/art70_9_e.htm.
[55] Mavroidis, above n 30, 402.

Appellate Body. The outcome of dispute settlements can lead to the suspension of concessions or the repayment of compensation.

So far, there has not been a measure undertaken based on human rights considerations before a WTO Dispute Settlement Body (DSB). Aaronson and Zimmermann argue that it is unlikely that countries that have violated human rights would want their case to be examined by a WTO adjudicating body. For example, the US has imposed sanctions on Burma due to its long history of human rights violations.[56] Thus far, Burma has not initiated a complaint against the US and is unlikely to do so before the WTO.

There has been one dispute settlement case in which human rights concerns were initially mentioned. In late 2002, India requested the establishment of a panel, challenging clauses of the General System of Preferences (GSP) established by the European Commission related to labour rights, protection of the environment, and prevention of drug production and trafficking.[57] Less than 3 months after initiating the claim, however, India withdrew the arguments regarding labour and environmental rights from the complaint, without explaining its motives. Its amended claim simply maintained that the preferences given to some countries for their initiatives in combating drug production and trafficking were awarded in a discriminatory manner. The dispute settlement panel found for India, and the EU agreed to amend its GSP to reflect the recommendations in the panel's report.

The India case generated discussions on whether the final decision prevents countries from promoting human rights in their GSPs;[58] its impact on human rights protection is thus debatable. Nevertheless, it is noteworthy as the first complaint in which human rights were brought before a WTO dispute settlement body, even though the human rights aspects of the complaint were never investigated by the panel. One can only speculate on whether the panel would have agreed to investigate the part of the complaint related to labour and environmental rights.

Many scholars have grappled with the question of how WTO

---

[56] Aaronson and Zimmermann, above n 42, 46.

[57] Panel Report, 'European Communities—Conditions for the Granting of Tariff Preferences to Developing Countries', WT/DS246 (1 December 2003).

[58] Professor Howse expresses concerns that, after this decision, countries could only refer to the General Exceptions in order to introduce human rights considerations in their GSPs. Professor Bartels is less concerned and contends that, if the GSP policies are developed in a non-discriminatory manner regarding all developing countries with particular human rights issues, human rights can still be introduced. See R Howse, 'India's WTO Challenge to Drug Enforcement Conditions in the European Community Generalized System of Preferences: A Little Known Case with Major Repercussions for 'Political' Conditionality in US Trade Policy', 4 *Chicago Journal of International Law* 385 (2003). See also L Bartels, 'The WTO Appellate Body Report in EC—Conditions for the Granting of Tariff Preferences to Developing Countries and its Implications for Conditionality in GSP Programs 482' in Cottier et al, above n 40.

adjudicating bodies would or should address human rights issues. WTO scholar Gabrielle Marceau contends that, in the case of a conflict between human rights and WTO law,

> WTO adjudicating bodies do not appear to have the competence ... to reach any formal conclusion that a non-WTO norm has been violated, or to require any positive action pursuant to that treaty or any conclusion that would enforce a non-WTO norm over WTO provisions, as in doing so the WTO adjudicating bodies would effectively add to, diminish or amend the WTO 'covered agreements'.[59]

The author recognises that WTO law prohibits violations of *jus cogens*:

> Arguably, because of its very nature, *jus cogens* would be part of all laws and thus would have direct effect in WTO law ... Situations of pure conflicts between WTO provisions and *jus cogens* are, however, difficult to conceive. In most, if not all, cases, the strong presumption against a violation of *jus cogens* will lead to an interpretation of WTO law which avoids such a violation. Some may argue that WTO panels and the Appellate Body do not have the capacity to determine the nullity of a WTO treaty provision for violation of *jus cogens*, as they only have the capacity to recommend that a national measure be brought into conformity with the covered agreements.[60]

In addition, Mavroidis points out that, with the exception of the TRIPS Agreement, requirements under WTO law are usually negative and do not anticipate the protection of human rights or even regulation of this field at all. In his opinion, the only positive requirement to protect human rights is provided by general public international law—the Vienna Convention on the Law of Treaties (VCLT). The VCLT stipulates in Articles 53 and 64 that membership in international agreements does not excuse states from their obligation to respect *jus cogens erga omnes*.[61] Joost Pauwelyn also supports the view that, as part of *jus cogens*, human rights have direct influence on WTO law.[62]

There is the possibility that right-to-food considerations could be invoked in a WTO dispute settlement procedure even without recourse to customary international law constructions. Disputes based on the AoA, the International Dairy Agreement and the International Bovine Meat Agreement can be settled directly through the WTO DSU system. In other words, even if it is not possible to introduce the right-to-food and food-security concerns on a human rights basis, there might be the opportunity to invoke them as matters related to WTO law. All of the above-mentioned agreements incorporate some food security

---

[59] G Marceau, 'WTO Dispute Settlement and Human Rights' (2002) 13 *European Journal of International Law* 753.
[60] Ibid, 759.
[61] 'Compelling toward all'. See Mavroidis, above n 46, 244.
[62] J Pauwelyn, 'The Role of Public International Law in the WTO: How Far Can We Go?' (2001) 95 *American Journal of International Law* 535.

considerations. For example, the International Dairy Agreement distinguishes between normal commercial transactions and transactions 'for relief and food-related development purposes' (Article V IDA; see also Article 3.7 Annex on Certain Milk Products). Articles I and IV of the International Bovine Meat Agreement consider the specific situation of developing countries. Multiple provisions of the AoA refer to agricultural and rural development, such as the provisions on prevention of circumvention of export subsidy commitments (Article 10), the provisions on special and differential treatment, and the provisions on least-developed countries and net food-importing developing countries (Parts IX and X).

Thus, some aspects of international agreements provide opportunities for countries to raise concerns in WTO processes related to food security. Countries are allowed to challenge non-compliance with domestic support limitation commitments, as well as to challenge the dumping practices of their trading partners. Practices that were possible under the Peace Clause can now be challenged since its expiration in 2004. Although it is unclear how likely it is that countries would invoke such complaints, at least theoretically they have the opportunity to bring such matters under the DSU. Thus, in this way, countries potentially have recourse to the WTO's system of complaints for food security-related issues.

The DSU reproduces the types of complaints found under the GATT. It distinguishes between violation complaints (Article XXIII.1a GATT), non-violation complaints (Article XXIII.1b GATT) and situation complaints (Article XXIII.1c GATT). So far, however, no situation complaints have been submitted.[63]

Most complaints are violation complaints. Through a violation complaint, the complainant claims that the defendant has violated a provision of the body of law covered by the DSU and that a benefit accruing to the complainant has been nullified or impaired. The complaining party carries the burden of proof. The WTO Appellate Body has established that the complainant has to make a prima facie case, ie provide sufficient evidence that its claim is true, which then reverses the burden of proof to the defendant.[64] The practice requiring the complainant to make a prima facie case has been consistently followed by the dispute settlement bodies. This strict requirement aims to discourage

---

[63] It seems that this type of complaint is envisioned to cover any complaints that are not violation complaints or non-violation complaints, and arise out of other objective circumstances: 'a situation'. According to Mavroidis, the only time the GATT practice refers to situation complaints is in a 1982 request for consultations by the European Communities against Japan on the grounds of 'the Japanese lifestyle'. A panel was never established. See Mavroidis, above n 30, 415.

[64] Appellate Body Report, 'United States—Measure Affecting Imports of Woven Wool Shirts and Blouses from India', WT/DS33/AB/R (25 April 1997).

members from raising claims that they cannot prove sufficiently well; to date, parties have complied with this rule made by the Appellate Body, even though it has not been incorporated into the DSU.

In the context of the right to food, violation complaints may be invoked only when the violation of the right to food and/or food security can be subsumed under a WTO law violation, such as a violation of the AoA or a violation of another relevant agreement. It would probably be possible to amalgamate the human rights violations with the WTO law violations, but in order for the claim to have standing before the DSB, the leading arguments must focus on the WTO law violation and the nullification or impairment of a benefit accrued to the complainant.

Non-violation complaints (NVCs) are described in Article XXII.1.b of the GATT:

> 1. If any contracting party should consider that any benefit accruing to it directly or indirectly under this Agreement is being nullified or impaired or that the attainment of any objective of the Agreement is being impeded as the result of . . .
>
> ...
>
> (b) the application by another contracting party of any measure, whether or not it conflicts with the provisions of this Agreement . . .

NVCs exist in recognition of the fact that even GATT-consistent behaviour can nullify or impair benefits of WTO members, and that members also should refrain from 'legal' behaviour that harms the benefits of trade liberalisation. Needless to say, the opportunity to contest GATT-consistent behaviour could open a dangerous door in the dispute settlement procedures. Therefore, to bring a complaint, certain conditions must be met cumulatively: (i) a measure that could be GATT-consistent, (ii) has occurred after concluding a tariff concession, (iii) which could not have been reasonably anticipated at the time of the conclusion, and (iv) which has nullified or impaired a benefit accrued to the complaining party. All those conditions have to be met in order to successfully raise a NVC. Mavroidis points out that those conditions significantly diminish the opportunity to challenge human rights-related issues through NVCs:

> [The deterioration of a concession] will be hard to prove for most human rights-related concerns: how can one establish, for example, that the advent of an oppressive regime which restricts freedom of speech has caused a reduction in the volume of foreign goods consumed? Many (if not most) human rights are largely unrelated to trade flows. A change is necessary for a non-violation complaint to succeed.[65]

---

[65] Mavroidis, above n 46, 254.

B. Advantages and Disadvantages of Invoking the Right to Food in Dispute Settlement Procedures

There are several potential benefits of invoking the right to food in WTO dispute settlement procedures. This chapter has already briefly outlined the impact that trade liberalisation has on access to food, food security and development in rural areas; thus, the relevance of raising those issues before the multilateral free trade forum is easily explicable. As opposed to the early GATT years, the reports of WTO panels or the WTO Appellate Body could—at least in theory—result in the payment of compensation or the suspension of concessions. In addition, at least in theory, a country that is targeted by a complaint might also change its human rights violating behaviour. Moreover, the DSP decision-making system is fast; the whole procedure, including appeals, takes up to 3 years, which is much shorter than the reported average time-span of an international court case.[66] Panels generally manage to comply with the imposed time frame.

Panels, which are established ad hoc at the discretion of the parties or with the intervention of the WTO Director-General, have very broad investigative powers both in terms of law as well as facts, and must investigate and adjudicate objectively.[67] Article 13 of the DSU allows panels to seek any information that they consider appropriate, including information from expert review groups (Article 13.2). So far, no advice has been sought from expert review groups, although some individual experts have submitted opinions to the panels. Nevertheless, this is an important opportunity for experts (including non-WTO experts) to participate in the proceedings. Similarly, the submission of briefs by amici curiae is possible, which potentially provides an opportunity for the involvement of human rights advocates in the investigating procedures. The participation of amici curiae is not an explicitly granted right, but rather an implied opportunity. Even though it is not specifically listed in the DSU, it has already occurred in practice during the *US-Shrimp* Appellate Body procedure.[68]

Another possible advantage of using dispute settlement procedures to raise right-to-food concerns is that it would benefit from the DSU require-

---

[66] For comparison, the average time span of a case before the European Court of Justice is 10 years. See C Edmond, 'ECJ Case Duration Dips to 10 Year Low', *Legalweek*, 27 March 2007, available at www.legalweek.com/legal-week/news/1156046/ecj-duration-dips-low. More than 23% of the cases before the European Court of Human Rights last three to more than five years. See European Court of Human Rights, 'Analysis of Statistics' (2005), available at www.echr.coe.int/NR/rdonlyres/496D9551-8C1A-42A4-8270-B7D5B6E-B6EC4/0/AnalysisOfStatistics2005.pdf.

[67] The Appellate Body only has review powers regarding law. In practice, however, almost any matter of fact can be presented as a matter of law and reviewed by the AB.

[68] Appellate Body Report, 'United States—Import Prohibition of Shrimp and Certain Shrimp Products', WT/DS58/AB/R (12 October 1998).

ment regarding shifting the burden of proof. Due to this requirement, a defendant cannot reasonably choose to remain passive, but must take a proactive role in order to rebut the presumption after the claimant has established a prima facie case. This practice protects the WTO system from members raising unsubstantiated claims; at the same time, it ensures that disputes will not simply be ignored by defendants or discharged easily with reference to the General Exceptions or National Security Exception Clauses.

There are two types of sources of information to which panels refer during the dispute settlement procedure. The sources of law for the dispute settlement procedure, both primary and secondary, are decided by the governments of WTO member states; the supplementary, interpretative elements are determined by the WTO panels and the Appellate Body. Some secondary sources of law in dispute settlement have the potential to be used in human right-related complaints—as they include, for example, the WTO agreements with the World Bank and the IMF. An even better opportunity to introduce human rights considerations into DSP, however, seems to be provided by the supplementary sources, despite their interpretative role. So far, practice shows that the following sources have been used for case interpretations: international agreements not incorporated in WTO law, decisions of international courts, domestic legislation of member states, customary international law provisions and scholarly opinions. Article 3.2 of the DSU refers to 'any other relevant rule of public international law applicable in relations between the parties' as sources for interpretation; the Appellate Body in *US-Gasoline*[69] has already explicitly established one source as the Vienna Convention on the Law of Treaties. To date, the VCLT has been used only as a tool for interpretation of the meaning of terms. As the right to food is recognised by all states parties to the ICESCR and is generally considered to be part of the general principles of law (or of customary international law), the right to food is therefore part of general public international law. Consequently, it can be referred to in interpretations, together with WTO law, pursuant to the VCLT.

An additional advantage of using the WTO DSP is that compliance with the panel report or Appellate Body report is monitored. Members have the opportunity to contest non-compliance through compliance complaints. In addition, parties have the opportunity to resolve the dispute at any time before, during or after the dispute settlement procedure through consultations, which occur before, or binding arbitration, which can occur during or after the dispute settlement procedure.

---

[69] Appellate Body Report, 'United States—Standards for Reformulated and Conventional Gasoline', WT/DS2/AB/R (29 April 1996).

This opportunity enables fast, mutually acceptable and cost-efficient solutions.

All of these potential benefits of invoking the right to food before the WTO in a dispute settlement procedure are only theoretical examples. To date, there has not been a case in which the right to food has been invoked, or in which there has been any direct reference to another human rights issue. Conversely, one can also imagine potential disadvantages of using WTO DSP as a forum in which to discuss the right to food or human rights in general. Most importantly, complaints before the WTO dispute settlement bodies can be initiated only by member states. It is therefore not possible for right-to-food advocates in a given country or region to raise a complaint before the WTO unless they persuade their government to do so. How realistic is it to expect cooperation from the states, given their own reluctance to bring human rights issues to the WTO? The lack of precedent and the prompt withdrawal of human rights matters from the only complaint that ever raised them (the India GSP case) do not indicate that state cooperation is likely. Furthermore, complaints cannot be initiated *ex officio* under the DSU, so a direct intervention by the WTO bureaucracy in protection of the right to food also cannot be expected. Considering the significance of this obstacle, Ernst-Ulrich Petersmann suggests that a new human rights paradigm on global integration should be developed and that individuals should be recognised as subjects under WTO law.[70]

Apart from the procedural difficulties, there is the additional concern that the enforcement of WTO obligations through the DSP does not work in practice. Kyle Bagwell and Robert Staiger point out the notable asymmetry in the dispute process and the lack of cases in which countries with smaller economies have enacted countermeasures against large trading partners.[71] The practical impact of such countermeasures is unclear, and might even be harmful, for the small economies of the complainants. Mavroidis also criticises the DSP outcome as institutionalising the interim measure—suspension of concession—without necessarily leading to the desired outcome, compliance.[72] Needless to say, neither proponents of multilateral trade liberalisation nor human rights advocates are interested in achieving such results.

Considering the difficulties of trying to raise right-to-food concerns in the WTO DSP, it is important to consider how the WTO system could better facilitate the inclusion of human rights concerns within the

---

[70] E-U Petersmann, 'Time for Integrating Human Rights into the Law of Worldwide Organizations: Lessons from European Integration Law for Global Integration Law', Jean Monnet Program Working Paper 7/01 (2001), available at www.jeanmonnetprogram.org/papers/01/012301.pdf.

[71] K Bagwell and R Staiger, 'Enforcement, Private Political Pressure and the GATT/WTO Escape Clause' (2004) 34 *Journal of Legal Studies* 471.

[72] Mavroidis, above n 30, 426.

organisation. For example, David Kinley, acknowledging that methods to protect human rights in current WTO DSP are limited, suggests that if human rights are to be considered within the organisation there is a need to reform the dispute settlement mechanism. Kinley stresses that calls for reform have come from both outside and within the WTO. He refers to the suggestions made by James Harrison to establish a monitoring system for the impact of trade rules on human rights in order to promote better understanding of international human rights instruments among trade specialists and WTO Dispute Settlement Procedure panellists and, ultimately, to insert specific references to human rights in the WTO treaties.[73] Similarly, in his Mission to the World Trade Organization report, the UN Special Rapporteur on the right to food recommends to WTO member states that they assess the human rights impact of their undertakings within the organisation and prior to concluding trade agreements. The Special Rapporteur also points out the need for a paradigm shift to reduce the excessive reliance on international trade in food security matters and to foster the development of flexibilities and domestic policies that protect the right to food and food security.[74]

V. CONCLUSION

Invoking the right to food before the WTO is not entirely unrealistic. At least theoretically, there are opportunities to do so through the dispute settlement procedures or the other discussed avenues outside the DSU. It is doubtful, however, that any of these possibilities is a way to achieve sustainable solutions to the right-to-food and food-security problems. Rather, in the context of the WTO, the genuine and lasting resolution of those problems depends on the willingness of members to discuss development and rights in the WTO. So far this has not happened.

Representatives of the civil society sector have successfully started discussions on trade liberalisation and the right to food at the WTO level. In 2008, the UN Special Rapporteur on the right to food and the WTO Director-General participated in such a discussion followed by meetings between the Special Rapporteur and WTO country delegates. This was the first official opportunity to discuss the right to food and food security at the WTO level, and the positions advanced by the Special Rapporteur received the support of several member states—mostly

---

[73] Kinley, above n 25, 76. See also J Harrison, *The Human Rights Impact of the World Trade Organisation* (Oxford, Hart Publishing, 2007) 227–45.

[74] O De Schutter, UN Special Rapporteur on the Right to Food, 'Mission Report to the WTO, ¶ 50, delivered to the Human Rights Council', UN document A/HRC/10/5/Add.2, 4 (4 February 2009).

developing countries. During the 2009 WTO Public Forum, an annual informal meeting for NGOs hosted by the WTO Secretariat, debates around the right to food and achieving a new global contract for food and agriculture dominated the forum's agenda. The fact that these discussions are happening with the participation of officials from the WTO Secretariat and that they are being met with strong interest indicates the great relevance of the issue. It also provides hope that more substantial developments could follow. However, until the political will of WTO member states is harmonised, and until mutually acceptable rules for trade liberalisation in agriculture and food are negotiated in accord with the Millennium Development Goals and international human rights standards, there is no way to settle the frictions between practices under the WTO and the right to food.

8

Food Aid: How It Should Be Done

LORETO FERRER MOREU

FOOD AID HAS historically been a very important tool of international relations. As such, it has been used to try to satisfy a number of different goals: promoting international trade, helping advance development and assisting relief efforts. One clear example of this diversity of purposes is found in the US Food for Peace Act (Public Law 480),[1] which describes a food aid scheme intended to 'promote the foreign policy of the US by enhancing the food security of the developing world' with a variety of goals:

(1) combat world hunger and malnutrition and their causes; (2) promote broad-based, equitable, and sustainable development, including agricultural development; (3) expand international trade; (4) foster and encourage the development of private enterprise and democratic participation in developing countries; and (5) prevent conflicts.[2]

The use of food aid to fulfil a number of purposes, which is in violation of the Tinbergen principle of 'one policy instrument per objective', has had severe consequences for aid effectiveness and, in many instances, has curtailed its legitimacy.[3] The international community has progressively come to terms with the need to redefine assistance policies in order to improve their quality and effectiveness.

---

[1] The Food for Peace Act, 7 USC.S §§ 1691 et seq (2008), which was formerly referred to as Public Law 480 and originally enacted as the Agricultural Trade and Development Assistance Act, is broken down into three Titles. Title I provides for the sale of agricultural surpluses to developing countries. Title II provides for donations of free food to countries for emergency and non-emergency purposes. Title III provides for donations of food to be sold in recipient countries, under the condition that the generated revenue be used for development purposes; it has not been used in recent years. See US Department of Agriculture, Foreign Agriculture Service, Public Law 480, Title I, available at www.fas.usda.gov/excredits/foodaid/pl480/pl480.asp.

[2] 7 USC.S § 1691 (2008).

[3] See CB Barrett, 'Food Aid: Is it Development Assistance, Trade Promotion, Both or Neither?' (1998) 80(3) *American Journal of Agricultural Economics* 566.

240 *Loreto Ferrer Moreu*

The goals, uses and types of food aid have been discussed at successive international conferences, where several agreements have been reached and declarations have been made. The international community has repeatedly expressed its commitment to cooperate in the eradication of hunger and has adopted different strategies pursuing that goal. There is an important gap, however, in the implementation of the commitments and guidelines adopted, in terms of both quantity and quality of the assistance provided. Indeed, food aid flows have fluctuated during the last decades and, contrary to international commitments, have decreased.[4]

The first section of this chapter addresses the current international framework of food aid. It briefly examines the various international summits, conferences and declarations on food aid. It identifies three main tendencies: (i) consolidation of a human-rights-based approach to food aid; (ii) revitalisation of the obligation to cooperate; and (iii) emergence of the concept of food security. The second section analyses the actual implementation of food aid programmes, projects and emergency assistance. It shows a lack of political will to implement effectively the aforementioned international agreements. Finally, the last section sets forth suggestions on how food aid should be done.

I. INTERNATIONAL FRAMEWORK AND TENDENCIES

During the last five decades, the fight against hunger has gained increasing weight within the international agenda. Simultaneously, the right to adequate food has been developed in international human rights instruments and its normative content has been clarified. States have gradually assumed stronger commitments to cooperate towards the alleviation of hunger, increasingly sharing the responsibility of the fulfilment of the right to food. Hence, in successive declarations and conferences, the international community has consistently stressed its political will to eradicate world hunger, looking to different strategies and approaches. Throughout the process, the role played by food aid in the broader context of the fight against hunger has been gradually shaped and subjected to certain conditions. A brief overview of the main conventions, conferences and agreements reached during the last 50 years points towards three trends: the consolidation of a rights-based approach to the fight against hunger; the increased recognition of an obligation to cooperate; and the identification of food security as the cornerstone of every strategy aiming at the eradication of hunger. Food

[4] CB Barrett and DG Maxwell, *Food Aid After Fifty Years: Recasting its Role* (London, Routledge, 2005).

aid has become, therefore, a quasi-residual instrument, required only in specific situations to combat immediate starvation.

A. The International Human Rights Framework

The right to food was first discussed as an international human right in the Universal Declaration of Human Rights (UDHR). The UDHR, adopted by the UN General Assembly in 1948, included the right to an adequate standard of living as a key element for human dignity and, therefore, for the achievement of freedom, justice and peace in the world.[5] Although not articulating the right to food as a human right, Article 25 of the UDHR listed food as a critical requirement to achieve a healthy life and well-being.[6] Subsequent to the UDHR, and most importantly for the recognition of a human right to adequate food, Article 11 of the International Covenant on Economic, Social and Cultural Rights (ICESCR) expressly stated the fundamental right of everyone to be free from hunger.[7]

According to the ICESCR, the primary responsibility for the implementation of this right rests on the sovereign states, which must develop national policies aiming at the development of the agricultural sector and equitable distribution of resources. Traditionally, the nation-state has the main responsibility for the fulfilment of human rights for those in its jurisdiction. States have been reluctant to accept obligations imposed by others to cooperate or provide international assistance towards the realisation of internationally recognised human rights. However, certain international commitments to cooperate have been voiced in different instruments. For example, the Charter of the UN affirms that all members will take joint and separate action in cooperation with the UN for the achievement of, inter alia, higher standards of living and universal respect of human rights.[8] Similarly, Article 2(1) of the ICESCR states that each state party 'undertakes to take steps, individually and through international assistance and co-operation, especially economic and technical, to the maximum of its available resources, with a view to achieving progressively the full realisation of the rights recognised

---

[5] Universal Declaration of Human Rights (UDHR), GA Res 217A, pmbl, Art 25, UN GAOR, 3d Sess, 1st plen Mtg, UN document A/810 (12 December 1948).

[6] Ibid, Art 25: 'Everyone has the right to a standard of living adequate for the health and well-being of himself and of his family, including food, clothing, housing and medical care and necessary social services, and the right to security in the event of unemployment, sickness, disability, widowhood, old age or other lack of livelihood in circumstances beyond his control'.

[7] International Covenant on Economic, Social and Cultural Rights, GA Res 2200A (XXI) Art 11, UN GAOR, Supp (No 16), 49, UN document A/6316 (3 January 1976).

[8] See UN Charter, Art 55–56.

in the present Covenant'. More specifically, Article 11 of the ICESCR emphasises the essential importance of international cooperation in the realisation of the right to be free from hunger. It also encourages states to take both the individual and collective measures that are needed to improve the methods of production, conservation and distribution of food, and to ensure equitable distribution of world food supplies.

In 1999, the Committee on Economic, Social and Cultural Rights issued General Comment 12, which focused on the right to adequate food.[9] It defined the specific content of the right to food to include 'physical and economic access at all times to adequate food or means for its procurement'.[10] It also identified three levels of obligations on states parties: the obligations to respect, to protect and to fulfil (facilitate and provide). While the primary responsibility to fulfil these obligations rests on the sovereign states, the General Comment also affirms that 'States parties should take steps to respect the enjoyment of the right to food in other countries, to protect that right, to facilitate access to food and to provide the necessary aid when required'.[11] That inclusion of state obligations to third countries regarding the right to adequate food confirmed a trend that has been consistently expressed in international conferences on food and nutrition: the idea of a shared responsibility for the progressive fulfilment of economic, social and cultural rights and, more specifically, for the eradication of hunger.

B. The Evolution of the Position of the International Community

In 1974, barely 2 years before the ICESCR came into force, 135 state representatives participated in the first World Food Conference. They addressed the global problems associated with food production and consumption, and adopted the Universal Declaration on the Eradication of Hunger and Malnutrition, which, introducing the language of rights, affirms the 'right of every man, woman and child to be free from hunger and malnutrition'. The declaration calls on individual states to formulate national plans integrating food and nutrition policies into overall socio-economic and agricultural development strategies. It also stresses the need for integrated rural development. The main emphasis of the declaration, however, is the idea of a shared responsibility of the international community in the eradication of hunger and the need for international cooperation. Thus, the eradication of hunger

---

[9] UN Economic and Social Council (ECOSOC), Committee on Economic, Social and Cultural Rights, 'General Comment 12 (Art 11), Right to Adequate Food', UN document E/C.12/1999/5 (12 May 1999).
[10] Ibid, ¶6.
[11] Ibid, ¶ 36.

Food Aid: How It Should Be Done   243

is presented as 'a common objective of all the countries of the international community, especially of the developed countries and others in a position to help'.[12]

The declaration urges developed countries to take effective international action to provide developing countries with sustained technical and financial assistance sufficient to address their needs, developed on the basis of bilateral and multilateral agreements, with favourable terms and limited conditionality. The declaration referred to specific fields in which international cooperation was required in order to advance the eradication of hunger: improvement of food production in developing countries; transfer, adaptation and dissemination of appropriate technology; cooperation to preserve the environment; improvement of food trade conditions; and, finally, cooperation in the provision of food aid.[13] Food aid was presented as an instrument to achieve two specific goals in the process of eradicating hunger: first, to meet emergency and nutritional needs; and secondly, to stimulate rural employment through development projects. Specifically, the conference encouraged the forward planning of food aid[14] in order to insulate food aid from the effects of excessive fluctuations in production and prices. It also urged all donor countries to provide commodities or financial assistance to ensure adequate quantities of food.[15]

By 1992, despite the decline in the prevalence of undernutrition, more than 800 million people still did not have access to enough food to meet their basic daily needs. Responding to a call by the Food and Agriculture Organization of the UN (FAO) and the World Health Organization, 159 states gathered at the International Conference on Nutrition[16] and reaffirmed their commitment to fight against hunger in the World Declaration on Nutrition. Again, the declaration's emphasis was on the right to adequate nutrition and the right to an adequate standard of living.[17] While recognising that each government had the primary responsibility to protect and promote the rights of its people, the declaration stressed the role of international cooperation in the promotion of the nutritional well-being of the world population. Hence, states pledged to 'act in

---

[12] World Food Conference, Rome, Italy, 5–16 November 1974, Universal Declaration on the Eradication of Hunger and Malnutrition, ¶ 1, UN document E/CONF 65/20 (1974).

[13] Ibid, 8–10 (adopting resolution XVIII on 'An improved policy for food aid' and recommending the reconstitution of the WFP's governing body, as well as the establishment of the World Food Council (WFC), the International Fund for Agricultural Development (IFAD) and the FAO Committee on World Food Security (CFS)).

[14] Ibid, 9: '[States] should make all efforts to provide at least 10 million tons of grain as food aid every year . . .'.

[15] Ibid, 7.

[16] 159 states, the European Community, 15 UN organisations and 144 non-governmental organisations participated in the conference.

[17] International Conference on Nutrition, Rome, Italy, 1–3 December 1992, World Declaration on Nutrition, ¶1, ¶14.

solidarity to ensure that freedom from hunger becomes a reality'.[18] To reach that goal, the declaration called for an increase in each country's official development assistance to achieve the accepted UN target of 0.7% of the gross national product (GNP),[19] as well as for further alleviation of external debt.

An interesting element of the declaration was the call for national nutrition improvement plans, which were to be developed through collaboration between the government, academia, local communities, non-governmental organisations (NGOs) and the private sector.[20] Consequently, the consensus reached was that international cooperation should respect the priorities and goals established in those plans and proceed appropriately with a focus on agriculture, rural development, environmental issues and improvement of trade conditions. Food aid was mainly consigned to assist in emergencies, to provide relief to refugees and displaced persons, and to support household food security. Food aid was nevertheless also assigned a minor role in the promotion of economic development. The parties to the declaration further defined some critical aspects of food aid that were to be met in every action: (i) it must be sufficient and stable; (ii) it must avoid creating dependency and negative impacts on food habits, local food production and marketing; and (iii) it should include the participation of local communities and long-term planning.

This global commitment to the fight against hunger was renewed at the highest political level in 1996, when world leaders met at the World Food Summit (WFS). At this occasion, representatives from 185 countries and the European Community (as it was then) reaffirmed the right of every person to have access to adequate food and be free from hunger.[21] Both the language of rights and the concept of food security were reinforced in the Rome Declaration that emerged from the summit. The Rome Declaration set a target of reducing the number of undernourished people to half the (then) present level by 2015. That target was to be achieved through two means: national policies aiming at sustainable development, stability and peace; and international cooperation directed towards the achievement of food security for all.

---

[18] Ibid, ¶1.
[19] UN Conference on Environment and Development, Rio de Janeiro, Brazil, 3–14 June 1992, Agenda 21, §33.13.
[20] These plans should identify short- and long-term priority areas for action; specify goals, which should be quantified where feasible, to be achieved within specified time frames; define the roles of relevant government ministries, local communities and private institutions; and, as appropriate, include estimates of resources that are required. The plans should take into account the goals set forth in the World Declaration on Nutrition. See International Conference on Nutrition, Rome, Italy, 1–3 December 1992, 'Plan of Action For Nutrition', available at www.fao.org/docrep/U9920t/u9920t0b.htm.
[21] World Food Summit, Rome, Italy, 13–17 November 1996, Rome Declaration on World Food Security.

The Rome Declaration included a wide range of measures to achieve food security, including implementing agricultural and productive policies, as well as improving the international trade conditions. Food aid, in this context, was only referred to in respect of natural disasters and man-made emergencies, as a way to meet transitory and emergency food requirements. But the declaration also made it clear that food aid should not stand as a substitute for long-term strategies aimed at food security: instead, it had to be directed towards rehabilitation and development, and had to create capacities to satisfy future needs (ie self-sufficiency).

A significant outcome of the WFS was the plan of action to achieve food security. In accordance with the declaration, that document presents food aid as a solution for hungry people facing immediate starvation during emergency situations, but clearly not as a long-term solution to the underlying causes of food insecurity. The WFS Plan of Action stressed the need for emergency preparedness, early warning systems and complementary measures such as conflict prevention and resolution, as well as rehabilitation and development promotion activities, which would prevent the recurrence of food insecurity and reduce the vulnerability of populations to food emergencies.

Unfortunately, despite the good intentions expressed in the Plan of Action, in 2002 the international community had to admit that very few advances had been made in the alleviation of hunger. The FAO thus convened the 'World Food Summit: Five Years Later' to track the progress that had been made since the 1996 summit and to consider new ways to accelerate those efforts. Parties—including governments, international organisations, civil society organisations and the private sector—were called upon to work as an international alliance against hunger, to raise the political will to address hunger and to reinforce their financial efforts in order to achieve the WFS target of halving the number of undernourished people no later than 2015. At the 2002 summit, the participants reaffirmed both the important role of food aid as an instrument for development by supporting safety networks and its importance in humanitarian crises. Specifically, parties were encouraged to improve the effectiveness of emergency actions, integrating them into sustainable development efforts to achieve food security. They were also called to promote safety nets for vulnerable and food insecure households, through, among other things, the implementation of school feeding programmes. State parties resolved to accelerate the implementation of the WFS Plan of Action and invited the FAO to create a set of voluntary guidelines to support member states' efforts to achieve the progressive realisation of the right to adequate food in the context of national food security.

By 2009, however, the global food crisis raised the number of people suffering from hunger to more than one billion. World leaders, gathered at the World Summit on Food Security, pledged to reinforce their efforts to meet by 2015 the targets of Millennium Development Goal One and the prior World Food Summits.[22] They reaffirmed the right of everyone to have access to safe, sufficient and nutritious food, and called for the implementation of the FAO Voluntary Guidelines to support the progressive realisation of the right to adequate food in the context of national food security, which are based on the principles of participation, transparency and accountability.

C. The FAO Voluntary Guidelines

Following the 2002 World Food Summit recommendations, the FAO established an intergovernmental working group. Its main goal was to provide states with practical guidance to fulfil their obligations under the right to food. The final document, the FAO Voluntary Guidelines, was passed in 2004; it stressed the need to adopt human-rights-based strategies for the progressive realisation of the right to food in the context of national food security.[23] The FAO Voluntary Guidelines represented the 'first attempt by governments to interpret an economic, social and cultural right and to recommend actions to be undertaken for its realization'.[24]

Even though the guidelines are voluntary and therefore do not set any legally binding obligations on states, they identify the various actions states should adopt in order to further the progressive realisation of the right to food. Although states hold the primary responsibility for their own economic and social development, the guidelines note the critical importance of international assistance in this task. The guidelines assign to the international community duties involving two main aspects of the right to food:

1. Responsibility to respect: 'States are strongly urged to take steps with a view to the avoidance of, and refrain from, any unilateral measure . . . that impedes the full achievement of economic and social development by the populations of the affected countries and that hinders their progressive realization of the right to adequate food.'[25]
2. Responsibility to fulfil: 'Consistent with commitments made at various international conferences . . . developed countries should

---

[22] World Summit on Food Security, Rome, Italy, 16–18 November 2009, Declaration of the World Summit on Food Security.

[23] FAO Council, 127th Sess, Voluntary Guidelines to support the progressive realization of the right to food in the context of national food security (November 2004).

[24] Ibid, pmbl.

[25] Ibid, §III.3.

assist developing countries in attaining international development goals . . . States and relevant international organizations . . . should actively support the progressive realization of the right to adequate food at the national level.'[26]

The FAO Voluntary Guidelines helped to revitalise the obligation to cooperate. Now, states are expected not only to respect, protect and fulfil the right to food of their own populations, but also to take positive action through international assistance to fulfil this right elsewhere. In this context, food aid is considered one of the many possible instruments of international assistance.

The conditions and circumstances under which food aid should be provided, however, are circumscribed in the FAO Voluntary Guidelines. Indeed, the guidelines use strong language regarding state obligations to provide food aid only in the cases of emergencies and as support for safety nets. Thus, in the case of natural or human-made disasters, '[s]tates should provide food assistance to those in need'.[27] Also, '[i]n situations where it has been determined that food plays an appropriate role in safety nets, food assistance should bridge the gap between the nutritional needs of the affected population and their ability to meet those needs themselves'.[28] However, Guideline 15, which addresses international food aid overall, uses a softer and more careful approach. It affirms that those states that provide international assistance in the form of food aid should regularly examine and review their relevant policies to progressively realise the right to adequate food in the context of national food security. Apart from the two cases mentioned above— emergencies and safety nets—food assistance is not encouraged as a form of international assistance. Moreover, the guidelines place strict conditions on food aid: in order to avoid the creation of dependency, it should be provided in a participatory manner, taking into account national food security and the importance of not disrupting local food production, respecting the nutritional and dietary needs and cultures of recipient populations, using the local and regional commercial markets, and containing a clear exit strategy.[29]

The FAO Voluntary Guidelines are an attempt by the international community to define and coordinate specific actions aiming at the eradication of hunger. Similarly, donor states and recipients have come together to define and improve the policy framework for international development assistance, in order to improve not only the quantity but also the quality of international official assistance.

---

[26] Ibid, §III.4.
[27] Ibid, §II.16.6.
[28] Ibid, §II.14.5.
[29] Ibid, §II.15.1.

D. The International Framework for International Development Assistance

In 2000, 139 heads of state gathered at the UN Millennium Summit. They issued the Millennium Declaration, recognising that

> in addition to our separate responsibilities to our individual societies, we have a collective responsibility to uphold the principles of human dignity, equality and equity at the global level. As leaders we have a duty therefore to all the world's people, especially the most vulnerable and, in particular, the children of the world, to whom the future belongs.[30]

The participants established eight goals—the Millennium Development Goals (MDGs)—to be achieved by 2015. With this initiative, the heads of state aimed to coordinate and galvanise the efforts of the international community to meet the needs of the world's poorest. The first goal is to eradicate extreme poverty and hunger. Specifically, states are committed to reduce the proportion of people who suffer from hunger by half.

As a way to achieve the first seven goals, state parties committed to develop a global partnership for development that, inter alia, would provide more generous official development assistance for those countries committed to poverty reduction.[31] At the Millennium Summit, heads of state acknowledged that, despite their consistent expressions of commitment to fight against hunger, developing countries face important obstacles in mobilising the resources needed to finance their sustainable development. Thus, in order to address that issue and try to remove those obstacles, the summit participants called for a High-level International and Intergovernmental Conference on Financing for Development, which was be held in Monterrey, Mexico, in 2002.

In order to achieve the MDGs, the Monterrey Consensus not only explored new sources of financing, but also addressed the issue of the effectiveness of official development assistance (ODA). Heads of states pledged to commit themselves to mobilising domestic resources; attracting international flows; promoting international trade as an engine for development; allowing for sustainable debt financing and external debt relief; enhancing the coherence and consistency of the international monetary, financial and trading systems; and increasing international financial and technical cooperation for development. ODA was presented as an essential complement to other sources of financing for development; it was also viewed as a crucial instrument to enhance food security. Developed countries were encouraged to achieve the target of 0.7% of GNP as ODA, as well as to devote 0.15–0.20% of their GNP to

---

[30] UN Millennium Declaration, GA Res 55/2, ¶ I.2, UN document A/RES/55/2 (14 December 2000).
[31] Ibid, §VIII.

least-developed countries.[32] The consensus also called on governments to enhance ODA effectiveness, adopting recommendations such as harmonising procedures, untying aid, enhancing the absorptive capacity of recipient countries and enhancing recipient countries' ownership of ODA-financed projects.

In 2005, the new focus on the improvement of ODA effectiveness was given expression in the Paris Declaration on Aid Effectiveness, which was endorsed by more than 100 states, international organisations and civil society organisations. The Paris Declaration laid down practical guidelines to improve the quality of aid and its impact on development, based on five key principles: ownership, alignment, harmonisation, managing for results and mutual accountability. A critical aspect of the Paris Declaration was that it promoted transparency and mutual accountability, providing a set of 12 indicators as a way to track progress. In September 2008, the Paris Declaration was reviewed at the Third High Level Forum on Aid Effectiveness, which took place in Ghana, and then elaborated on by the Accra Agenda for Action.[33]

E. Implementation Gaps

As seen in the discussion above, all major strategies to fight hunger hold the achievement of food security as their main objective. According to the FAO, food security exists when all people, at all times, have access to sufficient, safe and nutritious food to meet their dietary needs and food preferences for an active and healthy life.[34] Food security can and must be pursued through various channels, including improving agricultural productivity, strengthening good governance and the rule of law, improving international trade and investment conditions, alleviating external debt, and advancing gender equality. International assistance, particularly food aid, is seen as a complementary and sometimes subsidiary instrument that can help to advance food security both at the national and the household level.

In assessing the effectiveness of international assistance, governments and other interested parties have stressed the importance of placing conditions on the use of food aid. Its role in the promotion of food security has been identified as crucial to address immediate starvation

---

[32] International Conference on Financing for Development, Monterrey, Mexico, 18–22 March 2002, 'Monterrey Consensus of the International Conference on Financing for Development', ¶ 42, UN document A/CONF.198/11 (2003).

[33] See OECD, 'The Paris Declaration on Aid Effectiveness and the Accra Agenda for Action: 2005/2008', available at www.oecd.org/dataoecd/30/63/43911948.pdf.

[34] FAO, Commodity & Trade Division, Commodity Policy & Projections Service, 'Trade Reforms and Food Security: Conceptualizing the Linkages' (Rome, 2003) 25–26.

in emergency situations and complex crises, but food aid has been eschewed as an instrument to address the root causes of food insecurity and advance sustainable development. This understanding, however, has often been consigned to the realm of theory. Despite the apparent international consensus on the inappropriateness of using food aid to advance development, donors continue to use food aid for development purposes, unveiling discrepancies in the implementation of international agreements.

Similarly, the discourse of a rights-based approach to development has framed the design of every major strategy to fight against hunger. That, however, does not mean that the core human rights principles have been effectively implemented by governments. A rights-based approach to food aid—acknowledging that states, through the provision of food aid, are fulfilling the right to food and not just meeting basic needs—has major policy implications; yet those policy implications have been ignored or improperly addressed in most cases. The UN Special Rapporteur on the right to food has outlined what those implications are in a report to the Human Rights Council.[35] First, international human rights law imposes a certain obligation to cooperate internationally.[36] Secondly, the way international assistance is delivered must comply with the requirements of transparency, accountability, participation and non-discrimination. Finally, evaluations of food aid effectiveness should take into account the normative components of the human right to adequate food.[37]

The next section will address the actual role of food aid, its goals and procedures, and its impact on development. The discussion shows that there is a wide gap between discourse regarding food aid policies and the implementation of international agreements.

II. TYPES OF FOOD AID: WEAKNESSES AND OPPORTUNITIES

Food aid has been traditionally subdivided into three categories: programme, project and emergency food aid. Contrary to what people

---

[35] O De Schutter, UN Special Rapporteur on the Right to Food, 'Background Document: The Role of Development Cooperation and Food Aid in Realizing the Right to Adequate Food: Moving from Charity to Obligation, delivered to the Human Rights Council, 10th session', UN document A/HRC/10/005 (March 2009).

[36] Ibid, 5–6. The UN Special Rapporteur on the Right to Food argues that this obligation has at a minimum three components. First, countries should not diminish pre-existing levels of aid calculated as ODA in percentage of GDP. Secondly, the assistance should comply with the principle of non-discrimination. Finally, donor countries must follow up on commitments made for the assistance to remain predictable (non-retrogression, non-discrimination and predictability).

[37] Ibid, 14–15.

often think, the goal of food aid is not always to feed the hungry. Programme food aid, for instance, is simply foreign aid provided in the form of food. As explained below, its purpose is to influence the balance of payments and promote economic development in the recipient country. Project food aid, on the other hand, is typically free in-kind aid distributed as part of a development project. It has two different uses: first, it is used to strengthen safety nets for vulnerability reduction, which in many cases consists of providing food to vulnerable groups; and secondly, it is used to promote development. The goal of emergency food aid, which is the third type of food aid, is humanitarian relief in cases of imminent starvation.

Programme food aid dominated international food aid flows until the 1990s, when there was an important shift of aid tendencies in the world. At that time, emergency food aid became the dominant type of food aid; it has continued to be so since then. The decline of programme food aid can be explained by several factors. First, the end of the cold war led to a decrease in programme food aid used for political reasons. In addition, during the mid-nineties, there was a decrease in surpluses of food in developed countries, especially those in the EU. Finally, there was a significant shift in the European food security policy towards more need-oriented food aid.[38]

Food aid flows can also be subdivided into three categories, based on the delivery channel in place: bilateral food aid, multilateral food aid and food aid delivered by NGOs. Historically, food aid was mainly delivered bilaterally, from one country to another country. Since the late 1980s, however, one-quarter to one-third of world food aid flows have been delivered through the Word Food Programme (WFP).[39] It has been argued that this shift responds to the progressive disengagement of food aid from donor country farm programmes.[40] Finally, NGOs play an increasingly significant role in the delivery of food aid through the implementation of WFP projects as well as their own projects.

As discussed in the previous section, whereas governments and other actors generally recognise the crucial role played by food-based safety nets and emergency food aid to combat imminent starvation, increasing doubts have arisen regarding the advisability of using food aid to advance development. This section addresses the weaknesses and opportunities of the different uses of food aid. It concludes that food aid should only be used for development purposes in very limited situations, if at all.

---

[38] F Mousseau, *Food Aid or Food Sovereignty? Ending World Hunger in Our Time* (Oakland, CA, The Oakland Institute, 2005) 13.
[39] Barrett and Maxwell, above n 4, 14. The WFP is an agency of the UN that receives support through contributions from member states.
[40] Ibid.

A. Program Food Aid

Until recently, programme food aid was the dominant type of food aid. It is typically an in-kind transfer from one government to another. The food commodities are grown in the donor country, which ships them to the recipient country. Commodities are then sold on the domestic market of the recipient country and the money is allocated to a counterpart fund. This type of aid differs from what is traditionally understood as food aid in two main ways. First, the aid does not target vulnerable groups, but rather is used for macroeconomic purposes, such as budget support and relief of foreign exchange constraints. Secondly, it is not free aid, but is typically attached to concessional loans with lower-than-market interest rates. Donors usually impose conditions on the provision of this type of aid. Hence, it could be linked to diplomatic measures, commercial deals or the implementation of development objectives such as investment in health care, education or rural development.

Programme food aid originated in 1954. At that time, the US agricultural policy had generated large surpluses; the US government consequently decided to enact the PL 480 programme. The PL 480 was conceived as a way to advance the US agricultural sector both by reducing storage costs through shipping agricultural surpluses abroad and by opening new markets to US products. Since then, commercial and political interests have driven programme food aid. During the cold war and, more recently, in the so-called war on terror, programme food aid has been used as a political tool to further donors' interests in friendly countries. The US has traditionally been the largest food aid donor, providing 54% of global food aid in 2004, and programme food aid continues to be the most significant part of its food aid programme.[41]

Programme food aid is used as a type of international financial assistance. It is expected to help advance economic development in two main ways. First, it allows the recipient country to save on foreign exchange, supporting the balance of payments and allowing for new imports that could, if used well, advance industrialisation. Secondly, money that is generated by selling the food in local markets and then allocated to counterpart funds can be used for social development projects. However, programme food aid has been subjected to several criticisms: it is rarely development oriented, it is highly inefficient, and it has a negative impact on local producers and consumers. The following subsections address each criticism in turn.

---

[41] Ibid.

(i) Program Food Aid is Rarely Development Oriented

Programme food aid is typically donor driven. This is especially significant with respect to the US, the largest food aid donor, where the interests of farmers and agribusiness are the primary focus of its food assistance policies. Critics argue that US food aid policy does not even support the entire American agricultural sector, and that a handful of actors that have the most political leverage—agribusiness (wheat, rice, milk powder, corn, and soybean oil producers and exporters), shipping companies and large relief organisations—effectively control the US food aid policy.[42] A clear indicator of the fact that this type of aid is donor driven is the negative correlation between international grain prices and food aid flows. Thus, when international prices are low and there are larger food stocks in developing countries, international food aid flow increases. Similarly, when international prices are high and recipient countries are facing a scarcity of food, the volume of food aid decreases. Therefore, food aid often has procyclical effects, rather than alleviating scarcity periods. Furthermore, any relief on foreign exchange constraints may have Dutch disease effects[43] on domestic tradables, hurting the local food sector's competitiveness in international markets.[44]

In addition, programmes are often tied to related trade agreements that are beneficial for the donor country, such as transport agreements or export limitations. A clear example of this is the usual marketing requirement (UMR) clause imposed on food aid recipient countries. The UMR is a commitment by food aid recipients to 'maintain a normal level of commercial food imports in order that food aid does not displace trade'.[45] This sometimes prevents recipient countries from effectively using any relief regarding foreign exchange constraints to advance investment for development.

Finally, money resulting from selling the donated commodities is not always used for development purposes. US food aid to Vietnam and Indonesia in the 1960s and 1970s, for instance, resulted in an increase in military expenditure.[46] Many recipient countries lack the strong institutions, good governance and rule of law needed to effectively turn programme food aid into national sustainable development.

---

[42] For example, just four freight forwarders handle 84% of the shipments of food aid from the US and a few shippers rely extensively on US food aid for their existence. See Mousseau, above n 38, 50.

[43] The 'Dutch disease effect' refers to two negative consequences arising from an increase of the value of the national currency: first, a decrease in price competitiveness and thus exports, and secondly, an increase of imports.

[44] See Barrett, above n 3, 567.

[45] Barrett and Maxwell, above n 4, 69. URM is operationalised as the average of the preceding 5 years' commercial imports for the particular recipient country and commodity in question.

[46] See Mousseau, above n 38, 8.

(ii) Program Food Aid is Highly Cost Inefficient

Financial assistance in the form of food aid is extremely expensive. First of all, it involves large shipping expenses: for example, the US 1985 Farm Bill required that at least 75% of US food aid be shipped by US vessels, which charge high prices. Also, preference given to food produced in the donor country raises the commodities' prices. It has been stated that 'the premiums paid to suppliers and shippers combined with the increased cost of food aid due to lengthy international transport raise the cost of food aid by over 100% compared to local purchases'.[47] In addition, many developing countries do not have the institutional capacity to manage the counterpart fund effectively. This means that additional complementary resources, either financial or managerial, are required in order for the recipient country to effectively benefit from the programme food aid. Assessments of the managerial and programmatic capacity of the recipient countries to handle the food resources are therefore essential, although costly.

As a whole, programme food aid is highly cost inefficient, to the extent that counterpart funds are usually 23% below the actual financial cost of the aid.[48] That means that programme food aid has a high opportunity cost in terms of alternative development programmes that could advance the economic development of the recipient country at a much lower cost.

(iii) Program Food Aid Can Have a Negative Impact on Local Producers and Consumers

At the micro-level, programme food aid can have significant effects on both producers and consumers. Injection of food aid commodities in the local markets may drive down food prices in the recipient country. This leads to lower revenues for local producers and therefore lower incentives to produce. This dynamic can undermine local agricultural production, raising the dependence of a recipient country on external aid or imports in the long term.

Disincentive effects, however, could be mitigated if counterpart funds were used to increase agricultural productivity. The relief on foreign exchange constraints may provide fiscal resources, which the government can invest in creating public goods, such as the infrastructure required to better link farmers to markets, agriculture research, and rural health or education services.[49] Governments could also use those fiscal resources to compensate local producers for the loss of income, although from a

---

[47] Ibid.
[48] F Tar, *Foreign Aid and Development: Lessons Learnt and Directions for the Future* (London, Routledge, 2000) 159.
[49] See Barrett, above n 3.

right-to-food perspective such compensation would be a poor substitute for allowing local producers to produce and sell their crops at a fair price. A different potential solution to combating the disincentive effects is to target, exclusively, vulnerable groups through segmented markets (by regions, commodities or channels of distribution). Price discrimination, through sufficiently low prices or wage payments in kind, could lead to increased demand by the poor. This would favour vulnerable groups and local producers that are net food buyers. However, these measures are highly complex and usually have imperfect results. As mentioned above, many recipient countries do not have the institutional and financial capacity to implement these mitigation measures, as targeting can have huge administrative costs, and additional financial and managerial assistance would be required to do so.

Another aspect to consider is that food aid can adversely affect consumers. Consumers of course benefit from lower prices; however, because the commodity composition of food aid is fixed by donors, it often creates a problem of acceptability by consumers, and diets may evolve in ways that are detrimental to health. With time, this may lead to a shift in local food preferences and, in turn, to an increased dependency on imports and food aid in the long term.

Therefore, as a whole, it is difficult to defend programme food aid as an effective and efficient instrument to help advance development or address food insecurity. However, developmental uses of project food aid, discussed next, may be justifiable under certain conditions.

B. Project Food Aid

Project food aid is typically free in-kind aid distributed as part of a development project. The provision of in-kind aid, however, is being increasingly monetised by NGOs, which use the proceeds for project activities. Such projects have two 'uses' and thus pursue two main goals: strengthening safety nets for vulnerability reduction and financing development. The distinction between these two uses, however, is usually blurred.[50] Although traditionally channelled through NGOs and the WFP, there are also significant cases of bilateral government-to-government projects. The USAID Food for Peace programme is one of the most prominent examples.

A crucial use of project food aid is the creation of safety nets for vulnerability reduction and asset protection. In-kind or monetised food aid is used to strengthen social safety nets during no-crises periods, in order to protect the poorest from short-term shocks and reduce longer-term

---

[50] See Barrett and Maxwell, above n 4, chs 7 and 10.

food insecurity. This is especially needed in least-developed countries, where community-based systems of solidarity have been weakened by famines, scarcity, diseases—particularly HIV in sub-Saharan Africa—natural disasters and conflicts. The goal is to 'help people to defend current consumption without having to sacrifice future opportunities by selling off productive assets to cope with adverse shocks'.[51] Food safety nets thus play a key role in shock situations of insufficient food availability by preventing the targeted population from falling into poverty traps and by providing insurance against the violation of basic human rights during those periods. Safety nets mitigate the negative effects of a shock and help recovery after the shock. However, populations who are already chronically food insecure need more comprehensive assistance to climb out of the poverty trap.

For that reason, project food aid is used for developmental purposes as well. This means that food aid is used not only to prevent the targeted population from entering the poverty trap, but also to help them climb out of it.[52] Developmental food aid involves 'investing in community activities that reduce vulnerability while increasing productive potential'.[53] Thus, contrary to food safety nets, their aim is not only asset protection but also asset accumulation. Some potential interventions are: support for community food banks; diversification of livelihoods; creation of microfinance schemes that focus on the hungry; and support for rural financial systems that offer consumption credits. Food aid for development is typically provided to populations either for free or in exchange for participation in social activities. The most common interventions involve food-for-work and food-for-education projects.

Both the WFP and the USAID Food for Peace programme, two of the world's largest donors, have prioritised free food aid for young children and pregnant and lactating mothers as a long-term investment in human capital accumulation. In addition, the WFP has long advocated for the implementation of school feeding projects; it was praised for that advocacy by participants at the 2002 World Food Summit. School feeding projects serve three main purposes: (i) to protect the nutritional status of children; (ii) to improve learning development; and (iii) to create parental incentives to keep children in school.[54] Similarly, a new kind of programme called 'food for schooling' provides families with rations of food based on their children's school attendance.

Donors have also promoted food-for-work projects, which provide in-kind wages to working-age individuals who are employed in building

---

[51] Ibid, 124.
[52] Ibid, ch 7.
[53] UN Millennium Project, Task Force on Hunger, *Halving Hunger: It Can Be Done* (London, Earthscan, 2005) 150.
[54] Ibid, 16.

public goods. These projects have two complementary effects. First, they increase immediate food access through interventions in the labour market; secondly, they can simultaneously raise productivity and income flows through such activities as road building and watershed management.[55] Work can be directed towards the construction of public goods, such as roads, irrigation systems, schools, hospitals and the rehabilitation of degraded environments, that would enhance productivity and promote long-term sustainable development.

Both food-based safety net projects and developmental food projects have been criticised. Empirical data on the effects of project food aid is limited. While its crucial role regarding asset protection and vulnerability reduction is generally accepted, experts suggest that the real capacity of project food aid to advance development is overestimated. The main criticisms raised against project food aid are that it is often poorly designed and managed, it is cost inefficient, and it fails to allow participation and ownership.

(i) Project Food Aid Is Often Poorly Designed and Managed

Empirical studies show that project food aid is often poorly designed and managed. Transfers of food aid require complex logistics as well as accurate assessments of the needs and the absorptive capacity of the targeted community. Most of the time, NGOs lack the managerial capacity and human resources necessary to implement the projects effectively. Moreover, cases of corruption in the local distribution and implementation of the projects often divert resources, which hurts results. There is thus a need for stronger monitoring and accountability mechanisms of such projects. Project food aid is also criticised for not addressing the most vulnerable groups in rural communities. Targeting aid recipients therefore must be improved when designing the projects. Ensuring the participation of women is generally recommended, as they are better positioned to distribute the aid and manage the household resources.

One of the factors underpinning the inefficient design of these interventions is the instability of food aid flows. Project food aid does not guarantee sustainable nutritional effects because it is usually tied to three- to five-year funding cycles. For instance, food safety nets are crucial to mitigate the impact of the HIV/AIDS pandemic in many communities in sub-Saharan Africa. In those communities, orphans may require support from infancy to adulthood, so long-term multi-year agreements are required to guarantee stable flows of food aid. However, donors' funding cycles and commitments continue to be limited to the short term.

[55] Ibid, 150.

In addition, another fundamental aspect of food aid project design is to decide the commodities composition of food aid. This should always be based on needs assessments and participatory mechanisms. The selection of those commodities that may strengthen incentives for producing complementary local crops is also highly recommended. As an example, in the Baringo District food-for-work project in Kenya, the food received (maize, beans and vegetable oil) works as a gross complement to millet and sorghum, two widely produced commodities in the local economy.[56]

(ii) Project Food Aid Can Be Cost-Inefficient

As seen in the previous section, in-kind aid is attached to a number of expenses related to transportation, storage and distribution. Most of the time, the best alternative ways of addressing the needs expressed by recipients are not explored. Often, development assistance in cash would be preferable. When food aid is advisable, purchasing the commodities in local or nearby markets is highly recommended. Also, there is often a need to mobilise complementary resources in order to implement project food aid. For example, in the case of food-for-education projects, different root problems that limit the effectiveness of interventions must be addressed, such as the bad quality of education. Only after addressing that problem can education help prevent chronic poverty and promote development in the long term.

Overall, if food aid is required—ie only when food aid is the advisable type of intervention—NGOs should purchase or import only the exact amount of food needed that can be used effectively with the complementary existing managerial and financial resources.

(iii) Project Food Aid Often Lacks Participation and Ownership

It is not clear that in-kind remuneration is the best way of implementing work or educational projects. There are different examples in Latin America of projects in which families receive cash incentives instead of food aid—for example, the praised Mexican programme Oportunidades. Most of the recipients of aid who have been asked about their preferences have affirmed that they would rather receive cash-based remuneration, which would allow them to decide on family expenditures. This could also assist in the ownership of a project by its recipients, who would be empowered as active decisionmakers. With the same purpose, participatory approaches must be encouraged at all levels, including the design, implementation and evaluation of any project.

---

[56] There was a cross-price elasticity of demand of −1.5. It also complemented meat, milk, eggs and fish with a cross-price elasticity of demand of −0.05. M Bezuneh and B Deaton, 'Food Aid Impacts on Safety Nets: Theory and Evidence—A Conceptual Perspective on Safety Nets' (1997) 70 *American Journal of Agricultural Economics* 672, 674.

c. Emergency Food Aid

Relief or emergency food aid is free in-kind aid typically delivered by the WFP and NGOs, as well as some governmental agencies, in three situations: Ii) transitory shortfalls, typically in low-income economies dependent on rain-fed agriculture with small interannual grain inventories; (ii) natural or man-made disasters; and (iii) refugees.

The first two situations require short-term emergency food aid; in the case of refugees, relief food aid may be extended over a long period of time. The most common uses of food aid in the three emergency situations described above are: (i) general nutrition support, primarily through direct distribution of a basic food ration to vulnerable groups; (ii) correcting malnutrition via supplementary or therapeutic feeding for especially acutely affected subgroups; and (iii) food-for-work projects in those cases in which intervention has occurred rapidly enough to begin before people have been badly affected by the crisis.[57]

Emergency food aid has experienced a major increase since the mid-1990s, becoming the dominant type of food aid distributed multilaterally. Indeed, in 2003, the FAO reported that 90% of WFP resources were devoted to emergencies. Experts, donors and multilateral agencies agree on the crucial role that emergency food aid plays in protecting the lives of thousands of affected people during acute crises. However, much work remains to be done to improve the effectiveness and maximise the positive impact of emergency food aid. Some of the critical issues that need to be addressed are targeting, timing, food bias and political influence.

(i) Problems with Effective Targeting

Effective targeting involves getting 'the right kind of food in the right quantity to the right people in the right place at the right time, and getting it only to those people who actually need it'.[58] In widespread acute emergencies, geographical targeting is more common that household targeting, which, for example, could be based on income levels. This means that emergency food aid is focused on the hardest hit areas of the countries with the most important food deficits. Although targeting mechanisms and strategies have improved during the past few decades, there is still an important problem of imprecise and incorrect targeting both by inclusion and by exclusion. On the one hand, agricultural producers are concerned about targeting errors by inclusion, because the provision of food aid to people who can actually purchase

---

[57] See Barrett and Maxwell, above n 4, 123.
[58] Ibid,155.

food in the market could displace commercial sales and cause market prices to fall. On the other hand, humanitarian agencies are concerned about targeting errors by exclusion, which could leave people who are not able to cover their basic nutritional needs out of reach. In order to improve targeting mechanisms, information systems must be developed and local organisations that are familiar with the local needs, institutions and structures must be assigned leadership roles.

(ii) Problems with Timing

One of the consequences of deficient early warning mechanisms is a late response to emergencies. This has devastating effects on recipient populations. First, most vulnerable groups, such as children and the elderly, usually do not have the means to cope with the crises, and many of them do not survive long enough to see emergency aid arrive. Secondly, mistimed food aid has negative effects on local markets by lowering prices and displacing local producers.

The causes of the mistiming problem are found not only in deficient early warning mechanisms, but also in the inefficient and slow reactions of donor countries. Sadly, there are a number of examples that illustrate this dynamic. In July 2001, the government of Malawi requested international assistance following the bad harvest of June 2001. The international community, apparently sceptical, did not meet the request. Hundreds of people starved during the first months of 2002, when local prices peaked at their highest level. Then, in March 2002, following reports of starvation, donor countries overreacted and sent large amounts of food aid:

> Malawi was flooded with food one year after the failed harvest, with serious adverse effects on the country's budget, economy and agriculture, as well as on the Mozambican farmers who were seriously affected by the depression of the regional market.[59]

Similar situations arose in Niger in 2004 and in Ethiopia in 2000.

There is a need, therefore, to improve early warning mechanisms and information systems. In addition, donors should promote the participation of local institutions and organisations in all stages of the intervention. Welfare systems and agricultural services with permanent staff and resources are often more efficient and flexible, and able to react more quickly than international organisations that have to bring international staff, recruit local personnel, call for international funding and set up offices.[60]

---

[59] Mousseau, above n 38, 15.
[60] Ibid.

Mistiming problems are related not only to late reaction, but also to longer implementation than required in the recipient countries. Emergency food aid should persist only while local markets and institutions are unable to fulfil the population's right to food. Greater prolongation than necessary may create external dependencies.

(iii) Relief Responses Can Be Biased Towards Food Aid with Negative Effects

Even though the provision of food is typically crucial during the first stages of emergency operations, it can be achieved through a variety of efforts, including cash when local markets work and where food availability is ensured, and support for local producers. However, because the US, the largest food aid donor, provides most of its relief aid in kind, there is a clear bias towards food aid in the design of relief responses.[61] This may result in negative effects on local agriculture; poor cost effectiveness (as discussed above, in-kind food aid involves high transportation and storage costs); lack of flexibility and delays in the needed reactions; and lack of appropriateness in terms of the commodities composition of food aid. Furthermore, the food bias could impede other needed measures such as sanitation or health care. Emergency responses must be based on needs assessments that indicate the kind of response that is required.

(iv) Emergency Food Aid Can Be Politically Oriented

Emergency food aid is sometimes used for political reasons, addressing situations that, at least initially, are not strictly emergencies. In fact, out 'of the first fifteen food aid recipient countries in 2004, only five [had] significant numbers of internally displaced persons or refugees, including only three facing civil strife or conflict, and one having experienced a natural disaster'.[62] Hence, North Korea has led the food aid recipient countries for a number of years. According to Barrett and Maxwell,

> each of the donors uses food aid to extract concessions from the DPRK regime. Japan uses aid as a bargaining chip with North Korea as it tries to resolve kidnappings, hijackings and missile tests. China and South Korea use their own rice surpluses to try inducing cooperation with the North over refugees. The US meanwhile has grave concerns over North Korea's nuclear and long-range missile capabilities and its suspected support of terrorist organizations and has manipulated food aid shipments to the country explicitly so as to bring the North Koreans to the negotiating table.[63]

Similar patterns can be deduced from the emergency food aid flows

---

[61] Ibid, 29.
[62] Ibid, 22.
[63] See Barrett and Maxwell, above n 4, 35.

to Iraq and Afghanistan during recent years. Yet another example is when the US and the WFP pressed Zambia in 2002 to accept genetically modified food aid against its national regulations, which some observers interpreted as intended to ensure that it would open its markets to products from the US.[64]

In addition, the lack of political will of donor countries has serious consequences regarding the effectiveness of emergency food aid. As seen above, international flows of food aid depend on world prices and have, most of the time, procyclical effects. Moreover, despite the repeatedly expressed commitment to international assistance, the volume of international aid flows is not enough to cover global needs. Again, emergency food aid should be based on needs assessments.

III. AN ASSESSMENT

Experts and successive donors' conferences have concluded that food aid is not the appropriate instrument to address the roots of food insecurity or to help advance sustainable development. It is, however, an essential tool when facing immediate starvation in emergency situations and acute shortfalls of food availability. The only justifications for food aid rest in three key roles:[65] (i) short-term humanitarian assistance to food-insecure populations; (ii) provision of longer-term safety nets for asset protection; and (iii) very limited, targeted developmental interventions for asset building among chronically poor or vulnerable populations when food aid is relatively efficient.

In any case, food aid is merely one resource to employ; it is often not the most appropriate. Food aid should be used if and only if pproblem of food availability and market failure underpin the lack of access to food. Therefore, an appropriate response must address two main issues. First, if local markets are functioning well, food aid in kind is not needed. Cash transfers and the provision of jobs would be the best solution to guarantee access to food and to stimulate local production. Secondly, if local markets do not function well, food must be purchased in nearby markets. Hence, food aid should be provided primarily through local purchases or triangular transactions.[66] Finally, only if food cannot be purchased in the region may intercontinental shipments be appropriate.

When the provision of food aid is advisable, it must follow certain

---

[64] See Mousseau, above n 38.
[65] See Barrett and Maxwell, above n 4.
[66] Triangular transactions are those whereby food is purchased in one country (not the donor's) for use as food aid in another country. Triangular transactions contribute to the broader goal of development when food is purchased in a developing country, ideally from the same region as the final food aid recipient.

conditions. Some of those conditions are expressed in FAO Voluntary Guideline 15.1:

> Donor States should ensure that their food aid policies support national efforts by recipient States to achieve food security, and base their food aid provisions on sound needs assessment, targeting especially food insecure and vulnerable groups. In this context, donor States should provide assistance in a manner that takes into account food safety, the importance of not disrupting local food production and the nutritional and dietary needs and cultures of recipient populations. Food aid should be provided with a clear exit strategy and avoid the creation of dependency. Donors should promote increased use of local and regional commercial markets to meet food needs in famine-prone countries and reduce dependence on food aid.

When purchasing from local and regional markets, donors should make efforts to buy from small producers, avoiding large multinational corporations. This would help advance the development of the local economy. In addition, food aid must be participatory at all levels in order to strengthen local capacities and institutions. Also, the international community must devote more resources to improve need- and capacity-assessment methodologies.

To conclude, the effective implementation of a rights-based approach to food aid—understanding food aid as an instrument to fulfil the right to food—would have significant consequences for the quality and effectiveness of the food aid provided. 'Because [human rights] provide a framework which is grounded in the international obligations of both donors and recipient States, and because they emphasize the values of participation and accountability',[67] they can light the way for policymakers and have concrete consequences at the operational level.[68]

IV. CONCLUSION

Strategies for the fight against hunger, both at the national and international levels, must take a step forward and pursue the achievement of food sovereignty beyond food security. Food sovereignty is defined as

> the people's right to define their own policies and strategies for the sustainable production, distribution and consumption of food that guarantee the right to food for the entire population, on the basis of small and medium-sized production, respecting their own cultures and the diversity of peasant, fishing and indigenous forms of agricultural production, marketing and management of rural areas, in which women play a fundamental role.[69]

---

[67] De Schutter, above n 35, 16.
[68] Ibid.
[69] Global Forum on Food Sovereignty, Havana, Cuba, 7 September 2001, Final Declaration.

It involves a strong commitment to the right to food, self-sufficiency and autonomy, stressing local access to and control over territories and natural resources. In this framework, every strategy of the fight against hunger should develop four different areas of work: the right to food; access to productive resources (water, natural resources and biodiversity); food production through sustainable agro-ecological processes; and the promotion of fair and equitable trade conditions. Food sovereignty as a development model addresses the root causes of hunger and allows national states to fulfil their obligation to respect, protect and fulfil the right to food.[70]

---

[70] J Ziegler, UN Special Rapporteur on the Right to Food, 'Report on the Right to Food, delivered to the Commission on Human Rights', UN document E/CN.4/2004/10 (9 February 2004).

Index

Introductory Note
References such as '178–9' indicate (not necessarily continuous) discussion of a topic across a range of pages. Wherever possible in the case of topics with many references, these have either been divided into sub-topics or only the most significant discussions of the topic are listed. Because the entire work is about 'food', the use of this term (and certain others which occur constantly throughout the book) as an entry point has been minimised. Information will be found under the corresponding detailed topics.

accessibility, economic 125–6, 213
accountability 22, 24, 42, 138, 182, 246, 250
   mutual 249
adequate food, right to 23, 137, 143, 180–1, 213, 240–2, 244–7
adjudicating bodies, WTO 22, 229–31
adjustment, structural 17, 154–5, 167
ADM *see* Archer Daniels Midland
advanced technologies 97–8, 110
Afghanistan 145, 197–8, 262
Africa 4, 41, 55, 73–4, 151–6, 159–60, 197–8
   Sub–Saharan 2–3, 51, 139, 152–3, 156–7, 159, 256–7
   West 37–8
Agreement on Agriculture (AoA) 143, 144–51, 162–3, 175, 216–19, 222–3, 231–3
   reform process 164, 185, 190
Agreement on Subsidies and Countervailing Measures (SCM) 201, 222
agribusiness TNCs 13, 27–33, 35, 37, 39–41, 43–53, 57–63
   biotechnology 44, 48, 55–6, 61
   impact on right to food 27–63
   recommendations 58–63
      for governments and policy makers 62–3
   sector analysis 32–58
agricultural commodities 2–3, 20, 137–8, 142–3, 157–8, 160–1, 172
agricultural export credits 164–5
agricultural labourers *see* agricultural workers
agricultural markets 21, 119, 194, 203, 208–10, 218–19
agricultural producer support 199–200
agricultural producers 19–21, 82, 146, 151, 153–4, 156, 199
agricultural production 27, 29, 72, 101, 139, 170, 172
   modes of 171–2, 188

agricultural productivity 5, 164–5, 172–3, 254
agricultural subsidies 18, 160
   phasing out 21, 193–210
   reform of rich country 209–10
   trade-distorting 19, 202
   United States and Europe 198–201
   and World Trade Organization (WTO) 198–203
agricultural workers 4, 31–2, 41, 60, 62, 76, 142
   wages 7, 188
agriculture, subsistence 6, 30, 47, 157, 206–7
agrochemicals 13, 29–30, 44, 52, 56
aid, food *see* food aid
allocative efficiency 149, 179, 183
antitrust policy *see* competition policy
AoA *see* Agreement on Agriculture
Aquila Food Security Initiative 203–4
Archer Daniels Midland (ADM) 7–8, 34–5, 39
Argentina 19, 35, 66, 91, 98–100, 105, 148
asset protection 22, 255–6, 262
Australia 37, 54, 98, 165, 196, 204
availability, food 18, 24, 141, 213, 261–2
available land 102, 112, 124, 131

balance of payments 20, 139, 160, 166, 183, 185, 251–2
Bangladesh 142, 145, 154, 162
bargaining power 8–11, 70, 79, 90, 93
basic foodstuffs 164–6, 185, 190
BEFSCI *see* Bioenergy and Food Security Criteria and Indicators
bilateral investment treaties 114, 221
bilateral trade agreements 220–5
biodiesel 97, 99–100, 104, 106, 112, 117–18, 127
   market 99, 127
biodiversity 16, 128, 204, 264
   and biofuels 110–15
   loss of 47, 97

265

Bioenergy and Food Security Criteria and Indicators (BEFSCI) 119–20
biofuels 15–17, 95–7, 99–129, 131–4, 196, 208–9
  banning 131–4
  boom 96–106, 119, 121, 124, 130, 132–3
  debate 96–8
  and economic power 115
  and employment opportunities 117–22
  and fertilisers 117
  first-generation 95, 97–8, 131
  and food prices 106–10
  industrial 98, 113
  and intellectual property rights 115
  in international trade 103–6
  and land availability 101–3, 112, 124, 131
  land use, deforestation and biodiversity 110–15
  and local energy supply 95, 98, 109–10, 122–3, 131
  market 98, 105, 109, 118–19, 126
  and pesticides 117
  policies 95–6, 98, 102–3, 105–9, 124, 127–30, 133–4
    domestic 95–6, 98–101, 128
  possible impacts 106–23
  and private actors' responsibilities 130–1
  production 15–17, 97, 101–6, 109, 112–13, 115–18, 124–6
  and right to food 95–134
  second-generation 97–9, 109–10, 115–17, 131–2
  and states' obligations towards the right to food 124–30
  sustainable 120
  and water 116–17
biomass 15, 118, 122–3
biotechnology agribusiness TNCs 44, 48, 55–6, 61
biotechnology companies/firms 13, 29, 49, 52, 54, 56
Brazil 35–6, 96, 98–102, 104–5, 110–11, 132–3, 148
breeding companies 56–7
Bretton Woods 214
Bunge 7, 35
Burkina Faso 145, 176, 193
Burma 230
Burundi 145, 197
buyer power 9, 33, 83–9, 187
  retailer 14, 83
buyers 8–12, 79, 83–5, 87–8, 93, 119–20, 161
  commodity 3, 7, 11, 33, 91, 167–8, 187
  dominant 12, 126
  net food 6, 106–7, 118, 121, 142, 185, 189
by-products 102, 104, 108, 128, 140

Cambodia 142, 145, 225
Canada 37, 54, 98, 165, 187, 196, 204
capital 11–12, 78, 127, 155, 173
  investments 75, 79
carbon 111, 130
  credits 16, 130
carbon dioxide 111, 140, 170, 172
Cargill 7–8, 34–5, 39
Carrefour 71, 74
cash crops 16, 20, 172, 174
cash transfers 18, 22, 262
cashew industry 73, 76–7
cassava 97, 208–9
CDM *see* Clean Development Mechanism
Central African Republic 145, 197
centralisation 72, 119
cereals 145, 166, 183, 195–6
certification schemes 120–1
CESCR *see* Committee on Economic, Social and Cultural Rights
CFF *see* Compensatory Financing Facility
Chad 145, 197
chemicals 51, 131
child labour 37, 39–40, 226
children 23, 27, 30, 38, 58, 137, 256
Chile 19, 66, 70, 154, 194, 206
China 8, 69–71, 74, 93, 98–100, 194–5, 225
chocolate manufacturers 42–4
cities 7, 17, 67, 69, 100
  large 4, 67, 69
civil society 180, 182, 191, 245, 249
Clean Development Mechanism (CDM) 99–100
climate 16, 100, 173–5
  change 17, 95, 98, 100, 139–42, 170–2, 188–9
co-products 98
cocoa 33, 35, 37–9, 42–3, 60, 159, 167–8
  farmers 33, 38–9, 42–4
  grinders 38, 168
  industry 8, 13, 38, 40–2
  products 37, 39, 42
  traders 28, 38
coffee 9, 33, 159, 167
  farmers 9, 27, 60
  roasters 60, 167
Colombia 19, 98–100, 120, 154, 168
Committee on Economic, Social and Cultural Rights (CESCR) 23, 30, 170, 181, 185–7, 213, 242
commodities 28–30, 32–3, 59–60, 159–60, 190, 199, 252–5
  export 20, 160, 174
  food 17, 19, 32, 37, 53, 139–41, 160–1
commodity buyers 3, 7, 11, 33, 91, 167–8, 187
commodity markets 34, 70
commodity prices 7, 33, 44, 53, 60, 107, 119
  speculation 196–7

commodity processors *see* commodity traders
commodity traders 31–7, 39–40, 42, 167–8
 market power of 13, 29, 34–5
 recommendations for 59–60
Common Agricultural Policy 146, 200
Compensatory Financing Facility (CFF) 166
competition 16, 20, 33, 80–1, 109–12, 153–5, 168
 direct 109, 202
 food-versus-fuel 109, 112, 125
 increased 14, 66, 140, 170
 laws 14, 66, 82, 88, 126, 187
 policy 9, 66, 68, 82–9
 unfair 6, 151–2
competitiveness 6, 45, 47, 66, 89, 96, 162–3
complaining party 232–3
complaints 131, 222, 230, 232–4, 236
 non-violation 232–3
 situation 232
 violation 232–3
compliance 8, 75, 77–8, 90, 92, 114, 235–6
 costs 78, 91
concentrated markets 37, 68, 80, 119
concentration 8–9, 33, 35, 37, 44, 80–1, 167–9
 excessive 11, 187
 horizontal 33–4
 increased 12, 168
 vertical 34
concessions 119, 138, 185, 221, 223, 233, 236
 suspension of 230, 234
conditionality 155, 163, 166, 230
conflict diamonds 228
conservation 16, 200–1, 208, 242
consistency 78, 176, 215, 248
consolidation 8, 12, 22, 33, 68, 80, 240
consumers 8, 10–11, 59–60, 74, 84, 184–5, 254–5
 and supermarket procurement practices 80–1
 welfare of 84, 86–7
consumption 47, 97, 126, 129, 139, 170, 173
 local 11, 139
contract farming 31, 34, 57–8, 79, 93, 126, 169
convenience stores 67, 69, 71
conventional crops 54–5
conversion 98, 113, 116, 123, 172
 process 97–8
cooperation, international 19, 23, 140, 226, 242–4
cooperatives 8, 39, 92–3, 119, 122, 169
 family 119–20
 farmer 34, 122
coordination 82, 90, 176, 191
 costs 72–3
 vertical 33–4
corn 32–3, 66, 95, 97, 99–101, 107–8, 116–17
Costa Rica 19, 154

costs 12, 78, 81, 83–5, 89–90, 92, 188–9
 adjustment 147, 155
 coordination 72–3
 hidden 185, 188
 labour 54, 74, 168
 production 53–4, 148
 property 81, 83
 transaction 11, 72, 75, 78, 91, 141
 transportation 75, 123, 208
Côte d'Ivoire 33, 38–40, 42, 162, 197
cotton 54, 145, 148, 159, 183, 190, 202
crop failures 50, 207
crop residues 108, 117, 132
cropland 101–2, 111, 142
crops 9–12, 15–16, 51–3, 106–9, 114–15, 124–6, 161–2
 cash 16, 20, 172, 174
 conventional 54–5
 export 28, 31, 33–4, 159
 food 16, 95, 97, 107–8, 123, 126, 196
 fuel 111, 116–17, 119, 123, 125
 GM 52, 54–5, 62, 115
 oily 97, 99, 127
Cuba 194, 263
cultural traditions 30, 125, 213
cycles of debt 31, 45, 48–9, 52, 56, 58, 61

de minimis threshold 146, 149
debt 31, 48, 50, 52, 58
 cycles of 31, 45, 48–9, 52, 56, 58, 61
 external 244, 249
declining prices 3, 119, 138–9, 162–3, 183
deforestation 16, 36, 104, 128, 131, 170–1, 206
 and biofuels 110–15
Democratic Republic of Congo 145, 197
denatured ethanol 104–5
dependence 17, 89, 159, 172, 190, 223, 254
 excessive 144, 152, 189–90
dependency 17–18, 20, 143, 148, 156, 159–61, 163
 creation of 247, 263
desertification 112, 170
developed countries 18–19, 100–1, 145–7, 150, 153–4, 174, 217–18
 trade-distorting subsidies of 19, 154
developing countries 18–21, 45–53, 55–63, 142–9, 151–6, 161–4, 201–7
 food-importing 164, 204–5, 210
 importing 185, 188, 216, 218
 poor 17, 151
development
 economic 5, 110, 119, 121, 215, 244, 251–2
 rural 5, 79, 124, 127–9, 148, 206, 217
 sustainable 15, 145, 171, 213, 215–17, 239, 244

268   Index

development assistance
  international 247–8
  official 2, 152, 165, 204, 244, 248
differential treatment 143, 148–9, 153, 165, 184, 219, 232
dignity 30, 241, 248
diligence, due 59, 77, 130
direct investment 3, 7
  foreign 3, 15, 69
direct payments 146, 149, 200, 205, 217
discrimination
  price 85–6, 255
  unjustifiable 226–7
disease 1, 45, 57, 104, 173–4, 256
disguised restrictions 226–7
disincentive effects 254–5
displaced persons 244, 261
displacement 16, 47
dispute settlement procedures *see* World Trade Organization (WTO), dispute settlement process
Dispute Settlement Understanding (DSU) 137, 177–8, 229, 232–7
diversification 3, 5, 145, 152, 156, 176, 256
division of labour, international 3, 144, 155, 157–9
Doha Development Round 138, 143–4, 149–50, 152, 154, 201–2, 219–20
domestic markets 20, 106, 141, 160–3, 167, 184, 190
domestic policies 16, 90, 93–4, 127, 132, 155–6, 176
domestic support 105, 146, 150, 153, 175, 184
  trade-distorting 149, 219
dominance 9, 88
dominant buyers 12, 126
dominant positions 10, 88, 126, 167–8, 187
donors 2, 181, 204, 250, 252–7, 259–60, 262–3
  largest 197, 252–3, 256, 261
Dreyfus 7, 35
drought 45, 106–7, 139, 173, 198
DSU *see* Dispute Settlement Understanding
dualisation of farming 167–9, 186–8
due diligence 59, 77, 130
dumping 19, 21, 105, 142, 146, 218, 222–3

economic accessibility 125–6, 213
Economic and Social Council (ECOSOC) 30, 154, 213, 242
economic development 5, 110, 119, 121, 215, 244, 251–2
economic growth 122, 154–5, 157, 206, 223
economic power 16, 126
  and biofuels 115
economic sanctions 137, 186
  threat of 177

ECOSOC *see* Economic and Social Council
effectiveness 55, 121, 172, 239, 248–9, 258–9, 262–3
efficiency 77, 80, 84, 87, 95, 98, 133
  allocative 149, 179, 183
Egypt 37, 194, 204
elasticity 83
  cross-price 258
emergency food aid 22, 197, 204, 250–1, 259–62
emergency situations 197, 239, 243–5, 247, 250, 259–62
emissions, GHG 95–7, 99, 103, 111, 113–14, 117, 170–3
employment 19, 28, 41, 63, 73, 76, 214–15
  opportunities 16, 109, 126–7
  and biofuels 117–22
energy 15, 55, 97, 104, 114, 122–3, 128 *see also* biofuels
  green 127, 131
  solar 129, 140
energy independence 96, 101, 208
Energy Sector Management Assistance Program (ESMAP) 96, 101, 107
energy supply, local 95, 98, 109–10, 122–3, 131
environment 14, 107, 144–5, 170, 172–3, 188, 243–4
environmental impacts 95, 130–1, 172
environmental rights 224, 229–30
EPZ *see* Export Processing Zones
Equatorial Guinea 145, 197
equitable distribution 106, 241
  of world food supplies 23, 140, 242
Eritrea 107, 145, 197
ESMAP *see* Energy Sector Management Assistance Program
ethanol 96–7, 99–101, 104–7, 116, 127, 196, 208–9 *see also* biofuels
  denatured 104–5
  industry 99, 104, 208
  maize-based 208–9
  markets 96, 119, 127
  plants 116–17, 131
  production 104, 107, 116, 196
  undenatured 104–5
Ethiopia 15, 142, 145, 197, 204, 260
EurepGap 73, 77
European Court of Human Rights 234
European markets 89, 104, 145, 168, 223
European Union 88–9, 98–102, 104–6, 112–15, 145–6, 199–200, 217–24
  Commission 88–9, 97, 99, 102, 113–14, 151, 200
  Court of Justice 88, 234
excessive dependence 144, 152, 189–90
exclusion 259–60
expensive inputs 45, 48, 50, 56–8, 61
experts 54, 82, 116, 209, 234, 257, 259

Index 269

export commodities 20, 160, 174
export credits 150, 164–5, 187
export crops 28, 31, 33–4
   incentive to specialise in 159–67
export-led agriculture 3, 155, 173
export markets 11, 153
Export Processing Zones (EPZ) 225
export revenues 3, 20, 145, 160, 190
export subsidies 147–50, 153, 175, 202, 218–20, 222
export taxes 38, 105, 107
exporters 20, 38–9, 151, 160, 202, 253
   largest 37, 39, 99
exports 34–6, 38–40, 138–41, 145–6, 158–9, 172–4, 228
   grain 28, 168
extreme poverty 198, 248

FACs *see* Food Aid Conventions
fair prices 9, 122, 128, 255
families 7, 43, 104, 126, 188, 210, 241
   poor 126, 194
family cooperatives 119–20
family farmers 120, 209
famine 6, 213, 256
FAO (Food and Agriculture Organization) 1, 15–18, 28–30, 97–8, 119–25, 193, 197–8
   Investment Center 71, 79, 203–4
   Jatropha Report 98–9, 101, 127
   voluntary guidelines 246–9, 263
farm gate prices 39, 168
farmer cooperatives 34, 122
farmers 8–14, 31–2, 34–63, 78–9, 88–94, 119–20, 150–3
   cocoa 33, 38–9, 42–4
   coffee 9, 27, 60
   developing country 201, 206, 209
   family 120, 209
   poor 7, 15, 50–2, 55, 61, 144, 209
   poorest 60, 92, 106
   poultry 9, 162
   small 4–5, 49–50, 57–8, 60–2, 125–7, 168–9, 222–3 *see also* smallholders
   soy 33, 40
   supermarket-channel 73, 75–6
   traditional-channel 73, 75
farming
   organic 52, 188
   small-scale 5–6, 31–2, 125, 187
farmland 3, 14–15, 110, 141, 171
   leases 14, 16
FDI *see* foreign direct investment
Federal Trade Commission (FTC) 82–3, 85–7
feedstocks 95–8, 114–15, 118–20
fertilisers 16, 52, 75, 89, 93, 103, 132
   and biofuels 117

natural 98, 117, 132
   prices 196
FIAN 41, 104, 111, 129, 162
field burning 104, 117, 131
financial assistance 164, 166, 243, 254
financing 100, 164, 166–7, 204, 207, 248–9
first-generation biofuels 95, 97–8, 131
flexibility 13, 20, 153, 156, 181, 184, 190
flexible demand 75
flexible production 74–6
food *see Introductory Note and detailed entries*
Food, Conservation and Energy Act of 2008 (United States) 200–1, 254
food aid 17–18, 22–3, 108, 164–5, 185–6, 204–5, 239–63
   assessment 262–3
   commodities composition of 258, 261
   conclusion 263–4
   domestic 147, 201
   dominant type 251–2, 259
   emergency 22, 197, 204, 250–1, 259–62
   evolution of international community position 242–6
   FAO voluntary guidelines 246–9, 263
   flows 240, 251, 253, 257
   implementation gaps 249–50
   in-kind 197, 261
   international framework and tendencies 22, 240–50
   programme 22, 251–5
   project 22, 251, 255–9
   types 250–62
   US 253–4
Food Aid Conventions (FACs) 18, 108, 164–5, 218
Food and Agriculture Organization *see* FAO
food and beverage companies 8, 13, 29, 32, 40–2
   recommendations for 60
food availability 18, 24, 141, 213, 261–2
food chain 9, 11, 13–14, 71, 79
food commodities 17, 19, 32, 37, 53, 139–41, 160–1
   basic 2, 162
   prices 17, 19, 139, 141, 160–1, 166, 178
food crises 53–5, 138, 143, 195–8, 208
   global 3, 37, 245
food crops 16, 95, 97, 107–8, 123, 126, 196
   productivity 79, 188
food-exporting countries 23, 140, 160, 207
food-for-education projects 256, 258
Food for Peace programme, USAID 255–6
food-importing countries 19–20, 140–2, 147, 160–1, 164, 202–7, 210
food imports 20, 23, 140–1, 161, 163
food industries 8, 13, 28–9, 35, 65–6, 91, 168
food insecurity 1, 34, 57, 79, 154, 181, 245
   see also food security
   responses to 203–4

food markets 66, 197–8
food prices 4, 10, 16, 19, 193–8, 204–5, 209–10
  and biofuels 106–10
  crisis 3, 21, 193–7, 208
  global 107, 109, 194–5, 198
food processors 8–10, 13, 29, 32, 167, 187
food producers 10–11, 143, 179, 196
  local 4, 19
food production 4, 6–8, 30, 33, 125, 141–2, 242–3
  local 131, 244, 247, 263
food retail
  traditional 66–7, 70–2, 90, 168
  transformation of 65–94
food riots 33, 37, 53
food safety 8, 263
food safety nets 256–7
food security 137–8, 147–9, 188–91, 216–20, 222–3, 244–6, 248–9 *see also* food insecurity
  box 218
  global governance of 191
  local 116, 130
  national 109, 181, 245–7
food sovereignty 6, 22, 62, 138, 251, 263–4
food subsidies 204–5
food supplies 91, 97, 128, 141, 144, 189, 207
  world 23, 140, 242
food systems 7, 11, 24–6, 34, 58, 63, 171
  global 4, 13, 24, 27–8, 32, 35, 58–60
food-versus-fuel competition 109, 112, 125 *see also* biofuels
foods *see Introductory Note and detailed entries*
forced labour 38–40
foreign direct investment (FDI) 3, 15, 66, 69–70, 168
foreign exchange constraints 252–4
forests 16, 36, 97, 111–13, 129, 133
  clearing of 128, 171
  tropical 111, 172
fossil fuels 95, 101, 118
Framework Convention on Climate Change (UNFCCC) 99–100
France 14, 89, 99, 204
Free Trade Agreements (FTAs) 49, 181, 220–3
freedom from want 212, 214
fresh fruit and vegetables 66, 151
FTAs *see* Free Trade Agreements
FTC *see* Federal Trade Commission
fuel crops 111, 116–17, 119, 123, 125 *see also* biofuels

G-20 193–4, 202
Gambia 107, 145
gasoline 96, 99–100

GATS (General Agreement on Trade in Services) 143, 226
GATT (General Agreement on Tariffs and Trade) 137, 139, 148, 150, 214–15, 226–7, 232–3
General Agreement on Tariffs and Trade *see* GATT
General Agreement on Trade in Services (GATS) *see* GATS
General Exceptions 226–7, 230, 235
general international law 176–7, 231, 235
General System of Preferences *see* GSPs
genetically modified seeds *see* GM seeds
Germany 89, 99, 204, 220
Ghana 42–3, 57, 160, 162, 249
GHG (greenhouse gas) emissions 95–7, 99, 103, 111, 113–14, 117, 170–3
GHG (greenhouse gas) savings 99, 103, 114, 117
Glencore 7
global agricultural markets 21, 194, 203, 209–10
global food prices 194, 195–8
global food systems 4, 13, 24, 27–8, 32, 35, 58–60
global hunger 6–7, 20, 24, 98, 191
global markets 8, 15, 66, 70, 91, 105, 152
global retailers 8, 14, 167, 169, 187
global supply chains 7, 11–12, 14, 20, 70, 75, 168–9
globalisation 34, 159, 171
GM crops 52, 54–5, 62, 115
GM seeds 27–8, 31, 44–5, 51–5, 62, 115, 262
  promotion of 52–3, 55
GM technology 53–5
goods, manufactured 3, 5, 145, 158
governance 8, 75, 120, 145, 249, 253
  global 129, 186
grains 7, 53, 100, 183, 195–6, 243, 253
Green Box 150, 184, 217
greenhouse gases *see* GHG emissions
groundwater 41
growth
  economic 122, 154–5, 157, 206, 223
  population 4, 6, 103, 140
GSPs (General System of Preferences) 145, 230
Guatemala 73, 75, 194
Guinea 145, 197

Haiti 197
Harkin-Engel Protocol 42–3
harvesting 104, 117–18, 122, 127
harvests 47–8, 112, 161, 169
  bad 120, 161, 260
health 61, 82, 123, 131, 144–5, 157, 187
  risks 1, 52, 123

Index 271

High Commissioner for Human Rights 46–7, 49–50, 143, 180
high prices 10–11, 31, 52–3, 83–4, 106–8, 161, 209–10
high-value markets 2, 11, 151, 159, 167–8
HIV/AIDS 206, 228, 257
Honduras 126, 162
Hong Kong 66, 71, 149, 220
horizontal concentration 33–4
human rights 21–2, 46–7, 58–9, 176–8, 211–16, 223–31, 233–7
　fulfilment of 23, 177, 186, 241
　invocation of 22, 212, 225–6
　law 49, 95, 177–8, 224, 250
　obligations 176–9
　violations 129–30, 230, 233
Human Rights Council 27, 72, 121, 133, 137, 188, 250
hunger 1–7, 11, 21–4, 140–2, 191–4, 203–5, 240–6
　development of safeguards against 203–9
　eradication of 240, 242–3, 247
　global 6–7, 20, 24, 98, 191
　recommended government responses 204–8
　and rich country reforms 208–9
　risk of 139, 198, 204–5, 207–10
　threat of increasing in developing countries 197–8
hypermarkets 67, 69, 71, 82

ICESCR see International Covenant on Economic, Social and Cultural Rights
IEA see International Energy Agency
IFAD see International Fund for Agricultural Development
IISD see International Institute for Sustainable Development
IMF see International Monetary Fund
import surges 156, 161–3, 178, 183–4
import tariffs 17, 103–6, 154–5, 184, 205, 210
imports 73–4, 141, 159, 163, 173–4, 223, 253–5
　food 20, 23, 140–1, 161, 163
in-kind aid 197, 251, 255, 258–9, 261
incentives 9, 45, 50, 70–1, 104–5, 157–9, 161
　financial 130, 199
income support 150, 209, 217
incomes 4–5, 31, 69–70, 93, 108–9, 117–19, 142–4
　insufficient 31–2, 39
　sufficient 29–30, 36, 41, 43, 45, 48, 55
India 8, 49–50, 52, 98–100, 126–7, 193–5, 230
indirect land-use changes 99, 109, 112–14
Indonesia 19, 42, 66, 69–70, 98–9, 113–14, 168

industrialised countries 20, 66–7, 69, 74, 119, 153–4, 158
　high-value markets of 11, 151, 159, 167
inflation 82, 109, 195–6
information 11, 52, 96, 111, 128, 133, 234–5
　market 75, 90, 93
infrastructure 11, 82, 90, 109, 128, 164–6, 197
　rural 147, 158, 187, 207
　transport 9, 152
inputs 5, 10, 28–9, 51–2, 54–7, 78–9, 83–4
　expensive 45, 48, 50, 56–8, 61
　necessary 52, 57, 90
　patented 56
insecurity, food see food insecurity
integration 32–4, 72, 143, 207, 220–1
　vertical 54, 84
integrity 129, 177–8
intellectual property rights 13, 16, 45–51, 55, 61–2, 115, 228
intercropping 126, 131
intermediaries 38–9, 73
international agreements 22, 114, 176, 186, 216, 231–2, 250
international assistance 241, 246–7, 249–50, 262
international bioenergy trade 99, 106
International Bovine Meat Agreement 231–2
international commitments 177, 240–1
international community 138, 152, 190–1, 224, 239–40, 242–8, 260
International Conference on Nutrition 243–4
international cooperation 19, 23, 140, 226, 242–4
International Covenant on Economic, Social and Cultural Rights (ICESCR) 23, 137, 140, 176, 187, 212–13, 241–2
International Dairy Agreement 231–2
international division of labour 3, 144, 155, 157–9
International Energy Agency (IEA) 98, 112, 122, 171, 204
international financial institutions 154, 181, 191, 204
international food aid 150, 204, 210, 247
International Fund for Agricultural Development (IFAD) 15, 204, 243
international grain prices 183, 253
International Grains Agreement 165, 218
International Institute for Environment and Development (IIED) 15–16, 73
International Institute for Sustainable Development (IISD) 66, 169, 217
international law 94, 137, 143, 176–7, 180, 224, 230–1
　fragmentation of 176–7
　general 176–7, 231, 235

Index

international markets 2–4, 10–11, 17–19, 148–9, 159–61, 183–5, 189–90
International Monetary Fund (IMF) 57, 76, 129, 154–5, 166–7, 204, 216
international organisations 129, 186, 203–4, 216, 224, 245, 249
international trade 7, 20–1, 137–91, 214, 224, 226–7, 239
    Agreement on Agriculture (AoA) 143, 144–51, 162–3, 175, 216–19, 222–3, 231–3
    as component of national strategies for realisation of right to food 181–2
    control of market power 186–7
    discontents of current regime 151–3
    fragmentation challenge 176–9
    and incentive to specialise in export crops 159–67
    level playing field illusion 153–6
    limiting dependency on 182–4
    maintaining flexibilities 184–6
    procedural dimensions 179–82
    and right to food 137–91
    substantive dimensions 182–8
    towards socially and environmentally sustainable trade 188
    trade liberalisation 156–75
investment agreements 180, 221
Investment Center, FAO 71, 79, 203–4
investments 2, 19, 51, 70, 76, 78, 252–3
investors 14–15, 91, 125, 170, 221
    private 2–3, 15
Italy 37, 162, 203–4, 243–4, 246

Japan 18, 99–100, 165, 199, 204, 220, 232
jatropha 97–8, 112, 117, 123, 126–7
Jatropha Report, FAO 98–9, 101, 127
jus cogens 231
just in time delivery 14, 72, 74–6

Kenya 57, 73, 99, 162, 197, 258
Kimberley Waiver 227–8
Kyoto Protocol 100, 132

labour 12, 37, 75–6, 92, 117–18, 157–9, 229–30
    child 37, 39–40, 226
    conditions 36, 42–3
    costs 54, 74, 168
    forced 38–40
    illegal 39, 60
    international division of 3, 144, 155, 157–9
    productivity 138, 153
    rights 145, 225, 230
land
    additional 101–3
    arable 16, 73, 106, 125
    availability 101–3, 112, 124, 131
    marginal 112, 116, 125
    most fertile 115, 125
    prices 119, 125
    title 109, 119, 128
land-grabbing 14–15, 110
land use
    and biofuels 110–15
    changes 99, 104
    indirect 99, 109, 112–14
LDCs *see* least-developed countries
least-developed countries (LDCs) 3, 17, 19–20, 144–7, 153–4, 164–6, 218–19
Lesotho 107, 145
level playing field notion 144, 153–6, 194, 201
liberalisation, trade *see* trade liberalisation
Liberia 145, 197
life sciences 29, 44
linkages 5, 212, 249
livestock 12, 16, 31, 35, 44–5, 47, 56–8
loans 11, 36, 39–40, 126, 152, 154–5, 166
local communities 111, 121, 123, 131, 244
local economies 5, 67–8, 118, 258, 263
local energy supply 95, 98, 109–10, 122–3, 131
local markets 7, 10–11, 18, 22, 142, 155, 260–2
local producers 18, 20, 81, 160–3, 186, 254–5, 260–1
local production 147–8, 162, 262
long-term interests 144, 155, 183, 189
low-income countries 3–4, 165, 193, 197
low prices 10, 29, 31–2, 38–9, 42, 80–1, 161
low wages 29, 65, 104, 148

Madagascar 15, 142, 145, 197
maize 54, 162, 193, 196, 258
maize-based ethanol 208–9
Malawi 98, 108, 114, 145, 162, 260
Malaysia 19, 98–9, 122, 127, 154, 178
Mali 123, 145, 202
malnutrition 1, 4, 24, 141, 144, 191, 242–3
manufactured goods/products 3, 5, 145, 158
marginal lands 112, 116, 125
marginalisation of smallholder farmers 65–94
market concentration 68, 80
market information 75, 90, 93
market knowledge 89, 92
market power 13, 20, 28, 31–7, 44, 83, 87–8
    of commodity traders 13, 29, 34–5
    control of 186–7
market prices 12, 105, 128, 260
    support 199, 206
    world 146, 218
markets 9–12, 34–5, 50–1, 55–6, 70–2, 82–3, 141–2

biodiesel 99, 127
biofuel 98, 105, 109, 118–19, 126
commodity 34, 70
  concentrated 37, 68, 80, 119
  domestic 20, 106, 141, 160–3, 167, 184, 190
  ethanol 96, 119, 127
  European 89, 104, 145, 168, 223
  export 11, 153
  food 66, 197–8
  global 8, 15, 66, 70, 91, 105, 152
  high-value 2, 11, 151, 159, 167–8
  international 2–4, 10–11, 17–19, 148–9, 159–61, 183–5, 189–90
  local 7, 10–11, 18, 22, 142, 155, 260–2
  regional 30, 47, 247, 260, 263
  relevant 82, 87–9
  seed 48, 52, 55–6, 115
  selling 9, 12
  traditional 66, 73
  wet 67, 71
  world 19, 39, 58, 168
Marrakesh Agreement 201, 215–16, 224, 229
Marrakesh Decision 149, 164–6, 185, 190, 216, 218
Mauritania 145, 197
Mauritius 165, 176
MDGs *see* Millennium Development Goals
mechanisation 117–18, 127, 148, 173
mergers 33, 68, 81, 84, 87–8, 190
  downstream 87–8
  supermarkets 86–7
  upstream 88
methane 170–2
Mexico 17, 98, 107, 148, 193–4, 204, 248–9
middlemen 38–9, 42
milk 27, 57, 67, 205, 258
Millennium Development Goals (MDGs) 203–4, 213, 215–16, 220, 238, 246, 248
millet 51, 258
minimum standards 45–6
mistiming problems 260–1
modernisation 67, 69–71, 89
  procurement 14, 66, 72–81
Mongolia 197
monoculture production 34, 47
monopsony power 86–7
Monterrey Consensus 248–9
Mozambique 15, 98, 145, 162
multilateral agreements 70, 181, 243
multilateral trade regime 23, 137
  taking into account right to food 182–8

NAFTA *see* North American Free Trade Agreement
natural disasters 2, 245, 256, 261
natural factors 158–9

natural fertilisers 98, 117, 132
natural resources 14–15, 264
negotiating positions 119, 180, 202, 217
negotiations 143–4, 149–50, 164–5, 179–82, 189, 202, 229
  agricultural 194, 202, 217
Nepal 118, 145, 197, 225
Nestlé 8, 42–4
net food buyers 6, 106–7, 118, 121, 142, 185, 189
net food-importing developing countries (NFIDCs) 17, 21, 148, 153, 164–6, 185, 218–19
Netherlands 133, 204
NFIDCs *see* net food-importing developing countries
NGOs *see* non-governmental organisations
Niger 145, 197, 260
Nigeria 162, 194, 204, 208
nitrous oxide 170–2
non-GM seeds 53–4, 62
non-governmental organisations (NGOs) 14, 43, 111, 130–1, 243–4, 251, 257–9
non-trade concerns 148, 217
non-violation complaints (NVCs) 232–3
North American Free Trade Agreement (NAFTA) 107, 120
North Korea 197, 261
Norway 129, 165, 176, 199
nutrition 20, 33, 46, 144, 157, 169–70, 242–4
NVCs *see* non-violation complaints

ODA *see* official development assistance
OECD (Organisation for Economic Co-operation and Development) 2, 82–3, 91, 151, 160, 199, 206–7
  countries 2, 10, 17, 151, 154, 159, 199
official development assistance (ODA) 2, 152, 165, 204, 244, 248–50
oil prices 96, 106, 109, 122–3
oils 35, 127, 195–6
  palm 33, 97, 99, 106, 122–3, 127, 162
  vegetable 106, 122, 258
oilseeds 123, 127, 148, 183, 190
oily crops 97, 99, 127
oligopsony 83
organic farming 52, 188
Organisation for Economic Co-operation and Development *see* OECD
outgrower schemes 90, 92, 169
output payments 199
overproduction 2, 138, 146, 160–1, 163, 209

Pakistan 27, 178, 194, 197
palm oil 33, 97, 99, 106, 122–3, 127, 162
Paraguay 99, 194
Paris Declaration on Aid Effectiveness 249

participatory mechanisms 189, 258, 263
patentability 46, 48
patented seeds 48, 50, 53
patents 45–7, 49–52, 56, 115, 129, 132, 222
payments 14, 62, 91, 146, 199, 206, 234
    balance of 20, 139, 160, 166, 183, 185, 251–2
    direct 146, 149, 200, 205, 217
    output 199
Peace Clause 218, 232
peatlands 112–13
pesticides 16, 52–4, 77
    and biofuels 117
pharmaceutical products 29, 67, 228–9
Philippines 19, 69, 79, 98, 154, 194, 197
Piauí 104, 111
plant varieties 46–9
plantations 29, 32, 39, 117, 122, 130–1
    large-scale 5–6, 32, 120
pollution 16, 41, 116, 128, 132
poor countries 4, 11, 17–18, 189–90, 194, 201–4, 208–10
poor farmers 7, 15, 50–2, 55, 61, 144, 209
poorest countries 51, 206–7
poorest farmers 60, 92, 106
population 4, 17–19, 140–1, 185–8, 205–7, 245–7, 256
    growth 4, 6, 103, 140
    world 4, 13, 243
poultry farmers 9, 162
poverty 4, 6, 53–4, 65–6, 108, 118, 152
    alleviation 124, 157, 220
    extreme 198, 248
    reduction 5, 24, 248
    rural 2, 10, 17, 94, 155
Poverty Reduction Growth Facility (PRGF) 166
power 7, 14, 27, 33, 35, 63–5, 82–3
    buyer 9, 33, 83–9, 187
    economic 16, 115, 126
    market 13, 20, 28, 31–7, 44, 83, 87–8
    monopsony 86–7
    purchasing 24, 141
Preferential Trade Agreements (PTAs) 220–1
preferred supplier relationships 14, 74, 78–80
PRGF *see* Poverty Reduction Growth Facility
price discrimination 85–6, 255
price signals 153, 157, 161
price support 146–7, 199, 206
price takers 119, 122, 126
price transmission 86, 106
prices 9–13, 32–40, 59–60, 79–84, 106–10, 159–64, 205–9
    commodity 7, 33, 44, 53, 60, 107, 119
    declining 3, 119, 138–9, 162–3, 183
    domestic 167, 199

export commodities 20, 160
fair 9, 122, 128, 255
farm gate 39, 168
food 4, 10, 16, 106–9, 193–8, 204–5, 209–10
food commodities 17, 19, 139, 141, 160–1, 166, 178
high 10–11, 31, 52–3, 83–4, 106–8, 161, 209–10
land 119, 125
local 118, 260
low 10, 29, 31–2, 38–9, 42, 80–1, 161
market 12, 105, 128, 260
oil 96, 106, 109, 122–3
retail 85–6, 168
volatility 109, 122, 160–1, 175, 183–4, 190, 208
world 184, 196, 199, 262
private investors 2–3, 15
private sector 2–3, 14, 90–1, 151, 156–7, 191, 244–5
private standards 3, 8, 14, 74, 76–8
privatisations 8, 70
processed foods 3, 8, 68–9, 74, 158–60, 174
processing 11, 29, 77, 127
    equipment 119, 122
    local 118
    plants 9, 103, 116, 118
processors 31–5, 38, 40, 42, 56–7, 59–60, 184
    food 8–10, 13, 29, 32, 167, 187
procurement 8, 30, 72, 78, 88, 185, 212–13
    modernisation 14, 66, 72–81
    systems 8, 14, 65–6, 74
produce regulation 74, 76–8
production chains 31, 34–6, 39–40, 44, 60, 122, 126
production-reducing commitments 146, 149
productive resources 7, 143, 169, 207, 264
productivity 60, 79, 104, 142, 152–3, 170, 257
    labour 138, 153
profits 37, 39, 43–4, 60, 83, 119
programme food aid 22, 251, 252–5
progressive realisation of the right to food 23, 109, 178, 181, 245–7
project food aid 22, 251, 255–9
protectionist measures 132, 224, 227
PTAs *see* Preferential Trade Agreements
public goods 254, 256–7
public-private partnerships 92–3
public sector 2, 47, 151
purchasing power 24, 141

rainfed agriculture 139
rainforests 36, 110
rapeseed 53, 97, 99, 106, 117
raw materials 3, 105, 110, 120, 158, 217
recipient countries 204, 239, 249, 251–5, 261, 263

recipient populations 247, 260, 263
refugees 244, 259, 261
regional markets 30, 47, 247, 260, 263
regional trade agreements 49, 214
relevant markets 82, 87–9
research 50–1, 55, 61–2, 92–3, 97–9, 131–3, 200
residues 98, 104, 108, 117, 132
resources 9, 13–14, 29–30, 45, 47, 58, 262–3
  available 23, 241
  natural 14–15, 264
  productive 7, 143, 169, 207, 264
restraints, vertical 84–5
restrictions
  on agricultural practices 170
  child-labour-related 226–7
  export/import 150, 155, 222–3
  disguised 226–7
  on seed 31, 45. 48, 61
retail 67, 69–70, 84–5
  food 14, 65, 69–71, 89
  prices 85–6, 168
  supermarket *see* supermarkets
  traditional 66, 70–1, 168
retailers 8–10, 30–2, 35, 69–70, 72–4, 76–86, 91–2 *see also* supermarkets
  food 14, 71, 222
  global 8, 14, 167, 169, 187
  traditional 70–1
revenues 10–12, 44, 141, 188
  export 3, 20, 145, 160, 190
rice 1, 7, 33, 57, 160–2, 167, 172
rich countries 3, 21, 159, 172
  phasing out of agricultural subsidies 21, 193–210
right to food
  and agribusiness TNCs 27–63
  and biofuels 95–134
  development of contemporary definition 212–23
  evolution of modern understanding 212–14
  impact of trade agreements on 179–81
  and international trade 137–91
  perspective 51, 108–9, 209, 255
  progressive realisation 23, 109, 178, 181, 245–7
  small farmers 53, 223
  and WTO dispute settlement process 21, 211–38
rights
  environmental 224, 229–30
  human *see* human rights
  labour 145, 225, 230
  political 180, 225
  social 104, 154
  trade union 13, 65
rights-based approach 133, 240, 250, 263
Rome Declaration 244–5

Roundtable on Sustainable Palm Oil 120, 132–3
rule of law 225, 228, 249, 253
rural areas 4–6, 11, 16–17, 30, 69, 143, 154–5
rural development 5, 79, 124, 127–9, 148, 206, 217
rural infrastructure 147, 158, 187, 207
rural poverty 2, 10, 17, 94, 155
Russia 8, 70, 204–6
Rwanda 145, 228

safe drinking water 31, 40–1
safety nets 175, 185, 203, 245, 247, 255–8
safety standards 73, 90, 92
sanctions 137, 186, 230
school feeding projects 256
schools 123, 256–7
SCM *see* Agreement on Subsidies and Countervailing Measures
seasons 10, 48, 50, 79, 120, 171, 193
second-generation biofuels 97–9, 109–10, 115–17, 131–2
security 19, 31, 57, 90, 93, 204, 206
  food *see* food security
  smallholders 14, 66, 89–94
    government policies to ensure 90–1
seeds 13, 27–31, 44–5, 47–53, 75, 89, 115
  GM 27–8, 31, 44–5, 51–5, 62, 115, 262
  markets 48, 52, 55–6, 115
  non-GM 53–4, 62
  oily *see* oilseeds
  patented 48, 50, 53
self-sufficiency 144, 149, 189, 245, 264
sellers 9, 12, 32–3, 83, 85, 87
selling markets 9, 12
semi-processed foods 8, 69
Senegal 145, 151–2, 204
services 5, 67, 84, 105, 120, 157–8, 215
Sherman Act 86
Sierra Leone 145, 197
situation complaints 232
small farmers 4–5, 49–50, 57–8, 60–2, 125–7, 168–9, 222–3 *see also* smallholders
  right to food 53, 223
small-scale farming 5–6, 31–2, 125, 187
smallholders 6, 10–12, 14, 16, 90, 121–2, 169
  government policies to ensure security 90–1
  increasing competitiveness and security 89–94
  marginalisation 65–94
  role of private sector and other organisations in supporting 91–4
  security 14, 66, 90, 90–1
social rights 104, 154
soil depletion 112, 128, 170
soil quality 102, 109, 112
solar energy 129, 140

solidarity 244, 256
Somalia 145, 197
sorghum 51, 97, 112, 116, 258
South Africa 19, 98, 154, 160, 194, 204
South Korea 159, 204
sovereignty, food 6, 22, 62, 138, 251, 263–4
soy 32–3, 35–6, 40, 54, 100–1, 105, 116
soybean oil 33, 97, 105
soybeans *see* soy
Spain 171, 204
Special Rapporteurs, UN 30–1, 95–6, 108–10, 121–2, 125–6, 129–32, 237
specialisation 17, 149, 157–9, 172, 183
speculation 109, 196–7
standards 8, 77–8, 90, 92–3, 151–2, 168–9, 177
  minimum 45–6
  private 3, 8, 14, 74, 76
  safety 73, 90, 92
staple foods 1, 108, 195, 198, 205, 209–10
starvation 241, 245, 249, 251, 260, 262
storage 11, 77, 258
  facilities 10–11
structural adjustment 17, 154–5, 167
  policies 2, 152
  programmes 154, 157, 163
Sub-Saharan Africa 2–3, 51, 139, 152–3, 156–7, 159, 256–7
sub-standard conditions 4, 6, 32
subsidies 2, 18–19, 21, 104–5, 146–9, 217, 222
  agricultural *see* agricultural subsidies
  export 147–50, 153, 175, 202, 218–20, 222
  food 204–5
  trade-distorting 19, 154, 201–2, 209
subsistence agriculture 6, 30, 47, 157, 206–7
suburban areas 67, 69, 80–1
Sudan 15, 145, 197
sufficient food 29–30, 37, 39–40, 45, 48, 58–61, 125
sufficient income 29–30, 36, 41, 43, 45, 48, 55
sugar 33, 95, 97, 104, 112, 145, 159
sugarcane 97, 99, 101, 104, 111, 116–18, 131–2
supercentre format 80–1
supermarket-channel farmers 73, 75–6
supermarkets 7, 65–71, 73–5, 77–82, 84–5, 89–94, 168–9
  chains 66, 69–70, 168
  large 67, 80
  mergers 86–7
  proliferation 68–9
  rise 67–72
  supply chains 66, 72, 75–6, 90
  UK 65, 76, 84, 169
suppliers 8–9, 12, 43, 59–60, 78–9, 83–5, 88–9
supply chains 11, 16, 43, 59, 65, 72, 77–8
  global 7, 11–12, 14, 20, 70, 75, 168–9
  expansion 20, 168–9, 178
  food 156, 167, 175, 187, 191
  supermarket 66, 72, 75–6, 90
supply management schemes 161, 184, 190
surpluses 24, 105, 140–1, 146, 239, 251–2
sustainability criteria 102–3, 106, 113–14
sustainable agriculture 143, 203
sustainable biofuels 120
sustainable development 15, 145, 171, 213, 215–17, 239, 244
sustainable trade 188
sweet sorghum 97, 112
Switzerland 165, 199

tariff escalation 145, 150, 152, 159, 174
tariff peaks 145, 152, 159
tariff reductions 149, 214
tariffication 145, 163
tariffs 2, 104–5, 143, 145, 150, 159, 208
  agricultural 145, 202
  higher 118, 150, 152
  import 17, 103–6, 154–5, 184, 205, 210
taxes 72, 81, 84, 103, 105, 126
  export 38, 105, 107
tea 33, 159, 167
technical assistance 75, 92, 120, 163
technologies 45–7, 49–50, 54, 72, 75, 89–90, 114–15
  advanced 97–8, 110
  GM 53–5
technology transfers 62, 99–100, 172, 207
Tesco 71, 74
Thailand 19, 27–8, 55, 69, 71, 74, 79
TNCs *see* agribusiness TNCs
Tokyo Round 215
TPRs *see* Trade Policy Reviews
tracing requirements 76–7
trade, international *see* international trade
trade agreements 176–9, 181–2, 184, 189, 237, 253
  bilateral 220–1
  free 49, 220
  negotiating 181, 185
  preferential 220–1
  regional 49, 214
trade balance 20, 141
trade barriers 105–6, 159
trade-distorting domestic support 149, 219
trade-distorting subsidies 19, 154, 201–2, 209
trade law, international 143, 224
trade liberalisation 20, 143–4, 179, 183–4, 189–90, 233–4, 237–8
  and creation of the World Trade Organization (WTO) 214–16
  environmental impact 170–4
  history 21, 212–23

macroeconomic impacts 157–67
microeconomic impacts 167–9
non-economic impacts 170–5
nutrition and health dimensions 174–5
programme 148–9
and right to food 156–75
trade negotiations 141, 143–4, 149, 176, 179–82, 189
  transparency and participation in 182
trade-offs 79, 84
trade policies 106, 115, 175, 177, 180–1, 217–18, 228
Trade Policy Reviews (TPRs) 228
trade union rights 13, 65
traders 7, 10, 31, 35, 40, 218
  cocoa 28, 38
  commodity 32–7, 39–40, 42, 59–60, 167–8
  international 38, 167–8
traditional-channel farmers 73, 75
traditional food retail 66–7, 70–2, 90, 168
traditional markets 66, 73
transaction costs 11, 72, 75, 78, 91, 141
transfers 12, 100, 147, 243
  technology 62, 99–100, 172, 207
transformation of food retail 65–94
transition 19, 21, 67–8, 89, 91, 142
transnational corporations *see* agribusiness TNCs
transparency 60, 138, 182, 187, 246, 250
transport(ation) 11, 15, 74–5, 95–8, 100–1, 118, 170–1
  costs 75, 123, 208
  infrastructure 9, 152
trees 111, 123, 126–7
triangular transactions 22, 262
trickle-down effect 157
TRIPS Agreement 45–6, 48–9, 172, 228–9, 231
tropical products 145, 150, 175, 183, 190
two-prong test 226–7

UDHR *see* Universal Declaration of Human Rights
Uganda 27, 49–50, 57, 145, 154, 197
UMR (usual marketing requirement) 253
UN (United Nations) 1, 28, 33, 138, 186–8, 212–13, 241
  Charter 176, 186–7, 212, 241
  Committee on Economic, Social and Cultural Rights (CESCR) 23, 30, 170, 181, 185–7, 213, 242
  Conference on Trade and Development *see* UNCTAD
  Development Programme *see* UNDP
  Economic and Social Council (ECOSOC) 30, 154, 213, 242
  Environment Program (UNEP) 172, 188

Food and Agriculture Organization *see* FAO
Framework Convention on Climate Change (UNFCCC) 99–100
General Assembly 6, 31, 55, 101, 215, 228, 241
High Commissioner for Human Rights 46–7, 49–50, 143, 180
Human Rights Council 27, 72, 121, 133, 137, 188, 250
Millennium Declaration 203, 213, 248
Millennium Project 6, 142, 256
Security Council 178, 227
Special Rapporteurs 30–1, 95–6, 108–10, 121–2, 125–6, 129–32, 237
uncertainty 12, 22, 98, 102–3
UNCTAD (UN Conference on Trade and Development) 3, 133, 151, 153–4, 156, 160, 166
undenatured ethanol 104–5
UNDP (UN Development Programme) 18–19, 96, 139
UNEP (UN Environment Program) 172, 188
unfair competition 6, 151–2
UNFCCC (UN Framework Convention on Climate Change) 99–100
United Kingdom 37, 68, 70, 77, 84, 171, 204
  Competition Commission 12, 82, 84
  supermarkets 65, 76, 84, 169
United States 48, 56–8, 85–6, 98–102, 199–202, 208–9, 220–3
  2008 Farm Bill 200–1, 254
  Congress 86, 200, 212, 220
  Federal Trade Commission (FTC) 82–3, 85–7
  food aid 253–4
  Sherman Act 86
  USAID Food for Peace programme 255–6
Universal Declaration of Human Rights (UDHR) 23, 176, 186, 212–13, 241
UPOV Convention 45–6, 49, 222
upstream mergers 88
urban areas 67–8
urbanisation 5, 69–70, 174
Uruguay 19, 148, 154, 194
Uruguay Round 45, 141, 144, 148, 215–16, 218
US *see* United States
USAID Food for Peace programme 255–6
usual marketing requirement (UMR) 253

VCLT *see* Vienna Convention on the Law of Treaties
vegetable oils 106, 122, 258
Venezuela 177, 193–4
vertical concentration 34
vertical coordination 33–4

vertical integration 54, 84
vertical restraints 84–5
Vienna Convention on the Law of Treaties (VCLT) 177, 231, 235
Vietnam 8, 57, 74, 142, 168
villages 123, 128
violation complaints 232–3
violations 63, 86, 130, 185–6, 190, 231, 233
volatility of prices 109, 122, 160–1, 175, 183–4, 190, 208
Voluntary Guidelines, FAO 109, 181, 246–7, 263
voluntary schemes 114, 121
vulnerability 139, 141, 148, 156, 174, 181, 183
  increased 160, 184, 194
  reduction 251, 255, 257
vulnerable groups 165, 251–2, 255, 259, 263
  most 198, 257, 260
vulnerable populations 21–2, 194, 203, 210, 262

wages 5, 13, 36, 60, 62, 65, 154
  of agricultural workers 7, 188
  living wage 5, 9
  low 29, 65, 104, 148
waivers 227–9
Wal-mart 68, 79, 87, 93
waste materials 108–9, 132
water 6–7, 13–15, 40–1, 131, 138–40, 167–8, 187
  and biofuels 116–17
  pollution 16, 41, 116
  safe drinking 31, 40–1
  shortages 116, 132
West Africa 37–8
wet markets 67, 71
WFC see World Food Council
WFP see World Food Programme
WFS see World Food Summit
wheat 33, 35–7, 66, 97, 162, 167–8, 195–6
WHO see World Health Organization
wholesalers 8, 10, 75, 78, 82, 93
  specialised 73
women 23, 68–9, 109, 123, 137, 174, 179
workers 5, 9, 32, 36, 43, 63, 76–8
World Bank 14–16, 28, 44–5, 51–2, 75–6, 101–3, 152
World Declaration on Nutrition 243–4
World Food Council (WFC) 166, 243
World Food Programme (WFP) 197–8, 204–5, 243, 251, 255–6, 259, 262
World Food Summit (WFS) 213, 219, 244–6, 256

World Health Organization (WHO) 1, 174, 243
World Summit on Food Security 138, 203, 246
World Trade Organization (WTO) 20–1, 137–91, 194, 211–12, 214–26, 228–31, 236–8
  Agreement on Agriculture (AoA) 143, 144–51, 162–3, 175, 216–19, 222–3, 231–3
  and agricultural subsidies 198–203
  Appellate Body 177–8, 202, 222, 227, 230–5
  creation 214–16
  discontents of current regime 151–3
  dispute settlement process 21–2, 211–38
    advantages and disadvantages of invoking right to food 234–7
    raising of human rights concerns 229–33
  Dispute Settlement Understanding (DSU) 137, 177–8, 229, 232–7
  GATS (General Agreement on Trade in Services) 143, 226
  GATT (General Agreement on Tariffs and Trade) 137, 139, 148, 150, 214–15, 226–7, 232–3
  General Exceptions 226–7, 230, 235
  history 212–23
  and human rights 223–33
  impact of trade agreements on the right to food 179–81
  level playing field illusion 153–6
  Marrakesh Agreement 201, 215–16, 224, 229
  Marrakesh Decision 149, 164–6, 185, 190, 216, 218
  negotiations and agricultural subsidies 201–3
  non-violation complaints (NVCs) 232–3
  situation complaints 232
  TRIPS Agreement 45–6, 48–9, 172, 228–9, 231
  Uruguay Round 45, 141, 144, 148, 215–16, 218
  violation complaints 232–3
  waivers 227–9
WTO see World Trade Organization

Zambia 98, 142, 145
Zimbabwe 79, 92, 108, 162, 194, 197, 206